Is there a Nordic feminism?

Gender, change and society

Series editors: David Morgan, Department of Sociology, University of Manchester, UK and Gail Hawkes, Department of Sociology and Interdisciplinary Studies, Manchester Metropolitan University, UK.

Books in the series include:

Is there a Nordic feminism?

Nordic feminist thought on culture and society

Drude von der Fehr

University of Oslo

Bente Rosenbeck

University of Copenhagen

and

Anna G. Jónasdóttir,

University of Ørebro

UCL PRESS
· UCL ·
PRESS
Taylor & Francis Group

First published in 1998 by UCL Press

UCL Press Limited
1 Gunpowder Square
London EC4A 3DE
UK

and

325 Chestnut Street
8th Floor
Philadelphia
PA 19106
USA

The name of University College London (UCL) is a registered trade mark used by UCL Press with the consent of the owner.

British Library Cataloguing-in-Publication Data
A CIP catalogue record for this book is available from the British Library.

Library of Congress Cataloging-in-Publication Data are available

ISBN: 1–85728–877–7 HB
         1–85728–878–5 PB

Typeset by Graphicraft Limited, Hong Kong.
Printed by T.J. International, Padstow, UK.

Contents

CONTENTS

List of illustrations

Notes on contributors

Inga Dóra Bjørnsdóttir is a research associate and teacher of social anthropology at the Department of Anthropology at the University of California, Santa Barbara. The title of her dissertation is "Nationalism, gender and the contemporary women's movement in Iceland". Bjørnsdóttir has published several articles on nationalism and gender and the Icelandic women's movement. She has also done research on and made a documentary film, *Love and War*, about Icelandic war brides in the United States and is a co-author of the book, *Kvinner, Krig og Kjærlighet* (Oslo, Norway: Cappelen, 1995). She is currently studying the role of song in the shaping of the Icelandic national consciousness.

Kirsten Drotner is director of the Centre for Child and Youth Media Studies, University of Copenhagen. She holds a DPhil and her research interests include media history, qualitative methodology and young people's gendered experience of media. She has contributed extensively to Nordic and international journals and anthologies and published one book in English, *English children and their magazines, 1751–1945* (London: Yale University Press, 1988).

Kjersti Ericsson, a psychologist by training is now working as Professor of Criminology at the Department of Criminology, University of Oslo. The author of several books on juvenile delinquency, social welfare, gender relations, and feminist strategy, she has also published eight volumes of poetry.

Drude von der Fehr is Senior Lecturer in Comparative Literature, Department of Scandinavian Studies and Comparative Literature, University of Oslo. She holds a PhD in comparative literature (1989) and her current research spans semiotic theory, text analysis, aesthetics and literary theory, and cross-disciplinary gender-related studies in epistemology, ethics, feminist theory and medical semiotics. Among her publications are Semiotics and feminism (1990); Feelings and epistemology: Alison M. Jaggar and Charles S. Peirce (1991); Body, gender and action. A pragmatic point of view (1992); Pragmatism and gender (1994); Feminism, pragmatism, and literary criticism (1994); The aesthetic experience (1996), The symptom as sign (1996); Similarity and relevant difference in a pragmatic and feminist perspective (1997).

Hanne Haavind is Professor of Psychology at the University of Oslo. She was formerly Research Director at the Secretariat for Feminist Research of the Norwegian Research Council. Her research is directed at the way in which children grow up and develop gendered subjectivities, and how men and women handle love and power in intimate relationships. She has edited and written books and articles on feminist theories and methods within psychology/social sciences.

Elina Haavio-Mannila is Professor of Sociology at the University of Helsinki, Finland. Since 1964 she has conducted gender and equality research on the position and roles of women and men in politics, work, family and sexual life from a comparative perspective. She has also studied the health professions, immigration, and the history of sociology. At present she is comparing sexual life styles in Finland, Russia and Estonia on the basis of survey data and autobiographies.

Sara Heinämaa is Docent in Philosophy, Department of Philosophy, University of Helsinki, and also lectures at the Christina Institute for Women's Studies, University of Helsinki. She has published two books and several articles on existentialist phenomenology and the philosophy of sexual difference. She has recently co-edited a collection on *Commonality and particularity in ethics* (Macmillan) and is currently working on a book entitled *Body, wonder and difference: a study in the phenomenology of sexuality.*

Hanne Nexø Jensen is Associate Professor, at the Institute of Political Science, University of Copenhagen. She has a PhD in political science and teaches courses on public administration and on gender in relation to public organizations and change. Her work includes: Feminization of the central public administration (1978); Gendered theories of organizations (1994) and Public administration in a gender perspective (1995).

Anna G. Jónasdóttir holds a fellowship from the Swedish Council for Research in the Humanities and Social Sciences and is affiliated to the Department of Social Sciences, University of Ørebro. She has published widely on feminist theory in Swedish and English. Among her books is *Why women* *are oppressed* (1994). She is also co-editor, with Kathleen B. Jones, of *The political interests of gender* (1988).

Gunnel Karlsson, Senior Lecturer in Social Science, University of Ørebro, holds a PhD in history entitled *From brotherhood to sisterhood. The Swedish Social Democratic Women's Federation's Struggle for Influence in the Social Democratic Party* (1996). Her other relevant works are: *To the male society's Pleasure?* (1990); and two articles: "A red streak on the horizon: research on the women in the workers' movement" (1991) and "From support group to conflicts of interest, or, should women follow men?" (1994).

Anna Lyngfelt, holds a PhD from the University of Göteborg, Department of Literature, entitled *Disarming intimacy: one-act plays in Sweden 1870– 90* (1996).

Martina Reuter is a postgraduate student in the Department of Philosophy, University of Helsinki. She lectures on the history of feminist theory at the Christina Institute, University of Helsinki. She has published articles on feminist readings of Plato and Descartes, as well as a phenomenological analysis of eating disorders. Her doctoral thesis is a study of the philosophical foundations of feminist readings of Descartes.

Bente Rosenbeck is Associate Professor at the Centre for Gender and Women's Studies and the Department of Nordic Studies, University of Copenhagen. She has an MA in History and Philosophy from the University of Odense (1977), a PhD from the University of Aaalborg (1984), and a DPhil. From the University of Copenhagen (1993). Her main publications are *Body politics: about gender, culture and science* (1992); *Modern times: European history*, with Karin Lützen (1992) and *The female gender: the history of modern femininity, 1880–1960* (1987).

Kerstin W. Shands teaches English literature at Stockholm University. She holds a PhD and has published books and articles on women writers and feminist theory, among them the pioneering studies of two contemporary American writers, Gail Godwin and Marge Piercy: *Escaping the castle of patriarchy: patterns of development in the novels of Gail Godwin* (1990); *The repair of the world: the novels of Marge Piercy* (1994). Her current project aims to explore the significance of spatial metaphors in feminist texts.

Sighrúdir Helga Sigurbjarnardóttir is Cand. Sociol. at the University of Oslo. She has taught social science and history at colleges in Iceland and Oslo, Norway. She presently works as an organizational adviser on equality of status.

Anne Scott Sørensen is Associate Professor at the Department of Feminist Studies, Institute of Literature, Culture and Media, University of Odense. She is the head of a research project and the editor of a volume on *Nordic salon culture: a study in Nordic Salon Milieux* 1780–1850 (1998).

Karen Sjørup was educated as a sociologist at the University of Copenhagen. She is currently employed as Associate Professor in Humanist Feminist Studies at the Institute of History and Social Science, Roskilde University and as Pro rector at the same university. Her published articles include "Gender in sociology" (1990); "New professional genders" (1990); "Towards a new sociological concept of gender" (1994) and "Equality or the feminization of culture" (1994).

Hildur Ve is Professor of Sociology, Department of Sociology, University of Bergen. She holds a PhD on *Social class differences in socialization and reproduction of the labour force* (1975). Her main works include: "*Society and the working class: Parson's view of the workers' situation in a Marxist theoretical perspective*" (1977); "*Class and gender: role model considerations and liberation in advanced capitalism*" (1981); "*Sociology and the understanding of gender*" (1991); "*Action research and gender equality work in school*" (1992) and "*Education for change: action research for increased gender equality*" (1998).

Lis Wedell Pape is Associate Professor in Danish Modernism and Theory of Humanistic Science at the Department of Scandinavian Studies, University of Aarhus. The holder of a PhD, she has edited readings of Inger Christensen's work *Shadows of language* (1995).

Christina Carlsson Wetterberg holds a PhD in history. She is Senior Lecturer at the Centre for Women's Studies, Lund University. Her research focuses on modern political and social history, with special attention to the role of the women's movement. Among her publications are: *Perceptions of women and women's politics: a study of Swedish Social Democracy 1880–1910* (1986); "Money, love and power. The feminism of Frida Stéenhoff" (1994); "Mouvement des femmes et Etat Providence – L'exemple suedois" (1998). She has also written several articles on theoretical issues within women's/gender studies.

Foreword

The editors of this collection have performed a considerable service in introducing to an English-speaking readership the range of ideas and writing
that represent Nordic feminism today. This task is long overdue. As will
be apparent from the lists of references, such a body of work has been
developing over a period of some years although, from the perspective of
Britain, this endeavour has sometimes been obscured by the writings of
French or American feminist scholars.

It would be wrong, of course, to present an over-unified impression of
the writings from the range of countries, as well as the range of academic
disciplines, represented in these pages. The question of the identity of
Nordic feminist writings is addressed specifically in the concluding chapter.
There are complex historical differences and interrelationships between the
countries represented here as well as differences within each of the specific
countries along ethnic, religious and regional lines. Nevertheless, some unifying themes do emerge. These include the development of a solid welfare
state tradition within each country and the way in which this has established the parameters within which much subsequent political and social
debate has been conducted. Linked to this has been a detailed and often
profound exploration of the meaning of "care", both formal and informal,
going beyond the simple documentation of those in need of care or the
needs of the carers. Finally, there has been the significant representation of
women in many areas of public life in all the Nordic countries. This has led
to a searching examination of the character of patriarchy and the extent to
which it has been significantly altered by such developments, or merely
modified.

These themes will be found in the chapters that follow. But the reader
will also be impressed by the range of voices included here and the subjects
covered. Some of the names, and certainly some of the topics, will be

familiar, others less so. There is certainly no forced unity, and this recognition of diversity is one of the volume's many attractive features. I hope the reader will enjoy listening to these voices and appreciating the differences and the unities represented here. I, for one, found it a fascinating and informative experience.

David H.J. Morgan
University of Manchester

Preface

The idea behind this book is the attempt to understand some of the complex changes in culture and society that concern women and feminists in the Nordic countries today. This volume comprises part of the response to the editors' invitation, addressed to feminist scholars in Denmark, Finland, Iceland, Norway and Sweden, to join together in this attempt. This is not the first time that Nordic feminist scholars have worked together across the boundaries of their different countries and different languages. Yet, what is unique about this particular volume is that it results from a co-Nordic work process in which many academic borders have also been crossed. The basis on which the contents of this book have been structured – where, for example, literary essays and film analysis are integrated with research on women's struggle in parliamentary politics as well as with gendered interactions in work organizations and in identity production – expresses this crossing of established boundaries. In the introduction we will elaborate on the themes and concepts around which the contents of the book are organized.

A book on feminism from a particular country or region could be attempted in more than one way. Usually, articles taken from journals and books already published would be collected together in order to give a representative overview of the history of a country's feminist theory and research, or to present in one volume the most influential pieces of work by feminist scholars in that particular country (see, for instance, the series on feminist thought in different countries published by Routledge and Basil Blackwell in the early 1990s). Our way of preparing this volume has been different. With the exception of Chapter 2, which is a substantially revised version of an essay published earlier in Swedish (cf. Wetterberg this volume), all the articles included here have been specially written for this volume.

The eighteen chapters that comprise the edited contents of this book are the result of a selection process which started with more than sixty submitted abstracts and papers. Our book does not offer a comprehensive history of Nordic feminism nor should the selection of essays be seen either as representative or as a distillation of the most influential work being done in this field. What we invited, and thus what we try to catch glimpses of rather than cover *in toto*, are some of the different themes and modes of inquiry concerning culture and society that Nordic feminists are dealing with at the end of the twentieth century.

Had it not been for Margareth Whitford this project would never have been undertaken. Thanks are due to her for pushing for a book in English on Nordic feminism. Once begun, many individuals and institutions have supported this project. First, we would like to thank all those who sent us their papers knowing that only a few would be included. We would like also to express our special gratitude to all the contributors for their willingness to follow us through the many phases of this project and for their patience as time went by. For their help in correcting our English we acknowledge the following: Mary Bjaerum, Malcolm Forbes, Kathleen B. Jones, Mika Mänty, Anka Ryall, Linda Schenck and Margaret Whiting. Thanks also to the Centre for Women's Research, University of Oslo for their help in arranging a working conference during the early stages of the project. Financial support from four research councils made the conference, as well as several editorial meetings, possible: thanks to the Research Council of Norway (NFR), the Swedish Council for Planning and Co-ordination of Research (FRN), the Nordic Cultural Fund, and the Joint Committee of the Nordic Research Councils (NOS-H). In addition, NOS-H gave us a grant to cover some of the printing costs, support that deserves particular acknowledgement. Last, but not least, it has been a great pleasure to communicate with David Morgan, the series editor, as well as with Caroline Wintersgill, Senior Editor at UCL Press.

CHAPTER ONE

Introduction: ambiguous times – contested spaces in the politics, organization and identities of gender

Anna G. Jónasdóttir & Drude von der Fehr

Is there a Nordic feminism?

It would be easy to answer yes, of course, there is a Nordic feminism. Look at the consequences feminist thinking has had for women in the Nordic countries! The question, however, implies much more than that. We know for a fact that feminism in the Nordic countries has had a great impact on most women's lives, but is there something specifically *Nordic* about the movement and the modes of thought that lie behind it? A related question is whether there is one Nordic feminism or many. In other words, what is feminism in the Nordic countries about? The authors of this edited volume address these questions indirectly. At its close, in Chapter 18, one of the editors, Bente Rosenbeck, deals directly with the questions: "What is the Nordic?" and "What is Nordic feminist scholarship?"

Generally speaking, the situation today in the Nordic countries and in Europe as a whole is radically different from that in the late 1960s and early 1970s when contemporary feminist scholarship emerged. Throughout the 1980s and up to the late 1990s, much in the economic and political structures of these countries has been more or less fundamentally transformed, as too has much in their social and cultural life. Not least, practically every kind of intellectual orientation or belief system – philosophical, theoretical, politico-ideological – that dominated people's modes of thinking 20–25 years ago, has been somehow displaced or altered, and feminist thinking is no exception.

Our reason for producing this book is the widely felt concern with present changes; concerns with changing conditions and changing modes of living,

1

loving, working, acting, thinking and writing among women in this part of the world. The substantial aim of the book is, therefore, to identify and elaborate on some of the different historical, social, political, cultural and theoretical *breakups* which are currently taking place in the Nordic countries. By "breakups" we mean profound and in some respects sudden shifts which seemingly put an end to, radically transform or alter the course of on-going cultural and societal processes. Needless to say, our ambition is not to register historical changes in any strict sense, that is, to compare some precisely measured items between one moment of time and another. We aim to come up with some understanding of the different situations or contexts in which changes happen and are acted upon; to obtain more adequate concepts of women's experiences as well as new knowledge about changing gender relations more generally.

How, then, are women in various Nordic contexts situated today, and how do they act on their situations, socially, politically and culturally? What can be said about female–male relations in these contexts, and what kind of gender problematic is expressed in cultural production? What is the prime concern of Nordic feminist theory and research at present? How has it changed? In what direction(s) is it moving? In short, what does this book tell us about all this?

The outcome of the relatively open-ended premises we started with, and the subsequent interactive process of dealing with the material, will now be summarized and clarified somewhat before we proceed with a more substantial account and discussion of the chapters that comprise this book.

Themes and central problematic of the book

At first glance, the nature of the chapters which follow is such that the book could have been neatly divided into four or five sections according to the aspect of the subject with which they appear to deal. On the surface, the chapters cluster around topics such as "women and politics", "women and men at work", "changing forms of experiences among Nordic women", "women and cultural history", "gender and subjectivity in postmodernity (or late modernity)", to name just a few. Also, if organized solely on this concrete level – the social science and history contributions on the one hand, the aesthetic and philosophical on the other – these contributions would most likely be seen only in isolation.

However, beneath these divisions we also detected another pattern, a number of main *themes* that connected the various chapters somewhat differently and which thus warranted a more analytically grounded division of the whole collection into three distinct, but not wholly separate parts. Having chosen this alternative mode of presentation, the volume is structured so that three internally connected themes are arranged around the key concepts "politics", "organization" and "identity/subjectivity". These concepts, of course, still relate to the fields of different concrete subjects at the most immediate level (distinguished above), but they are also intended to function more analytically to help present and discuss the various subject areas or themes, now understood as both distinct yet connected. To take an example: even those chapters that deal most concretely with women in politics (Chs 2 to 4), show that women, in acting politically, often also problematize and try to politicize organizational fundamentals of society and culture at large. Likewise, we see in these chapters how women in politics struggle with issues of identity both in relation to men and among themselves. In other words, politics cannot be analyzed or discussed for long before questions regarding such issues as rationality, identity and subjectivity also emerge.

By distinguishing such themes with the help of key interlinking concepts, we were able to see connections which made the crossing of disciplinary boundaries to construct the three parts seem natural. To take another example. The process of reading and thinking about women in early modernity as they sought self-realization in arranging literary salons (Chs 7–8) in which men – and women, too – had access to the most pleasant room, the most receptive listeners and thoughtful responses, suggests some obvious similarities with the mode of making life pleasant at work – not least for their male colleagues – which the women gynaecologists in the Danish case study practise almost two hundred years later (cf. Ch. 12). This leads to the next analytical level by which we transcend the division into parts, or rather it leads to another sense in which the parts are connected.

A central *problematic* runs through the whole collection: women's variously situated and historically shifting struggle with men or male-dominated preconditions concerning how to organize and run society, and how to set and ground its cultural premises. Thus, also, this problematic entails women's various and shifting strategies and negotiations undertaken in order to make room for themselves and their concerns; all this on societally and culturally existing ground that seems to be constantly contested. To speak about struggle in this connection does not mean that women never benefit from the existing conditions they live in and act on. But to "see" the issue of struggle in this sense as it runs through the chapters is also to see relational complexity that demands a particular mode of thinking relationally. It should be underlined, perhaps, that differences or conflict-ridden relations between women are not glossed over or veiled here; the point is rather that the complex of male–female relations and the various same-sex relations do not necesarily exclude each other altogether, theoretically or empirically.

It seems to us that if, on the basis of this book, we are to speak generally about changes or discontinuities in the situation of Nordic women today, seen through changes in what Nordic feminist scholars deal with, we might say the following. If we take as a point of reference the situation, say, ten years ago, then a main focus was on *women's participation and visibility* in politics, in paid work, in cultural activities. It was a question of women becoming as much valued as men, although, or even because, they acted differently. While today the issue of participation and visibility continues to be addressed, in spite of advances, the focus has widened. Also, concentration seems to have moved more decisively to engage with the very *preconditions/premises* on which women were "let in" in the first place, as well as with those which frame their possibilities today. This means that *equality and difference* – both as institutionalized principles (in law and other formal rules) and as rhetorical arguments – have come into focus. This pair of principles also runs through the present volume in the form of a shifting problematization and arguments that characterize, or rather comprise, a part of what was formulated above as the central problematic of the whole collection.

The last point in this account of our analytical elaboration of the book's contents concerns the question of how to deal theoretically with issues of equality/difference; that is, is it possible to *think about* this notoriously difficult dichotomy in a non-dichotomous way? We think so. As a matter of fact, the ambition to do precisely this in the field of philosophy is the main thrust of Chapter 14 below (Heinämaa and Reuter). While neither primarily nor exclusively following these philosophical tracks, we assume that we show – by the very way in which we arrange and present the book's contents – that we embrace a view that may be called dialectical on how to practise a mode of *thinking relationally*. Three important aspects of this view need to be mentioned here. First, it goes beyond dichotomies in that things can be both equal and different at the same time. Secondly, instead of thinking in terms of closed or discrete categories of meaning and societal facts, this view is directed at processes in which people interactively – and through some form of dynamic practice or struggle – create various kinds of social and cultural value, including the social value of people. Finally, this view allows for "seeing" things, events and conditions as multilayered, that is, as being and happening at various levels. Therefore, investigations on different levels of analysis and of abstraction are needed.

Regarding the stance taken above and in addition to the more often expressed dichotomy criticism, the adequacy of the equality/difference concept as an analytical tool to be used empirically in history and the social sciences is open to question. This is because the concept is most often applied on the level of philosophical ideas about human nature rather than as a theoretically elaborated concept constructed for empirical use. The result is that questions about women's positions, possibilities or outlooks being equal to or different from men's receive a reductionistic treatment as different levels of abstraction are conflated. Confusion often arises as to when these concepts are being used as philosophical and logical categories and when they are being used as empirical concepts aimed at generalizations and ideal–typical descriptions. In Chapter 2, Christina Carlsson Wetterberg takes issue with the kind of approach to women's history that uses the equality/difference duality as a conceptual tool to determine shifting views and standpoints in the women's movement and, thus, to understand women's strategies in various contexts. The abstract either/or thinking that this entails does no justice, she argues, to the complexity of the concrete circumstances from which women's political strategies emerge. The approaches must also allow space for both/and thinking.

Politics in ambiguous times

Perhaps the most conspicuous and most discussed example of the breakups or changes mentioned above is the contested and uncertain situation of the Nordic welfare state. This issue is partly connected to another one, widely held to be of great importance for the future and further development of the relatively "women-friendly" Nordic societies. In question here is, of course, the emergence and the highly uncertain future of the so-called "New Europe" in general and the European Union in particular. For instance, the fact that women are numerous and comparatively strong in the parliaments and governments of the Nordic nation–states does not necessarily mean that women would be influential to the same extent in a centralized Europe governed by procedural means and principles basically different from those in which women won their political power in the first place.

However, rather than addressing the welfare state debate or the discussion on the EU as such, the chapters in the first part of the book problematize *the premises on which Nordic women are, and have been, politically influential.* Grounded in material mainly from Sweden and Iceland, they show how women have struggled politically among themselves as well as with men – and not in vain. Looking back, in all the Nordic countries we can easily discern increasing levels of participation and greater visibility of women in politics – a story of success can obviously be told. However, the authors included here have chosen to raise somewhat different questions. Who has the power effectively to define what is common ground and which are the areas of cleavage between women? Although we can see from the historical evidence given here, both from the more remote and the recent past, that men resist women's political action in various ways, why is it that women have not to a greater degree acted in a unified manner (Ch. 2)? How does it come about that some issues tend to be women's issues and others not? On what premises do male politicians claim that women shall obey and "follow the men"? Moreover, when women politicians, such as the Swedish Social Democratic women in the late 1970s, grow desperate and feel forced to revolt against party discipline in order to fight for their core issues, how should this particular kind of party in-fighting be framed, that is, in what scholarly terms should it be conceptualized and interpreted (see Ch. 3)? *Gendered interests* seem to be intricately woven into the structure of social cleavages on which the modern party system as a whole has been built. At least, after reading Wetterberg's and Karlsson's contributions here, one begins to wonder why, over the years, it has been considered so much more threatening to famous Swedish party discipline when a group of women joins together and acts for the common good than when men (happen to) act in single-sex groups for the same purpose.

In cases such as that of the Icelandic Women's Alliance, when women decide to organize and conduct politics "on their own premises", how do they do it and what do they themselves think is different about their way? On the other hand, do phrases and arguments taken from an idiom of women acting on their own premises necessarily mean total separation from men and a categorical difference thinking? And what are the strengths and weaknesses of the Women's Alliance strategy, to organize separately and differently within the existing political system (Ch. 4)? Furthermore, when actually successful in their own terms, what premises *are* women acting on, which may, somehow, explain their success in the first place? If, for instance, Icelandic women can be said to have benefited politically from the specific peaceful version of nationalist difference thinking that prevailed in Iceland in the nineteenth century, during the struggle for independence from Denmark, is there a cost too of this benefit (Ch. 5)? Finally, what is the political and ideological message to women around the world of a writer such as the American Camille Paglia who today actually advocates far-reaching separation; a writer who claims not only that women and men are fundamentally different but also applies radically biological and sexualized difference thinking to the whole of human culture as well as the rest of the cosmos (Ch. 6)?

All but one of the chapters brought together in Part I problematize the ambiguous terms on which women as a differentiated collective are and have been able to act as an interested party in the organized power struggle of democratic politics. We believe that the kinds of issue discussed here may open the door to raising other highly relevant questions, such as how to understand and analyze the possibilities and barriers for women with regard to moving on and enhancing their power in more or less transformed political decision-making arrangements.

These chapters, moreover, show clearly that the "ideological duality", to borrow Wetterberg's phrase, that comes from the abstract use of equality versus difference thinking, comprises a vital element in the ambiguity that characterizes the premises on which women and men, as well as women and women, relate politically – in consensus and contest. Hence, we find it interesting to connect to these concrete and historically located studies a politically concerned critique by a literary analyst, of a writer whose radical difference thinking and cultural criticism go against feminist claims to sexual equality and the dissolution of gender divisions, as well as against the more general abandonment of limits found in deconstructionism and post-modernism. In her chapter, "Postmodernist space in Camille Paglia's *Sexual personae*", Kerstin Westerlund Shands focuses on the spatial metaphors in Paglia's work. Thus, it may equally be read in relation to the chapters that make up the book's second part, arranged as they are around the theme of organization and contested space. Either way, it stimulates further questions: Is Paglia's extreme difference thinking radically liberating or is it conservative? Further, from what textual levels do these words derive their political meaning? Can Paglia's polemical dichotomizing moves against feminism be read as an expression of a widely felt cultural anxiety in an era when the traditional dichotomies are in general dissolution?

Another question, then, is how we are to understand the relationship between philosophical discourses and rhetoric on the one hand and people's acting and thinking in socially structured situations on the other. As a part of recent postmodernist debate, this has become – in a new way, we might add – a fairly open question. Precisely this issue becomes urgent with respect to Inga Dóra Björnsdóttirs revealing analysis of the male-authored maternalist element in Icelandic nationalism, derived initially from the Herder variant of German Romanticism. What connection, if any, is there between the Romantic ideas about the nature of Iceland, idealistically constructed by male poets and liberation heroes, as the Mother of the land's sons, and the political impact Icelandic women today may have as they profile their electoral programme around women's and children's social and economic disadvantages? What is at issue here seems to resemble Wetterberg's questioning of the meaningfulness of deriving knowledge about concrete historical realities from analyses of ideas about human nature (see Ch. 2).

Organization and contested spaces

Although the aim of this book is to understand the present, the fact that some of the historical analyses found in Part I concern the nineteenth century does not make their inclusion here less appropriate, quite the contrary. That was the time when nationalism emerged, an ideology which, as we can see from Björnsdóttir's contribution (Ch. 5), relied heavily on the dualist symbolism of femininity and masculinity. Politically, the late nineteenth century saw the birth of the party system, and it was the formative period for the first wave of the women's movement as well as the labour movement. So, looking back with gender-seeing eyes into this period of transformation elicits knowledge about *variously situated gendered interactions and struggles that actually centre around fundamentals and basic premises.* They centre around such fundamental matters as how society – *including the production and reproduction of its people, of life* – should be organized;

and around how politics – *including* socio-sexual politics – should be institutionalized; and they imply the repeatedly contested question of what makes humanity human and where – in *what kind of room/space* – the practice(s) necessary for *that* value creation take(s) place.

Part II also starts with history, this time the history of culture and aestheticism. Chapter 7 is about the importance in Nordic cultural history of the literary salon hostess as a feminine aesthete, while Chapter 8 is about a specific "feminine dramatic tradition, the one-act play", which originated in the salon culture. In the first of these contributions, "Taste, manners and attitudes – the bel-esprit and literary salon in Scandinavia *c*. 1800", Anne Scott Sørensen points out that, initially, the salon was a form of institutionalized public taste within the private sphere, during a period when public cultural institutions had not yet been established. In the second one, "The dream of reality: a study of a feminine dramatic tradition, the one-act play", Anna Lyngfelt tells us that later the salon also offered the women writers of the "breakthrough of modernity" (1870–90) the possibility of using a medium of entertainment to express things that, according to the norms of the time, were not to be spoken of in polite society. By such means women could participate in the contemporary debates about the institution of marriage as well as the whole issue of women's position in society.

If they were to be seen only as isolated subjects of study in the cultural history of modernity, it would make little sense to place these chapters together with studies of organizational changes and various kinds of women–men interactions in the contemporary workplace. However, in these chapters on culture, we read several stories. Most importantly, within the context of this book, they tell us a story of the historical genesis of a kind of "room" where women could create/produce their femininity by acting on their particular capacities and bringing their feminine powers into play; and as a matter of historical fact, it should be added, that *this creating and elaborating of particularized femininity was undertaken in direct or indirect communicative relation to men for whose creative/productive personal development this "room" was also a precondition.*

Scott Sørensen and Lyngfelt tell an exciting story about how women's spatial agency is closely connected to aesthetic, erotic and performance modes of expression. The question is whether contemporary methods of organizing and reorganizing societal space, and the opportunities for women to act, to use their powers and to express identities – in direct interaction with or as compared to men – somehow resemble the salon culture. This question is as fascinating as it is frustrating. Does it really make sense to think that even the gendered opportunity structures of today can be understood against the background of the salon's special intermediate as well as temporary position, that is, as constituting a temporary interspace between the private and the public sphere? Does it make sense to think that even the growth of Nordic women's power and opportunities since about the 1970s is temporary and in various respects conditioned by an overriding value – the furthering of men's power and opportunities? The point is not to answer decisively yes or no. Yet we wish to play a little with this resemblance, the salon as a metaphor. Perhaps, still, our possibilities for acting are more or less tied down to premises comparable to the ones that were shaped in the early modern salons and reformulated by, among other things, women's experimentation with the one-act play.

One hundred years later (*c.* 1970–90) we could, to paraphrase the literary expression above, speak about the "late-modern 'breakthrough' of wage-earning women". During this period women have used their "taste, manners and attitudes" to create and arrange another kind of room, another "salon" – the workplace. In particular, this concerns the part of the public sector, the welfare state, that opened up for women in this period, expanded fast and became, as it were, "feminized". It became feminized in the quantitative sense and, many would say, in a qualitative sense as well. It is here, in the new private/public interspace, that the elements of a new kind of social rationality have been developed, the kind of rationality which Norwegian feminist sociologists identified in the late 1970s and termed "responsible rationality" and "care-work rationality" (cf. Chs 10 and 17 below). In a thought-provoking contribution, Hildur Ve discusses the simultaneous disintegration of both the Nordic welfare state and the meaningful use of the concept of responsible rationality in feminist analyses (see Ch. 17).

Closely connected to the expansion of the Nordic welfare state has been the massive number of women entering paid work. As a matter of fact these two processes are interwoven. Furthermore, if there is any one social practice that – apart from the wage nexus – links the two processes, it is care work, which to a certain extent has "gone public". However, such work is still and to a much greater extent carried on in private and still mostly done, or co-ordinated, by women. Not surprisingly, then, the question of whether there is any common trait that characterizes Nordic feminist scholarship often elicits the answer – with respect to the social sciences – that it is strongly work-oriented, theoretically, empirically and ideologically.

Much has been written about work: women in paid and unpaid work, the different working conditions of women and men, the possibilities of achieving gender equality at the various workplaces and through work. Still, not much has been done on gender issues from an organizational perspective nor on the complex of questions raised here, that is: *what, actually, is produced at the workplace? Which values* are created there?

Statistics derived from various sources as well as other kinds of evidence continue to show a seemingly ineradicable pattern of gender segregation at work, an increasing or stagnating gap in wages between women and men, and almost no increase in the number of women holding high positions in any power structure other than the state-political one. This apparent inconsistency usually perplexes people, not least many foreigners who have a picture in their minds of the Nordic countries as the mainstay of sexual equality. How are the anything but fragile, albeit changing, patterns of inequality being produced and reproduced?

In the four chapters that comprise the rest of the second part of this book, various organizational aspects of work and what occurs at work are investigated and theorized. What happens, Hanne Nexø Jensen asks, when a public organization in which the majority of the employees are women undergoes a process of change (Ch. 9)? Who pushes for and who restrains the new status quo? What kinds of conflict between men and women are revealed in this process? In short, what does gender mean to organization and what does organization mean for the possibility of reforming unequal gender arrangements?

The workplace seems to be neither solely nor simply a place where work is done and products made for markets. *The workplace is also a place in which people – as socially conditioned sexes – are "made"*, a "room" in which gendered value is created. Perhaps not only labour power but also "love power" is being "exchanged" and "consumed" at the workplace.[1] If so, where does the one dimension (economy/work) end and the shift into the other (sexuality/love) begin? What theoretical views and what conceptual keys should be used to approach such "mixed" processes? In Chapter 10, Kjersti Ericsson argues persuasively that some of the concepts which have been developed for studying sexual harassment may shed light on the gendered character of qualifications for work that other conceptual keys cannot.

When students of organizations and the workplace have begun to "see" the dimension of sexuality in their field, sexual harassment has tended to be the area on which they have focused. However, in Chapter 11 Elina Haavio-Mannila shows that there is more to "sex at work" than harassment. Love is there too. She presents the results of a comparative study from four cities in four different countries (Copenhagen, Helsinki, Stockholm and Tallinn) of people's varying experiences of attraction and love in the workplace. Although the boundaries between oppressive and non-oppressive love relationships at work or anywhere else are by no means clear, and the difference, we might say, does not speak for itself, we agree with the author that it is "worth noticing that 76 per cent of women get happiness and joy from workplace romances and only 25 per cent get heartache". But what does this tell us if the aim is to interpret or explain the inconsistencies and ambiguities in the prevailing working conditions of Nordic women and men? At the very least Haavio-Mannila's tables tell us that the more or less eroticized interactions between women and men in the workplace often lead to quite different consequences for the two sexes. This in turn may imply that women and men in the seemingly socio-sexually and socio-economically advanced Nordic countries, still function under profoundly different conditions when it comes to living out in practice matters of sexual desire. When this desire is acted out in the ambiguously located interspace between public openness and private closure – the kind of room which intimacy at the workplace occupies – women's greater vulnerability becomes particularly accentuated.

How complex most matters of equality and difference are in the whole set of relations through which women and men interact, is clearly demonstrated in Karen Sjørup's case study (Ch. 12). Also at a highly professionalized and equalized workplace, such as the contemporary Danish hospital, although other things *are* equal, women and men as socio-sexual subjects are not. As already mentioned, opposite as the two settings are, the early modern salon seems to reappear – if somewhat modified – in the contemporary gynaecology department.

Without doubt, equality between women and men in the Nordic countries has advanced considerably and in many respects over the preceding 25 to 30 years. Their best-known achievement is probably the unusually large amount of women wielding power at all levels of electoral politics and even, in some of these countries, in government. Also, while there are variations, of course, between the five countries, the figures from Denmark relating to waged work and higher education that Sjørup presents are roughly equivalent to those for the other countries. About the same proportion (90 per cent) of women and men are in paid work, and of university students now half, or more, are women. Furthermore, during the 1970s and 1980s, particularly in Denmark, Norway and Sweden, the number of day-care facilities for children increased markedly. At the same time, sexual segregation in the workplace and in the choice of education programmes continues. And in practically all hierarchically organized social settings, other than party-based politics, the absence of women is glaring. As in the rest of the world, here too the economic, bureaucratic and scientific-technological power elites remain male. However, this seemingly insuperable and entrenched male dominance does not go wholly unchallenged; nor is it intact in each and every segment of society.

The subject of Sjørup's wider concern is the change that she argues is occurring in the construction of gender within the professions, among them the medical profession. Inspired by the theories of Foucault as well as of Weber and Parsons, she is also concerned more generally with changes in how power is produced in the form of society which she characterizes as postmodern. In assuming that the professions contain the central key to the understanding of societal power production, she thinks that women's intervention in the professions entails one of the essential changes. *What, then, is the result of this intervention? On what conditions does it take place?* What kind of power is produced *within* the professions? *Who become empowered when women enter the professions?* In her case study Sjørup finds an obvious break in the traditional gender-divided rationale; that is, the rationale that directed an almost male-only, scientifically oriented medical profession in its interdependent connection with an almost female-only, care-working semi-profession, the nurses. The break, however, is not clear-cut. Women – young women – are now in the medical profession in great numbers; and similarity between men and women in education, professional ethics and skill – but not gender difference in "taste, manners and attitudes" as in the salon – is a precondition for women's integration. Still, the women in Sjørup's study operate on very different conditions from the men, as professionals and as people. Even if they are many and even if they are young and skilled, the women *professionals*/the professional *women*, seem to be forced into a multifaceted dilemma – *because they are women*.

The point is, that even in institutional settings, which contain so many of the elements necessary for genuine equality between women and men, a certain pattern of gendered differences tends to develop, a pattern that actually *follows the conventional division between the sexes*. Although new in form, this pattern is all the more intriguing if we connect the organizational matters revealed here to recent issues in the field of subjectivity and personal identity-making. Here we are thinking of the widely held belief that people today, particularly young people, are free from earlier norms when it comes to constructing their own selves. A much greater scope is now thought to exist for each and every one to construct her or his own identity and consequently, it is assumed, to fashion her or his own social existence. Anyway, a part of the problem of the apparent inconsistency or paradox revealed above interlocks with the key issues in the third and last part of this volume, the part where questions on the subject and the making of gendered identities constitute the primary theme.

Identity/subjectivity – between equality and difference

In the third part of this edited collection we have brought together contributions from psychology and philosophy, a film analysis as well as a literary essay and, finally, a piece of work from the discipline of sociology. The five chapters are connected in two ways. First, they all take up problems of identity, rationality and subjectivity on the individual level of analysis rather than on the institutional or structural levels of politics and the organized production of social and cultural values. Secondly, the implicit and explicit concern with the equality/difference issue here takes a somewhat new turn. In Parts I and II actual or idealized differences are more central than *de facto* or potential equality. Here the view shifts insofar as a wider potential equality between the sexes is put into focus as a possibility to strive for. The point is not to search for a model of identity or equality for humanity as a whole. All the chapters here, in one way or another, deal with the intricate question, *what must be equal and on whose premises in the gendered condition, so that differences cease to be oppressive.*

To begin with, when viewed from a psychological perspective, which approaches should be used to investigate women's ways of becoming women and of handling their personal existence in the various settings of society? In Chapter 13, Hanne Haavind argues for an interactionist approach to make women's experience and self-creating agency intelligible; not only as such, but also as women themselves understand their living conditions and opportunity structures historically. On the basis of several empirical studies of women in Denmark, Norway and Sweden, she discusses methodological and theoretical issues of wider, essential interest.

Just as Sjørup, Haavind speaks about changes in the social circumstances under which gendered life is lived. She thinks that women are no longer forced by social norms to develop fixed feminine needs or otherwise to satisfy a certain feminine role model. On the contrary, the force of today's circumstances, thought to be particularly strong in the Nordic countries, predicates that women and men should be integrated equally into all social settings and that gendered stereotypes in attitudes and activities should disappear. At the same time the pressure to be – and remain – "one's gender" is at least as forceful as before. According to Haavind, these are the paradoxical terms on which women and men have to handle the making of their identities, the creation of their own personas. And to make oneself into a unique person is thought to be the "solution" of otherwise inherently conflict-filled situations. However, that which is and that which happens continuously in the "room" between opposing demands – to be equal and to be different simultaneously – should be termed *power*; and power for Haavind equals male dominance and its inversion, female submissiveness. This means that even if the notion of a freely and autonomously *negotiating subject*, which is now widely used to replace the concept of a naturally or socio-culturally determined person, is somehow in tune with the times, it does not necessarily follow that all negotiating subjects are equally positioned or equally empowered.

A phrase from Haavind (also included here) that has for many years had wide currency throughout the Nordic countries says that *a woman today can do everything as long as she does it in relative subordination to a man.* This statement expresses the core distinction of the contemporary form of the linguistic code which, according to Haavind, *is* gender and which in that cultural-contextual capacity "acts as a forestructure of experiences", a "matrix" that frames the relations and interactions between women and men. Leaving aside many intriguing questions as to the usefulness of thinking gender only or primarily as the "making of meaning" and as a code that "acts through language and resides in language", we ask instead whether *the gendered condition which Haavind's statement above is meant to characterize, can be demolished – in thought as well as concretely, in practice.* Obviously, if understood – as Haavind understands it – as an empirical generalization, it is often demolished, individually, without any measurable consequences for the larger context. But can it be done away with more definitely? If so, how?

Considering Sara Heinämaa and Martina Reuter's "Reflections on the rationality of emotions and feelings" (Ch. 14), one answer to the above questions might be that the first step to subvert this condition should take place within philosophy. Doing away with beliefs about systematic differences, differences that also mean the inferiority of women, must begin by breaking with some of the most central dichotomies in classical philosophy, particularly the traditions that oppose reason to emotions and mind to body. This very mode of thinking, in its various versions, Heinämaa and Reuter argue, is a much greater problem for feminism than open antifeminist attacks. In their discussion, they confront two of the most prominent women philosophers of today, Martha Nussbaum and Amélie Rorty, who have tried to solve this problem. As against Nussbaum and Rorty's attempts, Heinämaa and Reuter suggest an alternative mode of thought, sustainable enough effectively to transcend the mind–body dualism, namely the phenomenology of Maurice Merleau-Ponty. They think that his notion of the *human body as actively intentional, experiencing subject* is one that fits feminism, and that in this basic bodily respect women and men are alike.

What happens, however, when women, in concrete life or in cultural performances, live actively and intentionally in and through their bodies and act powerfully "towards a world" which as a matter of fact is dominated by men? What happens, for instance, when a woman takes a "posture in the midst of the world" – to speak further with Merleau-Ponty – as an erotic body subject? These questions, together with interesting and seemingly contradictory answers, are raised in a reading of Kirsten Drotner's essay (Ch. 15). Drotner writes about Asta Nielsen, one of the greatest stars of the silent screen, who, according to Drotner, is today also one of the least known. This actress was great in every sense in which a film actress is great. It is estimated that before the First World War she was seen by 2.5 million cinema goers every day in about 600 cinemas. One of the prominent directors she worked with compared her with Greta Garbo – to Nielsen's advantage. While Garbo may have been "godlike", for him Asta Nielsen was "human". Drotner argues that Asta Nielsen, through the powerfully eroticized persona she created, offered "new forms of cinematic pleasure to both sexes, if for different reasons". Why, then, Drotner asks without, however, giving a definite answer, is it "the childlike Mary Pickfords and not the eroticized Asta Nielsens who have gone down in film history as the early film stars?"

"A woman who uses her sexuality as a means of power is never liked", a woman journalist wrote recently in a Swedish newspaper article about the American film actress Sharon Stone.[2] Considering Drotner's analysis of Asta Nielsen's eroticized, even violent performance, in relation to the historical facts about her achievements and popularity, statements such as that above are not universally true. Nielsen's star status was shaped, Drotner points out, in a period of rapid changes in the Nordic countries, an "era of sexual struggle" too. We assume that whether an actress is liked or disliked depends on *when and how, and on whose premises*. It depends on how truly such "use" of sexuality is felt and thought by the audience to be in tune with their own experience and intentions as bodily subjects *vis-à-vis* the world of their particular time and place – to connect back into the Merleau-Pontyan view and add to it an historical dimension. Another question is which and whose truth remains alive and which does not survive the "sex struggle" of shorter "periods of rapid changes".

It is interesting to note that of the three different female personae mentioned in Drotner's chapter as having been created on the silent screen – the godlike, the childlike and the human – the human is the one that soon fell into oblivion. This suggests that D.H. Lawrence may have been right in thinking that women's humanity is an essentially contested matter (to paraphrase Gallie's frequently used words) in the sex struggle. Lawrence wrote:

> Man is willing to accept woman as an equal, as a man in skirts, as an angel, a devil, a baby-face, a machine, an instrument, a bosom, a womb, a pair of legs, a servant, an encyclopedia, an ideal or an obscenity; the only thing he won't accept her as is a human being, a real human being of the female sex.[3]

The complex and dynamic human woman whom Nielsen created in her artistic practice and brought into the open had to compete with the ethereal "ideal" woman as well as with the "baby-face", and lost – at the time. This leads into Lis Wedell Pape's chapter which takes us further into the contested field of subjectivity and rationality (Ch. 16).

Taking the questioning of the classical modern and, as she puts it, androcentric subject as a point of departure, Pape turns to Heideggerian phenomenology and to the poetic discourse of the Danish woman poet, Inger Christensen, in an attempt to show what a genuine alternative to the rational, autonomous, self-centred subject might be. By an analogous reading of Heidegger and Christensen, Pape wishes to thematize the particular power or capacity ascribed (by Heidegger) as a privilege to poetry – or to art more generally – to bring immanence into existence. Such particular poetic practice, Pape thinks, can be understood and named by the phrase from Derrida as "writing 'as woman'". The privilege of poetry/writing "as woman" means, to borrow from one of Pape's quotations from Heidegger: "the inaugural naming of being (to bring into the open for the first time) all that which we then discuss and deal with in everyday language" or, in short, to let truth happen. Viewed thus, poetic language "keeps open the manifestation of the world". In her reading of Christensen's work Pape demonstrates what writing "as woman" might be.

In her poetic practice Inger Christensen establishes a dialogue, not only with "things" already "defined", but also with "the logic /still/ not defined / . . . / the logic left /as/ an uneasiness, a despair, a pulse with no body /which/ is a criticism of the body because it's a criticism of life" (cf. the poem "det/it" Christensen 1969). To write – or to act – "as woman" means to "de-realize", to decenter the subject. It is to be a pro-ducer (Latin *pro* + *ducere*) in the "interplay of difference". It is to intervene in affairs of "inaugural naming" as both listener and speaker, both receiver and deliverer.

To lead on from Christensen and Pape into the subject matter of the collection's penultimate essay, by Hildur Ve. What if, now, the capacity to "listen" and to "relate itself" to that which is "left out" or "concealed" behind that which is already "defined" and "described", is the capacity of "beings" to write "as wom/e/n" in *poetic* practice and in *philosophy*; and if the capacity and privilege to write "as woman" is that which brings about new manifestations of the world – in *texts*? What powers and privilege are there in living people that would manage to do all this in social reality? If a fundamental *rethinking* of rationality takes place in poetic work, as Pape tells us (after Heidegger and Christensen), and if this work is essentially gendered, as Pape also suggests, by adopting the phrase "as woman" from Derrida, where, then, in the social world, through what kind of "real work", occurs the *remaking* of things and conditions that ratio(nality) – rethought or not – is needed for? And is this remaking and the rationality that "works" (operates) in society also gendered?

Yes! was the practically unanimous answer of feminists to the last question, from the late 1960s and until about the late 1980s. Among Nordic feminist scholars, not least in Norway, the genderedness of the rationality that "worked" at home as well as outside the home, was brought into the open in the contemporary process of remaking both these areas. As mentioned earlier in this introduction, Norwegian feminist sociologists in the late 1970s and early 1980s began to rethink and reconceptualize rationality as they met various forms of it in their research. In the process of remaking that started in the Nordic societies in the early 1960s an immense new private/public interspace has been created. This creation contains more or less strong elements of a new kind of social rationality, in other words a new kind of guiding principle for how to organize and carry out the new tasks which the advanced industrial/postindustrial societies call for. Most importantly now, and increasingly, people themselves – young and old, sick and healthy, skilled and unskilled – are simultaneously the workers, the work objects and, to a great extent, the means used in the work process.

The elaboration of the Weberian conception of rationality and its basic distinction between instrumental and value rationality, which resulted in the concepts of "responsible rationality" and "care-work rationality", comprised an important part of a wider development of feminist thought that, at the time, occurred mainly within the broad context of the social sciences. This means that the measure of the fruitfulness of concepts was first and foremost their empirical sensitivity and usefulness for generating new ideas, and not criteria set by philosophical logic or epistemological principles. Of course, philosophical or metatheoretical issues are never wholly absent from empirically oriented conceptual and theoretical work. In this Norwegian case, what concerned the women sociologists and motivated them to rethink rationality was of course the prevailing one-dimensional, either/or view of it, frequently used in their discipline. Either people were rational or they were irrational, difference from the one and only *ratio* was *irratio*, at best a lack that could be and should be remedied – in the image of the One.

What has emerged worldwide since the 1960s is an intellectual movement or movements whose message is that the main struggle or "interplay of difference" that feminists should be concerned about is not that between the sexes, particularly not the concrete things that happen to women and men. What matters, according to this message, is the interplay of all (other) differences, not least those among women.

In her chapter, Hildur Ve shares with us her deeply considered experience from what she calls a "decade of chaos". Her phrase refers to the last ten years and the results of the "simultaneous signs of disintegration of the welfare state within Western societies, and postmodernist deconstruction of theories and concepts within feminist thought". The former development, she continues, "constitutes a serious threat to the public sector which – however inconsistently – has served as a basis for job security and influence for women. The latter implies a dissolution of the analytical tools which have enabled women to understand and criticize – at least in the Nordic countries – part of the ideological basis for male dominance and power, and consequently achieve some political influence." Rather than looking back in anger or despair, Hildur Ve makes a thorough assessment of the rights and wrongs of the "chaos", particularly the conceptual part of it.

We would like to conclude this introduction by connecting again to the first chapter in this collection, "Equal or different – That's not the question. Women's political strategies in a historical perspective" (Ch. 2). Here, Wetterberg offers insight into the feminist debates in Sweden around the turn of the century. Among others she discusses Frida Stéenhoff, a radical socialist feminist writer who met with both appreciation and silence from the labour movement. Sténhoff opposed the internationally well-known Ellen Key's idealization of motherhood as being the determination of woman, and perhaps more importantly she opposed the terms on which the "woman question" was debated. In a letter to Ellen Key in 1903, Wetterberg tells us, Sténhoff wrote the following, and we conclude by embracing and emphasizing her point:

> It is true that I differ with you on one point – on the special nature of woman. . . . I no longer occupy myself with that point. I am less

interested in describing the nature of woman than I am with ensuring a place for her nature, be it flesh or fowl. Either is fine with me.

At this late hour of the twentieth century we are, if anything, still "less interested" in dealing with "the nature of woman" than with the question of "ensuring a place" for women in culture and society – be their nature "flesh or fowl". Perhaps the most important issue for feminism to address, now and in future, concerns the possibility for combining social constructivism and the critique of essentialism with ontological realism. We believe in this possibility and that there are modes of thinking that offer various ways to ground such combinations. Philosophical pragmatism, the phenomenology of Merleau-Ponty and the research tradition of critical realism are examples of such modes of thought. Directly or indirectly the combined use of constructivism and realism as a way of approaching gender issues characterizes most of the contributions to this collection. For us that is one of the most interesting results of this project. There is no *one* Nordic feminism and, thus, no unitary focus or a sole mainstream in the Nordic countries' feminist scholarship. We think, however, that one of its streams, some of which runs through the pages of this volume, focuses on the organization of everyday life, on dialogical or interactive individuality, on the importance of ethics in the formation of gendered individuality, and on ontological realism. This focus, we believe, can be seen as significantly Nordic. At the same time it connects us to several equally fascinating contemporary schemes of thought being developed in other parts of the world.

Notes

1. The concept "love power" (compare "labour power") was coined and used in Anna G. Jónasdóttir's *Why women are oppressed* (1994). Originally this book was published under the title *Love power and political interests* (1991).
2. *Dagens Nyheter*, 27 May 1995.
3. Quoted after Morgan 1970: 633.

References

Christensen, Inger 1969. *det*. Copenhagen: Gyldendal. *Dagens Nyheter* (a large-circulation Swedish newspaper), 27 May 1995.
Jónasdóttir, A.G. 1994. *Why women are oppressed*. Philadelphia: Temple University Press. (A slightly revised version of *Love power and political interests. Towards a theory of patriarchy in contemporary Western societies*, Ørebro Studies 7, University of Ørebro, 1991.)
Morgan, R. 1970. *Sisterhood is powerful. An anthology of writings from the women's liberation movement*. New York: Vintage.

PART ONE

Politics in ambiguous times

CHAPTER TWO

Equal or different? that's not the question. Women's political strategies in historical perspective

Christina Carlsson Wetterberg

Introduction

From the end of the nineteenth century, when the modern political party system was born, women have made various attempts to organize themselves across party and class boundaries.[1] However, the predominant trend has been that women have more or less fully conformed politically to the various party doctrines which were gradually established.

Why haven't women to a greater degree acted in a unified manner in politics and is it possible to discern a common interest among women? This chapter focuses on these questions in a historical perspective. The concrete examples are taken from Sweden during the period 1880–1930 and the emphasis is on the social democratic women's movement. The empirical discussion is aimed at illuminating the more general question of how women's political action should be analyzed and understood.

Much of the research on the history of the women's movement, especially in America, has been structured around the concepts of equality/ difference. The analyses have focused on how the different parts of the movement have conceptualized the question of women's nature. In other words, whether women are inherently similar or different from men. The concept of feminism has as a rule been reserved for a political strategy, which takes its point of departure from the conviction that men and women are alike. If one accepts this premise, one has also taken a stand about what kinds of politics can be said to be in the interest of women, namely, politics that have as their starting-point the conviction that men and women are alike.

Questions about the concepts of equality/difference and about the presence of common interests for women, as a group, have also arisen within Nordic research and debate. In Sweden, Yvonne Hirdman has used this pair

21

of concepts in her analysis of the women's movement and stated that women social democrats supported the ideology of difference quite early on and, further, that the continued development of the social democratic, the liberal and conservative women's movements can be seen as an oscillation between the two alternatives (Hirdman 1983, 1986).

Two questions arise here. First, is it possible to discern two distinctly different lines of thought within the women's movement? Secondly, is this question of women's innate nature the most relevant question around which to structure analysis? Of late, a good deal of criticism has been directed towards this model of analysis, both empirically and in principle, since it has proved difficult to categorize the different women's movements according to the equality/difference dichotomy. Indeed, these two ideas have often existed side by side.[2] When I analyzed the Swedish social democratic women's self-image and political action around the turn of the century, I chose to emphasize the variations and incongruities, both ideologically and in everyday life, experienced both by the individual woman and by women collectively (Carlsson 1986). Instead of focusing on the more abstract "nature of woman" and placing the discussion in the realm of ideas, we ought to strive to widen and concretize the discussion. In order to understand the contradictions and incongruities that characterized women's political action, one must see them in relation to women's everyday life, which was not homogeneous. Women's differing positions in society constantly created divergent loyalties and different needs.

What is political?

Ever since the days of Plato and Aristotle women's role in society and their nature have been objects of speculation within philosophical, religious and political thought. The household, both in Athenian society and in the western agricultural society, was the economic nucleus of the communal structure and therefore the status of women had a given place in discussions about the nature of society. Woman was defined principally in relation to the family and she was seen as innately inferior to man.[3] Quoting Aristotle, "With regard to the differences between the sexes, man is by nature superior and leading, woman inferior and led" (from Eduards & Gunneng 1983:32). Or, as Martin Luther stated, "Rule and supremacy belong to man and by the command of God woman must obey and submit to him, he shall rule in the home and in society . . ." (from Åsbrink 1959:33).

With the growth of modern society and industrialization the household lost its earlier role as the foundation of production in society and thus the family as a theme for philosophical and political thought tended to disappear. The family and the relationships between men and women were relegated to the private sphere, and politics were defined with regard to the new, public sphere. The question of the relationship between the sexes did not, of course, simply cease to exist. If anything, it was discussed more fervently than ever during the nineteenth century, especially within medicine, but what I want to point out here is that the discussion was separated from the area that later would be defined as political.[4]

From the point of view of European women the nineteenth century was paradoxical. At the same time as modern ideas of women's liberation were being articulated ever more clearly, a new family form was being consolidated – starting in the upper classes – where women were increasingly being relegated to the domestic sphere. However, the contrasting political ideology was based on the role of the individual in industrial society as opposed to that of the household in earlier times. In accordance with this – and to a great extent out of economic necessity – the formal emancipation of women took place (Qvist 1960, 1978). The previous unequal treatment meted out to women by the law, such as legal incapacity and a smaller share of any inheritance, disappeared, but the family lived on – children were born and needed to be cared for, the household needed to be run. Of course, these everyday matters did not become obsolete when ideology started to focus on the individual or when labour was redefined to mean paid labour only. Home and children continued to be the responsibility of women and, in spite of the new ideology, women and men did not have the same opportunities to participate in politics and in the public sphere.

The so called "woman question" meant different things for different groups of women. For women of the middle class it coincided for the most part with the drive for formal emancipation, where they sought to create opportunities for unmarried women to make their living and strived to strengthen women's status within marriage. For women in the lower social strata there were no formal barriers to work. The main difficulty for these women was the struggle against poverty and the childcare problems that resulted when mothers were forced into the labour market.

Ideas of women's emancipation were first expressed in an organized manner during the French Revolution, but they were thwarted. Women's organizations were forbidden and some leading feminists were executed (Abray 1975). The ideas persisted, though, both in liberal and socialist form. They were developed most consistently by groups within the utopian socialist movement, who opposed all forms of oppression. Their goals were often formulated as a struggle against the three evils: religion, private ownership and marriage. Among other things, they strove to create socialist oases within the framework of contemporary society, where the individual could live in a socialist society in which free love was central. It would prove difficult to live up to these ideals, owing to the fact that people did not arrive as clean slates but instead were creatures of their backgrounds, which was particularly true in regard to relations between the sexes (Taylor

1983). But even if these experiments did not succeed, it is interesting to note that during the early 1800s, the possibility still existed to formulate all-embracing ideological alternatives. These utopian socialists represent an early attempt to create a broad concept of politics, a concept that also encompassed relations between men and women.

Both liberals and other groupings of socialists were influenced by the utopians, especially with respect to their views on the relations between the sexes. John Stuart Mill was a staunch supporter of sexual equality, even if he did not profoundly question the family and woman's role within it (Mill 1869). August Bebel, the leading Social Democrat, spoke of two types of oppression, that of women and that of the working class, and he argued that the labour movement had to fight on both these fronts (Bebel 1879). These thoughts existed but the prevailing trend during the nineteenth century was that politics was defined ever more narrowly. Gender relations disappeared from the definition, and politics was defined solely by class. Politics was about the public sector, production, distribution, etc. That the woman's sphere was primarily limited to the family became a premise within ideology and in the practical political work for both liberals and social democrats. This premise was challenged, however, within social democracy due to the prevailing reality – that many working-class married women were forced into the labour market out of economic necessity. This resulted in the above-mentioned conflict between the need to support oneself financially set against the need to care for the children.

The problem of combining work with motherhood is of course not a creation of modern society, it has affected poor women throughout history. However, the problem takes on a different, more structural character, as production becomes increasingly separated from the household and, as a consequence, women are forced to leave their children in order to work. At the close of the twentieth century, we are all familiar with this conflict, but at the turn of the century it was almost only women of the working class who were affected. How, then, did the labour movement handle this situation in ideological terms and in practical politics? By studying this phenomenon, we may be able to uncover some mechanisms which can help us better understand the conditions that create the framework for women's political action.

The conflict between work and motherhood

The leading Swedish Social Democrats during the 1880s and 1890s in part derived their ideas on equality between the sexes from prominent social theorists, among whom were Friedrich Engels and August Bebel. They spoke of a future society where men and women would work side by side and participate in public life on equal terms, where children would be cared for by the community and where everything would be utopian. The rate of women's paid employment would of necessity increase, something which should be seen as a primarily positive development, as Engels stated in his theoretical discourses about the relationship between women's liberation and contemporary social development. The negative effects of women's paid employment on children and family life within the working class, which he described in detail in other contexts, were omitted entirely from the theoretical argument and were not problematized politically (Engels 1978).

The discrepancy between the depiction of reality on the one hand and theory and practical politics on the other was also evident within Swedish social democracy. The press, newsletters and pamphlets presented many dreary depictions of the difficult situation working families were put in when women were forced into the labour market and children were left alone without supervision. In 1895 the following comments appeared in a social democratic newspaper:

> Among the poorer classes . . . marriage as an institution for eco-
> nomic support for a woman is but a memory, because to a larger
> and larger degree she is drawn into every different possible area of
> labour outside of the home. . . . The children are neglected and
> uncared for and the degeneration of the family will be the inevit-
> able consequence (quoted in Carlsson 1986:176).

This is representative of other, similar articles. Moreover, its author could see no immediate solution to the problem – other than an entire transformation of society. From our perspective, it is significant that the problem was discussed but was not made the subject of concrete political measures. Suggestions for communal childcare were made, but only rarely. When the party discussed concrete demands and political programmes, the absence of the issue of women's double work load and opportunities for financial support was painfully obvious. Women were seen either as paid workers, who together with men should organize themselves and fight capitalism, or it was assumed that they were housewives and mothers in the home – never both.

Why didn't women join political and union organizations? Why did they compete with men and yet work for inferior wages? Why didn't they see socialism's blessings? Instead of relating these problems to women's vulnerable situation, they were reduced to questions of attitude. Women's lack of solidarity was the answer (Carlsson 1986:178).

When, after the turn of the century, the Swedish social democratic movement began to give up hope of a speedy social transformation and began to concentrate instead on long-term efforts at reform, more concrete discussions about the relationship between women's paid labour and family life started taking place. However, the vision was not of equality in the labour market or the obsolescence of the family as an economic unit. Instead, the importance of keeping the mother in the home was stressed. This was to be accomplished by raising men's wages, which meant that demands for equal working conditions both men and women were no longer emphasized. This change of attitude was expressed more concretely in discussions suggesting that women be banned from working night shifts. The Social Democratic Party leadership supported this suggestion in spite of the women's protests.

Women's labour within industry is in no way a liberation of the working-class woman, stated Hjalmar Branting, leader of the Social Democratic parliamentary group in 1909. He thereby repudiated the assumption that labour was liberating and that women's labour was a necessary result of capitalist development. In support of his views he quoted a Dutch woman social democratic:

> For women of the working class industrial labour means nothing else than a means of feeding themselves, no liberation from her spiritual poverty, no possibilities for a spiritually richer life. The proletarian labour is without spiritual value and dull for women; it raises her in no way above the level of housework . . . With respect to her housework, the woman is at least to some degree an independent producer: she can regulate her work as she sees fit, she can take a moment's rest from her work now and then, play with her children etc. . . . For her, work in factories and work shops does not mean financial independence and spiritual liberation, but a new form of slavery, even crueler than the former (Carlsson 1986:243).

At that time there was a basic ideological duality with respect to the official view on women within social democracy. On the one hand there was socialism's theoretical ideal of equality between men and women while on the other there was a burgeoning articulation of a housewifely ideal; and the latter ideal ultimately came to prevail. Both perspectives were characterized by their one-sidedness and failure to grasp the complexity of women's situation at that historical point in time. In the original socialist conception, attention focused on women's roles as paid workers; family and children disappeared when politics was formulated. This was at best an ideology for those women who could act in the labour market under the same terms as men – and there were not many who could. The rethinking that occurred after the turn of the century meant that family and childcare issues, which had become acknowledged problems for the working class, comprised a new point of departure. In this case, the issue of women's paid labour tended to take a back seat. This was an ideology for the married housewife. The housewifely ideal, which was to be achieved by raising men's wages to a level which would enable them to support their families as sole bread-winner, provided guidelines for politics, creating a scenario which did indeed solve many problems for married women. However, it also meant even tougher circumstances for those women who did not have the financial support of men – unmarried mothers, widows and divorcees.

None of the officially acknowledged ideologies took its point of departure in working-class women's actual situation at the time, namely, that married women often had a double work load and that many were independently responsible for supporting their families. Opposing interests among working-class women and between men and women of the working class were consequently neither recognized nor acknowledged.

The basic assumption of social democracy was that the family was a harmonious unit, no conflicts existed between men and women of the working class and to the degree that one spoke of women's more vulnerable situation, it was viewed as an effect of a more pervasive class oppression. When women directly or indirectly questioned the "ideal" division of labour between the sexes, or when they brought up the question of male dominance, they were most often met by a lack of understanding, arrogance or even aggression. These issues were not viewed as politics.

Through studying social democracy's formative decades we can see how the definition of what is political becomes narrower with time and how a stereotypical picture of women is formed – a real woman is a woman who marries, has children and sees her primary role in fulfilling her caring and nurturing responsibilities. This image became a guideline for politics and, as we shall see later, it also became an obstacle when women articulated their demands, which were derived from a multifaceted and non-stereotypical reality.

Women and politics

In other social groupings, such as farmers and the urban middle and upper classes, the gender division of labour was not questioned in the same manner as it was in the growing working class. The wealthier, married women, who at the turn of the century chose work outside the home over full-time mothering had the economic resources to provide for childcare. However, few made this choice. The women who prioritized their professional work were usually single. The difficulties encountered by single, middle-class women trying to earn a living were seen by public debaters and decision-makers to constitute an important social problem, which demanded a solution. However, the solutions that were offered and implemented did not have equality as a goal. Instead, the actual solution was a strict division of labour with women as a rule ending up in the lowest positions in the hierarchy. Those women who entered male-dominated professions were viewed as anomalies and often met strong opposition. This held true not least for academic women (see, for example, Ohlander 1987, Florin 1987, Odén 1988). The woman who renounced the chance to have a family was often seen as very threatening, a fact demonstrated in an article which warned against the "third sex" published in the social democratic news-paper *Arbetet*. According to the article, the concept of a "third sex" was coined by the Italian Doctor Ferrero to designate the growing group of perman-ently unwed women. The unsigned article made the following claim:

> a woman who is neither wife nor mother is an incomplete woman
> . . . She can – thanks to her chastity – concentrate all her physical
> and mental abilities on her work, she is not disturbed by family
> relations, she is often by virtue of her unrestrained egoism victorious
> in the struggle for existence at the expense of men (*Arbetet*,
> 29 January 1895).

Women's situations differed greatly between the different social classes. However, in the labour market women, irrespective of their social status, were treated differently because of their sex and they encountered similar problems when they joined established organizations and political parties. There was often both opposition to and fear of the women's movement, even if the degree of opposition did vary. What, then, did women do when they encountered these problems and this opposition? Did they attempt to reformulate the concept of politics? How did they organize themselves? Were the women united? First a few words on the women's movement in Sweden at that time.

The organization of women

The first conservative/liberal women's organization in Sweden was the Organization for Married Women's Right to Private Property, which was founded as early as 1873. The Fredrika Bremer Federation, which con-sistently fought for the formal emancipation of women, was founded in 1884. During the same decade the first social democratic women's organiza-tions were started. With time, in step with the development of the modern political party system, women increasingly organized themselves in line with existing political divisions. Thus, by the beginning of the 1920s the most important political parties all had special organizations for women.[5]

Attempts had been made to organize women across party, class and other divisions. One example of this is the national organization for women's suffrage, Landsföreningen för kvinnans politiska rösträtt (LKPR), which was established in 1903. Along with liberals, women from conservative as well as social democratic groups were represented here, even if the latter were in a minority. As long as none of the parliamentary parties was willing to support the demand for women's right to vote, there were no problems with this sort of all-embracing organization. However, when the Liberals and the Social Democrats changed their positions on the issue in face of the 1911 elections, the situation became more problematic. Social democratic and liberal women wanted the organization to support the left wing, which was, of course, totally unacceptable for the conservative women and therefore resulted in friction within the organization (Björkenlid 1982:79ff).

The social democratic women had been faced with a similar conflict earlier when the Social Democratic Party had decided in 1902 to remove the issue of women's right to vote from the political agenda. At first the women seemed to accept this decision as it was not entirely apparent which strategy was to be preferred: to win the right to vote for all men thereby increasing the number of workers in the parliament or the right for women to vote yet in accordance with contemporary voting rules. The latter alternative would most likely result in a strengthening of the conservative forces in parliament. The social distance between women was very apparent at this point. Getting maids to co-operate in the suffrage movement with women who otherwise were their employers and counterparts in union organizations was not without its share of problems.

When, in 1921, women had finally won the right to vote, an initiative was taken to create a Swedish Women's Citizen Organization, which was intended to continue to promote women's interests and replace the suffrage organization. However, there was little support for this initiative among politically active women: "We women find our political home amongst those men that share our views, not in some sort of neutral zone amongst women with differing views", as the conservative Berta Wallin put it (Nicklasson 1992:124). The federation was founded in spite of the low levels of interest, but without ambitions to function as a political party. Thus, the need to build a separate women's party or federation continued to be discussed during the 1920s and yet another attempt along these lines was made in face of the elections in 1927 and 1928, when a special Women's List was introduced. This list, initiated by the liberal women, did not, however, receive enough votes to gain parliamentary representation (Torbacke 1969).[6]

On the men's side, these attempts by women to co-operate across party boundaries were seen as threatening due, among other things, to a fear of losing the women's support, which became especially pressing once women had won the right to vote. Even where such co-operation has involved founding separate women's organizations within party boundaries, we see the same pattern, especially in those cases when women were seen as politically unreliable. Hesitance has been tangible and women have often met with overt opposition when they have attempted to establish their own organizations. There were fears that these organizations would be "battle organizations against the men", as a male social democrat expressed it at an early party congress (Carlsson 1986:134).

Women's strategies

In clear contradiction to the gender-neutral outlook that constituted the theoretical premise for both liberal and social democratic ideology, the pervasive view on woman, which in many ways came to guide official politics, was that her main role was that of wife and mother. This perspective was expressed, among other things, in special laws for women in the labour market and in separate scales for men's and women's wages. Women's actual divergent situations in life were not taken into account. Perhaps it is precisely this failure to account for women's differing roles that is of central importance, or as a male supporter of women's emancipation stated in 1908 with regard to the parliamentary debate concerning the proposed banning of women from the night shift, "The proposal seems crude in the sense that it, without further reflection, treats the entire womankind alike" (ibid.:230). Women also reacted against this in their concrete political actions.

This pattern of thought, where the point of departure was an assumption of profound differences between men and women, was present within parts of the women's movement as well (Losman 1980, Wikander 1994). Such was the case with Ellen Key, an important figure in the contemporary debate, whose ideas were discussed and well received not least within social democratic circles. In 1896 she gave a lecture entitled "Missbrukad kvinnokraft" ("Misused women's strength") which caused a sensation. She was up in arms over the women's movement because, in her opinion, its adherents had gone too far in their efforts for emancipation and were trying to turn women into men. The natural differences between men and women served as her point of departure. Man represented intellect, activity, creativity and progress, while characteristic for woman was her "quick intuition, her spontaneous devotion, her strong instincts and above all her connection to nature through her fertility and mothering abilities" (Key 1896:53).

On the other hand, there were also women who tried to formulate an ideological alternative, one that did not rest upon a notion of absolute equality or difference, but endeavoured to transcend this dichotomy. The author, Frida Stéenhoff, attempted such a formulation during the decades around the turn of the century.

The century of the child and the woman – an ideological alternative

Frida Stéenhoff wrote literary dramas as well as pamphlets on social issues and was in addition a popular lecturer. She produced the majority of her work during the period 1896–1913. While she was a very controversial and well-known writer in her day, today she is a relatively unrecognized figure in the world of research.[7] There are similarities between Ellen Key's and Frida Stéenhoff's points of views. Both took up specific problems experienced by women such as the double work load and sexual liberation, issues which were invisible in the discourse of traditional ideologies. Women's sexual and economic independence was central for both of them, but their views on the nature of women and their role in society differed profoundly. While Ellen Key argued for the essential differences between the sexes and believed that a woman's life was designed for motherhood, Frida Stéenhoff tried to formulate an alternative that would give women (and men) the right both to work outside the home and to have children. She was well informed about and influenced by the international debates concerning these questions and we find similar ideas to hers in the thinking, for example, of Grete Meisel-Hess in Germany and Katti Anker Møller in Norway (Melander 1990, Blom 1991). It was Frida Stéenhoff who introduced the concept of feminism into the Swedish debate, explaining what she meant by feminism in an essay entitled "Feminismens moral" ("Feminism's morality"), published in 1903. The essay was a sharp attack on the prevailing sexual morals and also a vision of an entirely different social order:

> The ideal should be that every person is both sensitive and intelligent. *A whole personality.* The prevailing morals have tried to roll over all sensitivity to women and all reason to men and by aiming to maintain the subordination of women to men, they have distorted the true spirit of the sexes (Stéenhoff 1903:15).

The core of Frida Stéenhoff's feminism was a defence of free love, by which she meant love free of monetary concerns. In her opinion, the basis for women's subordination was the fact that love had become a commodity. This in turn was the result of women's role as "bearer and rearer" of the nation's children. It was this extra work load that destroyed her position, she wrote, but this was not superfluous labour. "On the contrary, this is one of the most important tasks for the nation and yet it had turned women into constrained and dependent beings." Childbearing had placed women in a relationship of charitable reliance on men and woman was seen as a parasite, feeding on the fruits of men's labour. Her work was not recognized and it was in this respect that Frida Stéenhoff intended that changes should be made. Women must be made economically independent of men, she argued, which in turn presupposed the economic independence of children (ibid.:20f).

Stéenhoff and socialist theorists had in common a belief that economic dependence was at the root of women's subordination, but the similarities ended there. In socialist theory, developed by among others Friedrich Engels, children were somewhat cynically seen as a problem or obstacle to women's complete equality and pursuit of free love and were in future to be dealt with through socialized childcare. Frida Stéenhoff, however, took as her point of departure the wellbeing and welfare of children, reflections on the importance of motherhood and fatherhood, and the nature of love. As a result her perspective was entirely different from that of the socialists. The next century would be the "century of the child" says a character in one of her dramas, and thereby she coined an expression which would later be used as the title of one of Ellen Key's best-known books.

On general political issues Frida Stéenhoff took a radical standpoint and in this she was close to the ideology of the labour movement. The liberation of women and a radical restructuring of society were for her synonymous. She was not a revolutionary but preferred a process of gradual change, in which people's growing "spiritual awareness" was important. In spite of their descriptions of such prevailing miseries as prostitution, poverty and infanticide, her writings are permeated with an enormous optimism and faith in the innate goodness of humanity.

It is not possible to categorize Frida Stéenhoff's ideas according to prevailing patterns, neither in a general political nor a feminist political context. She remained politically independent and while committed to the suffrage movement, was not a leading light. Nor did any of the established organizations take her ideas to heart. They sympathized with her, but only in part.

Frida Stéenhoff received considerable criticism both for her radicalism and for her feminism – which she saw as one and the same. When she took a standpoint on questions that were defined as *political*, she received both strong support and appreciation from the labour movement. But where questions of love and marriage were concerned the male-led movement was more hesitant. Its members did not openly protest this aspect of her feminism, which in fact was really the core of her ideas, but instead remained silent. In certain female circles within the labour movement her ideas were well received, especially when they were concretely expressed as demands, for example, for the right to birth control or better conditions for unmarried mothers. Not surprisingly, the conservative grouping recoiled at her radicalism and her feminism. The conservative/liberal women's movement at the turn of the century was not a social revolutionary movement; its adherents saw their main task as ridding legislation of obstacles to women's full participation in public life. Above all they wanted to solve the unwed, middle-class woman's problems in supporting herself. However, where questions of morality and the nature of love and marriage were concerned, the women were not unanimous, as witnessed by a dispute between the two feminist journals, *Dagny* and *Framåt* in the 1880s (Qvist 1978:221ff). However, in official contexts they usually defended the family and tied primarily into the prevailing ideology, which stated that men and women were by nature different, that woman was most suited for the role of wife and mother and that her professional work should be secondary to her domestic work and should be consistent with her nature.

I said earlier that it is difficult to categorize ideas within the women's movement in a simple framework according to whether one views women and men as equal or different by nature. This categorization does not seem meaningful when applied to Frida Stéenhoff's ideas. She did not share Ellen Key's notion of a social motherliness, but argued simultaneously that the nature of woman was a question of lesser importance. In a letter to Ellen Key in 1903 she wrote:

> It is true that I differ with you on one point – on the special nature of woman . . . I no longer occupy myself with that point. I am less interested in describing the nature of woman than I am with ensuring a place for her nature, be it fish, flesh or fowl. Either is fine with me (quoted in Carlsson Wetterberg 1994:81).

It is this determination not to become bogged down in a discussion on the nature of women and men that permeates Frida Stéenhoff's writing.

In conclusion, Frida Stéenhoff's feminism did not take as its point of departure an abstract concept of equality; it was a socially committed feminism that included demands for women's right to develop in all areas of society while at the same time emphasizing the value of motherhood and the rights of children. It is this composite picture that I find interesting for it is one which I believe may hold true for many other women authors, thinkers and debaters if we look carefully enough at their words and work.

The conflict between work and motherhood in practical politics

Around the turn of the century and within social democracy there were, then, two suggested solutions to the prevalent and predominantly working-class conflict between motherhood and work. On the one hand there was the socialist theorist's solution which required a combination of paid labour for women and socialized childcare, and on the other hand there was the solution that the Social Democratic Party stood for in practical politics, which effectively entailed increasing men's wages so that their work alone could support the family thus enabling mothers to stay at home. The early social democratic women's organizations did not support either of these alternatives whole-heartedly. They did not seize upon the extremes of ideological equality and thus demand the abolition of marriage and socialized childcare, but nor did they accept women's total economic dependence on men. Frida Stéenhoff's proposal for a nationally financed system of childcare does not seem to have been well-received either. We can, however, discern ideological influences from all three of these suggestions in the material at hand (Carlsson 1986:249ff, Carlsson Wetterberg 1989).

The actions of social democratic women at this point may therefore seem incongruous. On the one hand they fought energetically for equality in the labour market, for example by demanding equal pay or rejecting the ban on night shifts for women, yet on the other they often expressed the hope that

mothers would be able to stay at home. Their journal *Morgonbris* simultaneously published a series of articles by Clara Zetkin which were far-reaching
in their demands for equality and articles that glorified motherhood and
more or less promoted the home as women's own sphere.[8]

Accordingly, both on a more general ideological level and on a level of
practical politics we find incongruities. Even when we turn our attentions to
the varying standpoints of different individuals, we are faced with a seemingly inconsistent picture, where views supportive of equality exist side by
side with concepts of difference and where at times solidarity with the party
is promoted and at others the subordination of women is evident.

How, then, should we interpret this picture, so full as it is of contradictions? I believe it must be viewed in light of the working-class woman's
reality around the turn of the century and the composition of the social
democratic women's movement. Working-class women did not comprise a
homogeneous group but an extremely heterogeneous one with respect to
their economic and family situations, and this heterogeneity characterized
the social democratic women's movement as well. There were married and
unmarried women, those with jobs outside the home and housewives,
women with children and those without. Above all there were a number of
unmarried, working mothers, a situation that did not accord with the prevailing ideal. The limitations of the established perspective become apparent when women try to define their own situation and formulate political
demands. Their scope for action was limited by the predominant ideology
and practical politics.

The situation faced by the unmarried mother can be seen as a core issue,
which illuminates the dominant perspective. The male-oriented workers'
movement prefers to avoid the issue entirely. Of course, the question is of
central importance for women, yet it is a difficult one to solve. At an early
women's congress the social democratic women declared that motherhood
was every woman's right, be she rich or poor, married or unmarried. But
how? Besides being a question of morals, it was also a question of economic possibilities, especially for the working-class woman. Was it up to
the government to intervene? Many women in feminist circles, including
Frida Stéenhoff, thought so. They believed that a system of insurance for
motherhood plus child benefit would solve the problems of financial support
and promote the liberation of women by making them economically independent of men.[9] However, such a solution was problematic for the social
democratic women, as they associated the public sector and different forms
of aid with power and their own subordination. They had greater faith in
class solidarity than solidarity with the government, however; with regard to
unmarried and abandoned mothers, class solidarity was called into question! This example is a clear illustration, I believe, of the narrow space for
women's actions. The limits to their possibilities for action were set by

society's mode of organizing labour, childbirth and childrearing as well as by their own, male-dominated political movement.

Where the scope of women's actions is concerned, it is insufficient to refer only to external conditions. It is also important to consider the conflict of interests among women which created an ideological duality and opposing views on concrete issues. At the turn of the century the Social Democratic women's movement represented different categories of women with different and sometimes conflicting pressing needs. A general wage raise for men was to be desired by women who lived in a stable family unit with responsible husbands, while it was undesirable for single mothers, whose chances of supporting themselves would thus worsen. In time the social democratic women came increasingly to embrace an ideology of the housewife and, perhaps predictably, they also tended to organize mostly housewives.

The conflict between paid work and motherhood was not a burning issue within other contemporary women's organizations that were directed at and organized women from other social classes. Wealthier married women who wished to work outside the home had the financial resources to arrange childcare. On the other hand there were rules drawn up by the labour market that prohibited married women from working as, for example, teachers or secretaries. This negative attitude towards married women work was something that at times also affected working-class women. It was not until 1939 that it became illegal to fire a woman because she married. In any case, the question of a married woman's right to work outside the home was never a core issue within other women's organizations during the first decades of the twentieth century. Yet in spite of this, there was a fundamental discrepancy in the message from those organizations that aimed to promote women in the labour market – for example, the Fredrika Bremer Federation – since it was inconsistent to demand equality in the labour market and equal pay for men and women while at the same time accepting that the married woman be supported by her husband. An interesting item on the agenda of the "Women's List" was a demand for equal wages with the proviso that the support of the family be separated from the system of wages. This financial support should be achieved in another way (Torbacke 1969:151). Such demands challenged the deeply rooted principle of man as bread-winner.

During the 1930s and in the wake of the population crisis, the question of the conflict between work and motherhood found renewed vigour. Within social democracy ideas of a socialized childcare, first expressed by socialists around the turn of the century, were revived. Alva Myrdal argued for a system of rational childrearing and day nurseries, proposals which Yvonne Hirdman has viewed as a step in the direction of putting "life in order", which characterized social democracy at this point. Women's liberation would be achieved by introducing the rationality of the labour market into the private sphere (Hirdman 1990). We can discern during the 1930s a simultaneous revival of radical feminist alternatives, in the footsteps of Frida Stéenhoff and others.[10]

However, within those sections of the women's movement that have been actively committed to the fight for equality, the tendency has been not to question the basic principle of man as supporter of the family. This tendency was thus responsible for the above-mentioned ideological incongruity and the principle was not effectively challenged until the 1960s.

Power and the conflicting interests of women

When I analyzed the women's politics of the early period of social democracy I was faced with the question of how to characterize such a politics. Was it male politics in conflict with women's interests? How else could the question be formulated? Lacking a better alternative, I used the terms *male* or *patriarchal* and discussed this question from two angles: first, the contents of the politics and, secondly, the way women were received within politics.

With respect to the contents of politics, I argued that it was not the abandonment of the concept of equality, as stated by socialist theorists, that could be characterized as patriarchal and in conflict with women's interests. Thoughts of equality were abstract and did not problematize issues concerning children and family relations, and such thoughts were therefore as one-dimensional as the later housewife ideal that only saw a woman in her role as wife and mother. As I discussed above, Frida Stéenhoff's perspective was entirely different, with its determination to see the whole person. The problem with both the perspectives within social democracy was the inability/unwillingness to see the complexity of the women's reality coupled with the inability/unwillingness to see men in any work or care relationship within the home. The ideal woman worked in the home, was caring and married and supported by her husband's wages – an ideal that poorly mirrored the reality around the turn of the century. Yet this ideal served to legitimize differences in wages between men and women and provided implicit support for restrictive laws in the labour market.

Ideas about the ideal division of labour and the assumption that there were no gender conflicts came to characterize the formation of social democratic politics. Parallel with this was the old and deeply rooted idea of women's inferiority which continued to exist, even if disguised. Party politics and public life belonged to men. Women should not bother to get involved – and if they really must do so, then they had to accept the premises of the system. (Naturally, this is a generalization; there are and always have been men who have given women their support.)

Inevitably this leads on to a discussion of how women were treated in politics. The social democratic women around the turn of the century had a difficult time gaining sympathy for their opinions where those opinions differed from those held by the leadership. I have already mentioned the question of banning women from working night shifts. Another question concerned the right to vote. Moreover, when women made so bold as to attempt to widen the scope of politics to include close relations between the sexes, they met even tougher opposition. For example, they failed to get the party to brand a man who had abandoned a pregnant woman as harshly as they would a strike-breaker, or to issue a directive against "open brutality on the work site". In the first case, congress notes tell us that although the male delegates looked shame-faced, no measures were adopted. In the second, the party leadership turned against the

> particularly offensive comment directed at a large group of workers, with the categorical statement that ideas about the situations mentioned are "relatively widespread". The leadership cannot suggest any admonishment of male workers based on such loose grounds (Carlsson 1986:269).

This problem was compounded by the fact that the organized women did not themselves present a unified front. Some of the women's leaders supported the party leadership, even over the issues of banning women from the night shift and letting up on the demand for women's right to vote, which of course was appreciated by the leadership and strengthened the argument for the political line that was taken. With respect to questions more directly concerned with relations between men and women, the same pattern can be seen. For example, Kata Dahlström, one of the leading female agitators within social democracy, once warned women not to make the sexual question the central plank in the workers' movement, an allusion to the stance adopted by Frida Stéenhoff and others, "when other issues are of much greater importance" (ibid.:271).

Political discussions on women's issues and the treatment of women in other political parties have run along similar lines to those within the Social Democratic Party. When women have questioned stereotypical views on women and challenged male power, they have met with opposition, yet at the same time there existed different opinions among organized women with regard to these questions. I will conclude by giving an example of this from the conservative party of the time, Allmänna Valmansförbundet (AVF), where opposition to women's right to vote and to female participation in politics was perhaps most pronounced at this point in history. The federation established by the conservative women in 1915, Sveriges Moderata Kvinnoförbund, never succeeded in gaining recognition as an independent organization within the AVF. This may seem strange, considering that the women constantly declared their support for conservative ideological premises and did not question society's prevailing view on women. Within right-wing politics there seems to have been a generalized and forceful opposition to female participation in politics. Perhaps these women were seen as a threat, not because of what they said but because of who they were. For many of them were unmarried, self-supporting professionals, who nevertheless seemed reluctant to politicize that side of their lives. As was the case within the social democratic movement, the conservative leadership was able to exploit the divisions within the female collective. They succeeded namely in founding a rival women's organization, Centrala Kvinnorådet, which was situated within and subordinate to the party. This rival organization acquired the largest membership and constituted the basis for the independent women's federation founded at the close of the 1940s (Nicklasson 1992).

We can see here, too, how the women fluctuated between solidarity with their social class and political party and solidarity with other women and, as experienced by their female counterparts within the Social Democratic Party, the reality for these women was varied and discordant. Here were independent professional women, some of whom had entered male-dominated areas and others who were active in female-dominated areas, such as nursing. Here were also the upper-class married women, as well as women representative of all the different conditions prevalent in urban as opposed to rural environments.

Concluding remarks

This chapter began by asking whether it is possible to discern a common interest among women based on an analysis of their political actions. It has been shown that women have seldom co-operated across class and party boundaries, but have instead, over time, organized themselves within parties; although even here women have had difficulty presenting a unified front. Different opinions have held sway on concrete political questions and there have even been differences in opinion about whether women should organize themselves separately at all. Based on the evidence of such differences one might well question the assumption of a common interest among women. Yet I would like to redirect the discussion and argue that it is these very conflicts that are of central importance. In today's society there is a prevailing stereotypical definition of femininity, set ideas about what is feminine and what is masculine and about how men and women ought to be and to act. However, the concept of the ideal woman or norm should not be confused with real women. There was also such a concept of the ideal woman current in early agricultural society – the married, productive housewife and mother who was subordinate to men, but this image did not coincide with reality, neither in respect to the scope of her work nor to the realm of her power. At the same time there were always women who would never be able to live up to that ideal. The same is true of modern society. The disagreements among women should be seen in light of the differences in their everyday lives. Some are able to live up to the social ideal and create a worthwhile existence within the framework of the prevailing division of labour and even achieve power and influence within this framework, while others suffer under the same system.

There is still a branch within feminist research that aims to analyze the status of women with the help of a separate theory about the patriarchy or gender system.[11] Others have, on different grounds, dismissed the idea of developing a separate theory to explain the subordination of women, emphasizing instead that the subordination of women cannot be isolated from the historical context or other social power relationships. Historians have been especially sceptical of attempts analytically to discern a uniform subordination of women or a universal form of male domination.[12] I am inclined to align myself with the latter group.[13] But, of course, the way we approach the problem in our concrete analysis is based on certain fundamental theoretical assumptions. I believe that research which aims at studying the role of sexuality and childbirth in the construction of society is still very dynamic and, further, that we ought to remain open-minded in our search for new concepts to encompass gender relations.

When examining the political action of women, as here at certain historical moments, it is evident that there has often been overt male opposition to women in politics, yet this has not resulted in any marked increase in unified action among women. Instead, one finds varied strategies for political action and even conflicts among women. I believe that it is important to incorporate both of these aspects in any explanatory historical analysis of women's political strategies. Women did not act only with reference to their subordination, and the discussions were not about whether women were equal to men in an abstract sense; they were about concrete social relations to husbands, children, employers and other women. Women formulated their ideas and politics based on their experiences of everyday life and the conflicts experienced there. Even if it is important for feminist research to uncover male opposition and structural obstacles directed at women as women, it is at least as important to make visible women's own actions and own alternatives – how women have adapted, been in opposition, succeeded and failed – in relation to a larger context of which they were a part both historically and socially.

Notes

1. Cf. for instance, Sigurbjarnardóttir's contribution (Ch. 4 below).
2. With respect to this, see, e.g., Scott 1988:167ff, Offen 1988.

3. With respect to the idea of historical development see, e.g., Ekenvall 1966, Okin 1979, Eduards 1983. A central question within feminist historical research has been to what degree this image has coincided with reality, to what degree have women been subordinate in everyday life, a question which in turn ties into the constant on-going theoretical discussion about what is meant by the concepts of oppression, patriarchy, male society, etc.
4. Among others, Anna Jónasdóttir (1991:118–49) has spoken of this in her analysis of the thinking of Hobbes and Locke.
5. For a concise overview of the Swedish women's movement during the period, see Wahlström (1933) and Rössel (1950). With respect to early organizations see also Ambjörnsson (1974:58ff) and Manns (1992). Since this chapter was written, the research on this topic has increased; see, for example, Taussi Sjöberg & Vammen (1995), Karlsson (1996), Östberg (1997), Manns (1997), all of which material I have been unable to take into consideration here.
6. Recent research has shown that during the 1930s there existed a well-developed and sometimes quite sucessful co-operation between women from different parties and organizations. See Hobson (1993), Karlsson (1996:120–30), Andersson (1997), Carlsson Wetterberg (1997), Frangeur (1997), Östberg (1997).
7. See also Zade's biography (1935), Kyle (1984), Levin (1982) and Carlsson Wetterberg (1992).
8. See, for example, *Morgonbris* 1905 (nos 2,3,4) and 1906 (nos 2,3,4) where Clara Zetkin's article "The working class woman's and today's feminist question" from 1889 was published in series form and contrast the article, "Women in the socialist movement" in no. 7 (1909) where only the negative effects of women's labour outside the home are discussed.
9. These thoughts are expressed within the Federation for Motherhood and Sexual Reform in Germany. See Allen (1985).
10. With respect to this see Eskilsson (1991). The 1930s are interesting because of the scope of discussions. Lindholm (1990) makes an interesting comparative analysis of Alva Myrdal's and Elin Wägner's feminism.
11. With respect to the Swedish debate see, for example, Carlsson et al. (1983), Hirdman (1989) and Jonasdóttir (1991).
12. For an interesting addition along these lines see, for example, Gordon (1991).
13. I develop this further in Carlsson Wetterberg (1992). For the debate on this question see also Hageman (1994) and Sommestad (1994).

References

Abray, J. 1975. Feminism and the French Revolution. *American Historical Review.* **43–62**.
Allen, A. T. 1985. Mothers of the new generation. Adele Schreiber, Helene Stöcker and the evolution of a German idea of motherhood, 1900–1914. *Signs. Journal of Women and Culture* **10** (3), 418–38.
Andersson, I. 1997. Vem skickade Lullu Lous och Thora Knudsen brev till i Sverige? Svenska kvinnors nätverk, skandinaviska och nordiska kontakter med utblickar mot Europa 1915–1940. See Gullikstad & Heitman (1997), 182–205.
Ambjörnsson, R. 1974. *Samhällsmodern. Ellen Keys kvinnouppfattning till och med 1896.* Göteborg. Unpublished PhD thesis, Göteborg University.

Bebel, A. 1972 (1879). *Kvinnan och socialismen.* Göteborg: Partisan.

Björkenlid, B. 1982. *Kvinnokrav i manssamhälle. Rösträttskvinnorna och deras metoder som opinionsbildare och påtryckargrupp i Sverige 1902–21.* Uppsala: Avd. för litteratursociologi, Litteraturvetenskapliga institutionen.

Blom, I. 1991. Voluntary motherhood 1900–1930: theories and politics of a Norwegian feminist in an international perspective. In *Maternity and gender policies. Women and the rise of the European welfare states 1880s–1950s,* G. Bock & P. Thane (eds), 21–39. London and New York: Routledge.

Carlsson, C. 1986. *Kvinnosyn och kvinnopolitik. En studie av svensk socialdemokrati 1880–1910.* Lund: Arkiv förlag.

Carlsson, C., Esseveld, J., Goodman, S., Widerberg, K. 1983. Om patriarkat – en kritisk granskning. *Kvinnovetenskaplig tidskrift* (1), 55–69.

Carlsson Wetterberg, C. 1989. Likhet och särart. Den tidiga arbetarrörelsens kvinnopolitik. *Arbetarhistoria* **13** (51), 47–54.

Carlsson Wetterberg, C. 1992. Från patriarkat, till genussystem – och vad kommer sedan? *Kvinnovetenskaplig tidskrift* (3), 34–48.

Carlsson Wetterberg, C. 1994. Penningen, kärleken och makten. Frida Stéenhoffs feministiska alternativ. See Wikander (1994), 80–102.

Carlsson Wetterberg, C. 1997. Kvinnorörelse och välfärdsstat – Sverige/Schweiz. Några tankar kring en komparativ studie. See Gullikstad & Heitman (1997), 155–81.

Eduards, M. (ed.) 1983. *Kön, makt, medborgarskap. Kvinnan i politiskt tänkande från Platon till Engels.* Stockholm: Liber Förlag.

Eduards, M. & H. Gunneng 1983. Medborgaren och hans hustru. Om Aristoteles' syn på kvinnan. See Eduards (1983), 27–39.

Ekenvall, A. 1966. *Manligt och kvinnligt – idéhistoriska studier.* Göteborg: Akademiförlaget.

Engels, F. 1978 (1884). *Familjens, privategendomens och statens ursprung.* Stockholm: Arbetarkultur.

Eskilsson, L. 1991. *Drömmen om kamratsamhället. Kvinnliga medborgarskolan på Fogelstad 1925–1935.* Stockholm: Carlsson.

Florin, C. 1987. *Kampen om katedern. Feminiserings- och professionaliserings processen inom den svenska folkskolans lärarkår 1860–1906.* Stockholm: Almqvist & Wicksell.

Frangeur, R. 1997. Feminismen och statmakten i Sverige på 1930-talet. See Gullikstad & Heitman (1997), 130–54.

Gordon, L. 1991. On difference. *Genders* (10), 91–111.

Gullikstad, B. & K. Heitman (eds) 1997. *Kjønn, makt, samfunn i Norden i et historisk perspektiv. Konferenserapport fra det 5. nordiske kvinnohistorikermøte, Klaekken 08. – 11.08.96.* Dragvoll: Senter for kvinneforskning.

Hageman, G. 1994. Postmodernismen användbar men opålitlig bundsförvant. *Kvinnovetenskaplig tidskrift* (3), 19–34.

Hirdman, Y. 1983. Den socialistiska hemmafrun. Den socialdemokratiska kvinnorörelsen och hemarbetet 1890–1939. In Åkerman Brita et al., *Vi kan, vi behövs. Kvinnorna går samman i egna föreningar,* 11–60. Stockholm: Förlaget Akademilitteratur.

Hirdman, Y. 1986. Särart – likhet: Kvinnorörelsens scylla och karybdis. In *Kvinder, mentalitet og arbejde,* I. Fredriksen & H. Rømer (eds), 27–40. Aarhus: Aarhus Universitetsforlag.

Hirdman, Y. 1988. Genussystemet – reflexioner kring kvinnors sociala underordning. *Kvinnovetenskaplig tidskrift* (3), 49–63.

Hobson, B. 1993. Feminist strategies and gendered discourses in welfare states: married women's right to work in the United States and Sweden. In *Mothers of a new world: maternalist politics and the origins of welfare states*, S. Koven & S. Michel (eds), 396–429. New York/London: Routledge.

Jónasdóttir, A.G. 1991. *Love, power and political interests*. Örebro: Örebro Studies.

Karlsson, G. 1996. *Från broderskap till systerskap. Det socialdemokratiska kvinnoförbundets kamp för inflytande och makt i SAP*. Lund: Arkiv förlag.

Key, E. 1896. *Missbrukad kvinnokraft och naturenliga arbetsområden för kvinnan: Tvenne föredrag*. Stockholm.

Kyle, G. 1984. Kvinnorörelser 1880–1920. Traditionalism, reformism och revolutionär feminism. In *Rapport från nordiskt kvinnohistoriskt seminarium*, A. Korppi Tommola (ed.), 2–30. Helsinki.

Levin, H. 1982. Frida Stéenhoff- feminist och födelsekontrollpionjär. *Kvinnovetenskaplig tidskrift* (4), 76–9.

Lindholm, M. 1990. *Talet om det kvinnliga. Studier i feministiskt tänkande i Sverige under 1930-talet*. Göteborg: Department of Sociology, Göteborg University.

Losman, B. 1980. *Kamp för ett nytt kvinnoliv. Ellen Keys idéer och deras betydelse för sekelskiftets unga kvinnor*. Stockholm: Liber Förlag.

Manns, U. 1992. *Kvinnofrågan 1880–1921. En artikelbiografi*. Lund: Arkiv.

Manns, U. 1997. *Den sanna frigörelsen. Fredrika-Bremer-förbundet 1884–1921*. Stockholm/Stehag: Symposion.

Melander, E. 1990. *Den sexuella krisen och den nya moralen. Förhållandet mellan i könen i Grete Meisel-Hess' författarskap*. Stockholm: Almqvist & Wicksell.

Mill, J.S. 1906 (1869). *The subjection of women*. London.

Morgonbris: 1905, 1906, 1909.

Nicklasson, S. 1992. *Högerns kvinnor. Problem och resurs för Allmänna Valmansförbundet perioden 1900–1936/37*. Uppsala: Acta Universitatis Upsaliensis.

Oden, B. 1988. Kvinnostrategier i studentmiljö. *Scandia* **1**, 71–86.

Offen, K. 1988. Defining feminism. A comparative historical approach. *Signs. Journal of Women and Culture* **14** (1), 119–57.

Ohlander, A.-S. 1987. Kvinnliga nordpolsfarare. De första kvinnliga forskarna i Sverige. In *Kvinnliga forskarpionjärer i Norden*. Rapport från ett seminarium 27 November 1986, 61–99. Stockholm: Delegationen för Jämställdhetsforskning.

Okin, S.M. 1979. *Women in western political thought*. Princeton, NJ: Princeton University Press.

Östberg. K. 1997. *Efter rösträtten. Kvinnors utrymme efter det demokratiska genombrottet*. Stockholm/Stehag: Symposion.

Qvist, G. 1960. *Kvinnofrågan i Sverige 1809–1846. Studier rörande kvinnans näringsfrihet i de borgerliga yrkena*. Göteborg: Scandinavian University Press.

Qvist, G. 1978. *Konsten att bliva en god flicka. Kvinnohistoriska uppsatser*. Stockholm: Liber Förlag.

Rössel, J. 1950. *Kvinnorna och kvinnorörelsen i Sverige 1850–1950*. Stockholm: YSF's Förlag.

Scott, J.W. 1988. *Gender and the politics of history*. New York: Columbia University Press.

Sommestad, L. 1994. Mejerskor, industrialisering och välfärd – argument för en komparativ genusforskning. In *Fra kvinnehistorie till kjønnshistorie. Rapport III. Det 22. nordiska historikermøte*, K. Tønnessen (ed.), 107–120. Oslo.

Stéenhoff, F. 1903. *Feminismens moral*. Stockholm: Wahlström & Widstrand.

Taussi Sjöberg, M. & T. Vammen (eds) 1995. *På tröskeln till välfärden. Välförenhetsreformer och arenor i Norden 1800–1930*. Stockholm: Carlsson.

Taylor, B. 1983. *Eve and the new Jerusalem. Socialism and feminism in the nineteenth century.* London: Virago.

Torbacke, J. 1969. Kvinnolistan 1927–28 – ett kvinnopolitiskt fiasko. *Historisk tidskrift* (2), 145–84.

Wahlström, L. 1933. *Den svenska kvinnorörelsen. Historisk översikt.* Stockholm: Norstedts Förlag.

Wikander, U. 1994. *Det evigt kvinnliga. En historia om förändring.* Stockholm: Tidens Förlag.

Zade, B. 1935. *Frida Stéenhoff. Människan, kämpen, verket.* Stockholm: Bonniers.

Åsbrink, E. 1959. *Genom portar I. Studier i den svenska kyrkans kvinnosyn kring 1800-talets början.* Stockholm: Almqvist & Wicksell.

CHAPTER THREE

Social Democratic women's coup in the Swedish parliament

Gunnel Karlsson

Being politically active is certainly no easy task, neither for men nor for women, but I venture to say that it has in several ways been more difficult for women. According to men's conception there are only two types of female politician: those that sit quietly and shyly and never dare to speak up and as a result are judged bad bets, or those women who do speak up and dare to have their own opinion and who are said to be so enormously unruly that one cannot have anything to do with them in a political context. There does not seem to be anything in between.[1]

The above quotation is taken from a letter which Olof Palme read out at the Swedish Social Democratic Worker's Party (SAP) Congress in 1972, when he spoke under the heading, "Women's equality". He had received the letter from a female party member and, stating that the writer's words contained a "profound truth", he maintained that the party needed to increase its efforts to recruit and educate women. He added, "It is true, as has been said, that women must fight for a place through their own strength, however that is not enough. It is a mutual responsibility for the entire workers' movement."[2]

Some of the problems which the social democratic women have encountered in the party can be explained by the formulation that women must "fight for a place". Indeed, for years women have complained about male opposition, about being forced literally to *fight* for a place in the party. The uneven gender distribution within the membership in the early 1970s, 27 per cent women and 73 per cent men,[3] confirmed the existence of a problem which could not be ignored at a time when the party emphasized "equality" and when, simultaneously, a new women's movement was emerging and women's issues were being heatedly debated.[4]

For the Social Democratic Women's Federation (SSKF) it was significant that it was the party chairman himself who gave a speech at the congress about women's equality and emphasized that responsibility for achieving it was shared by the entire workers' movement. Olof Palme conferred status on the question of gender equality, a goal which had hitherto been striven for by the women's federation alone, with little support from the rest of the party. According to Björn Elmbrant, author of a biography of Olof Palme, Palme's speech on equality became "a turning-point in the very male-dominated party. What Palme spoke of had up until then been reserved for the ladies, in other words the Social Democratic Women's Federation."[5]

It was a turning-point in the sense that questions of equality between women and men – what came to be known in Sweden as *jämställdhet*[6] – became party questions, as Elmbrant argues. However, was it also a turning-point for the women and the women's federation with respect to opportunities to participate in debates and influence party policies on equality? If I look at what happened a few years later, in 1976, when half the women in the social democratic parliamentary group, acting against the advice of the party leadership, staged a coup on a motion on paternity leave in parliament, the answer to the question is extremely uncertain.

The coup occurred during what was a successful period for the women, when questions of equality were among those most frequently aired in public debate, and when the number of politically active women increased sharply. The prospects for advancing women's interests within the social democratic government party appeared good, even without the coup. But the women's federation staged the coup in desperation at their failure to win support for women's interests from the party leadership. The latter group condemned the women's action and chose to view it as a serious breach of party discipline, finding no grounds for the women's complaints. This divergence of views thus led to an intractable problem for the parliamentary group. Before I describe the conflict in detail, I will begin by relating it to feminist research's theories on women's conditional participation in politics. The discussion will be confined to a few of the issues concerning women and politics which I have found most relevant to my study of the history of the Social Democratic Women's Federation.[7]

Women's conditional participation in politics

One of the problems experienced by women in the party, and something that is revealed in the letter to Olof Palme, inheres in the men's separation of women into two unrealistic groups, one quiet and obedient, whose members were never entrusted with any serious work within the party, the other strong and unruly, and deemed wholly unsuited to politics. Such an attitude was premised on the feeling that women have no place in party politics

– implying that the "normal" party member was a man. It is also about women being assigned a role in the party that felt both foreign, defined as it was by men, and constricting. Moreover, the two roles that were on offer must have appeared impossible to fulfil for any woman who wanted to accomplish something by her political work. The implicit message seemed to be that women did not belong in the party, or in politics. According to Berit Ås, who analyzed the situation in terms of domination techniques, the alternatives described in the letter can be classified as a double bind: "damned if you do, damned if you don't".[8]

The problem that the letter writer indirectly articulated is one often expressed within feminist research as the fact that women's participation in politics is *conditional*. Women have had to insinuate themselves into an already complete political system, which was created by and for men, and where the political activitist has been by definition male.[9] Women have, moreover, been in a minority – representation of Swedish women in parliament has risen from less than 2 per cent in 1922 to 40 per cent following the elections in 1994, but women are still in the minority.

For a long time women's relative absence from party politics was explained, both within research and among politicians, with reference to a shortage of suitable women.[10] The tendency to put the blame on women for being so few in politics – to blame what was "on offer", which is also a domination[11] – was also prevalent within the workers' movement.[12] Feminist research has questioned that perspective and stressed that the problem lies with the political system and not with the women. In our formally democratic, Western society, the political system seems to have functioned so as effectively to *hinder* their participation or *exclude* women.[13] Political scientists, among them Maud Eduards, Gunnel Gustafsson and Anna G. Jónasdóttir, have questioned how and why women are discouraged or excluded in today's Swedish society, where formal obstacles to equality no longer exist.[14]

Many of mainstream feminist research's questions about power and gender are relevant to my study of the Social Democratic Women's Federation, especially those concerning the relationship between the party and its female and male members in their roles as political figures. Bearing in mind that this concerns a party which had held government office continuously from 1932 to 1976[15] and which was, moreover, strongly male dominated, it is reasonable, together with Eduards, Gustafsson and Jónasdóttir, to ask what is significant about the fact that men most often make the decisions on issues which concern women. Why do men dominate in politics (as well as in the Social Democratic Party)? Why do men have power, but not women? Why isn't male dominance seen as a problem,[16] while the risk of female dominance has, at least historically, been seen as very problematic – for example over the issue of women's right to vote, when men considered setting different age limits in order to counteract female dominance? This same fear, that due to their large numbers women would override men, was apparent too during the Swedish vote on prohibition in 1922. Then the men argued that women, despite their newly won right to vote, should not be allowed to participate in the voting because they did not drink alcohol.[17] To the best of my knowledge, no one has ever suggested that men be excluded from voting on, for example, abortion issues. Men have evidently viewed themselves as the legitimate representatives of the public interest while women have been seen as representatives only of special interests, in other words of women's issues.

With reference to the classic political-scientific discussion about how issues become politicized, for example, who decides who gets what and what issues make or *do not* make the political agenda, the Danish political scientist, Drude Dahlerup, has pointed out that there is a tendency within political parties to avoid politicizing questions on women's status.[18] Starting from political scientists' methods of analyzing the art of avoiding decision-making ("non decision-making"[19]), she emphasizes the importance of studying how certain (women's) issues are held back, in other words *not* politicized. In the same manner, I believe it can be rewarding to study which of the Social Democratic Women's Federation's issues were taken up by the party and which were not. It is perhaps particularly important to study the "non-issues" or "non-decisions", in other words how a party has actually behaved in order to avoid dealing with issues of gender conflict.

Related to the discussion of the political system's tendency to avoid issues of gender conflict, Drude Dahlerup has also formulated the hypothesis that the parties tend to bring up gender conflict issues in a *transformed* form. Instead of discussing the distribution of power and other values between women and men, the issue is transformed and presented in connection with, say, family policy, which, viewed from the perspective of gender conflict, is hardly a controversial political matter.[20] Yet even here the line of reasoning seems relevant for the Social Democratic Party and its women's federation. One example of this is the federation's demand for a 6-hour working day in the 1970s. What had once been an issue of equality was transformed within the party into a gender-neutral, family policy issue of the right of parents with small children to a shorter working day. The women's federation's demand was for a 6-hour working day for everyone, the ideal being that women and men would share both domestic and professional work equally.[21]

Women's interests

With respect to why it has been – and still is – so difficult to frame and advance women's interests, both generally in politics and within the workers' movement, I wish to tie into Anna Jónasdóttir's theoretical discussion of women's interests. According to Jónasdóttir, it is a matter of common

47

feminist interest that women are represented in politics, that they are represented on their own terms, as voices speaking for women as a group – "as women".[22] Her main focus is on women's common interest in participating in and influencing politics, in other words their mode of participation and action. This entails a distinction between political action to champion women's interests and the results of such action. What is important, according to Jónasdóttir, is that women participate in the decision-making process, that as a group they are given the opportunity to be present, which means that besides actual participation they are afforded access to the necessary knowledge and information to enable them to weigh up the conditions for and consequences of a decision – in other words, they are able to monitor the decision-making process. Jónasdóttir distinguishes between "*simple*" and "*controlling*" participation.[23] Simple participation denotes the formal right to participate in the decision-making process, women's right "to be present", while controlling presence denotes a more specific presence, where women as a group can successfully participate in and decide on public issues ("the demand for participation in and control over society's public affairs").[24] Casting a quick glance over the political history of both Swedish and social democratic women, it seems as if the women were welcomed into politics as long as they were satisfied with a "simple" presence, but often met with opposition when they demanded a "controlling" presence.[25]

This does not mean that in its role as a branch organization the Social Democratic Women's Federation has not had considerable influence on party policy with respect to women's issues. Nancy Eriksson, one of the organization's leading members for many years, describes the situation vividly:

> The fact that the women have influenced Social Democratic Party policy in many aspects is beyond doubt. For decades thoroughly discussed social policy reforms have been able to be taken from the women's federation's test kitchen and implemented in reality. One has often found greater radicalism among the women than in the rest of the party.[26]

Undoubtedly, women have taken advantage of opportunities to influence party policy; what they have lacked is an openly acknowledged power, "authority – as women", to quote Jónasdóttir once more.[27] She means that while women can indeed influence and affect political decision-making, they do not have authoritative power, in other words legitimacy, openly acknowledged authority.[28] Her separation of the concept of power into *authority*, which stands for legitimate power, and *influence*, which represents power that is not openly acknowledged, appears to apply when the women's federation is studied as an organization. Put simply, the women's federation can be said to have authority as an independent organization.

The problem, however, is that the federation was not able to exercise authority within the party organization. In their role of branch organization, federation members have instead had to be satisfied with exerting influence. The workers' movement's traditional emphasis on class, not gender, as comprising the fundamental conflict within society has also functioned as an obstacle to women's collective action within the party. While the women's demands for power in the form of influence in party politics were seen as legitimate, their demands to exercise authority, that is power for women as a group in relation to the power men as a group have always wielded within the party, were not seen as legitimate but rather as a threat to the party. Here I would like to refer to the work of the political scientist Maud Landby Eduards. She has written about women's collective action, and views patriarchal power as an obstacle to women's collective action.[29] The nub of patriarchal power's political expression is, according to Eduards, that *women are hindered in implementing personal experiences – by male oppression and conflicts of interest between women and men – into collective action as women*" (i.e., women cannot use their personal experiences as a basis for collective action).[30] This view is also relevant to the relationship between the women's federation and the Social Democratic Party, where class but not gender was an acknowledged basis for collective action.

The Social Democratic Women's Federation

The political scientists referred to here, Maud Landby Eduards, Gunnel Gustafsson, Anna Jónasdóttir and Drude Dahlerup, argue in general terms, something which I do not believe to be problematic when one applies broad elements of their discussion to the relationship between the women's federation, the Social Democratic Party and its female and male members. It has often been women, within or close to the women's federation, who have articulated the feminist interest and who have asserted that there have been gender conflicts within the workers' movement. The problems and the opposition within the party that women have encountered when they have presented feminist points of view are similar to the reactions many politically active women have met under similar circumstances.[31] Speaking openly about gender conflicts and conflicting interests of women and men has perhaps been even more taboo in the Social Democratic Party, where, more than elsewhere, the common interests of the working class were continually stressed. Already at the first social democratic women's conference in 1908, when the question of building a women's federation was discussed, the party leadership defensively declared that men and women "*always have the same interests*". No special women's federation was needed because, according to a representative of the party leadership, a women's federation's "*opinions would always coincide with the party's*".[32]

Already in 1908 it was evident that opinions did not always "coincide", at least not according to the women. It was difficult to politicize issues concerning women's status and consequently throughout its history the women's federation's leading lights have complained about their male party colleagues' lack of understanding for the women's demands.[33] It is even possible that one of the federation's most important tasks has been to "free" the party from issues that both suggest and provoke gender inequalities and conflicts. By this I mean (and at the risk of inadvertently misinterpreting Dahlerup and Jónasdóttir) that there has been an unspoken expectation in the party that the women's federation would not only take care of and prepare the difficult questions of women's equality, but would also see to it that these questions, when they actually came before the party for discussion, were framed in an acceptable way, such as under the heading of family policy – and not as gender-political questions.[34] From the viewpoint of the women's federation, participation in the transformation of questions from "women's issues" into more or less gender-neutral family issues can be seen as a necessary strategy to ensure that such issues actually reached party level, and did not fade into political oblivion. The transformation has often been a difficult and painful process, which has led to conflicts both within the women's federation and between the federation and the party.

In retrospect

While studying the history of the Social Democratic Women's Federation from the time of the first congress in 1908 up to 1978, I believe I have "heard" a constant, on-going dialogue between the women and their male party colleagues concerning women's place and role within the party.[35] If I link Jónasdóttir's grouping of the interest concept with the letter which Olof Palme read aloud at the congress in 1972, it is tempting to believe that it was the simple presence and obedient women which the men expected; in other words, a troupe of women offering unconditional support within the party. However, the women's demands for real influence (a controlling presence) collided with the men's expectations, and as a result women within the party were seen as unruly. Within social democracy (as well as elsewhere) more or less clearly stated and more or less consciously held conceptions and ideas about women and their place and role in politics were prevalent. Early on there was an expectation within the workers' movement that women would support the men in *their* class battle, which is perhaps related to the fact that women's path of entry into the party was different from men's. While the men were organized through unions and in the workplace, many women came into contact with the workers' movement through the family, as wives, daughters and sisters of male party members.[36] Maybe an explanation can be found here as to why the women literally had to fight for a place, as articulated in the letter to Olof Palme.

The politically active working-class women encountered obstacles both in the home and within the party.[37]

In other words, women have not been considered independent, political figures; on the contrary, they have been allocated the role of supporters of the men.[38] To the extent that the promotion of women's interests has been discussed, it has been a question of "women's issues" as a sort of extra issue; in other words, women have tried to supplement the political agenda with "their" concerns, such as child and maternity care, abortion, etc. In this way a pattern developed early on within social democracy (indeed, from what can be seen, the same was true in the other parties); it took the form of an expectation that women would concentrate on women's issues, whether within the framework of an organized women's federation or by delegation from another party organization.[39] It was a division of labour that in its simplest form meant that questions concerning the domestic and private sphere – those concerning the home, children, family, care, *became* "women's issues".[40] On the other hand, they were issues in which men normally took *no* interest (with the exception of financial decision-making, which men often monopolized). This development became entrenched during the 1930s, when the politically active women within the SAP, represented by the Social Democratic Women's Federation, increased in number and also took on the role of co-creator of the national home.[41]

During what I choose to call a difficult "politicization process", having its inception with the formal establishment of the Social Democratic Women's Federation in 1920 and continuing until the beginning of the 1950s,[42] a pattern of co-operation developed between the party and its women's federation. From their position as a separate organization, the federation women devoted their attentions to lobbying the party on issues of special interest for women, so-called "women's issues". The women turned to the party leadership with their demands, and it was also the party leadership that decided when and how their demands would be met.[43] The women's federation had had a co-opted deputy within the party leadership since 1948; she had the right to speak, but not the right to vote. In fact, with the growth of the women's federation in both number and strength, this pattern of co-operation came under increasing pressure. Inga Thorsson, the federation's spirited chairwoman between 1952 and 1964, refused to accept that she and the federation were allotted only a subordinate position within the party, in the "women's issues department", as she called it.

When, during the 1950s, the women started to assert their right to participate in the formation of party policy, for example with respect to the Swedish nuclear weapons issue,[44] conflicts arose between the party and the women's federation. Against the party's expectations of a loyal branch organization, there ranged the federation's demands for the right to exert influence in its role as representative of a large group of party members and voters – namely, women. The situation was exacerbated by the fact that a tacitly ignored gender conflict was actually built into the organization – in the very fact of the separate organization of women. The women's federation, comprising all its members and the even larger group of non-members whom the federation believed themselves to represent, did not have access to power within the party. At the leadership level, where women were few in number until well into the 1980s, the women's federation was seen as just another party organization, not as a representative of one of the party's largest interest groups. The federation was allocated the same representation as any other party organization. The fact that it was the only party organization that organized its members according to gender was not questioned. Gender, as previously stated, was not seen as a basis for interest; if the women spoke of gender conflicts, then these were seen by the party as "women's problems". If any criticism is to be levelled at the federation, one might suggest that the organization became the vehicle for a *denied gender conflict*.

The gender conflict was "carried" by the women's federation, where for years it was constantly being expressed in discussions about the form of the women's organization. Behind the spoken question of whether the women should be organized separately or more closely connected with the party, lay an unspoken question, namely, how should the women gain more influence in the male-dominated party? A related question was that of what place and role the women had in the party. It was evident, as I have already mentioned, that the party's women and men had very different views on the women's place and role within the party. During the 1920s and especially the 1930s there was an on-going discussion, which at times turned into an altercation. The party questioned the women's separate organization, while the women complained that they were seen as coffee-makers and "election fodder".[45] At the same time, the women stressed that their federation did not comprise a separate sector within the party and that their goals were synonymous with the party's – their goal was a better society.[46] The intractable gender conflict became a permanent fixture within the women's federation, whose goal was to function both as a band of supporters for the party and as a women's interest group within the party. These two goals have been difficult to combine. This was especially true in the 1950s, when the federation defined its role as an innovator, a leader, and a promoter within the party of issues of special interest for women.[47] The task for the women's federation was not to be "obedient", but just the opposite. According to Inga Thorsson, members were, if necessary, to cause a disturbance:

> If we really wanted to please male society we would have to change colours every hour like chameleons on a patchwork quilt. Now once and forever this is not our task. We will, like other progressive and radical powers, constantly agitate and provoke, continually question whether what is thought up and planned by men is always so sensible and right.[48]

If the task was to "constantly agitate and provoke" and "continually question . . . what is thought up and planned by men", there was a grave risk that conflicts would arise between the federation and the party. As mentioned above, this happened in the 1950s when the women's federation independently and without waiting for the endorsement of the party took a stand against nuclear weapons. It became clear that the party expected the women's interests to be subordinate to the party's or, as the party leadership expressed it then, that the women should follow the men's lead with respect to the nuclear weapons issue.[49]

The problem

If I return to the original question of the problems facing women in their fight for a place within the Social Democratic Party, it does not seem to be primarily a question of men and women holding differing opinions on political issues. Instead and at least from an historical perspective, it appears to be a question of men assuming both male precedence in interpretation and women's subordination.[50] When the women have promoted their particular standpoint it has often been interpreted as an "unfriendly act", as Lena Renström, chairwoman in the Ørebro women's district, remarked in connection with the women's recommendation in 1943 that a woman be selected as congress representative for the party district. It was a suggestion that was dismissed out of hand by the men as being "entirely absurd". While the women had no wish to become the men's enemies, Lena Renström wrote,

> it is unfortunately the case that proposals from our side are often received as if they were unfriendly acts. And if we always back down, then we are going to stand here, getting nowhere all the time.[51]

With these words Lena Renström has expressed in a nutshell what I see as the women's and women's federation's eternal dilemma. When the federation acted *for* women and "caused a disturbance", it was deemed to have acted *against* the men. If the women backed down – namely, were obedient – they got nowhere.

I will take Lena Renström's words as a starting-point as I turn to describe what happened when the Social Democratic Women's Federation "caused a disturbance" in 1976, virtually staging a coup by introducing a motion in parliament for compulsory paternity leave. The coup can be interpreted in different ways. One possibility within the party was to view it as an unfriendly act, as though the women had behaved "improperly" and committed a serious breach of party discipline. Conversely, within the women's federation the coup was seen as a tool for promoting a better image of

53

equality for the party in face of the forthcoming elections. The women chose to "create a disturbance" rather than obediently to "stand still and get nowhere". Further, the episode can be seen as an example of the opposition women encounter when they act collectively, especially if they are not satisfied with a mere presence as a minority deciding on already formulated and predetermined alternatives (a simple presence), but instead choose to act in order to influence the issue which the decisions concern (namely, seek a controlling or authoritative presence). This was really a question of the women's refusal to accept the recommendation on parental allowance which the party leadership had drawn up, and of their lobbying instead for a different type of parental allowance, namely paternity leave. The women's attempt to change the recommendation met with opposition, which was manifested in different ways: partly through the exercise of techniques of domination and partly through the use of the bureaucratic system whereby the party leadership, using its precedence of interpretation could transfer issues to areas to which the women had no access. Implementation of such strategies avoided the necessity for a debate on issues of gender conflict, which in this case concerned equality between women and men. It became, as we shall see, a "non-issue".

Feminist revolt and parental allowance

In the spring of 1976 the women staged what could best be called a coup in the parliament. It was a unique event. Eighteen of the 36 social demo-cratic women in the parliament met late one evening and penned a motion demanding compulsory paternity leave. They proposed that the present parental leave should be extended to include an eighth month, allocated to the child's father.[52] The motion was presented directly to the parliamentary chancellery without the party counsel (i.e., leadership of the (s) social demo-cratic parliamentary group) being informed.[53] This was a sensational occur-rence considering, first, that the party counsel had already twice advised the women against putting forward the motion and, secondly, that it was customary for representatives within the social democratic parliamentary group to follow the counsel's recommendations. Never before had a group of representatives openly defied the counsel and more or less staged a coup by introducing a motion behind the counsel's back. "*One only does such [a thing] when one is desperate,*" said the women's federation's chairwoman Lisa Mattson many years later.[54]

Background

The background to the motion was a recommendation from the social demo-cratic government concerning an extension of the parental leave allowance, a recommendation with which the women were disappointed.[55] Their dissatisfaction was a result of the government's failure to heed the women's long-standing demand for extended parental leave with an eighth month. Already in 1972 the women's federation had demanded such an extension in their family policy programme, *Family in the future*, and as late as 1974 had voiced their demands for an eighth month (to be allocated to the father) to Minister of Health and Social Affairs, Sven Aspling.[56] They argued that their goal was an improved "image of equality" in face of the forthcoming elections, and that was the reason why they introduced a motion seeking paternity leave.

The political issue of an extended parental leave with a special time allocation to the father was nothing new; what was new and surprising was that the women's federation protested by staging a coup. The coup consisted in the fact that the women introduced the motion without having previously informed the party counsel. This itself was a form of protest, and was afterwards toned down when chairwoman Lisa Mattson explained the absence of information as a result of her being on vacation at the time.[57] Nonetheless, the action illustrated the fact that the women's federation chose to act primarily as a women's organization, in spite of demands from the (s) parliamentary group that the federation act as a loyal party organization. There, at the intersection between the federation's role as a women's organization and as a party organization, lies the root of the conflict that arose around the motion.

From the women's federation perspective it was a question of cumulative dissatisfaction with the party's lack of sensitivity to the women's demands. Their disappointment was the greater after the hopes for change raised by the Year of the Woman in 1975. However, the public response generated by the federation's demand for a 6-hour working day was considerable. The demand was debated at the party congress that year, but even if the women's federation was gratified that it had managed to get the issue debated at party level – and even into the party manifesto – there was disappointment that no decision was taken on the issue. After the congress, the question simply "disappeared" into the realms of the party's internal inquiry system. However, at the congress held in the autumn of 1975, the federation loyally supported a recommendation concerning a 6-hour working day which it viewed as a compromise by the party leadership. In return, the women expected the party's support on the issue of parental allowance the following spring. When, in the election year of 1976, the social democratic government presented a recommendation on the extension of parental allowance, which the women felt that they had not been given the opportunity to influence, their patience ran out. A decision was made within the women's federation's leadership to "quarrel". That family policy would be one of the big issues in the forthcoming election campaign served as a point of departure. The women were disappointed with the government's recommendation;

it was nothing one "could enter the election campaigns with", according to Lisa Mattson. The women's federation wanted to give the proposal a "better image of equality" and to that end Lisa Mattson stated that "We have a congress decision, where we make the eighth month a priority."[58]

From the party leadership's point of view it was a question of the women, represented by the women's federation, having dared to do what was strictly forbidden: by their action they had flagrantly disregarded the unwritten rules traditionally followed by all representatives within the social democratic parliamentary group. Initially the party counsel, whose function it was to be informed of and approve social democratic motions, attempted to talk the women out of submitting their motion.[59] The party counsel was not, however, unanimous. In fact, the women's federation did receive support from one of its members, Lily Hansson, who backed the motion in order to "satisfy the voters' expectations".[60] Lily Hansson's support was important. She was a member both of the party counsel and the party leadership, but did not usually make a point of taking a stand on women's issues. Her participation showed that this was a question of a collective women's action and not just an action emanating from the women's federation. It should be noted that the federation's own members did not support the motion as a matter of course. This was true for example of Anna-Lisa Lewén-Eliasson, who recommended against showing internal disunity. She emphasized the importance of "creating a family policy synonymous with the party's policies".[61] In other words, while in her eyes party unity took priority, for those who proposed the motion it was a question of creating a better image of equality between women and men.

To recapitulate. Leading up to the motion was the women's accumulated disappointment over the lack of party support for their demands for extended parental leave, demands voiced since 1972. The disappointment deepened when the working committee for child and family policy, which had been appointed as a result of a decision by the 1975 congress at which Lisa Mattson had represented the women's federation, was, according to the women, denied the opportunity to review the recommendation to the proposal prior to presentation. The women had hitherto taken their participation for granted and when they felt outmanoeuvred by the party leadership, they decided to introduce the motion irrespective of the consequences to themselves. If the women's federation had followed the unwritten rules for the parliamentary group, they would not have acted, especially after two recommendations from the party counsel against such an action. While the party counsel could not in reality forbid the proposal of a motion, a recommendation against doing so was to be understood as a veto.

In light of this it was truly astonishing that 18 of the 36 (s) parliamentary representatives signed and delivered the motion proposing the extension of parental leave.[62] Yet the coup almost failed to happen. The motion was originally framed as a protest by a unified leadership of the women's federation, but when the number of potential signatories diminished sharply after the two negative recommendations from the party counsel, Lisa Mattson was close to giving up.[63] Among those who signed the motion were half the members of the executive committee, but only a handful of the federation leadership's ordinary members and not one of its five deputy members.[64] Viewed positively, however, this meant that half the social democratic women in the parliament supported the motion.

Apportioning blame

Olof Palme was not happy when the party counsel met after the motion had reached the parliament. He stated that never before had a motion been introduced *against* the determined recommendations of the party counsel. When he spoke of the incident in front of the entire parliamentary group that same day, his words took the form of a severe reprimand.[65] He adopted a tone both pained and accusatory. He began by saying that, with respect to the parliament's deliberations on parental allowance, he was forced to bring up "an issue that I find extremely unfortunate to have to raise". He then disclosed that questions had been asked about how a social democratic motion on parental leave "could have by-passed the party counsel".[66] The motion had not, of course, by-passed the party counsel, and here there was an unspoken accusation to which Palme returned with dramatic effect when he closed his speech by saying that it was a *"devastating disappointment"* to discover that there was such a large group of disloyal members within the parliament. He was moved to quote his predecessor, Tage Erlander, who after 23 years as Social Democratic Party chairman and prime minister was an important figure in the party. Erlander had written in his diary: "I have been confident that our enormous party could be led without a lot of fuss and without any party discipline other than the loyalty we all should have to the party."[67] Never in all his years as chairman of the parliamentary group, continued Palme, had Erlander been subjected to what he himself had experienced, namely "that a considerable fraction within the group went against the counsel's objection".

With such emotive language Palme apportioned both blame and guilt among the women at the party level. The women had acted disloyally as a group and in so doing had violated the requirements of party discipline. Earlier, Olof Palme had touched upon his own personal disappointment at the women's action, which in his eyes had been both wrong and badly timed. This was a very effective way of imposing blame and guilt; after all, a loyal parliamentary representative was not expected to disappoint the party chairman and prime minister so deeply. Moreover, and with respect to his own efforts to achieve equality, "to the extent that the party chairman's own work carries any weight", – Palme modestly stated that he had person-ally tried to break the old mould, the way of thinking which held that only women should be concerned with women's and family issues. He had done this by choosing and emphasizing one question at a time at the congresses: equality for women in 1972 and family policy in 1975. By tackling such fundamental issues one at a time he had hoped to demonstrate that these were indeed issues for the whole party, issues that concerned men as much as women. He continued:

> If we receive such petitions signed only by women, we fall back 20 years in time and then we are back to: this is an issue that only concerns women and the men concern themselves with the so-called firm realities. I personally find this tragic, that we should end up there again.[68]

The women's mode of action was thus unequivocally rejected by the party chairman. Sten Andersson, party secretary, also blamed the women. He was very critical, believing that there was now a serious risk of a split in the party because of their action. And he, too, had stern words: "You have not made things easier for us in the election campaigns with this. If you imagine that this would be the case, then you are wrong."[69]

Re-allocating the issue

Olof Palme explained the party counsel's negative response to the motion. In his view, the reasons for their rejection were both numerous and well founded. He referred first to public financial and political constraints and then proceeded to cite internal party divisions as further reasons for turning down the motion. He cited, too, family policy decisions agreed at the most recent congress, which were on this point entirely "clear". While he pointed out that congress decisions were certainly not sacrosanct, "we usually try to follow" them, an addition that ought to be seen as a reproach to the women. In effect, Palme said that the women had set themselves above congress's jurisdiction, above the party's highest descion-making body. He continued by showing how the minister for health and social affairs' recommendation both closely followed the congressional directive and (implying the opposite of the women's motion) was held to be within the planned economic framework. Yet this has been criticized by the women, said Palme, omitting to mention that the criticism was in connection with the lack of information to the working committee on child and family policy.

Palme made no mention either of the working committee on child and family policy which the women had cited and which had been appointed by congress. He did not refer to the women's criticisms, speaking instead about a *different* family policy working committee which was engaged with a *different* if equally controversial issue of family policy, the question of a shorter working day for parents of small children.[70] This particular committee was also supposed to look at the question of extended parental leave. It was in accordance with the congress decision a year earlier, stated Palme, that the party leadership tied the two issues of extended parental leave and a shorter working day for parents of small children together into a single package. However, the women protested against the artifice of joining the two issues into such a package. One reason for their desperation, as Lisa Mattson put it when they introduced the motion, was that their pet issue of a 6-hour working day was reformulated[71] and "disappeared" into a working committee after the 1975 congress. Their other pet issue, extended parental leave, met the same fate. The women's federation did not have any access to this committee, so in the women's eyes it appeared as if the party leadership, through the re-allocation of the issue, wilfully *impeded* the women's opportunities to exert influence.

The purport of Olof Palme's words was that the party leadership's methods of dealing with the issue were in total accord with the party congress's decision, which he had in part reiterated. Here ran an important dividing line between the party leadership and the women, who read the party congress's decision in an entirely different manner from Olof Palme. As has already been said, the women believed that the party by-passed the working committee for child and family policy where the women were represented. They argued that they also had a congress decision to follow, just as the party did. From their perspective, implementing congress's decision would entail no obstacles to the inclusion in the proposal of the women's now five-year-old demand for an eighth month of parental leave. The women supported their arguments with the help of party congress minutes, just as Palme did. The matter was brought to a head when Gördis Hörnlund, who had earlier participated in the inquiry on parental leave, said that this was a question of gender conflict:

> In the end, it's men versus women. It was after all not the aim that a small group of men should henceforth bear responsibility for all family policy. At times one almost gets that impression. It probably would not hurt if a little contact was kept with those of us, who have had to raise our voices alone for such a long time. We have not received much help in the past, but I am more than willing to share the responsibility.[72]

Asserting precedence in interpretation

Neither Olof Palme nor Sven Aspling understood the women's criticisms. Olof Palme did not bring up the women's criticisms, on the contrary he maintained that the party leadership had precedence in interpretation:

I wish strongly to dispute that this should in any way be in conflict
with the party congress's decision. There is no room for any other
interpretation of the congress decision than this one.[73]

He did not touch on the issue that was of the utmost importance for the
women, that of promoting an image of equality in face of the forthcoming
elections by allocating the eighth month to the father. This became a "non-
issue" in the party. Olof Palme wanted to turn the discussion back to what
he considered the most important issue, namely, that of party discipline:

> None of the speakers has brought up what I see as of principal
> importance. It has never happened before that anyone has openly
> expressed indifference when the party counsel has strongly recom-
> mended against a motion. And this is a humiliating disappointment
> for me.[74]

Olof Palme closed the discussion and hoped that the group would act
in a unified manner when dealing with the issue in the parliament.[75]
The parliamentary group did just that; the women's motion was rejected in
accordance with the committee's recommendation without any dissent.[76]

Splitting the women

The women were for the most part united in the debate in the parliamentary group and the majority of them who spoke out were among those who
had signed the motion. However, unity among the women was broken,
when Birgitta Dahl, who was an influential member of the party leadership
but not a member of the women's federation, said that she "was sorry about
the combative stance one had taken between the sexes". She supported
Olof Palme and clearly dissociated herself from the women's federation.
She thought it sad that all of those – including herself – who had worked for
so many years on family policy, should now hear that family policy could
be advanced only because the federation had acted.

A wedge was thus driven between the women's federation and the party
and between those women who were loyal to the party and the "gorillas".
That was the nickname the women behind the motion were given afterwards
– as if it were not enough that they were accused of disloyalty, of flouting
party discipline and of being the cause of Olof Palme's personal disappointment.[77] It was also – considering that it was women who had acted
– a remarkably gender-neutral nickname. No man spoke up when the "party
women" and the "gorillas" debated, in spite of the fact that this concerned
an issue on which men and women had different points of view, and thus
the conflict manifested itself as a disagreement between the women. In this

way the women's federation representatives became the stigmatized carriers of the conflict, a gender conflict buried under the discussion of party discipline, game rules for the conduct of the parliamentary group and of interpretation of congress's decision.

Denying the gender conflict

The record of events shows that the women met with strong opposition from the party leadership when they took collective action and sought to participate in the formation of party policy on parental leave. The discussion that followed can be seen from different perspectives. For Olof Palme it was a question of a group contesting and ignoring the agreed – if unwritten – rules of conduct for the parliamentary group. In a parliament where power was equally divided between the right wing and socialist blocs, as a party chairman and prime minister, Olof Palme needed to control and monitor the group and parliamentary happenings.[78] As a result, it was imperative for him to make this a warning for others: an action such as this would not be tolerated.

For the women it was a question of a protest action, born out of feelings of desperation at not being heard or able to exert influence without reverting to unacceptable and startling methods. What is of interest is what the representative for the party leadership did *not* mention, namely, the women's desire to imbue the recommendation with a better image of equality by allocating the eighth month to the father. It was a radical, innovative and complex demand, controversial even within the women's federation.[79] Olof Palme had remarked earlier that he did not believe that one could influence the father's behaviour, so it was perhaps no coincidence that the issue "disappeared" from the debate.[80] With it disappeared, too, the image of equality in the face of elections that Lisa Mattson had so vigorously sought. The fact that Olof Palme chose not to discuss the issue is illuminating. He neither looked at the protest's intention nor did he attempt through discussion, to arrive at some semblance of unity within the parliamentary group. Instead, he maintained that the women were wrong, had acted incorrectly and had interpreted the decision incorrectly, while his own interpretation was correct and the only one that was valid.

If one examines this incident from a gender perspective, meaning that it is about women versus men, as Gördis Hörnlund said during the debate, things become more complicated. One can still sympathize with Palme's demands for order within the parliamentary group, but would he have offered such a severe reprimand if the offending group had not been made up of women? Would he have been just as dismissive of the issue – presenting an image of equality – if half the men in the parliamentary group had introduced the motion?[81] Why didn't a single man bring up the issue of the need to improve the profile of equality? Why didn't a single one of their male party colleagues support the women? Why didn't they, too, fight for paternity leave?

My questions are of a speculative nature and there is, of course, no single answer. Of equal importance are questions concerning Palme's authority as party chairman, the invisible element in this context. The question is if gender was not a more important element; this was a matter of gender conflict, as Gördis Hörnlund said in the debate.[82] For once it was perfectly clear that a large group of women in the parliament wanted something entirely different from the party leadership, and they were ready to fight for it. The women's federation's chairwoman took responsibility for the motion and even if almost all the women who signed it were members of the federation, this was not solely a federation action but a *women's action*. The women wanted to improve their profile with the female voters; they acted as women in the parliament. As a result they ignored the normal game rules for the parliamentary group. They were reprimanded for their action, but in the eyes of the women it had been worth it. As a direct consequence of their "coup", the allocation of an eighth month's paid leave to the father was incorporated into the party's family policy programme in the autumn of 1976. While the party fell from office in the elections that year, the issue of paternity leave has, however, once again come to the fore. In 1994, and in the face of tough parliamentary opposition, the Swedish liberal party succeeded in allocating one month of the paid parental leave to the father only. The reform was, however, short-lived. When the social democrats regained power in 1995 the extra month of parental leave for fathers was pared down.

The question of whether or not the 1970s saw a turning-point for women, with respect to their influence on party policy on equality, remains unanswered. However, Lena Renström's words from 1943, on women's legitimate demands for influence being seen as "unfriendly actions" by men, seem to apply equally to the 1970s. The party leadership's refusal to speak in terms of women's and men's interests proved the conditionality of the women's participation: if they were not obedient and did not follow party policy, they were viewed as disruptive "gorillas" who did not fit into the parliamentary group. Prior to the elections in 1976, it seems that attempts were initiated at the highest level to remove two of the women who had taken leading roles in the coup from their parliamentary seats. However, this was unsuccessful.[83]

Notes

1. Letter quoted by Olof Palme in his congress address, "Equality for women"; minutes from SAP congress 1972, p. 234. Olof Palme was at the time prime minister and chairman of the Social Democratic Party, SAP. It was his first

congress as party chairman; he had replaced Tage Erlander at the 1969 congress.

2. Ibid.
3. Percentages calculated from membership statistics in SAP's and SSKF's annual reports 1972.
4. Equality (primarily between classes, but in the 1970s also between men and women, and what came to be called *jämställdhet* in Sweden) had been an important theme since the 1967 party congress, when the first equality working party was appointed under the direction of Alva Myrdal. The group presented its first report in 1968 and another at the 1972 congress. See also Karlsson 1990.
5. Elmbrant 1989:31; my italics.
6. Compare Yvonne Hirdman, who wonders if the name change is due to a desire to keep equality "*masculinely pure*" and both the French Revolution's slogan of "Liberté, egalité, fraternité" (freedom, brotherhood and equality) and socialism's ideology that the important conflict is that between classes, not that between the sexes. Yvonne Hirdman, "Genderless research. The women and SAP from a genus perspective", *Arbetarhistoria* **52** (4), 5, 1989.
7. Karlsson 1996.
8. B. Ås, *Women together. A guide for feminist liberation* (Malmö: Gidlunds, 1982), p. 49.
9. Eduards et al. 1991:30.
10. Ibid., p. 31.
11. Ås 1982, p. 54; Eduards et al. 1991, p. 31.
12. Karlsson 1991; Carlsson Wetterberg 1993:53. Complaints about women's lack of interest were also expressed within the women's federation, for example in their programme publication *Forward in SSKF* of 1956, which complains about the lack of political interest (cf. pp. 9 and 18).
13. A.G. Jónasdóttir, "On the concept of interests, and the limitation of interest theory" in *The political question of gender. Developing theory and research with a feminist face*, K.B. Jones & A.G. Jónasdóttir, 44 (London: Sage, 1988).
14. Eduards et al. 1991, p. 29.
15. The governmental rule was actually laid aside for three months in 1936 and during the Second World War. In my PhD thesis *From brotherhood to sisterhood*, I examine the women's federation's fight for influence up to 1978.
16. Eduards et al. 1991, p. 31: "The important question of *why* men dominate political life has not been researched by political scientists in any deeper sense." Compare, for example, with how power studies describe male dominance in the power elite: "Men are responsible for a dominant contribution to the 1989 power elite." Men made up 87 per cent of the power elite. See The Power Inquiry's main report, *Democracy and power in Sweden*, 44 (SOU 1990), p. 330.
17. A. Östlund, *Morgonbris* (1924:4); G. Karlsson "From support group to conflict of interests or should women follow men?" in *Viewpoint Sweden*, SIS bulletin, New York (14 March 1994).
18. Dahlerup 1984:34.
19. Ibid., p. 35f.
20. Ibid., p. 33ff. With Anna G. Jónasdóttir's formulation of Drude Dahlerup's thesis: "political parties have always tried to avoid a clear politicizing of the question of women, and have instead connected sex/gender conflicts with family politics or some other sub-issue" (Jónasdóttir 1988:44), with reference to Dahlerup.
21. Karlsson 1996, Ch. 7.

22. Jónasdóttir 1988:54. See also Jónasdóttir 1994: Ch. 7, esp. 154ff, 170ff.
23. Jónasdóttir 1988:54.
24. Ibid., p. 40.
25. Where hereafter I refer to Jónasdóttir's concepts "simple" and "controlling" I do so without quotation marks.
26. Eriksson 1969:163.
27. Jónasdóttir 1986:163. Here she separates the concept of power into *influence and authority*. Authority denotes legitimate power while influence is power that is not openly acknowledged. Women have influence but often meet opposition when "we demand authority as female beings", according to Jónasdóttir (ibid.).
28. Ibid.
29. Eduards 1992.
30. Ibid., p. 255.
31. Whether or not women meet male opposition tends to depend more on gender and (possibly) degree of "unruliness" than political persuasion. See, e.g., the Conservative Britt Mogård's memoirs, *Summa summarum. Roots, life and standpoints* (1991) and memoirs of Social Democrat Anna Greta Leijon, *All roses are not to be chastised!* (1991).
32. Taken from the minutes of the negotiations from Sweden's first Social Democratic women's congress in Stockholm in 1908 (p. 19). The women understood it as the party leaders having vetoed a women's federation; see Ruth Gustafsson's comment at the 1914 women's congress, Social Democratic women's congress notes 1914, p. 14; my italics.
33. Carlsson 1986. See also Karlsson 1996.
34. Drude Dahlerup (1984) and Anna Jónasdóttir (1988) speak of questions being "transferred" from gender-political to gender-neutral agendas.
35. When I speak of women's place and role in the party I tie into Yvonne Hirdman's thoughts on the genus (gender) system and the genus (gender) contract, about the ranking of gender and the distribution of places and functions at different levels in society. See Hirdman 1990:44, 1988:3.
36. Karlsson 1996: Ch. 3.
37. Ibid.
38. This was true both within social democracy and the other parties. About the support troupe function, see Karlsson (1990:47). M. Eduards, *Women and politics. Facts and explanations* (Stockholm: LiberFörlag, 1977), p. 39 and Hirdman 1984:267.
39. Karlsson 1996; Hirdman 1989, 1983.
40. Carlsson 1986.
41. Karlsson 1990:35, Hirdman 1989, Lindholm 1990.
42. Karlsson 1996: Ch. 3.
43. See discussion from women's federation's congress 1952 when Gunnel Olsson said, "We speak of our wishes and it is then up to the party and the government to formulate the proposal" (SSKF congress minutes, 1952, p. 45).
44. Nilsson Hoadley 1989.
45. Many women complained in letters to Hulda Flood, party secretary with responsibility for women's organization, over the inferior (i.e. subordinate) role allotted them by their party brothers. See Hulda Flood's collection and SAP:s archive vol. FXXVIaa 1–4, both to be found at Workers' Movements Archive and Stockholm Library. See also Karlsson 1996.

46. According to Anna Sterky at the women's federation's congress in 1920 (SSKF congress minutes 1920, p. 7).
47. *Forwards in SSKF*, p. 8.
48. *Morgonbris* 1964: 1, editorial, p. 28.
49. SAP party leadership minutes 1956, 21/12.
50. This is especially relevant with respect to defining politics, which the male social democrat did excellently at the beginning of the twentieth century; see Carlsson, 1986, Carlsson Wetterberg 1993:54f.
51. Letter from Lena Renström, chairwoman for Ørebro Social Democratic women's district, to the leadership for the Ørebro party district, 19 October 1943; Ørebro women's district's archive BI:1, Folk Movement Archive, Ørebro.
52. The Swedish parental allowance in 1975 guaranteed parents the right to seven months' paid leave for the birth of each child. Leave can be taken by both parents, one at a time or simultaneously. Because it was most often women who took up the entitlement to paid leave, the women's federation wanted to encourage men to do the same – hence their proposal for an eighth month's paid leave. Allocation meant that the parent who had already taken up the first seven months, was not entitled to the eighth month. In the case of single-parent families, the parent would have the right to the eighth month.
53. The leadership of the parliamentary group was called the party counsel; Olof Palme was chairman.
54. Taped interview with Lisa Mattson, 7 October 1987; my italics.
55. SAP, parliamentary group's minutes, 17 February 1976, para. 4.
56. SSKF annual report 1974, Supplement 13, pp. 60–2.
57. Parliamentary group's minutes, 16 March 1976.
58. Ibid.
59. SAP Party Counsel's minutes, 25 February 1976, para. 2b and minutes for 11 March 1976.
60. Ibid., 11 March 1976.
61. Ibid.
62. Motion 1975/766:2231; parl. minutes no. 119, 6 May 1976; interview with Lisa Mattson, tape dated 7 October 1987.
63. According to an oral report from Lisa Mattson via telephone conversation, 7 May 1994.
64. The federation's minutes reveal no internal discussions, but according to Kerstin Sandelius, who was the secretary for inquiries at the federation's office, there was strong criticism of the "father's motion" among the office employees (taped interview, 19 August 1992). Annie Marie Sundbom, federation secretary, was also very critical (taped interview, 24 April 1990).
65. From 1975 to 1976 the Social Democratic parliamentary group consisted of 156 representatives: 36 women and 120 men. The women's share was thus 23 per cent.
66. SAP parliamentary group minutes, 16 March 1976.
67. Ibid., quoted by Palme from Erlander's memoirs.
68. SAP parliamentary group minutes, 16 March 1976.
69. Ibid.
70. This was the so-called Fridhska committee, which was set up to look at the 1975 women's federation and party congress's controversial issue of a 6-hour working day for parents of small children. The result of the women's demands for a 6-hour working day was just that: an inquiry into the working hours of

parents with small children. The working committee's name came from Göte
Fridh, who led the committee.

71. In other words, an issue of shorter working hours for parents of small children
    – one example of gender conflict issues becoming questions of family policy.
    Compare Drude Dahlerup's hypothesis mentioned above concerning how gender
    conflict issues do not reach the political agenda other than in family policy form.
    A 6-hour working day was one such issue within the party (Karlsson 1996:
    Ch. 7).

72. SAP parliamentary group's minutes, 16/3 March 1976.

73. Ibid

74. Ibid.

75. Ibid.

76. Parliamentary minutes, no. 119, 1976.

77. Oral report on the nickname from SSKF official, confirmed by Lisa Mattson in
    conversation (7 October 1987) and via telephone conversation (9 May 1994)
    when she read and gave opinions on parts of this text. On stigmatizing as a
    strategy to remove issues from the political agenda, see Dahlerup 1984:35.
    There were women within the women's federation who were against staging
    the "coup", for example, federation secretary Annie Marie Sundbom. In a (taped)
    interview (24 April 1990) she emphasized that she had not participated in the
    action: "I am loyal to the party. They introduced the motion late one evening
    without it having gone through the group leadership."

78. The socialist bloc, the social democrats and the leftist-party communists had
    175 seats. Together the right-wing parties, the centre party, the conservatives
    and the liberal party, also had 175 seats. The parliament was called the "lottery
    parliament"; when the votes were even between the blocs, decisions had to be
    made by lottery.

79. The issue concerning the father's relationship to his child was not given time in
    the debates in the committees, where minutes were recorded. But at least
    among the officials within the women's federation there were those who thought
    that the federation leadership had acted too quickly and were uncertain about an
    obligatory allocation (interview with Kerstin Sandelius; tape dated 19 August
    1993). When the matter was discussed among the party leadership, differences
    of opinion among the women also surfaced; voiced, for example, by Lisa Mattson
    and Anna-Greta Skantz, the latter a member of the party leadership and former
    longtime representative of SSKF's federation's leadership; SAP party leadership
    minutes, 20 May 1976.

80. SAP parliamentary group minutes, 17 February 1976, when the government's
    proposal for parental leave was introduced.

81. Allowing that the evidence is scant: men seem more apt to follow the political
    game rules, at least if one is to believe S.U. Palme's inquiry on party loyalty
    among s-parliamentary women in "At the polls and in the parliament during
    the last 50 years". *Women's vote and right*, R. Hamrin Theorell et al. (eds), 90.
    (Stockholm: Allmänna Förlaget, 1969)!

82. The gender conflict could have been clearer if more women had supported the
    motion. In her capacity as representative of the federation leadership, Frida
    Berglund from Luleå, said that the motion would be introduced only if "we are
    united". The leadership was not united and Berglund was disappointed that
    the action occurred at all. Lisa Mattson was disappointed, on the other hand, at

the lack of support from their own federation leadership. There were, however, women outside the federation leadership who signed the motion.
83. According to Lisa Mattson, chairwoman of the Social Democratic Women's Federation (telephone interview, 9 May 1995).

References

The archives of the Swedish Social Democratic Party (SAP), the SAP Parliamentary Group and The Social Democratic Women's Federation (Arbetarrörelsens Arkiv och Bibliotek, Stockholm).

Carlsson, C. 1986. *Feminist perspective and feminist politics. A study of Swedish Social Democracy 1880–1910.* Lund: Arkiv dissertation series 25.

Carlsson Wetterberg, C. 1993. Women's political strategies in a historical perspective. In *Equality research, guide light on Sweden, equality's promised land,* L. Jakobsen & J.C. Karlsson (eds). Karlstad: Centre for Equality, Labour Science, Research Report 93:5, University of Karlstad.

Dahlerup, D. 1984. Overcoming the barriers. In *Women's views of the political world of men,* J. Hicks Stiehm (ed.). New York: Transnational, Dobbs Ferry.

Eduards, M.L. 1992. Against the rules of the game. On the importance of women's collective actions. In *Rethinking change. Current Swedish feminist research.* Uppsala: HSFR, Uppsala.

Eduards, M. Landby, Gustafsson, G., Jónasdóttir, A.G. 1991. Gender power and powerlessness in a nation state. In *Women's power and influence.* Jämfo-report no. 15, Stockholm.

Elmbrant, B. 1989. *Palme.* Stockholm: Fischer & Rye.

Eriksson, N. 1969. The women and the Social Democratic Party. In *Women's vote and right.* Ruth Hamrin-Theorell et al. (eds). Stockholm: Ab Allmänna.

Family in the future. A socialistic family policy. SSKF, Stockholm 1972.

Forwards in SSKF, programme publication from SSKF, Stockholm 1956.

Hirdman, Y. 1983. The socialistic housewife, the Social Democratic Women's Movement and housework 1890–1939. In *We are able, we are needed! Women unite in their own organizations.* Brita Åkerman (ed.). Stockholm: Akademilitteratur Publishers AB.

Hirdman, Y. 1984. The master's comfort – SAP and the women. *Tiden,* 1984, 5–6.

Hirdman, Y. 1988. The genus system – reflections on women's subordination. *Kvinnovetenskaplig Tidskrift* **3**, 49–63.

Hirdman, Y. 1989. *Att Lägga Livet till Rätta* (Studies of Swedish folk-home policies). Stockholm: Carlssons.

Hirdman, Y. 1990. *The genus system.* The Power Inquiry's main report, *Democracy and power in Sweden,* SOU, p. 44.

Jónasdóttir, A.G. 1986. Gender, power and politics. A summary of on-going theory development on the foundations of the formally equal society's patriarchy. *Feminism and Marxism. A love affair with impediments.* Stockholm: Arbetarkultur.

Jónasdóttir, A.G. 1988. On the concepts of interest, women's interests and the limitation of interest theory. In *The political question of gender. Developing theory and research with a feminist face,* K.B. Jones & A.G. Jónasdóttir (eds). London: Sage.

Jónasdóttir, A.G. 1992. Does gender have any implications for democracy? In *Contract in crisis. About women's place in the welfare state*, G. Åström & Y. Hirdman (eds). Stockholm: Carlssons.

Jónasdóttir, A.G. 1993. Patriarchy as a social theoretical problem. In *Equality research. Guide light on Sweden as equality's promised land*, L. Jakobsen & J.C. Karlsson (eds). Karlstad: Research Report 93:5, Centre for Equality, Labour Science, University of Karlstad.

Jónasdóttir, A.G. 1994. *Why women are oppressed*. Philadelphia: Temple University Press.

Karlsson, G. 1990. *To the male society's pleasure?* Stockholm: Tiden.

Karlsson, G. 1991. A red streak on the horizon. Research on the women in the workers' movement. In *Worklife and the workers' movement. Modern historical research in Sweden*, K. Misgeld & K. Åmark (eds). Stockholm: Workers' Movement's Archive and Library.

Karlsson, G. 1993. *Från Stödtrupp till Intressekamp*. Lecture given at the Conference for Women and Politics. Strategies for Change, arranged by the Forum for Feminist Studies, University of Ørebro, 15 May 1993. Unpublished manuscript in possession of the author, available in English as: "From support group to conflicts of interest or should women follow men?" Translated by Kersti Board in *Viewpoint Sweden*, no. 14 March 1994, a periodical issued by SIS, the Swedish Information Service, Svenska Generalkonsulatet i New York.

Karlsson, G. 1996. *From brotherhood to sisterhood. The Swedish Social Democratic Women's Federation's struggle for power in the Social Democratic Party*. PhD thesis, Department of History, University of Göteborg. Lund: Arkiv.

Leijon, A.G. 1991. *All roses are not to be chastised!* Stockholm: Tiden.

Lindholm, M. 1990. *Speech on the feminine. Studies in feminist thought in Sweden during the 1930s*. PhD thesis, Department of Sociology, University of Göteborg.

Mogård, B. 1991. *Summa summarum. Roots, life and standpoints*. Stockholm: Norstedts.

Nilsson Hoadley, A.-G. 1989. *Nuclear weapons as a party problem. Sweden's Social Democratic Women's Federation and the question of Swedish nuclear weapons 1955–60*. PhD thesis, Department of History, University of Stockholm (Acta Universitatis Stockholmiensis 40).

Palme, S.U. 1969. At the polls and in the parliament during 50 years. In *Women's vote and right*. Ruth Hamrin Theorell et al. (eds). Stockholm: AB Allmänna Förlaget.

Power Inquiry's Main Report, *Democracy and power in Sweden,* SOU 1990:44.

Ås, Berit 1982. *Women united, a handbook on liberation*. Malmö: Gidlunds.

CHAPTER FOUR

"On their own premises": the political project of the Icelandic Women's Alliance

Sighrúdur Helga Sigurbjarnardóttir

Since the beginning of the twentieth century, women of the Western world have fought for a place in the political arena. Although most have battled within "men's parties", there have always been some who dreamed of, and realized, separate electoral alternatives within the political system. Audur Styrkársdóttir (1995) has found examples of women's lists or women's parties not only in all the Nordic countries except Finland, for example in Denmark, Iceland, Norway and Sweden, but also in the USA, England, Belgium, the Netherlands, Germany, Israel, Japan and Australia. The oldest of these was a Women's Equal Rights Party, founded in California, which fielded its own candidate for the presidential elections in 1884 and 1888. A recent and remarkably successful example is the Icelandic Women's Alliance which was established in the early 1980s.

Women's repeated efforts to voice their political opinions through their own electoral arrangements is clearly testimony to the fact that many women are not comfortable at a table set by men. Styrkársdóttir finds that the arguments women have used to legitimize promoting separate ballots or forming political parties are similar around the world. She points to three main arguments among which the most salient is one or other version of maternalism or, rather, of a wider perspective of care, which stresses that women's experiences foster special qualities which society needs. Traditionally, such needs have not been voiced in the established political parties, and hence many women in so many different countries feel themselves responsible for politicizing them. Women also often lay claim to special interests as mothers and, finally, they state that as women they are denied the space and opportunities enjoyed by men within politics.[1]

It is thus evident that for these women the content of politics has been important. However, the form of politics (i.e., the methods and organization of political work) has also been of special concern to many women. Styrkársdóttir points out that for Christabel Pankhurst, for example, who founded the Women's Party in England in 1918, it was just as vital to change the rules of the game of politics. Pankhurst wanted "to create a new game", rather than to be an uncritical player in the existing one.

Such dual aspects of women's political concerns – with the form as well as the content of politics, are in line with Jónasdóttir's (1988, 1994) reformulated application of the concept of interest. She emphasizes that historically this concept has had a twofold significance which makes it meaningful to distinguish between the form and content of political interests, although the two aspects are connected.

In summary, the concept of interest has from the beginning had a dual significance consisting of two connected, though often hidden, aspects: that of *form* – the demand to "be among", otherwise the demand for participation in and control over society's public affairs; and that of *content* or *result* – which concerns the question of those substantive values that politics puts into effect and distributes, including what this process results in as it relates to various groups, needs, wishes and demands (Jónasdóttir 1988:40).

It is when women demand the right to participate in politics *as women* that the dual meaning of the concept of interest is most obvious. For these women it is not enough just to enter politics, shaped as it is historically by men. They demand a position that makes it possible for them to change the content of the politics as well as its form ("the game"), on the basis of their own values.

In this chapter I shall introduce Icelandic women's contemporary attempt to participate in politics on, as they put it, their "own terms". Of the many attempts, worldwide, to establish a separate women's alternative in electoral politics, the Icelandic Women's Alliance, founded in 1983, is the only one that has succeeded in gaining a significant position within the political system.[2] Of all the various strategies women use to win influence and make room for themselves and their concerns among the rest of humanity – that is, among men, this is but one. Whether the Icelandic alternative would be capable of realization in other contexts or, indeed, how effective generally from a feminist viewpoint this separate strategy might be, are issues too extensive to be taken up in any detail in this chapter. However, as a unique political phenomenon the Women's Alliance makes an interesting case study from the viewpoint of democratic politics in general and of feminist politics in particular.

I begin with some historical facts and a discussion of the ideological basis for the foundation of The Women's Alliance. The main aim of this chapter is to analyze the Alliance as a political project, to examine its agenda in order to understand what its women members mean when they claim as their (and other women's) interests the right to "participate in politics on their own terms". For this I use a four-dimensional model borrowed from Ann Phillips (1991). In each case, some criticisms are offered, followed by emphasis on the current dilemma of the Women's Alliance: the fact that it finds itself torn between different organizational levels, between a grass-roots movement on the one hand and ordinary political party business on the other.

The material here does not focus on the practical function of the Women's Alliance within the political system, but the chapter concludes with open-ended questions about separate women's lists/parties as a strategy in women's struggle to create a better society.[3] Nor is concentration centred on the practical politics of the Women's Alliance. Thus, for the most part, the connection between the theories and practice of the Alliance must be left for later analysis.

The start

As recently as the early 1980s the position of women in Icelandic politics was extremely weak. At the time women representatives held only three seats out of sixty (5 per cent) in the Icelandic parliament, the *Althingi*, this was the largest number of women ever to have held seats simultaneously in the *Althingi*. Icelandic women have been eligible for election to the national assembly since 1915, but until 1983, when the Women's Alliance came on the scene, the total number of women ever elected to the *Althingi* was twelve. Compared with the steadily increasing numbers of women entering the national assemblies of the other Nordic countries, the situation in Iceland was striking. In 1983 women's representation in the Finnish national assembly was 31 per cent, in Sweden (1982) it was 28 per cent, Norway (1981) had 26 per cent and Denmark (1981) 24 per cent.[4] Further, in the local Icelandic political assemblies the number of women representatives was very low – in 1983 only 6 per cent, a situation the more remarkable when compared with the rest of the Nordic countries where women representatives were far more common at local level. In the national election in 1983 women's representation in Iceland reached 15 per cent. Nine women were elected to the *Althingi*, three of them form the Women's Alliance.

The anomalous political position of Icelandic women is hard to explain, particularly after Iceland gained its New Women's Movement. In 1970 women in and around Reykjavik, the capital of Iceland, organized under the name "*Raudsokkarnir*" (the Red Stockings). In a way, the founding of the Women's Alliance can be seen as part of and a shift in the development of the New Women's Movement in Iceland. The Red Stockings were very active between 1970 and 1975, but in the years afterwards the movement suffered from bitter internal power struggles and its activity decreased considerably. In the beginning of 1981 there was almost no activity at all. The Red Stockings did not manage to mobilize ordinary women to any great degree; on the contrary, ordinary women were often alienated by the movement's activities and Marxist ideology and found it repellent. The Red Stockings never became a mass movement, and the organization was confined to the Reykjavik area.

In May 1981 a small group of women from the Red Stockings' organization took the initiative to assemble women to discuss their situation and to debate new ways of campaigning for the women's struggle in Iceland. This initiative resulted in calls for an open meeting on the 14 November 1981 where the idea of a separate women's alternative in the local 1982 election was to be discussed and decisions made.

From the perspective of their understanding of a basic commonality of interests among women, the speakers at the meeting emphasized the bonds that unite women. Stressing that the positive aspects of women's experience are essential for the future development of society, they held that women themselves must actively contribute to bringing about change. Neither right nor left, bourgeoisie nor working class were referred to. Those women who attended were addressed directly, in an effort to mobilize women's own potential for political change based on their unique knowledge and experience. Their words struck a chord with women who had previously participated neither in politics nor in the traditional women's struggle, with women whom the Red Stockings with their dogmatic separation of bourgeoisie and working-class women and allegations that "women are nothing but an unpaid proletariat", could never reach.

The exact number of participants in this open meeting is not known, but estimates vary from 400 to 600. It should be remembered that the whole population of Iceland at the time was about 250,000. What is beyond doubt is that the conference room was filled beyond capacity, and that an overwhelming majority was in favour of a separate women's list in the coming local election. In the local 1982 election the women's list in Reykjavik, called the Women's Alternative polled 5 per cent of the vote, and gained two seats on the city council. In the beginning most of the women involved intended the Women's Alternative to be a one-off campaign. But late that year some of them became interested in running for national election in 1983. In a short but intense debate it became clear that the women were unable to reach agreement. Those who wanted a new list for the national election decided to hold an open meeting along similar lines to that held on 14 November 1981. The result was a new list, the Women's Alliance. This organization has participated in every election since, both on a local and national level, and most of the members of the Women's Alternative have shifted their allegiance to the Women's Alliance.

In the 1983 election the Women's Alliance received 5.5 per cent of votes cast, and won three seats in the *Althingi*. In 1987 the women won 10.1 per cent of the votes and six seats, and in 1991, 8.3 per cent and five seats. Between 1987 and 1993 the polls have shown a variation giving between 8 and 28 per cent support. In the beginning of 1993, polls showed 10 per cent support, but between late summer and mid-September it rose to 17 or 18 per cent.

The ideological basis

The Women's Alliance entered Icelandic politics in 1983, with the realization that although women had to some extent battled their way into the political arena, they had hitherto failed to bring about any fundamental changes. Women had entered a system formed by men for men, and were really only allowed to participate as men's assistants. According to the Women's Alliance, women's greatest problem was not the very exclusion from participation in party politics; after all, experience had shown that "clever" women were allowed to participate.

The Women's Alliance felt that women's first and most pressing problem was that they had taken part neither in defining the political agenda nor in developing the work methods or modes of doing politics. The women in the Women's Alliance felt that the structure and working methods of the parties were inappropriate for women, and therefore effectively barred women's commitment. They also said that the number of women listed on a political party ballot was in fact immaterial unless it had some consequence for the respective party's ideology and programme. While the actual presence of women was a necessary precondition, in itself it was insufficient to deserve women's votes. In a newspaper article from the spring of 1982, one of the women behind the Women's Alliance states:

> Until men and women become equal in reality, a woman on a political party ballot is first and foremost a representative of a party founded by men, a woman who has made a place for herself in the world of men, and who has formed her political stance according to men's standards. We cannot call that *voting for women*; we call it *voting for party representatives*, that is all.[5]

According to the Women's Alliance, it was essential that the women who were elected based their political activities on an increasing feminist consciousness. They held that in Iceland, in 1982, the only way to do this was through a separate electoral alternative.

The single most important source of ideological inspiration for the establishment of the Women's Alliance was Berit Ås's theory of a women's culture. In 1981 Ås wrote:

> At this time in women's history, I pose a theory of women's culture as a counter culture . . . Fully understood, this theory will give the women's movement a tool to enhance self-confidence, group understanding, and a platform for a future strategy . . . Making women's culture visible is the first step in women's common struggle for freedom (Ås 1981:16).[6]

A great number of women in Iceland accepted Ås's challenge to make the concept of a women's culture into the strategic platform of their political struggle. The starting-point of the movement was the existence of a women's culture that is suppressed and hardly visible in society. This culture emerges from the differing position of women and men in society, and from the resulting division of labour. The arena for women's culture with its norms for human relations, its values, logic and language, is the private sphere. These cultural aspects differ markedly from those that have developed in the public sphere, and which, according to the women of the Women's Alliance, must be termed men's culture. From this consciousness emerged the goal of Icelandic women: to make women's culture as highly valued as that of men's in the development of society.

Let us take an example of how the Women's Alliance presents its platform by looking at a quotation from their 1984 pamphlet *From woman to woman. The Women's Alliance, history – agenda – structure.*

> Women's role has always been to protect life and to care for life. Women carry children, give birth, and raise them. Their workplace has traditionally been their homes, or close to their home. That is where women have developed their methods for cooking, production of clothing, midwifery, and upbringing of children. Women have cared for the sick and the elderly. In spite of women's different life situations, this is still their common world of experience, a heritage from generation to generation, and this is the reality that has shaped their worldview and culture . . . The ideology of our association is based on the belief that men's and women's values and views of life are shaped by their traditional division of labour, their upbringing, and gender. Men's culture has been more outward; hard competition dominates, and man's personal as well as his family's status depends on his ability to cope well in competition. Men's hard world often seems to hold no place for human co-operation and feelings, which, on the other hand, is a vital aspect of traditional women's work (1984:3).

To achieve a more positive development of society, the Alliance women felt it was vital that women should retain the values and norms from their own culture as a basis for their political activities.

The Women's Alliance as a political project

The goal of the Icelandic women who founded the Women's Alliance was to integrate their growing feminist consciousness with practical politics. As they did not articulate a fully defined ideology,[7] it is problematic to pinpoint the concrete implications of this goal. A process was started, and a course was set, without a projected goal. As Sandra Harding (1986) has pointed out, this is understandable, since there is no existing conception of a society with complete equality between women and men. The spokeswomen for the Women's Alliance in Iceland said that instead of taking the premises and working rules of the system for granted, they would always ask the question "why?" or "Is that necessarily so?" in order to make themselves aware of established truths. The issue was to enclose accepted conventions within parentheses, at least temporarily in clear opposition to the usual alternative practice for women entering traditional political parties who struggle first to gain power on men's terms so that they may later be able to work on those changes and for the issues they feel to be most important. The goal of the Women's Alliance is change – change in the balance of power between women and men, and not least fundamental change in the governing values and attitudes within society. Their goal is also to change the political system, indeed the entire political culture.

One difficulty in analyzing the Women's Alliance, is that their statements are often vague. Their goal, i.e., the notion of a society where the sexes are equal, is held to emerge through a process. The women claim that their political movement is based on a feminist system of ideas, a system the further development of which they themselves contribute to through their actions. On feminism they state:

> It [feminism] must never be entrapped in a closely defined and complete system. If that happens, it will die a definition death, as have all men's ideologies so far. As is life, so is feminism an eternal process of renewal. It can never be continual wellbeing (Hafstad 1988).

These Icelandic women demand access to the political system *on their own terms*, which they believe will have direct consequences for the form of politics, as well as for its content. This is in line with Phillips (1991) who claims that women's goal has generally been to strive for democratic practice in both the form and content of politics. According to Phillips, this means (a) cutting through pompous masculine rhetoric; (b) breaking down unnecessary hierarchical structures; (c) opening up the political decision-making process; and (d) creating a new world. The following section will examine the goals and practice of the Women's Alliance in the light of these points.

(a) Cutting through (pompous) masculine rhetoric

A concern among the women of the Women's Alliance has been to remind people that *politics* is about *our* lives. Given that, they hold that the words and concepts used should be comprehensible to women and to people in general. Thus, on the one hand, it is important for these women to peel off the difficult packaging of political concepts, to find their hidden meaning. On the other hand, it is equally important to bring words and concepts from women's everyday lives into the political language to avoid the sense of alienation many women express towards political language.[8] If this strategy were to succeed, the Women's Alliance women believed that politics would soon appear less complicated than it did when hearing politicians talking in the traditional way.

During the first elective period, it was both natural and necessary for the representatives from the Women's Alliance to use their everyday language. The three women elected to the *Althingi* had no previous experience of working in party politics or of participation in the organized women's struggle. Describing the first period, when she had her first-ever experience of taking part in a radio broadcast, of appearing on live television and at public meetings, all within the space of a few days, as a time of tremendous stress, one of the representatives commented: "I had nothing but sound reason and my inner voice to guide me." For these women, this meant using the language they already possessed.[9]

No research has hitherto been done on the language of the Women's Alliance, and it is something which needs to be examined from at least two angles. The first concerns the language the women employ in everyday, practical politics, where the impression is that they have to some degree succeeded in speaking a language people understand. While this is a point often made in discussions about the Women's Alliance and Icelandic politics, the language issue is still a live debate within the organization. At its 1993 Spring Convention,[10] several of the younger women held that the *Althingi* representatives from the Women's Alliance used a language free from political jargon within the movement, and that it was important that they spoke in the same way outside it.

The ensuing discussion showed that most agreed that it is important to be conscious of language. But it was also pointed out that women are different, have different backgrounds and hence also speak differently.[11] Some women emphasized that the point was also about being taken seriously in political debate, and that everyone should therefore speak the language that came most naturally to her.

The other angle regarding the language of the Women's Alliance concerns their wording of their major goals and political perspectives. One might argue that it is also difficult to cut through pompous feminist rhetoric to find the political substance. Here I refer to statements such as those asserting that the movement cannot be placed on the political scale, because the Women's Alliance is "the third dimension", that it "take[s] nothing at face value, but view[s] everything as new, this time through the eyes of women". Hence, it is often hard for other politicians and for people in general to grasp the real content of what is said. A valid question in this connection might be to ask through which women's eyes the Women's Alliance women view the world. As a matter of fact, though, and not surprisingly, in later years the question of the differences between women has increasingly been discussed among them.

(b)   Breaking down unnecessary hierarchical structures

The women of the Women's Alliance have a vision of human relations as non-hierarchical. One speaker at their 1987 National Convention puts it as follows:

> By refusing to elect a leader, refusing a structure of power, refusing an order of rank and thereby refusing to make this an aspect of our interaction, we are making a statement that we are all equal, and have equal opportunities for influence. Possibly, we are invalidating the conception that one individual's relation to another, one institution's relation to another, must of necessity be defined according to an order of rank.

The fundamental principle in the structure of the Women's Alliance is the aim of spreading power; of drawing as many women as possible into the decision-making process. The women define the Alliance as a women's movement. Accordingly, it has no elected leader, nor any form of elected leadership. The movement has chapters in all of Iceland's seven constituencies. These chapters are independent units with an executive committee, which bears certain responsibilities and monitors the chapter's activities. A guiding principle (not a statute rule) limits the period a woman may sit on the executive committee to between six and eight months at a time.

The National Convention, which is open to all women of the Women's Alliance, is their highest body and empowered to take all political decisions. The Alliance has one central authority, the executive council, which has overall financial responsibility for the movement and is partly in charge of distributing tasks among members. The executive council functions as a purely administrative body and it is through the so-called "back-up groups", which emerge according to the need to work on certain issues, that the real political work is done. Anyone can initiate a group to work on current topics and later present its findings to the women in the *Althingi* or on the city council. Alternatively, elected representatives of the Women's Alliance can request background reports from the back-up groups on specific issues. Thus, the back-up groups are voluntary working parties that start up when needed and dissolve themselves when a specific task has been completed.

This back-up group model conforms to the concept of the Women's Alliance as a movement where the political course is set through dynamic political activity at grass-roots level. However, reality has proven to be quite different. The grass-roots level has hardly ever functioned as intended, though in some periods it has done so more than at others. This shortcoming has worried the Women's Alliance for several years, and is invariably brought up as a theme at the spring and national conventions. At the 1990 spring convention, one of the *Althingi* representatives spoke at length on "The Women's Alliance – ideas, priorities and methods", examining the goals of the organization and their practical execution. Concerned at the lack of political debate within the Women's Alliance, she pointed out that as it was, almost all debates and activities were carried out within the *Althingi* group, where the political decisions were also made. It was evident, asserted the *Althingi* representative, that a political movement with democratic participation as one of its primary motives must find this state of affairs unacceptable.

A group of young women who entered the Women's Alliance after 1990 raised a similar problem at the 1992 spring convention. At the national convention the same year, these women made a concrete proposal to "reorganize the political programme efforts of the Women's Alliance". They were concerned that there were few decision-makers in the movement, that the *Althingi* representatives were isolated in their work, and that there was no body for on-going development of the political agenda within the Women's Alliance. Continual, process-oriented work, on practical politics as well as on the Alliance's basic principles, has always constituted an important goal for the organization.[12] As a result of these initiatives, women gather for brief periods before national conventions or elections for very concentrated agenda-building efforts. The negative consequence of this practice, however, is that there is no continuity. The proposal made by the young women was discussed at the national convention, which agreed that it was a basis to work from. But the fact that the Alliance's internal structural difficulties once again appeared on the agenda at the 1993 spring convention illustrates the chief difficulty confronting the movement – that of drawing out the conclusions of major discussions and of transforming them into action. An obscure mode of distribution of responsibility makes it difficult to say who is in charge of making the decisions, and of deciding whether or not to implement them.

At the 1993 spring convention, several factions made it clear that the organization and working methods of the movement pose major problems. Greater structure and more formalized opportunities for leading the organization were called for. Because the membership has always been so insistent that all women within the movement are equal and that decisions must be made jointly, they have been especially restrictive as regards formal delegation of power and responsibility. But, as one of *Althingi* representatives stated, "This 'model' is just not working any more." She felt that a body had to be established whose responsibility it would be to take political responsibility together with the *Althingi* representatives. She described how the

Althingi representatives often feel isolated within the system because while everyone can demand the right to participate, there is no body within the movement obliged to participate in the decision-making process. In reality, those "inside" the system all too often stand alone, feeling that they are making decisions in an undemocratic way.

At the end of the spring convention (1993), a group was established with the mandate to draft a proposal for new procedural methods and for changes to the structure of the Women's Alliance. The aim was to open up the organization so as to encourage greater political initiative at grass-roots level, and to formulate a structure with a clearer division of responsibility, thus clarifying the decision-making process. "Who will decide which women will head the cabinet ministries that the Women's Alliance is allocated in the next government?" is one of the questions this restructuring will answer. The working party was asked to present and discuss its proposal at all chapters of the Women's Alliance before the national convention held in November 1993.

It is worth noting that throughout the extensive discussions concerning the structure and working procedures of the Women's Alliance in later years there have been no demands to elect one single leader and a traditional governing body. What is currently happening in the organization is in accordance with the movement's aim to be a flexible institution, of learning from experience. Similarly, it is far from certain that the women will conclude that the traditional hierarchical party structure is the only alternative for a political movement.

(c)   Opening up the political decision-making process

An important principle for the women of the Women's Alliance was that politics should not be a profession, but an activity for ordinary people. For the Alliance this implies a radical practice of job rotation throughout their spectrum of activities both to contribute to women's insight into the processes of the political community, and to encourage such activity. Rotation would thus demystify politics, and counteract the feeling of alienation often experienced by those outside it. The rotation principle is also argued for from the perspective that the most important thing in politics is to keep in touch with your own roots, and with society. Rotation would ensure that women kept in contact with women's conditions in life, and with the everyday reality they wanted to change. Through job rotation the women hope that their representatives will keep their freshness, their sensation of coming from outside the system, and thereby also maintain their creativity within the system. Another important aspect is that the women also bring experience and knowledge back to the movement from the political system. It is vital that women who have held positions within the system do not disappear from the movement when they step down from those positions, but continue working at grass-roots level, and thus take part in the on-going development of the process. However, this latter aspiration has proven to be a problem for the Women's Alliance. When women leave their positions, they do tend to disappear from active political work with the consequence that the important knowledge and experience they have gained also disappear from the Women's Alliance. Finding a way to transfer experience and knowledge in a way that does not bar creativity and invention has been a topic for discussion, but has not yet been satisfactorily resolved.

A somewhat more problematic argument in favour of job rotation is that it is an arrangement that "works well for women". The women of the Women's Alliance emphasize women's obligations and responsibilities to home and family, which make women dependent on flexibility. They need to be very active for a period, and then able to take "a political holiday", as the women of the Alliance put it. This is possible in the Women's Alliance because the organization does not have the hierarchical rank or structure of the traditional parties. Women thus avoid the strenuous struggle for positions which often takes place within other parties. Indeed, it is this very rank or seniority principle that functions as one of the most effective barriers to women's political participation, according to the Women's Alliance. Its women feel that their own structure and working methods take this problem into account, so that women do not need to give up their role of caring for their family, but can allow themselves to participate in both the domestic and political spheres.

However, this line of argument is problematic on at least two counts. First, the women of the Women's Alliance have not made a critical assessment of women's position within the family, and have in fact been criticized for contributing to preserving the status quo in this area. Secondly, they employ expressions like "suiting women" without allowing for nuance. The women of the Women's Alliance seem to imply that all women are the same, and have the same interests and needs. Gudrún Agnarsdóttir[13] wrote in 1992 that while women demand that their special situation be respected, it is equally important that they respect the differences among themselves. However, although women are different, Agnarsdóttir argues, they may be on the same road. The Women's Alliance, she states, fights for *every* woman's right to choose.

In this connection, perhaps, it should be noted that the Women's Alliance's programmes and statements should not be taken as if they were aimed primarily to function analytically within a scholarly context. The Women's Alliance is a political movement acting in the ideological field of party political competition. When it speaks on behalf of "women", it refers to women who agree with its ideas and the political platform on which it bases its activities. It is a dilemma, perhaps even an impossibility, for the Women's Alliance to integrate into its ideology and political programme every group of women's interests. Most women who are active within the

Alliance, are aged between 25 and 45, and most are mothers. The political profile of the Women's Alliance is thus obviously influenced by the issues which strike closest to home among these groups of women.

Perhaps even more important for the opening up of the political decision-making process is that all meetings of the Women's Alliance are open to all its members. This also holds true for the meetings of the *Althingi* group, where all who wish to do so may take part in the political discussion and in making decisions. Women can thus actively participate in shaping the politics of the Women's Alliance even when they first join the movement, something illustrated by the experience of the young women mentioned earlier, who entered the Women's Alliance after 1990.[14] Just as every other member, they had open access to the *Althingi* group meetings, where they engaged in the political discussion. At national and spring conventions they worked hard to accomplish changes within the Women's Alliance. They deserve credit for having brought about what now seems to be real progress.

This group of young women described a meeting attended by members of the youth organizations from the various political parties. However, theirs was an experience quite different from that of members of the other youth organizations, who expended a great deal of energy on just making themselves heard and being seen, not to mention on obtaining positions in their respective parent organizations. A front-line position in formulating their party's political agenda was out of the question for them. In sharp contrast one of the women stated: "Although our grass roots are slightly wilted, we must appreciate the value of having a real opportunity to participate in work directly associated with the *Althingi*." This is perhaps the Women's Alliance's greatest contribution towards opening up the political decision-making processes.

(d)   Creating a new world

There is no doubt that the goal of the women of the Women's Alliance is "to change the world". How they will do it and what they will change it to is harder to pinpoint. The women have said that they will strengthen the welfare state, underlining that by so doing they do not mean providing more of the same thing. To be able to speak of a real welfare state, the women felt it necessary to think along entirely new lines, and to give priority to values other than purely materialistic ones.

When women speak of a necessary change to society they often compare the structure of society with that of a house. They use the metaphor of the house built by men, which men have planned, decorated and furnished on their own. For women to achieve the sort of freedom the Women's Alliance is fighting for, it is not enough that men allow women access to the men's house, planned, decorated and furnished as it is by men. The women believe fundamental structural change to be a prerequisite if women are to achieve political and economic equality of such power that the social and cultural concept "woman" is assessed as exactly equal to the social and cultural concept "man". However, the women do not see the Women's Alliance as a separatist movement; they work within the system and structure of power, and the long-term goal is integration. Their goal is to build a bridge between the two "houses", but when the time will be ripe for this is not clear.

The women are thus asserting their need to develop their own politics and visions in a scenario where they have no requirement to be in direct contact with men in order to be heard, and where they can employ their energy creatively. The future goal for a movement such as the Women's Alliance is to become superfluous.

This lack of a concrete vision has at times been commented on by the women of the Women's Alliance. At the 1993 spring convention one of the women raised questions about the Alliance's vague goals, stating, "What will we do if we gain political positions? We cannot just say we wish for a better society; so does everybody. What does a better society look like? We have to know what we want, where we are going."

This is a discussion of some urgency and a great challenge for the Women's Alliance. In 1992, for the first time, a serious political split occurred within the organization. One of the *Althingi* representatives supported the outcome of the European Economic Area negotiations, while the others felt this to be in conflict with the platform of the Women's Alliance. This led to fierce discussions at the 1992 national convention, in meetings closed to the press. In the end, the woman in favour of the negotiation results abstained from the *Althingi* vote on the European Economic Area issue, while the others voted against. The discussions around European Economic Area Co-operation have strengthened the awareness that it is necessary to sharpen the political profile of the Women's Alliance. However, this is a process that the Women's Alliance has yet to embark upon.

It is thus of fundamental importance for women of the Women's Alliance to gain support for their view that, based on women's culture, women develop different values from men. These values have not been represented in the fora where public opinion and interests are defined. The project of the Women's Alliance is to implement what it sees as women's legitimate demands, that is to function on their own terms within the system. This implies the right to choose the organization and working methods they feel to be suitable. The women want to demystify politics by employing their own language; they want to open up the political processes by letting women rotate positions. The women of the Women's Alliance believe that society needs both changes in organization and in attitude, and that new values must be given priority. These are their goals.

The Women's Alliance of 1993: what is it? What will it become?

Having been in existence for more than a decade, the Women's Alliance is still struggling with problems of identity, perhaps more so now than during the first phase; and these problems are in some ways built into its very emergence and existence. The Women's Alliance has always been defined by members as a movement founded at grass-roots level. Yet, it emerged as an electoral movement, and it is among the groups surrounding elected representatives and members of political councils and committees that the political activity of the Women's Alliance has taken place. It is also interesting to note that the Alliance has been less successful in mobilizing women for local and community politics. This is an important dilemma for a grass-roots movement that encourages members actively to engage in politics concerning their lives – local politics not least. Again, this was one of the issues raised at the 1993 spring convention.

The many unresolved questions regarding the Women's Alliance may be illustrated by the title of a half-day group session followed by a plenary debate at the 1993 spring convention: "What was the Women's Alliance meant to be; what has it become; what do we want it to become?" From the discussions it was clear that within the movement the three questions inspire answers that vary greatly, and are also quite vague. Some women said they had started out with the notion that the Women's Alliance would be a campaign lasting no more than four years. Others said they had always felt there would be a need for the Women's Alliance to continue for a long period. Most agreed that at its inception, it had been important to point out that the Women's Alliance would not be an institution or a party, but a political movement, the effect of which would be ruled by whether the Women's Alliance, having achieved its goals, was ready to close itself down. However, what the criteria for such a conclusion were was never defined.

If closing itself down is still a goal within the Women's Alliance, then it has been toned down considerably. In 1993, several of the women emphasized that they saw the organization as a "very serious political player", one at least as important then as in 1983. Even more to the point, one of the women stated: "We must stop talking about closing ourselves down. We have to realize what we are: a political party." However, there are always women who react strongly against using the concept *party* to describe the Women's Alliance. In response, some of the younger women held that, for them, the Women's Alliance was a political *channel*, whether the term *party* was used or not. It has always been part of the political Iceland they know. They stressed that they had joined the Women's Alliance to participate in politics.

The most important thing to many of the women was to avoid what they called the descriptive phase and to enter the phase of action. To achieve this, the Women's Alliance must have power, and power is what we will have, say the women who speak most directly about the new awareness within the Women's Alliance; that the movement must emerge from opposition into position. This is a difficult topic for the women, however, for how will power change them? How will they handle power if they have it? Up to now, women's vision has been to break down and distribute power. What happens if they actually end up in positions of power? Will they, as others have done, manoeuvre their own candidates into bureaucratic positions? "Is not that just what we need to change about things?" others ask.

Power is one of the masculine instruments that, until recently, women have felt a great aversion to using; but a change of heart is noticeable. Now the clear tendency is to stress that the Women's Alliance wants to take part in the decision-making process, a factor illustrated by the above-mentioned discussion concerning reorganization and structural changes. The topics included what terms ought to be used for new bodies of the Women's Alliance. Everyone agreed that the choice of terminology was important. In line with the previous standpoint, some felt that it was important not to introduce *masculine* attitudes. They suggested that a new body, which would share political responsibility with the *Althingi* representatives, might be termed the *consultative council.* However, others rejected this on the grounds that the movement now wanted to delegate power to certain women, and that it was important to signal this very fact.

Thus, as the movement enters its second decade, there is an on-going and lively debate on core organizational issues within the Women's Alliance, and the views of the women who work for it are still probing. However, it is not clear how the women want the Women's Alliance to evolve; whether as a party, a political movement which hopes to make itself superfluous or as some other form of grass-roots movement with a less defined future. What was evident was that everybody[15] wanted a more action-oriented organization.[16] As one member commented: "We want to be a strong political force now, as well as in the future." A quotation from one of the women at the 1993 spring convention sums up this approach: "We need to organize ourselves better; we must have faith in ourselves! But it is we ourselves who choose the way."

Political reality

So far, I have left undescribed the political context within which the Women's Alliance has existed for more than a decade. My aim here has been to interpret and to some extent analyze critically their own programmatic self-understanding, which includes their political organization and working methods, as well as policy content. As mentioned earlier, throughout the twentieth century, and all over the world, women have on occasion attempted to establish their own electoral alternatives.[17] Thus, separate women's electoral lists are neither new nor confined to Iceland,[18] but only in Iceland have women managed to become a political force through such a tool.[19] That makes the Women's Alliance in Iceland something quite unique. I have wanted to find out what is characteristic of this most successful of such women's alternatives. How do the women themselves define their movement and their politics? What do they want to achieve? And last, but not least, what, in fact, distinguishes such a women's alternative from the traditional parties?

The women of the Women's Alliance have often asserted that if women participated on their own terms, the form as well as the content of politics would change. It is easy to spot the different form of the women's alternative. Primarily, this concerns the structure and working methods of the movement. Political discussion in the Women's Alliance takes place in a different manner from that of the other parties, and politics is discussed in terms of relevance for the women, i.e., it is not discussed through abstract, political concepts.[20] Secondly, the Alliance women differ from other participants in public debate, both in the way they present and debate their issues, and in the way they behave. Women's Alliance representatives show greater respect for the opinions of others than is usually seen among politicians. And if they occasionally behave more like the others, they are nevertheless very rarely accused of arrogance. Their clear and matter-of-fact manner in debate as well as their respectful way of meeting and confronting others have repeatedly been stressed in opinion polls.

On the other hand, with respect to their political agenda it is difficult to argue that the Women's Alliance is unique, that it constitutes a "third dimension" of Icelandic politics. When the Women's Alliance women sum up their politics in the *Althingi*, they stress that the vast majority of issues raised by them concern concrete improvements for women and children in society. These are the same issues that women have contested in all the Nordic countries. Iceland's tardiness in this respect must be seen in relation to the traditionally very small number of women in Icelandic politics, a point often stressed by the Women's Alliance women. And at least with respect to the most important issues handled at the *Althingi*, they also seek to show how these issues affect women. This applies, for example, to issues of employment, education and social policy.

All in all, it is fair to say that women are concerned with issues connected to welfare and cultural politics, in addition to the traditional women's issues. The political agenda of the Women's Alliance resembles that of the socialists in that it stresses social responsibility and solidarity. When it comes down to the actual vote in the *Althingi*, however, the Women's Alliance tends to cast its vote further to the left than the socialists (Schneier 1992).

Now what?

What results has the Women's Alliance achieved, and what effect has it had on Icelandic politics in general and the country's woman-oriented feminist politics in particular? What influence has the Alliance had on political debate within the political system and in society at large? Has the Women's Alliance in any way changed the political culture? Of what importance has the Women's Alliance been for women's position in Iceland, and how has this affected women's struggle in other areas of society? Far more research on several levels is needed before anything resembling a complete answer can be formulated to such comprehensive questions.

Finally, however, let me add some further reflections on the importance of the Women's Alliance for the development of women's position in society. More precisely, where is women's struggle in Iceland today? What have been Icelandic women's experiences in bringing the women's struggle as openly and concretely as in their case into the political system? How much and what kind of room is there for actually furthering women's struggle within the system? These are questions some women in Iceland are beginning to pose, questions about the consequences the Women's Alliance has had for women's struggle in other areas of society, and whether it is possible for an independent women's movement to co-exist side by side with the Women's Alliance. Some consider that the Women's Alliance now constitutes an obstacle to the emergence of other forms of women's involvement, since women's commitment to social reform is often identified with the Women's Alliance, and is thus made political in a manner not all women want. This may also be so because the initiatives of other women are portrayed as opposed to those of the Women's Alliance, and are thereby seen as disloyal. Those who support this argument hold that it is very important at this point in time to separate the women's struggle from traditional political activity. A clearer profiling of the Women's Alliance may be implied. If it is to become a party, choosing to work within the political system – in fact it is accurate to say that this is just how the Women's Alliance acts – then it is important to accept the consequences and clarify which form of women's struggle is appropriate and possible within the political system. This will facilitate the compromises necessary for political collaboration, and will allow for an independent women's movement outside the system. The latter neither needs to – nor should – make political compromises, but may instead function as a pressure group and support for the women working within the system. The Women's Alliance is currently undergoing a necessary and challenging process of redefinition which may well be decisive for its future. The development of the Women's Alliance will thus have consequences for the Icelandic women's movement in general.

After more than a decade of activity by the Women's Alliance, a considerably larger number of women are active in politics and in most areas of society. All over Iceland, many women have become active either within the Women's Alliance or as a result of its activities. Those who follow Icelandic political debate know that there are "women's perspectives" on issues that concern society at large. This is important. However, much more research is needed before the Women's Alliance's actual influence within the political system and within the wider society can be definitively assessed.

Notes

I wish to thank Anna G. Jónasdóttir for her generosity and for her help with this text.

1. Styrkársdóttir's projection is not seen through a historical perspective; thus whether there have been changes over time in women's arguments of legitimacy and the basis of their ideas is not brought to light.
2. It should be noted that, as early as 1908, the year they won the right to vote in local elections, Icelandic women presented a separate women's list in Reykjavik. It was a great success and all four women on the list were elected to the city council. Icelandic women won the right to vote in national elections in 1915, and in 1922 the first woman was elected to the national assembly. She was also from a separate women's list.

    Until 1926, Icelandic women had occasionally, and in different parts of Iceland, presented their own lists. The difference between these early women's lists and the contemporary Women's Alliance is that while the early lists were established with the sole goal of the next election, the Women's Alliance is a political organization in line with the political parties.
3. It would also be interesting to see the Women's Alliance in a wider perspective, as an answer to the skills lacking in traditional politics for handling the urgent political issues of our times. In other countries there have been other grass-roots movements (e.g., the Greens in Germany), which in many ways can be compared with the Women's Alliance. Such an analysis is, however, outside the scope of this chapter.
4. Haavio-Mannila 1985.
5. Magdalena Schram, article in daily newspaper *Dagbladet og Visir*, 23 April 1982; translation from Icelandic by the author.
6. Berit Ås brought the concept of women's culture into the Nordic scientific debate. She defined it as "a collective set of values, interpretations and causalities which affect women, but which are difficult for men to understand, or invisible" (Ås 1995). Ås' point is that women and men inhabit separate spheres, which is why the sexes develop different norms and values.
7. All in all it is problematic to speak of an ideology behind the Women's List. The movement's structure, the organization of work and methods are dialectical elements that together constitute the ideology of the Women's list (Sigurbjarnardóttir 1992).
8. Sociologist Dorothy E. Smith (1987) is among those feminists who hold that women are excluded from men's concept of culture. Her point is, as Harding (1990) has underlined, that women's experience from their own activities is incomprehensible to men, and impossible to express by the use of the split abstractions of male schemes of concept.

9. According to Berit Ås, language and communication are among the cultural dimensions that tend to separate women and men.

10. The Women's Alliance holds a national convention every autumn. This is the movement's decision-making body. There is also a spring convention every year, but this has no power of resolution. Problems of a more existentialist nature are on the agenda, and the previous winter's political work in the *Althingi* is summed up. Both the national and spring conventions are open to all members of the Women's Alliance.

11. Because of the rotation principle, which the Women's Alliance employs consistently, none of the three women first elected to the *Althingi* is still there. Of the five Women's Alliance women presently in the *Althingi*, three have solid political experience from the feminist and/or student movements of the 1970s.

12. The women have always emphasized that the Women's Alliance is not a rigid and predefined institution. Their aim is that the structure, organization and working methods of the Alliance should be permanently open to change.

13. Gudrún Agnarsdóttir is one of the three women first elected to the *Althingi*.

14. Most of these women have an academic background, and entered the Women's Alliance as a group.

15. At the spring convention, not a single dissenting voice was raised against the need for a stronger organization and governing body; I have also not heard a single woman from the Women's Alliance disagree with this.

16. The discussions regarding what the women wanted the Women's Alliance to be, brought up the issue of the Women's Alliance's moral role. Women from the Alliance have been accused of pointing a finger at politics, an allegation which has been met with mixed feelings. At the spring convention, one of the *Althingi* representatives said that she precisely wanted to see it "as part of the Women's Alliance's role to improve the morals of politics".

17. An interesting attempt was made in Oslo in 1988, when women on the left of Norwegian politics tried what they called "The women's initiative". The effort crumbled away. In Sweden, there are various activities and mobilizations among women, including the women's party, the Net Stockings and the Support Stocking.

18. Styrkársdóttir (1995).

19. This raises another interesting question: Why have Icelandic women succeeded so well, while women in other places have not been successful? "The women's initiative" in Oslo in 1988, for which the Icelandic Women's Alliance was partly a model, comes to mind.

20. Such claims are difficult to substantiate, and I write from my own observations. I have attended national conventions of other parties, and have observed several political meetings of the traditional parties before the 1987 *Althingi* election. I also worked actively for the Socialist Party prior to the 1983 election.

References

Ég er forvitin rauð. 1980. Reykjavík, feminist movement magazine.

Grønseth, E. (ed.) 1976. *Familie og kjønnsroller; arbeid – forsørgelse – likestilling* (Family and sex roles: work – maintenance – equality). Oslo: Cappelen.

Haavio-Mannila, E. et al. (eds) 1985. *The unfinished democracy. Women in nordic politics.* Oxford: Pergamon Press.

Hafstad, I. 1988. The ideology of the Women's Alliance in Iceland. Unpublished paper.

Harding, S. 1986. *The science question in feminism*. Milton Keynes, England: Open University Press.

Harding, S. 1990. Feminism, science, and the anti-Enlightenment critiques. In *Feminism/Postmodernism*, L. Nicholson (ed.), 83–107. London: Routledge.

Jónasdóttir, A.G. 1988. The concept of interest, women's interests and the limitations of interest theory. In *The political interests of gender. Developing theory and research with a feminist face*, K.B. Jones & A.G. Jónasdóttir (eds), 33–65. London: Sage.

Jónasdóttir, A.G. 1991. *Love power and political interests. Towards a theory of patriarchy in contemporary western societies*. PhD thesis, Department of Political Science, University of Göteborg. Ørebro Studies 7, Ørebro University. Published, slightly revised, 1994, as *Why women are oppressed*. Philadelphia: Temple University Press.

Phillips, A. 1991. *Engendering democracy*. Cambridge: Polity Press.

Schneier, 1992. Icelandic women on the brink of power. *Scandinavian Studies*, vol. 64, no. 3.

Sigurbjarnardóttir, S.H. 1992. *Kvinnelisten i Island. Underveis fra kvinnepolitikk til feministisk politikk?* (The Icelandic Women's Alliance. On the way from women's politics to feminist politics?). MA, thesis, Department of Sociology, University of Oslo.

Skjeie, H. 1992. *Den politiske betydningen av kjønn. En studie av norsk topp-politikk* (The political meaning of gender. A study of top-politics in Norway). PhD thesis, Department of Political Science, University of Oslo. Oslo: Institute for Social Research.

Smith, D. 1987. *The everyday world as problematic. A feminist sociology*. Boston, Mass.: Northeastern University Press.

Styrkársdóttir, A. 1995. *Kvennaframbod. Barátta um vald* (The women's lists. A struggle for power). Department of Social Science, University of Iceland.

The Women's Alliance. History – agenda – Structure. Reykjavík: The Women's Alliance.

Ås, B. 1981. *Kvinner i alle land*. Oslo: Aschehoug.

Ås, B. 1995. On female culture; an attempt to formulate a theory of women's solidarity and action. *Acta Sociologica* **18**, 142–61.

CHAPTER FIVE

They had a different mother: the central configuration of Icelandic nationalist discourse

Inga Dóra Bjørnsdóttir

In 1944 Iceland became a republic after almost five hundred years of Danish colonial rule. Iceland's fight for independence was led by Icelandic nationalists who were influenced by European Romantic and nationalist thinkers, especially German ones. However, due to fundamentally different historical circumstances, nationalism in Iceland developed along different lines from its German counterpart. While German nationalism was characterized by militarization and aggressive foreign policy, Icelandic nationalism was peaceful and internally oriented.

The idea first developed by the German nationalist, Johann Gottfried Herder, that national resurrection involved a return to and a celebration of the country itself, the "mother", as well as the cultural and historical attributes believed to be embedded in and to emanate from her body, became central to Icelandic nationalist discourse. As will be discussed below, one of the major themes of this discourse involved the resurrection and revitalization of the "mother's" body and spirit, as her health and strength was believed to hold the key to the resurrection of Icelandic manhood, national selfhood and the Icelandic nation's political independence.

The positive configuration of identifiably female forces and attributes in Icelandic nationalist discourse situated the mother and the maternal at its symbolic centre, something which had an ambiguous effect on the social position of Icelandic women. It placed constraints on them since it was believed that only as mothers and housewives were they fully legitimate women and Icelanders. But as I will discuss later in this chapter, the effects were also liberating as such a configuration facilitated Icelandic women's access to the political sphere. Icelandic women have twice, first from 1906 to 1926 and again from 1981 to the present, succeeded in running their own political parties and in having their representatives elected to both the island's municipal councils and the Icelandic parliament.

Warfare and the resurrection of the nation

In much nationalist discourse nations are often presented as spiritually, morally and physically disintegrated and one of its central concerns thus revolves around the resurrection of the national body, the national spirit and the national sense of self.

The means by which a nation and the national self are to be resurrected is intimately connected to the prevailing notion of how man and the nation are constituted. In nineteenth-century German nationalist discourse man was believed to be eternally torn between his desire to serve his selfish, material needs, the "needs of flesh, matter and nature" as well as those of his immediate family, and his desire to rise above his own personal needs to attain spiritual heights and selflessly serve the needs of his nation (Fichte 1968). A nation was healthy and strong when its individual members set its welfare and interests above their own. However, the health of the national body and its spirit was in constant jeopardy as man so easily lapsed into self-seeking, and where such self-seeking prevailed, the spiritual order became lost, the citizens becoming like "isolated atoms" dissolved into a heap (Hegel 1964, Avineri 1972).[1]

To counteract the nation's tendency to dissolve, the nation–state had to provide consistent institutional means to sustain the forces of reason, spiritual freedom and a strong sense of community. Improved academic and physical education as well as active participation in sports were seen as appropriate means to resurrect the national spirit, unity and the national sense of self (Fichte 1968, Mosse 1985).[2] Another, even more potent means to abolish selfishness and revitalize the national body was, within German nationalist discourse, believed to be military training and active participation in war (Treitschke 1916, Clausewitz 1968).

The importance of warfare in German nationalist discourse was connected to the belief that prolonged periods of peace were the major contributor to the moral disintegration of the communal spirit and national unity, since they allowed men to slip back and immerse themselves in "ordinary" life and materialistic self-seeking. Warfare thus had to be embarked upon at regular intervals in order to shake man out of the comfort of his daily existence and preserve his ethical health and the national spirit (Treitschke 1916). In this context war was not simply to be instigated in a desire to expand one's territory for economic or political reasons, nor was its purpose to secure the life and property of the civic community. Security, as Hegel argued, could not possibly be obtained by the sacrifice of what was to be secured (Legge 1918). Within this discourse, warfare served a higher moral purpose. Risking his life and facing the perils of death in war, man was forced to overcome his selfish inclinations, his desire to gratify his bodily and material needs; instead, he reached a state of true spirituality and a sense of sharing in a greater communal good (Clausewitz 1968, Treitschke 1916).

Thus, in German nationalist discourse and in spite of its brutal, inhuman appearance, war was considered to be at a deeper level inherently ethical and humane. And not only was true humanity born through warfare, but nations as well; as Fichte stated, only "in war and waging of war a nation becomes a nation" (Fichte in Morgan 1970).

Herder: man, nature, nation

In the light of war-torn nineteenth- and twentieth-century German history, it may perhaps be a little difficult to imagine that at the turn of the eighteenth century one of Germany's leading nationalist thinkers, the Lutheran minister and philosopher Johann Gottfried Herder (1744–1803), promoted pacifist views articulating how nations could revitalize their national spirit and national sense of self and gain their political independence.

The major concern of Herder's writings was, in common with that of other German nationalists, the political weakness of Germany and the demoralized condition of the German people and German society. Unlike most other German thinkers of the period, Herder did not blame France for Germany's decay, nor did he blame it on Germany's lack of military strength. Instead, Herder's diagnosis of Germany's social ills was that Germans had become estranged from German nature, the source of their life, spirit, national identity and political power.

Herder was highly critical of the predominant notion in Western rational discourse that man and nature were fundamentally opposed, and of the belief that man could create himself and political units through his own will. This was an attractive but mistaken illusion on man's part. Man and nations, he argued instead, were an integral part of nature, and man's life, spirit and consciousness rested within the "maternal" body. It was not man's will but the supreme power of mother nature that ultimately decided the character and the fate of man and nations (Herder 1968).

According to Herder, since the natural contours on earth were nowhere exactly the same, the forces of nature in each and every region on earth were unique. The country's unique natural characteristics set their inalienable mark on its language, culture and history, aspects that were, according to Herder, organic forces rooted in nature, and thus played a key role in the construction of the national spirit, *das Volkgeist* (Herder in Ergang 1931).

Since no two countries had the same natural features, no two countries could generate the same kind of national spirit. Accordingly, there was no universal mind or a universal man, only a national mind and a national man. Only if one were true to one's origin and own national heritage would one be able to live a fruitful life and realize one's true human, national self.

The Germans, Herder claimed, had brought their own misery upon themselves by disobeying the laws of German nature. By doing so, they had jeopardized the wholeness of the national body and spirit as well as their own. Germans, Herder argued, had to reconsider their values and beliefs about the German language, history and culture, make amends and take their "mother" back into their fold. Further, a resurrection of German manhood and sense of national selfhood was to be an exclusively internal affair, for only through peaceful means could Germans and the forces of nature reunite and the German nation come into its own.

One of Herder's major contributions to political thought was his notion that nations were natural entities created by the unique forces of mother nature. All peoples thus had a legitimate claim to demand their political independence and sovereign status regardless of their size, political, economic and social advancement. Being the undoubted sons of their country, nurtured and shaped by its unique natural features, the sons did not have to prove their worthiness and legitimize their claim to rule their country through struggle and strife. Their authenticity was securely grounded from birth and it was their natural, inalienable right to reign and assume sovereignty over their country as the very source of their life, consciousness and spirit (Herder in Ergang 1931).

Icelanders, they had a different mother

Herder's notion of the *Volkgeist* and the existence of distinct national cultures also had a profound influence on nationalist discourses elsewhere than in Germany. However, Herder's vision that national man and nations came into being though an internally oriented, peaceful process did not, as indicated above, gain a hold in German nationalist discourse. It did so in Icelandic nationalist discourse.

In the late eighteenth century, when stirrings of nationalist consciousness first emerged, Iceland did not possess economic, political, or military resources on a par with those of Germany. Iceland was an underdeveloped, underpopulated Danish colony, which from the point of "rational" political discourse, had much too little to legitimize its claim for political independence. It is within this context that the significance of Herder's ideas becomes clear – that neither population size, nor economic strength nor military might justifies a country's claim to full recognition and independence.[3]

Icelandic nationalists had no difficulty in establishing their distinct cultural heritage, their possession of a language and a history that, as they claimed, was rooted in and shaped by the Icelandic natural environment, their unique "maternal" body, which was distinctly different from that of Denmark. The resurrection of manhood and the national spirit was not to be instigated through man's conquest of nature or other nations. Instead, the Icelanders' road to salvation lay through mother nature. And the representation of Iceland as a woman and a mother became the central national symbol in Iceland.

As in German nationalist discourse, there was from the outset a deep concern about Icelanders' moral disintegration and their loss of manliness, termed *manndóm* in Icelandic nationalist discourse. Blame for this was to some extent laid at the door of the Danish colonial rulers, especially the Danish merchants who had failed to meet their obligation to provide appropriate goods for farming and fishing but had instead always had plenty of alcohol on offer (Ólafsson 1832). However, the burden of blame lay primarily with the Icelanders themselves. In a Herderian spirit, the moral disintegration of the nation was traced to Icelanders' disloyalty towards the country itself, their "mother", and to her cultural heritage. The sons had neglected and abused their "mother" by adopting the language and mores of their "father", the Danish king, for in Icelandic nationalist discourse Icelanders referred to the Danish king as their father (Ólafsson 1832, Jochumsson 1936, Jónsson frá Bólu 1942). In the process they had inadvertently not only harmed their own "mother" but, more importantly, had also contributed to their own moral disintegration and loss of selfhood.

Since the "sons" were dependent on their mother for their very being, the reconstruction of the national body involved the reconstruction of the maternal body and the maternal spirit. The only way for the sons to regain their selfhood, and manhood, was through the nurturing provided by a wholesome and strong "mother".

One of Iceland's earliest nationalists, the natural scientist and poet Eggert Ólafsson (1832) first emphasized the symbiotic relationship between the country, the "mother", and her sons in his poem "Ísland" (Iceland) written in the late eighteenth century. The poem is narrated by the "mother", who mediates through her body the story of her life spanning a period of more than 800 years. It provides a graphic and detailed description of her changing bodily states, which in turn are reflected in her sons' own physical, moral and spiritual health. During her life, she has given birth to three sets of sons, each generation lasting for almost 300 years, the birth of each generation marking the beginning of a new period. The first was a time of glory and strength. Then Iceland was young and beautiful and her sons were, in their virtues, strength and courage, equal to the flower of manhood among the neighbouring countries.

When her first generation of sons grew old and started to die, the mother decided to give birth to another set of sons. But this period became one of decline and corruption, characterized by the loss of manly virtues, internal strife, vendettas, warfare and loss of faith. Their mother is forced to endure physical abuse until eventually her sons sell her to a foreign king. She becomes physically exhausted and her breast milk dries up.

Still, she gives birth to her third set of sons and a period of total moral disintegration and social discord ensues. Her last set of sons are effeminate, lacking all vitality and energy, poor, lecherous, lazy drunkards. Iceland herself had at this time become old, sick, blind and hairless, clothed in tatters, lying dormant in her bed almost all the time, totally lacking in beauty and sexual appeal.

Throughout the poem, blame for the wretched health of the mother is put on her sons. In order to secure her rehabilitation, the sons have to change their way of life. This theme is, however, not sustained. Towards the end of the poem the narrative takes a somewhat bizarre twist. Ólafsson, while greatly concerned about the resurrection of the dignity and manhood of Icelanders and the recognition of their distinct national and cultural identity, did not favour Iceland's separation from Denmark. He was a staunch royalist and in his opinion only the firm hand of the Danish king could guarantee order and social cohesion in Iceland. Thus, the Danish king and no longer the sons of Iceland becomes the only person capable of rejuvenating the mother and, by implication, her sons as well, through consummation of the sexual act. Out of his mercy the Danish king is willing to share Iceland's bed, who at this point is presented as a subservient wife to the Danish king. Through their sexual intercourse Iceland is revitalized; she becomes young again, and gives birth to a healthy set of sons, the generation of the future. But Ólafsson's message is clear: while the king is the ultimate source of political power, the mother is its mediator. It is through her that the king, the "father", is to rule his Icelandic subjects, his sons. The sons are not to leave their mother and join their father, but are to remain under their mother's wing while the king, the "father", is absent in a distant country.

Iceland: a Mountain Woman

After the French Revolution in 1830 the cause of nationalism gained serious momentum among Icelanders. At this time the goal of the nationalists was no longer simply to resurrect Icelandic culture and national identity, but also to fight for Iceland's political independence. The Herderian notion, that the possession of a distinct language, culture and history provided not only a legitimate basis for Icelanders' cultural independence but also for Icelanders' political independence gained increasing support (Óskarsdóttir 1982). Subsequently, the dynamics of the national narrative changed. Although Icelanders still referred to the Danish king as "father", Iceland and Denmark were no longer presented as a couple. The representation of the "mother" and the maternal body also changed. Ólafsson was a utilitarian and a man of the Enlightenment, and in his text Iceland the "mother" was carnal, sexual and mortal, afflicted with all the frailties and shortcomings of a suffering humanity. Now, under the influence of German Romanticism, the Icelandic nationalists envisioned "Iceland" as a royal figure in her own right; she became a queen and a divinity, a healthy, beautiful, independent mother. In the writings of the nineteenth-century Icelandic nationalists, the "mother" became the sole and ultimate source of her sons' life, spirituality and freedom (e.g., Gröndal 1900). At this point the bond between Icelanders and their native land was regarded as involuntary and the life of the sons and the life of the mother were viewed as totally intertwined. If the sons cut their tie with the mother they would cease to be themselves and would wither and die (see, e.g., Thomsen 1880).

In 1864, Eiríkur Magnússon, a professor of Nordic studies at the University of Cambridge of England had a vision of Iceland as a Mountain Woman. He made a sketch of his vision, but later hired a German artist, J.B. Zwecker who, in co-operation with Magnússon's brother Helgi, completed the painting that was soon to be widely reproduced throughout Iceland (Valdimarsdóttir 1990, Hjaltason 1986). Even though Magnússon's depiction of Iceland as a Mountain Woman appears uniquely Icelandic, he drew on an ancient source of archetypal Indo-European symbolism in his composition. But as Eric Neumann shows in his classical study *The great mother*, mountains have been worshipped throughout history and in various cultures as the Great Earth Mother (Neumann 1963).[4]

Magnússon's *Mountain Woman* symbolically embodies the key ideas that had been evolving in the nationalist discourse throughout the nineteenth century about the meaning of Iceland, her nature, culture and history and her crucial role in the construction of the Icelanders' sense of self and their national identity. While it is beyond the scope of this chapter to provide a detailed symbolic analysis of Magnusson's representation of the idea of the Mountain Woman, I will, however, discuss some of her most salient features.

The Mountain Woman's body is covered by a long-sleeved dress modelled after the dresses Icelandic women were supposed to have worn during the Saga period (the Middle Ages) (Gröndal 1874). As I have discussed at great length elsewhere, the *Mountain Woman*'s dress simultaneously symbolized Icelandic nature, Iceland's historical rootedness and maternal virtues, the key source of Icelandic men's life, spirit and distinct identity (Björnsdóttir 1992). A dress similar to that worn by the Mountain Woman was introduced as women's national costume by a prominent Icelandic nationalist Sigurdur Gudmundsson, an artist and the founder of the National Museum of Iceland (Gudmundsson 1857, Antonsson 1989). Icelandic women warmly embraced their new national dress and became (and still are) some of its strongest advocates. Indeed, for several decades it became very fashionable (Bjarnadóttir 1942).[5]

The belief in the total dependency of the sons on the mother for their spirituality and consciousness is most prominently expressed in the depiction of the nocturnal sky surrounding the Mountain Woman. With its luminous bodies the nocturnal sky is, according to Neumann, the most prominent manifestation of the Mountain Woman's spiritual powers. Its stars symbolize her sons who have been created by her spiritual force and whose spiritual resurrection has taken the form of a luminous birth in her nocturnal sky. Through their spiritual rebirth the sons have acquired full human consciousness; their souls have attained the highest form of earthly and material

Figure 5.1 *The Mountain Woman.* A drawing based on the vision of Eiríkur Magnússon. (Courtesy of the National Art Museum of Iceland)

human development; they have achieved the stature of immortal heroes (Neumann 1963, Gudmundsson 1903).

However, as immortal heroes, but unlike the sons of the Apollonian solar "patriarchal" spirit, they do not present themselves as pure spirits that have no ties to the maternal earth and as leading a "pure" existence in eternity. Even in their immortality, the mother does not release them but keeps a tight rein on their masculine activities and endeavours. They are stars in their mother's nocturnal sky and remain son-like, apprehending themselves as being historically generated (Neumann 1963).

The Mountain Woman is shown holding an ancient Icelandic manuscript firmly in her left hand and from the water surrounding her other manuscripts are seen to emerge. These manuscripts not only symbolize wisdom and learning, but, more importantly, they represent the manuscripts of Icelandic medieval literature, the Icelanders' supreme intellectual and artistic achievement that became the major evidence resorted to by them to prove their uniqueness and authenticity as a distinct nation.

The emergence of the ancient Icelandic manuscripts from the water, from the "maternal womb", further reinforces the notion that the country itself was the source, the *Drottning* or queen of the spiritual power of the writers of the Icelandic Sagas and Icelandic poetry. She had not only given birth to the writers, but also to their literary works. Hence, she was both queen of the Sagas and of Icelandic poetry (Gudmundsson 1903).

Finally in her sedentary, immobile position the Mountain Woman takes possession of earth and visibly rules over the land. The Mountain Woman, Neumann argues, represents the original throne, "the throne pure and simple". Thus, in this particular context, the "sons" of Iceland, her men, came to power by "mounting" the throne, by symbolically clambering on to their "mother's" lap (Neumann 1963).

From the symbolic to the social: the Mountain Woman and Icelandic women

In recent years some Western feminist scholars have argued that the construction of the Western rational male subject and the consolidation of Western political power are based on the denial and conquest of the forces of nature. These scholars argue that the deeply entrenched and powerful resistance to women's access to the political sphere is intimately connected to women's close association with nature and the belief that they are inferior to men by nature (Brown 1988, Di Stefano 1991, Braidotti 1991, Pateman quoted in Jónasdóttir 1991).

However, Jónasdóttir (1991) offers a different explanation for Western women's absence from the public sphere. She argues that from the seventeenth century onwards the idea of women's closeness to nature was not the most powerful anti-feminist argument. Rather, from then on resistance to women's participation in the public sphere was to a considerable extent related to women's usefulness in the domestic sphere. Women's capacity to reproduce and contribution to running the home were considered essential for the stability of the state and the pleasure of men.

In Icelandic nationalist discourse women were regarded as being in closer contact with nature than men and, by nature, as different from men. This, however, did not make women inferior to men, but rather superior, as women embodied and controlled the essential source of Icelandic men's life, spirit, identity and political power. This belief had ambiguous effects on the social position of Icelandic women. On the one hand it put constraints on them, as only in their role as mothers and housewives were they regarded as fully legitimate women and Icelanders. It was in the domestic sphere that women were judged to be of most use for the new nation. On the other hand, such a view of women facilitated their access to the political arena since women as housewives and mothers were believed to have legitimate grounds for involvement in public decision-making, especially with respect to issues concerning women and children (Bjarnhédinsdóttir 1907).

There have twice been political parties founded specifically for women in Iceland; the first was active from 1906 until 1926, the second was established in 1981 and is still active and going strong. The success not only of the earlier women's party but also of the contemporary one, the Women's Alliance, can, I argue, to some extent be attributed to their adherence to the ideas of the strong, benevolent and resourceful mother similar to the ones generated by nineteenth- and early twentieth-century Icelandic nationalist discourse.

The connection between the nationalist ideals of the mother and the early women's party in Iceland may seem obvious, since this women's party emerged at the height of the struggle for Iceland's independence. But this ideal became an inherent part of the Icelandic cultural hegemony and remained empowering and important for Icelandic women and to how men perceive and think about women. The persistence of this idea manifests itself in various ways with respect to the contemporary women's party and here I will mention a few examples.

First, the particular timing of the emergence of the Women's Alliance. During the late 1960s a small group of Icelandic women, many of whom had previously been active on the radical left, established a Women's Liberation Movement, "Raudsokkur" or the "Redstockings". In accordance with the predominant views within the international women's movement at the time, the Redstockings regarded the domestic and maternal role as the major contributor to women's oppression. They demanded a critical re-evaluation and total reconstruction of women's role and capacities. The division of labour along gender lines was to be abolished both within the home as well as in the public sphere (Kristmundsdóttir 1990).

Icelandic women reacted to the Redstockings' message with some ambivalence. They were in general sympathetic towards the Redstockings' demands for raising women's salaries and improved childcare. However, there was strong and persistent resistance to what was perceived as their anti-maternal message. Hence, the Redstockings enjoyed the active support of only a minority of Icelandic women and remained a small, radical fringe group.

In the late 1970s feminist thinkers on both sides of the Atlantic began critically to re-examine the ideas initially embraced by the women's movement concerning the similarities between men and women. Now, instead of denying and denigrating women's differences from men, women were to celebrate just those differences, the uniquely feminine. Women's culture and women's social and historical experiences were to become the major source for women's political ideas and actions (see Eisenstein 1983).

What is significant in the Icelandic context is that at a time when the international women's movement started celebrating the difference of women, the Icelandic women's movement first gained momentum and became a major political force. This, I argue, can to some extent be attributed to the consonance between Icelandic nationalist ideas about the feminine and the mother and the "new" ideas of the international women's movement.

The Women's Alliance emerged as a "counter-party" to the male-dominated political parties and from the outset it was its official policy not to play according to the rules of what was seen as a corrupt and corrupting men's politics. Now women in their maternal capacity were to infiltrate the bastions of male power and eradicate all political corruption. As I have argued at great length elsewhere, close scrutiny reveals that the Women's Alliance ideal of the radical mother is very similar to the nationalist ideal of the strict, resourceful but ultimately benevolent mother (Björnsdóttir 1992). Significantly, radical as the women sound, it has never been the intention of the Women's Alliance to take over the bastions of male power. Instead, it was their members' official goal from the outset that once the changes they are striving for have been implemented, the Women's Alliance should be abolished and women should seek new and different avenues in life. Harmony and co-operation between the sexes, as in the national ideal, were to prevail.

Finally, the young women's acknowledgement of their roots in the national heritage was reflected in their choice of the official emblem of the Women's Alliance. It is the *skotthúfa*, a cap which forms part of the women's national costume, at the top of the international women's symbol. The members of the Women's Alliance took the national costume to their hearts and wear it on festive occasions. At the second inauguration of Iceland's president Vigdís Finnbogadóttir in 1984, for example, one of the representatives of the Women's Alliance came in national dress, to the great admiration of the men present. Finally, one of the most dramatic instances of the adoption of the national dress by the Women's Alliance occurred in 1990 when Icelandic women celebrated the 75th anniversary of women's suffrage. Several members of the Women's Alliance wearing national costume joined women from other women's groups in a procession in downtown Reykjavík led by a woman dressed as the "Mountain Woman".

Above I have discussed how from the outset the Women's Alliance embraced the ideal of the mother, similar to the one celebrated in Icelandic nationalist discourse. In recent years the Women's Alliance has started to re-evaluate its great emphasis on the mother and motherhood as the ideological and practical foundation for women's participation in Icelandic politics. While the Alliance continues to regard women's biological and cultural difference from men as crucial for their political agenda, it has increasingly come to realize that in order to sustain and broaden its constituency it has

Figure 5.2   Icelandic women celebrating 75 years of women's suffrage in Iceland, 1990. In the middle is the Mountain Woman and above her a statue of the leader of the Icelandic nationalist movement, Jon Sigurdsson. (Courtesy Rut Hallgrímsdóttir)

to recognize the great variety and different interests *among* women. The details of this debate and its development will, it is to be hoped, form the subject of future research.

Notes

1. During the French occupation (1807–9), the German philosopher and nationalist Johann Gottlieb Fichte gave a series of public lectures, the "Addresses to the German Nation", which soon became one of the more important manifestos of German nationalism. In this text Fichte claimed that the Germans' passive reaction to the Napoleon invasion was due to their loss of interest in the welfare of the community and the German nation; the motive of all their vital activities was mere material self-seeking as they were content only if their material needs were met (Fichte 1968). "[T]here lived in the majority naught but flesh, matter and nature" (Fichte 1968:134).
2. In "The Addresses" Fichte advocated the creation of an entirely new German national self, through a total change of the existing German educational system.
3. While Herder's writings never became popular reading matter among the Icelandic public, his ideas on nature and its role in the construction of national self had a profound impact on Icelandic intellectuals and nationalists (Óskarsdóttir 1982). Tómas Sæmundsson, an Icelandic nationalist and intellectual who studied

in Copenhagen in the 1830s, stated for example in his "Ferdabók" ("Travelogue") that Herder's *Ideen zur Philosophie der Geschicte der Menschheit* was one of the most profound and sublime inquiries into world history which exists in German (Sæmundsson 1947).

Iceland acquired its first constitution in 1874, the same year as Icelanders celebrated the 1,000th anniversary of Iceland's settlement. In 1904 it won home rule, in 1918 it gained commonwealth status within the Danish empire and in 1944 it became a republic with its own president.

4. There were other nations that had, like Iceland, female national symbols. For example, Germania in Germany and Marianne in France. The meaning and significance of these symbols in their particular nationalist discourses were somewhat different from that of the Icelandic "Mountain Woman" (see Mosse 1985).
5. The popularity of the national costume has increased in Iceland during the 1990s, see, e.g., *Morgunbladid* 2 February 1992 "Skotthúfan má ekki gleymast." Also a programme on Icelandic National Radio about the national women's dress, broadcast 4 March 1992.

References

Antonsson, T. 1989. "Madurinn sem orti Aldahroll". "The man who wrote Aldahroll." In *Lesbók Morgunbladsins*, February 11, pp. 4–6.

Avineri, S. 1972. *Hegel's theory of the modern state*. Cambridge: Cambridge University Press.

Bjarnadóttir, H. 1942. "Heimilisidnadur," "Cottage industry." In *Hlín*, a yearly women's magazine, **25**, pp. 21–33.

Bjarnhédinsdóttir, B. 1907. *Kvennabladid, The women's magazine*, January 23.

Bjørnsdóttir, I.D. 1992. *Nationalism, gender and the contemporary Icelandic women's movement*. Ph.D. thesis, University of California, Santa Barbara.

Braidotti, R. 1991. *Patterns of dissonance. A study of women in contemporary philosophy*. Trans. E. Guild. Cambridge: Polity Press.

Brown, W. 1988. *Manhood and politics: A feminist reading in Political Theory*. Totowa, N.J.: Rowman and Littlefield.

Clausewitz, C. von 1968. *On war*. A. Rapoport (ed.). Baltimore: Penguin Books.

Di Stefano, C. 1991. *Configurations of masculinity. A feminist perspective on modern political theory*. Ithaca, NY: Cornell University Press.

Eisenstein, H. 1983. *Contemporary feminist thought*. Boston, Mass.: G.K. Hall & co.

Ergang, R.R. *Herder and the foundations of German nationalism*. New York: Columbia University Press.

Fichte, J.G. 1968. *Addresses to the German nation*. George Amstrong Kelly (ed.). New York and Evanston: Harper & Row.

Gröndal, B. 1874. *Skýring á minngarbréfum um thúsund ára byggingu Íslands. Explanation of the memorabilia of the thousand years anniversary of Iceland's settlement*. Reykjavík.

Gröndal, B. 1900. *Kvaedabók. Book of poems*. Reykjavík: útg. Sigurdur Kristinsson.

Gröndal, B. 1985. *Ljódmaeli. Poems*. Reykjavík: Bókmenntastofnun Háskóla Íslands og Menningarsjóds.

Gudmundsson, S. 1857. "Um kvenbúninga á Íslandi ad fornu og nýju". "Icelandic women's costumes today and in the past." In *Ný Félagsrit* 17 árg., pp. 1–53.

THE CENTRAL CONFIGURATION

Gudmundsson, V. 1903. "Ísland". "Iceland." In *Eimreidin* IX árg., pp. 69–70.

Hegel, G.F.W. 1964. *Hegel's political writings*. Trans. T.M. Knox. Oxford: Clarendon Press.

Herder, J.G. 1968. *Reflections on the philosophy of the history of mankind.* Abridged and with an introduction by F.E. Manuel. Chicago and London: University of Chicago Press.

Herder, J.G. 1969. *J.G. Herder on social and political culture.* Trans., edited and with an introduction by F.M. Barnard. Cambridge: Cambridge University Press.

Hjaltason, J. 1986. "Hvers vegna urdu Íslendingar thjódernissinnadir?". "Why did Icelanders become nationalists?" In *Lesbók Morgunbladsins* September 27, pp. 12–13.

Jochumsson, M. 1936. *Ljódmaeli. Poems.* Reykjavík: útg. Magnús Matthíasson.

Jónasdóttir, A.G. 1991. *Love power and political interests. Towards a theory of patriarchy in contemporary Western society.* Ørebro Studies **7**. Also published as Jónasdóttir, A.G. 1993. *Why are women oppressed?* Philadelphia: Temple University Press.

Jónsson, H. frá Bólu. 1942. *Ljódmaeli. Poems.* Reykjavík: Bókaútgáfa Menningarsjóds.

Kristmundsdóttir, S.D. 1990. *Doing and becoming: women's movements and women's personhood in Iceland 1870–1990.* Ph.D. dissertation University of Rochester.

Legge, J.G. 1970. *Rhyme and revolution in Germany, a study in German history, life, literature and character 1813–1850.* New York: AMS Press.

Morgan, R. (ed.) 1970. *Germany 1870–1970. A hundred years of turmoil.* London: BBC Publications.

Mosse, G.L. 1985. *Nationalism and sexuality.* New York: Howard Fertig.

Neumann, E. 1963. *The great mother.* trans. R. Manheim New York: Pantheon Books.

Ólafsson, E. 1832. *Kvaedi. Poems.* Copenhagen: S.L. Möller.

Óskarsdóttir, T. 1982. *Ideas of nationality in Icelandic poetry 1830–1974.* Ph.D. thesis from University of Edinburgh.

Sæmundsson, T. 1947. *Ferdabók. Travelogue.* Jakob Benediktsson (ed.) Reykjavik.

Thomsen, G. 1880. *Ljódmaeli. Poems.* Reykjavík: B. Jónsson & S. Pálsson.

Thomsen, G. 1969. *Ljódmaeli. Poems.* Sigurdur Nordal (ed.), Reykjavík: Mál & Menning.

Treitschke, H. von 1916. *Politics Vol.II.* London: Constable & Company Ltd.

Valdimarsdóttir, T. 1990. "Um gagnkvaema ást manna og meyjar" (fjallkonunnar). "About the mutual love between a man and a maiden" (the mountain woman). In *Yrkja, afmaelisrit til Vigdísar Finnbogadóttur, Cultivation, a tribute to Vigdís Finnbogadóttir on her 60th birthday.* Reykjavík: Idunn, pp. 288–294.

CHAPTER SIX

Make a line, so I can cross it: postmodernist space in Camille Paglia's Sexual personae

Kerstin W. Shands

Postmodernism has a horror of limits. The postmodernist craving for cen-
trelessness and absence of oppressive frameworks ultimately turns in on
itself in a claustrophobic embrace, creating a continuously shape-shifting
never-ending labyrinth of contingencies. Texts "looping" back on themselves
are seen as superior to commonplace linear and sequential texts. Hyperspace, for example, in its boundarylessness, becomes a postmodernist
heaven, as is obvious in Robert Coover's glorification of hyperspace's "intricate and infinitely expandable, infinitely alluring webs, its green-limned gardens
of multiple forking paths" (Coover 1992:23).

A common denominator in two major postmodernist modes of thought,
feminism and deconstruction, is precisely the desire to overcome, abolish or
erase boundaries and structures, be it in social or psychological codes or
barriers, or linguistic and logical systems. With her tome on Western culture, *Sexual personae: art and decadence from Nefertiti to Emily Dickinson*
(subsequent references abbreviated to *SP*), Camille Paglia – assessed by
Newsweek as a "Cultural terrorist" yet part of the cultural elite (5 October
1992:40) – is a writer who has managed to irritate feminists and deconstructionists alike. Paglia's book, according to herself "one of the great
books of the century", which "won't be understood for another 30 years"
(see Allen 1991, B4), has indeed, as Barrie Green contends in *The Harvard
salient*, "challenged standard academic thinking on both sides of the political
spectrum" (Green 1991:15).

While Camille Paglia has been discussed mainly in the United States, her
work has also received some attention in the Nordic countries. In my view,
her work does indeed deserve scrutiny here too, both for the self-criticism it
might inspire among feminists and for the vigilance its more reactionary
tenets ought to provoke. Resting on what during the most recent decades

has seemed "antediluvian" theories of nature, biology and culture, *Sexual personae*, in several respects, appears anomalous. Paglia's assertions on the incorrigibility of humankind and on the inescapable biological bondage of womankind send shivers down progressivist and constructionist spines. But Paglia's text is also an anomaly in another respect: correctly assessed on its cover as an "omnivorously learned work of guerrilla scholarship", its language and visions are bold and provocative, portioning out sadistic whacks and quips at traditional, timid academics who suppress, or simply miss, all the shocking, sexual and sacrilegious references in Western works of art and literature, who inflict on their students hateful books such as *Huckleberry Finn* and *Tom Sawyer* – woman-fearing "songs of innocence sixty years past their prime" (*SP*:623), and who have missed the theories of aggression in Spencer's *The Faerie Queen*, the sadism in Emily Brontë's *Wuthering Heights* or Blake's "Infant Joy", the decadence amid the social realism in Balzac, or the sex and violence in Emily Dickinson.

One cannot accuse Camille Paglia of being a deconstructionist. Her critique of the Judaeo-Christian emphasis on the word as concentrated upon by deconstructionists – in the wake of Freud – is too pugnacious, as is her critique of the "French" idea that "there is no person behind a text" (*SP*:34). Neither can she be placed with feminists. Paglia's pessimism as to whether we will reach feminism's goal of equal rights is profoundly disheartening. In both deconstructionist and feminist shops, then, Paglia remains a cool customer. Despite her posture as *voyeuse amusée* of the Western world and her disdain for some postmodernist theoreticians such as feminists and French-influenced academics, however, Paglia's visions and strategies seem peculiarly postmodernist in one, in my opinion fundamental, aspect, and that is in her attraction to the game of establishing distinctive dualities, discreteneses and divisivenesses, in order subsequently to puncture, transgress, or transform these entities. As she herself observes, in sadomasochistic and other, sexual or cultural, raptures, it is the erection of limits and the subsequent transgressions of those limits that is paramount: "make a line, so I can cross it" (*SP*:349).

Western culture rests upon a pagan foundation which Judaeo-Christianity has not been able entirely to suppress. The pagan is associated with nature or the chthonian or nether regions, the bowels of the earth, which are always threateningly present, even when hidden or not immediately visible. While the chthonian sometimes refers to subterranean or underworld deities, in Paglia, it also assumes connotations of the Dionysian and of nature's uncontrollable force, unbridled and irrepressible forces which Paglia posits against an Apollonian drive towards control and order. Paglia's theory of beauty, too, is spatially conceived along the lines of an Apollonian–Dionysian dichotomy. The horror of Apollonian minds at Paglia's attempts to lure them down into chthonian murk might obscure some less obvious points concerning Paglia's epistemological premises. In this chapter, those premises will be under scrutiny, through a focus on what I regard as basic metaphorical underpinnings in Paglia's theoretical structure, i.e., her spatial metaphors. Throughout *Sexual personae*, the master tropes are spatial, probing, for example, the significance of space(s) in Leonardo's paintings, closure versus containment in *Anthony and Cleopatra*, the womblike "bowers" or female zones in *The Faerie Queen*, the self-incarceration of Emily Dickinson and the whirlpool in Poe's *A descent into the maelström*.

Metaphors – the substitution of a word or a context for another or the combination of concepts into compressed analogies – have always been important in metaphysics and philosophy, and have more recently been debated by, among others, Jacques Derrida and Paul Ricoeur. There has been a movement away from a perception of metaphors as optional dashes of garnish added to "concrete" language, which is then held to be complete but rendered less vivid without them. As Jacques Derrida points out in "White Mythology", metaphor has been presented in textbooks along such lines ever since Aristotle. Derrida, whose own work is saturated with suggestive spatial metaphors (hinges, conchs, labyrinths, invaginations, edges, pockets, chiasmas, and so forth), has shown the fundamental unavoidability of metaphor in any discourse, arguing that it is not "a matter of inverting the literal meaning and the figurative meaning but of determining the 'literal' meaning of writing as metaphoricity itself" (Derrida 1977:15). For his part, Paul Ricoeur has seen the "opposition between figurative and non-figurative art" as "exclusively modern" (Ricoeur 1979:37). I take the view that metaphors can be partly unconscious features in literature at the same time as they are cognitive, an approach which may appear contradictory at first sight but which may allow a different passage into a work of literature or criticism, foregrounding, among other things, the ambiguity and ambivalence within a certain work. In Camille Paglia's work, the spatial metaphors reveal a particular ambivalence and angst which could be linked to the threatening and profound, unpredictable, re-figurations of space coming from previously marginalized corners such as feminist and postcolonialist theory.

In this chapter I will concentrate primarily on two major, interrelated domains in *Sexual personae*. First, I will examine Paglia's conception of nature and culture and of Apollonian and Dionysian forces, part of which discussion is also Paglia's theory of beauty and aesthetics. Secondly, I will consider her concepts of feminine and masculine, which are also related to Paglia's vision of art, culture and aesthetics. Although some parts of her theories are contradictory and controversial – such as her unquestioning acceptance of the variability hypothesis, much debated by twentieth-century scholars (see, e.g., Shields) – my aim in not to refute or reject her vision of the Dionysian and the Apollonian in Western art and literature. My chapter focuses instead on Paglia's use of spatial metaphors, which I see not as ornamentation but rather as unconscious features and as cognitive categories underpinning Paglia's epistemological and philosophical framework. It is that conceptual framework – and "all conceptualization is a framing" (*SP*:31) – that this chapter will examine critically. I will submit that despite important divergences, Camille Paglia, contradictorily, is writing within what I see as a postmodernist space, sharing many fundamental forms of conceptualization typical of feminist or deconstructionist thinking, but that an inspection of the spatial metaphors in *Sexual personae* suggests that there is, underneath and despite Paglia's engrossment with sexual syncretism, metamorphic identities and the collapsing of boundaries, a reactionary proposition. In my view, Paglia's text functioning as palimpsest makes visible a contemporary cultural angst and ambivalence, an angst agonistically and absolutistically evident both in the allure and in the apprehension of essentializing archetypes, often elided in feminist theory but well worth closer inspection.

The Apollo–Dionysos or culture–nature dichotomies spatially visualized

In Paglia's view, feminism is a construct of the philosophical model of Rousseau. Just as liberalism, from which it departs, it believes in humans' basic probity, a soundness disturbed and distorted mainly by society. It refuses to reckon with the permanently dark perimeters of human existence, that part associated with brutal and undifferentiating violence in nature, a side confronted in the writings of Sade and in Nietzsche's concept of the will-to-power. (Feminism's relation to Rousseau is, of course, more complicated than Paglia's assessment suggests. Liberal feminism, in fact, began as an anti-Rousseau impulse, with Mary Wollstonecraft's *Vindication of the rights of women* [1792] as an enraged response to Rousseau's presuppositions about women.) Camille Paglia chastises intellectual movements and ideologies such as liberalism and feminism for having swept their disparities under the carpet and for discounting nature's devastating force. Equality is desirable but unachievable, and feminism, aiming for this illusory goal, has eliminated contingency (i.e., the effects of nature and fate). Rape could be seen as an effect of nature – or male hormones – which occurs because there is too little social control, which Paglia, in Hobbesian vein, sees as necessary for reasonable harmony. Naïvely, feminism has assumed that natural forces, such as men's urge to rape, could be eradicated through the achievement of equality.

Nature, a problematic term in *Sexual personae*, seems to be both the natural world inclusive of the chthonian, threatening elements, and human nature. We have to civilize ourselves to keep nature in check, but the more we civilize the more repressed nature strikes back at us. One example is the *femme fatale*, who, rather than being a career woman *manquée*, as some feminists have suggested, represents a return of the repressed (and who, at this *fin-de-siècle* just as at the previous one, appears to be coming back with a vengeance in contemporary art and literature – a notable example being Margaret Atwood's novel *The robber bride* [1993]). In an anti-Rousseau and pro-Sade vision Paglia perceives nature as at best superficially beautiful, but really, fundamentally chaotic, perpetually in movement towards dissolution, re-creation and, again, dissolution in a perpetual, relentless process. With the complexity movement we may wish to ascribe to nature a propensity towards arranging its energies and quantum particles in particular, orderly patterns, but a deluge of liquidity and non-differentiation will, inevitably, delete all creation. As a defence mechanism, the Apollonian endeavours to rein in the Dionysian. Apollo's is an area of anxiety threatened by the Dionysian, "the chthonian whose law is procreative femaleness", and "liquid nature, a miasmic swamp whose prototype is the still pond of the womb" (*SP*:12). Attempting to control, the Apollonian names, classifies, categorizes: recognition, too, is our *apotropaion* or shield against the dangerous or incomprehensible, as is pornography, which tries to make explicit what never can be visible or comprehensible. Politics is another Apollonian strategy of control. Thanks to the Apollonian, however, which has dominated Western society, we have art and culture. But the Apollonian is a severance from immediate, earthy touch, a severing of the umbilical cord joining us to the chthonian mother or matrix, and involves a distancing emphasis on seeing: the visual has dominated the Western world. Sky-cult has replaced earth-cult, something that paradoxically "shifts woman into the nether realm" at the same time as it lifts her, since "male civilization . . . has lifted woman with it" (*SP*:8,9). Through art and through a fixation on the aesthetic, Western civilization has attempted to circumvent the abysmally frightening aspects of life and death, nature and woman. Life is an uncontrollable, menacing flux, a chaos, which art attempts to restrain through a ritualistic imposition of control:

> Art is a shutting in in order to shut out. Art is a ritualistic binding of the perpetual motion machine that is nature . . . Fixation is at the heart of art, fixation as stasis and fixation as obsession. The modern artist who merely draws a line across a page is still trying to tame some uncontrollable aspect of reality (*SP*:29).

In nature, Paglia asseverates, there are no objects, just a primal soup. Since woman is identified with the Dionysian, "thing-making" is, not surprisingly, a male obsession, part of male projection, progression and linearity, all of which are necessary for civilization to develop: "If civilization had been left in female hands", Paglia posits in a much-quoted statement, "we would still be living in grass huts" (*SP*:38). Logically, too, the ideal Apollonian genre is cinema. While Judaism is based on the word, Christianity, in Paglia's view, has been unable to suppress pagan pictorialism, underestimated by modern scholarship, which remains fixated on the word. In our epoch of the mass media, however, the image is taking precedence over the word. Scrutinizing the development in Western art history, Paglia takes as her point of departure the *Venus of Willendorf,* an image showing how mother (Latin *mater*) and materia are connected. This sculpture is formless, has "no lines" but "only curves and circles". "She is the formlessness of nature. She is mired in the miasmic swamp I identify with Dionysus" (*SP*:57). The *Venus of Willendorf* is nature. Only in Egypt did art in the Western, Apollonian sense arise, as non-utilitarian conceptualization, impermeability, intractability. However, it must be added that Egyptian culture did not attempt to extinguish the Dionysian, but fused "the conceptual with the chthonian" (*SP*:61), one of the reasons it lasted longer than its Greek counterpart. A symbol of this synthesis is the cat, along with the crocodile a venerated animal in Egypt. A similar synthesis was achieved during the Roman republic, but in Greek culture, as during Roman decadence, the Apollonian and the Dionysian remained unreconciled. For Paglia, then, the Apollonian is objectification, separation (as in Western personality and thought), while the Dionysian is identification, empathy – two forces which even split our brains into the higher cortex and the limbic.

Postmodernism might perhaps be seen as a Dionysian reaction to the Apollonianism of high modernism, a reaction so strong that it is presently causing a swing back towards the Apollonian, perceptibly so, at least, in *Sexual personae.* Paglia, who privileges the Dionysian but works out of the Apollonian, constructs her concepts spatially in a way that makes them accord very well with a postmodernist space. If we go to Ihab Hassan's Comparative Table, among the postmodernist qualities he defines are, for example, "Antiform (disjunctive, open) . . . Play, Chance, Anarchy, Exhaustion/Silence, Process/Performance/Happening, Participation, Decreation/Deconstruction . . . Dispersal . . . Desire . . . Polymorphous/Androgynous . . . Indeterminacy, Immanence" (Hassan 1982). With darker undertones, Paglia's concept of the Dionysian could be related to many of the items on Hassan's list: Hassan's "Play" and "Process/Performance/Happening" correspond to Paglia's idea of the Dionysian as the new, the energetic, "Chance" to the unpredictability of Paglia's universe, "Anarchy" to the chaos of promiscuity or *sparagmos* (a tearing apart or spasm), "Exhaustion/Silence", "Decreation/Deconstruction", and "Dispersal" to dissolution and death, "Participation" and "Immanence" to Dionysian empathy and identification; "Desire" to Dionysian promiscuity, the "Polymorphous/Androgynous" and "Indeterminacy" to the Dionysian plurality and puncturing of Apollonian contour. Paglia's delineation of the Apollonian, on the other hand, to a large extent coincides with Hassan's items on the modernist side: "Form (conjunctive, closed), Purpose, Design, Hierarchy, Mastery/Logos, Art Object/Finished Work . . . Genre/Boundary . . . Genital/Phallic . . . Determinacy, Transcendence". Paglia's master images might be lined up thus:

Apollonian	Dionysian
head	body
eye	viscera
externality	internality
definiteness	indefiniteness
transparency	opaqueness
condensation	ex-tending, sparagmos
line, form, contour	formlessness
transcendence	immanence
male	female
containment	openness, all-inclusiveness

The listed items can, of course, separately or synthesized, open up new dichotomies: femaleness, for example, which is "primitive and archaic" is opposed to femininity, which is "social and aesthetic" (*SP*:359), and the Apollonian and Dionysian as pagan forces can be placed together against Judaeo-Christianity. The fundamental dichotomy I see in Paglia's theoretical edifice, however, is containment versus openness. The "abyss" Paglia sees as opening up monthly for women, moreover, brings to mind the postmodernist spaces described by Alice Jardine in *Gynesis* as connected with Woman or with the non-knowledge of the master narratives, a rethinking by modernity visualized as

> a vast self-exploration, a questioning and turning back upon their own discourse, in an attempt to create a new space or spacing within themselves for survivals (of different kinds). In France, such rethinking has involved, above all, a reincorporation and reconceptualization of that which has been the master narratives' own "non-knowledge", what has eluded them, what has engulfed them. This other-than-themselves is almost always a "space" of some kind (over which the narrative has lost control), and this space has been coded as feminine, as woman (Jardine 1985:25).

Alice Jardine continues: "To give a new language to these other spaces is a project filled with both promise and fear, however, for these spaces have hitherto remained unknown, terrifying, monstrous: they are mad, unconscious, improper, unclean, non-sensical, oriental, profane" (ibid.:73). It is precisely such profane, terrifying and monstrous spaces that *Sexual personae* delves into. Moreover, "modernity [as] a rethinking not only of secular boundaries, but of sacred boundaries as well" (ibid.:80), is a rethinking present also in Paglia's concept of the *temenos* or ritual precinct. Jardine has also observed that "It is no accident that the interrogative return to our sources of knowledge must also be a return to the mother's body" (ibid.:139), an observation which could be applicable also to Paglia's project, and in which it, in turn, connects to theories in feminist psychology which explore and valorize the pre-Oedipal – or the pre-Antigonal, as Nina Lykke imaginatively reconceptualizes it. That space could be compared to Paglia's Dionysian matrix with its seeming seamlessness and boundarylessness, its fusion and identification but also, with a Kristevan term, its abjection. Interestingly, Dionysus himself is associated with women. Below, I will return to a discussion of the female or maternal spaces in *Sexual personae*, but for now, these comparisons may suffice to indicate that Paglia's modes of conceptualizing, in particular her spatial metaphors, place her closer to postmodernist thinking than her explicit or implicit critique of it suggests at first glance.

Masculinity and femininity, spatially conceived

Paglia places sexuality and eroticism at an intersection between nature and culture. From that spot, she departs into a jungle of intertwined analogies. As indicated above, Paglia uses a spatial metaphorics based on old mythologies or archetypes identifying the male with the discreet and the female, contradictorily, with uncontrollable boundarylessness at the same time as femaleness is enclosure, "the still pond of the womb". Furthermore, woman is connection rather than separation, as she "turns a gob of refuse into a spreading web of sentient being, floating on the snaky umbilical cord by which she leashes every man" (*SP*:12). The umbilical cord, the primary and concrete connective link between humans, is spun by woman and controlled by woman, hence men's – or humans'? – irredeemable, ineradicable archaic fear of women's power. It is not a male god, as men have wanted to believe, who initiated things. Puny man delivers a mere "gob of refuse" which woman, miraculously, transforms "into a spreading web of sentient being". Here, we have woman as weaver of webs, an image both pointing back to ancient myths and archetypes and forward to some branches of contemporary cultural and archetypal feminism. Where Paglia differs from mainstream feminists is in her assertion that those ancient myths and archetypes are inescapably real. Grounded in liberalism and utilitarianism, feminism has, she claims, understandably but uselessly, been engaged in wishful thinking.

However, Paglia's analogies between genitals and fertility systems on the one hand and male/female cultural achievements or psychological dispositions on the other, or her parallels between animals and humans must be questioned. Analogous with their erections and ejaculations, Paglia asserts, men crave linear progression towards conclusive goals, while women, with their diffuse and unlimited sexuality and their groundedness in the cyclicity and circularity of constantly recurring monthly cycles, need no such visions. In Paglia's vision, male sexuality is both linear and bounded, while woman's sexuality is diffused. At the same time as society's inhospitality to woman (in the form of oppressive patriarchy) is due to nature's awesomeness or awfulness, metaphorized as a female space, the public spaces of culture and society result from woman's feminizing powers. Although a much debated concept, in feminist analyses patriarchy concerns male power or control over women, but in Paglia's single-minded view, patriarchy is simply a male defence against man's disturbing sense of woman's power. If Paglia is correct, feminists' struggle to dismantle patriarchal structures will prove vain. Moreover, if Paglia is right in asserting that "Woman is in league with the irrational. Nature, more than society, is her true oppressor" (*SP*:591), then political struggle to improve women's lives will prove fruitless.

In Paglia's theory, it is thus no longer woman who is imprisoned in/ by patriarchy, as in feminist analyses, but man who is woman's prisoner: "Woman's body is a labyrinth in which man is lost. It is a walled garden, the medieval hortus conclusus, in which nature works its daemonic sorcery" (*SP*:12). At the same time, paradoxically, woman is enclosing herself. She is both encloser and enclosed, man merely enclosed, in this vocabulary grounded in archetypal thinking and associating woman with the garden and the labyrinth. But because woman in ancient times must have appeared self-contained or self-sufficient, requiring only a "gob of refuse" to be able to turn inward and sink back into maddeningly inscrutable, daemonic completeness, while man gazes upon the unfolding, enveloping mystery with awe, does that mean that contemporary humans, cognizant of the dual forces requisite for creation, should retain the archetypal vision of woman as mysterious nature? Pregnancy is indeed miraculous, but why should woman be more associated with mystery because her fertility apparatus is inside, hidden from sight? Just because the male contribution to the creation of new life is temporally less extended and spatially minuscule, almost invisible, is it *therefore* less mysterious or significant?

According to Paglia, male sexuality is an unenviably driven and anxiety-ridden, constant and paradoxical projection towards, and away from, awesome woman/nature. Woman as *temenos* invites veneration and profanation. Ironically, even if men in sky-cult attempt to soar above the chthonian, the places/spaces through which this goal is to be reached replicate woman's inner space. Superficially, Paglia's notions resemble Erik Erikson's ideas of a woman's inner space. The conclusions are different, however, almost at opposite poles. While Erikson looks benevolently upon woman's inner space, projecting upon the womb societal salvation in an extension of the "values" it creates and propagates, values of celebration and veneration of life itself, Paglia's vision is both darker and more dualistic, emphasizing the creative and destroying facets of this remarkable literal and metaphoric female space. In Paglia's analysis, propagation and procreation present no pretty spectacle. The painful, gory, chaotic aspects of pregnancy and childbirth are suppressed by feminist propagandists of feminine principles and Erikson-type advocates alike. Apparently, Paglia is inverting Simone de Beauvoir's long acclaimed words that one is not born a woman, one becomes a woman, by saying that biology is indeed destiny (although de Beauvoir herself counteracts her own statement in her catalogue of the biological horrors and suffering of womankind). In my view, Paglia, too, contradicts herself in asserting that woman is debilitated and disadvantaged by biology at the same time as she is so powerful that men, in terrified defence, have created patriarchal forms of control. Paradoxically, a pregnant woman, maddeningly complete and self-sufficient, may radiate power to a man yet she is really powerless before the chthonian forces which have taken over her life. Menstruation is another uncanny force which women cannot control, a "red flood", from the "female sea", a "chthonian matrix from which we rose" (*SP*:11). The womanly abyss of the vagina is another awesome space of female power, metaphorically expressed in the myth of the toothed vagina, another myth which Paglia holds up as literally true, since "every vagina has secret teeth, for the male exits as less than when he entered" (*SP*:13). Female genitals are another paradox, being charged with the cutting edge of dentated power yet vanishing into an aesthetic formlessness surpassing that of the *Venus of Willendorf*. To male and female sexual excitement are applied the same kinds of metaphor, an erection being architectural, while female arousal is "slow, gravitational, amorphous" (*SP*:91). Whether architecturally coherent or incoherent, the feminine and maternal spaces in *Sexual personae* are depicted as both alluring and menacing, spaces that are internalized, territories which men can never completely escape. In this vision, woman is a statically enclosed and enclosing space while man is perpetually in movement, towards or from that space, imaged as a *temenos*, a concept also applied to Paglia's discussion of art. The female body is a prototype of holy spaces. The female space is also water. Woman is *hygra physis*, which is not just plain water: it is "not free-flowing but contained water, fluids which ooze, drip, or hang in tissues or fleshy sacs" (*SP*:91).

Since women's key metaphor is the unseen, ambiguity becomes more tolerable for women, who realize and accept that a limited and subjective understanding is a normal predicament in life, something that makes women more realistic. Biology thus underlies epistemology. Moreover, as does everything sacred, the *temenos* of woman will invite, or provoke, profanation and violation in the form of rape. Feminists have debated the battle of the sexes as if there could be a double victory in the achievement of political equality. In Paglia's predictions, such a scenario will remain utopian since the sexes, endlessly engaged in warfare, are divided by an unbridgeable gulf.

Concluding thoughts

Reading *Sexual personae*, a strange picture forms in my inner mind. In a primeval landscape I discern a huge female figure, awesome, darkly silent and terrifying, towering above a multitude of frenetically scrambling little men who in their sexual anxiety hurl themselves again and again at this mysterious and impenetrable sexual persona, a goddess figure – but, alas, to no avail. Their concentrated and projecting movements forwards are part of a Sisyphean repetition-compulsion aimed at alleviating perpetual male anxieties in face of the chthonian. *Sexual personae* itself could be visualized along similar lines. Double-edged, paradoxical and contradictory, it is a celebration of ancient, ungraspable and unquenchable, ultimately inexplicable, natural forces, imaged as and identified with woman. It is also an *apotropaion*, an attempt to ward off our deepest fears of such forces, since Paglia's own perception of divisive and defining patterns, i.e., her closing-in of writers or aspects of their work in particular patterns while closing others out, is an edgy Apollonian generation of contour. Paglia's text is a *uroboros* (a serpent eating its own tail). It is both towering self-contained "femininity" and scrambling, anxious "masculinity". It erects looming structures in order to smash and demolish them. Central in Paglia's theory is the idea that ancient myths, such as the sexual stereotypes of woman attacked by equal rights feminists as male fabrications, have universal power simply because they are true. Such essentialist statements will make any cultural constructionist cringe. Paglia seems to be reaffirming the ideas Mary Ellman critiqued in *Thinking about women* in 1968: woman being identified with the formless, the hidden, the serenely self-contained, with nature. But one might instead argue, with Bell Hooks, that

> Stereotypes, however inaccurate, are one form of representation. Like fictions, they are created to serve as substitutions, standing in for what is real. They are there not to tell it like it is but to invite and encourage pretence. They are a fantasy, a projection onto the Other that makes them less threatening. Stereotypes abound when there is distance. They are an invention, a pretence that one knows when the steps that would make real knowing possible cannot be taken – are not allowed (hooks 1992:34).

Similarly, Yi-Fu Tuan writes that "Myths flourish in the absence of precise knowledge" (Tuan 1977:85).

Paglia's text straddles the Apollonian and the Dionysian, embracing the Western canon of art and literature while apparently rejecting postmodernist theories such as deconstructionism and feminism as grounded in Logos. What she rejects, I think, is the utopian mode of postmodernism rather than its reactionary mode. As I have shown, Paglia privileges the Dionysian, yet attempts an "Egyptian" synthesis of Dionysian and Apollonian drives. However, these two forces pull in different directions in her text, the synthesis failing to coalesce since the text remains studded with contradictions. While Paglia dismantles boundaries and valorizes transvestitism and hermaphroditism, Romantic incest and sexual ambiguity (at least figuratively), she wishes to leave intact the gulf between man and woman. Celebrating the wonderful progress of civilization which has made her own creativity realizable, she deems political progress impossible in the face of archetypal realities. *Sexual personae* embraces Dionysian dissolution and identification, yet falls into a Descartian trap of dividing body and soul. Paglia pities woman as the prisoner of gender, yet places her on an awesome pedestal, and in order to paint her picture uses a technique in art and literature she has termed gigantism (used by Michelangelo to create his "viragos" and by Emily Dickinson to transcend the limitations of her sex). But as she herself has pointed out, gigantism masculinizes, and thus blurs the very male–female dichotomy which placed woman on the pedestal. Paglia holds up ancient archetypes of woman prevalent in the West as explanatory of the primeval fears men have of women and of the existence of patriarchy. A glaring absence in Paglia's theory is her failure to explain why the different and more egalitarian interpretations of male and female archetypes existing in the East have not led to more egalitarian conditions on a social and political level.

Paglia's theories, then, as elaborated through her spatially conceived metaphors, on one level resemble postmodernist sensibilities. *Sexual personae* indeed shares with feminism a transgressive impulse. However, it is a transgression in a different direction. Is it moving "backwards" or "beyond"? In common with some postmodernist thinkers Paglia rejects the concept of a unitary personality, embracing instead a Dionysian, shape-shifting plurality. More fundamentally, however, Paglia solidifies the epoxy of the Western culture she (together with feminists and deconstructionists) loves to critique and fortifies the traditional hierarchical dualities such as masculine and feminine, culture and nature, transcendence and immanence, hieraticism and profanity, unity and *sparagmos*, and rationalism and irrationalism. Paglia observes that "Woman's current advance in society is not a voyage from myth to truth but from myth to new myth" (*SP*:16). What I see as a severe crack in her in many respects towering edifice is the absence of the insight that not only the advancement of woman as she analyzes it but also her own vision of nature may be a myth, a belief, or a construction. Unchangeably, nature is, in *Sexual personae*, liquefying Dionysian, chthonian miasma, a continuous dissolution of man-made patterns, demarcations, lines, or *objets d'art*. Indeed, male and female biology, as well as nature's agenda – if there is one – remain unfathomable and mysterious to us, and nature's indiscriminate cruelty manifested in eruptions, droughts, floods and other natural catastrophes is irrefutable. But does that mean that nature's breathtaking beauty is merely an illusion, temporary and vacuous? Paglia seems to adopt only one lens through which to look at both literature and life, the lens of de Sade, while discarding that of Rousseau. But perhaps two lenses are necessary for a balanced view? Perhaps the tyranny of Apollo and the vandalism of Dionysus should be gazed at through bifocals? Resting on a rock of reiterated "truths" about nature, man and woman, repeated with sometimes monotonous predictability, Paglia's telescope fixes most willingly upon the horrors and the perverse psychodramas played out in nature, in boudoirs and in literature, unfazed by how strenuously debated concepts such as "man" and "nature" have been in recent decades.

One of the best marks of scholarship is the stimulation of theoretical debate, and in this respect Camille Paglia has succeeded admirably. *Sexual personae* itself should, I think, be read bifocally. Laudable in *Sexual personae* is its comprehensive critique of Western canonical works of art and literature, with often original and stimulating discussions of English, French and American works, discussions often penetrated by unflinching and invigorating visions. But the underpinnings of Paglia's theoretical edifice need to be scrutinized. Is Camille Paglia, along with some reactionary postmodernist thinkers, building a theory which, as Alice Jardine suggests with respect to some recent French philosophers, is "satisfying a repressed desire in men (and women?) for what may turn out to be a very old, and, in any case, very readable plot" (Jardine 1985:37)? A scrutiny of the spatial metaphors in *Sexual personae* suggests that there is, underneath Paglia's interest in sexual syncretism, metamorphic identities and the collapsing of boundaries, a reactionary position, which ultimately might be used, politically, to condone totalitarian regimes and, privately, to "understand", if not applaud, male brutality against women. Despite Camille Paglia's self-advertised radicalism about masculinity and femininity, *Sexual personae* may thus be read as a bolstering of conservative ideologies. Furthermore, Paglia's staunch essentialism ought to motivate a response rather than a retreat since a scrutiny of her work might promote a more nuanced elucidation of differences within both essentializing and constructivist types of feminism. Some essentializing branches of feminism, while perceiving themselves as polar opposites of Paglia's kind of essentialism, may be much closer to it than they might like to think. As for the anti-essentialist materialists, they may, as Diana Fuss writes in *Essentially speaking*, "run the risk of too quickly dismissing both biology and psychology as essentializing discourses, often failing to recognize the irreducible essentialism informing their own theorizations" (Fuss 1989:50). In times of backlash, feminist self-scrutiny needs to be increased and the seductive nature of essentialist archetypes closely inspected since we need to examine the presuppositions that "nature and fixity go together (naturally) just as sociality and change go together (naturally). In other words, it may be time to ask whether essences can change and whether constructions can be normative" (ibid.:6). The reactions to Paglia's brilliantly idiosyncratic text point both to a general cultural angst in times of apparent dissolution and, more specifically, to realistic feminist fears of losing ground. Paglia's work adds fire to the essentialist/constructionist battlefield, a polemical dichotomization in feminist theory which in some quarters has led to deadlock and paranoia but which needs to be delved into rather than dismissed.

References

Allen, H. 1991. Camille Paglia's mad, mad worldview. *Washington Post*, 15 April, B1, B4.

Alter, J. 1992. The cultural elite. *Newsweek*, 5 October, 34–41.

Coover, R. 1992. The end of books. *New York Times Book Review*, 21 June, 1, 23–5.

Derrida, J. 1977. *Of grammatology*. Gayatri Chakravorty Spivak (tr.). Baltimore, MD: Johns Hopkins University Press.

Ellman, M. 1968. *Thinking about women*. New York: Harcourt Brace Jovanovich.

Fuss, D. 1989. *Essentially speaking: feminism, nature and difference*. New York: Routledge.

Green, B. 1991. Camille Paglia speaks out at MIT: as nasty as she wants to be. *Harvard Salient* (November), 15.

Hassan, I. 1982. Toward a concept of postmodernism. In *The dismemberment of Orpheus: toward a postmodern Literature*, 2nd rev. edn. Madison, WI: University of Wisconsin Press, 259–71.

hooks, b. 1992. Representing Whiteness in the Black Imagination. In *Cultural studies*, introduced by Lawrence Grossberg, Cary Nelson and Paula A. Treichler (eds), 33–46. New York: Routledge.

Jardine, A. 1985. *Gynesis: configurations of woman and modernity*. Ithaca, NY and London: Cornell University Press.

Lykke, N. 1989. *Rødhätte og Ödipus: brikker til en feministisk psykoanalyse*. Odense, Denmark: Odense Universitetsforlag.

Paglia, C. 1990. *Sexual personae: art and decadence from Nefertiti to Emily Dickinson*. London and New Haven, Conn.: Yale University Press.

Ricoeur, P. 1979. *The rule of metaphor: multi-disciplinary studies of the creation of meaning in language*. Tr. Robert Czerny, with Kathleen McLaughlin and John Costello, SJ. Toronto: University of Toronto Press.

Shields, S. 1982. The variability hypothesis: the history of a biological model of sex differences in intelligence. *Signs* **7**, No. 4 (summer), 769–97.

Tuan, Y.-F. 1977. *Space and place: the perspective of experience*. Minneapolis: University of Minnesota Press.

PART TWO

Organization and contested spaces

CHAPTER SEVEN

Taste, manners and attitudes – the bel esprit *and literary salon in the Nordic countries* c.1800

Anne Scott Sørensen

When the Schimmelmann mansion, one of the remaining architectural gems of the old Frederiksstad situated around Amalienborg Castle in Copenhagen,[1] burned down in April 1992, a great deal of public interest was aroused, and the press dug the story of the Schimmelmann salon out of the smouldering ruins. It was a fascinating tale about the liberal aristocrat and statesman Ernst Schimmelmann, a knowledgeable patron of literature and the visual arts in the late eighteenth and early nineteenth centuries. However, the story suffered from a significant omission – Charlotte Schimmelmann, his wife, who in fact was the hostess or *bel esprit*, as they were then called, was absent.

Just as Charlotte Schimmelmann, the other *beaux esprits* in the Nordic countries have been more or less forgotten, or shrouded in an ambiguous veil of myth. In the latter case, their houses, their social gatherings and the men of letters who attended them are looked back upon with nostalgia in a national and primarily literary tradition. Until now, even the content of academic research has been based on the highly anecdotal, and only recently have interdisciplinary gender and cultural studies prepared the ground for a more systematic study of the subject. Using this as a starting point, I shall sketch a different story of the *bel esprit* and of the predominantly literary salons that flourished in the Nordic countries around the turn of the nineteenth century,[2] and invite the reader inside two Danish ones to discuss similarities and differences in the theory and practice of the salon in the North, and between its northern manifestation and the form it took in the rest of Europe.

ANNE SCOTT SØRENSEN

The Utopia of the salon

In his paradigmatic thesis on the rise of the bourgeois public sphere, Jürgen Habermas described the salon[3] as a primarily French-inspired counterpart to the clubs and coffee-houses which spread from England to continental Europe during the eighteenth century, and to the budding German societies of the turn of the nineteenth century (Habermas 1990). According to Habermas, the salon was a forum for aesthetic judgement and training which moulded public taste but was privately managed by the well-to-do, most often aristocratic circles in a Europe where the idea of polite culture took its form mainly at the direction of literate and literary women. In contrast, the clubs, coffee-houses and societies represented an early public space instrumental in the formation of public opinion among bourgeois men and which anticipated the genuine political culture of bourgeois society. With his primary focus on this latter so-called classical public sphere, Habermas takes little interest in the salon and its various manifestations, but holds to an apprehension of a semi-private, semi-public phenomenon in the transition to embourgeoisement. However, in the preface to the 1990 edition of his *Strukturwandel der Öffentlichkeit* he proposes to operate within not only one authentic public sphere but several competing ones.[4]

This point has been developed in recent studies of the salon in Germany, England and France, in which the salon has been seen as part of a dynamic and multi-layered cultural process evolving towards modernity (Wilhelmy 1989, Heyden-Rynsch 1992, Seibert 1993). Nevertheless, such recent studies are inspired by the early Habermas in that they understand the salon as a step towards if not a bourgeois public, then the modern cultural institutions which represent an implicit ideal.

Petra Wilhelmy (1989), who has studied the Berlin salon of the nineteenth century (1780–1914), maintains a kind of network theory in arguing that after 1780 and up to 1850 the many different salons in Berlin appear as independent social entities, as socio-cultural organisms that in part lead a life of their own, in part are connected to each other and to other social gatherings, for example to reading societies. According to this analysis, they can be said to have formed larger cultural circles and thus to be the forerunners of the cultural institutions of modern Europe. Peter Seibert (1993), whose specific interest is the literary salon in Germany and the connections between literature and society from the late eighteenth through the nineteenth century, draws attention to the production and reception of literature and the creation of a literary public within the salons. Furthermore, he argues that the salon promotes oral and dramatic genres such as the proverb, the anecdote, the narrative or dramatic improvisation, and the so-called "*proverbes dramatiques*", and that the salon itself becomes a theme in, as well as a model of, contemporary literature in genres such as memoirs, diaries, letters and the salon novel (German *Salonstücke*).

122

However, both the abovementioned studies consider the original quality of the salon to be its existence as an informal social gathering, directed by the salon hostess who guarantees spirited conversation and an atmosphere of conviviality (German *Geselligkeit*). And it is this art of socializing which is the basis for Verena Heyden-Rynsch's study (1992). Hers is a broader interest in the European salon, which she understands as a coherent female-centred culture transported from Italy to Scandinavia, from Spain to Russia over an extended period dating from the early Italian Renaissance and continuing into the twentieth century, albeit with roots that can be traced back to antiquity.

Heyden-Rynsch's main thesis is that the salon marks a culmination of a now-lost women's culture. In her view, it represents the free rein given to intellectual, literate and aesthetic engagement not only for women but which also allowed for a unique interplay between the sexes during which taste, manners and attitudes were changed. In this respect, the members of the salon, and not least the salon hostess herself, according to Heyden-Rynsch the "playmaker of spirit", engage in an urban, cosmopolitan education which reorganizes the internal as well as the external world in the same process of modernity in which it is gradually subsumed, a process that already appre-hends a lost sense of the rituals of society, of the art of life, acted out as it was in a form of drama and through the Socratic rhetoric of gentle irony (ibid.:27).

In contrast to Wilhelmy (1989) and Seibert (1993), both of whom celeb-rate the perspective of modernity even if in common with Habermas they deplore the decline of the public sphere in late modernity, Heyden-Rynsch (1992) takes the salon as her ideal – even as her Utopia. However, she accentuates a very similiar point:

> The educational conversation which unfolded without any limita-tion on time or compulsion to agreement has receded in favour of the constrained opinion formation of the mass media. The recrea-tional talk has still more unmistakably encapsulated the type of dialogue already lauded by Nietsche when he talked about the playful atmosphere of humanity (27; author's translation).

In a recent paper, Ulrike Weckel (1996) has criticized these studies for being too apologetic, even if in another – feminist – sense than earlier studies (Drewitz 1965, Hertz 1991). In other words, she looks upon them as a part of a feminist project of historical documentation and celebration of "foremothers", and in so doing she moreover accords with the German, French and English feminist literature on the subject (e.g., Lougee 1976, Baader & Fricke 1979, Goodman 1989, Myers 1990). One of her main argu-ments is that research is still restricted in many ways – geographically, scientifically, etc. – which makes its conclusions very unreliable. Her critique seems reasonable in so far as scholarship on the subject is still young and tied into the academic centres of modern-day Europe, but also rather predictable when one considers the on-going shift of paradigms within international academic feminism. Consequently, the aim of the present chapter, which represents the results of the first extensive research project of its kind in the Nordic countries (Scott Sørensen 1998), is to contribute to the differentiation of the map of European salon culture and the process of on-going academic reflection in a dialogue with feminism.

The cultural history of the salon in Europe and the North

As in the rest of Europe around 1800, educated women in the North from both the aristocracy and the upper ranks of the bourgeoisie assembled the literate and the learned of their day in their homes and thereby positioned themselves at the centre of cultural events. The salons seem to have been concentrated in the metropolises of northern Europe, in itself a European backwater when viewed from the perspective of "central" Europe. But, as we shall see, there are also interesting exceptions which challenge the very idea of centre and periphery.

In the period under discussion, the contemporary North was an unstable entity. Before the Napoleonic Wars there existed on the one hand a united monarchy of the kingdom of Denmark-Norway and the now German states of Schleswig and Holstein, and on the other a Swedish kingdom which included Finland. The Kiel treaty of 1814 created a Danish monarchy without Norway and a union between Sweden and Norway under the Swedish king. Finland had already been made a principality of the Russian empire in 1809. Furthermore, the class of higher officials was to a great extent comprised of second-generation German immigrants (Denmark), the educated classes were German (Denmark) and French-speaking (Denmark, Sweden and Finland) and, still, the main language in Finland was Swedish, in Norway Danish. These circumstances make it reasonable to seek the inspiration for the Nordic salons in Germany and France in particular and their common roots in the generalized European history of the salon.

One of the main points made in earlier studies is that the origins of the salon can be traced as far back as the early Italian Renaissance and to its famous *beaux esprits*, such as the duchess of Urbino, Elisabeth Gonzaga (1471–1526), and the duchess of Mantua, Isabelle d'Este (1474–1539). Both were influenced by *Il Libro del Cortegiano* (*The book of the courtier*), a kind of handbook by the Italian Baldassare Castiglione on courtly manners, courtesy and refined language which mirrored an early Renaissance humanism. Another source of influence was the knight and troubadour culture of the late Middle Ages in other parts of Europe. Thus, European salon culture grew out of the court, and Heyden-Rynsch (1993) discusses how this culture of the nobility reached its peak and then gradually declined, leaving the innovative cultural role to the bourgeois educationalist project (German *Bildung*). However, she claims that court and salon functioned in counterpoint from the early seventeenth to the late nineteenth centuries, and that the court remains the negative basis of the salon in a continued process in which the bourgeoisie is mobilized and the aristocracy modernized. Consequently, the end of this process is also the grand finale of the salon.

The seventeenth-century French *precieuses* provide a relatively early if apposite example of such a rarified cultural milieu. The marquise de Rambouillet (1588–1665), the most renowned of their number, saw herself and her gatherings as an alternative to the dissolute and corrupt life of the French court. She took pride in refining the social niceties, especially the conventions of social relations between the sexes, and in beautifying the French language according to the new "exquisite" mode of socializing. Raised into a devotion to linguistic codes, bodily attitudes and social manners, her gatherings came in part to be ridiculed in their own day, in part victim of a dubious reputation in spite of their lofty intention. According to Mary Terrall (1996), the salon was already imbued with an ambiguity between the academy and the boudoir. This ambiguity, which was deliberately cultivated in the salons of the French Enlightenment, was influenced by the new discoveries in physics, chemistry and biology, concerned with the processes of life.

The French tradition reached its zenith in the salon of the author Germaine de Staël (1766–1817), daughter of the French minister of finance and the salon hostess Mme Necker and married to the Swedish diplomat Erik Magnus de Staël von Holstein. Just before and in the early days of the French Revolution, Germaine de Staël presided over a highly politicized salon in Paris which applauded Enlightenment ideas and was hugely popular with the radical male elite. Afterwards, during her political exile towards the end of the revolutionary period and during Napoleon's ascendancy, she held a mainly literary salon at Coppet by Lake Geneva in Switzerland, which had as its inspiration the trends of Sensibility and early Romanticism and was much favoured by all the European luminaries within literature, art and science. Among them was the Nordic *bel esprit* Friederike Brun who on several occasions lived at Coppet. De Staël also visited the North in 1812 where she held a temporary salon in Stockholm in Sweden. In the novel *Corinne* (1807), she has given the definitive interpretation of the salon culture of her day and of the often conflicting ambitions of the *bel esprit* who strove to transform their role into a professional career.

Following on the Parisian model, but also in a critical gesture towards the French tradition with its philosophical and erotic connotations, the Bluestocking Club was formed in the middle of the eighteenth century in England by a geographically widely dispersed circle of women interested in literature, among them Lady Montagu (1720–1800), "the queen of the blues", as she was known (Myers 1990). However, there seems to have been very little interchange between the Nordic salons and either the Bluestockings or the later London assemblies. Instead, the mainly musical salons of Vienna, but above all the mainly literary salons of the so-called Young Germany, served as inspiration for the North in the beginning of the nineteenth century.

In Berlin, the salons were then directed by a group of intellectual Jewish women, among them Henriette Hertz (1764–1847) and Rahel Varnhagen von Ense (1771–1833) (Hertz 1991). Nordic *beaux esprits* such as the Danish Friederike Brun (1765–1835) and the Swedish Malla Silfverstolpe (1782–1861) were greatly influenced by this milieu. Both visited Berlin, and Friederike Brun also kept up a regular correspondence with Caroline Humbolt,[5] while Malla Silfverstolpe wrote to Bettine von Arnim (1789–1855) and Amalia von Helvig (1776–1831) (Klitgaard Povlsen 1998a, Holmquist 1998).

The famous Jena group was formed with Dorothea Veit-Schlegel (1763–1839) and Caroline Schlegel-Schelling (1763–1809) at its centre. It was said to vitalize Goethe's idea of elective affinities (*Wahlverwandschaften* [1809]), but in recent German literary and gender studies a debate has arisen concerning the theory and practice of the relationship between the sexes within the group (Behrens 1981, Enzenberger 1988). The controversy has centred around the famous male authors who were the husbands, brothers and lovers, while Friedrich Schlegel's novel *Lucinde* (1800) has been read as a *roman à clef*, alternately praised and vilified (Scholz 1992). There was no single explicit bond between Jena and the northern salons but many connections, not least through the so-called Weimar circle which was formed around J.W. Goethe. For instance, the German *bel esprit* Amalia von Helwig, who kept salons in Weimar, Heidelberg and Berlin was married to a Swede. She held a salon in Stockholm between 1805 and 1810 and again between 1814 and 1816 and, moreover, lived with Malla Silfverstolpe in Uppsala for a short time in 1816 in a sort of Germano-Swedish salon community.

Many kinds of mutual influence grew out of the relations between the Danish-German aristocracy in Schleswig-Holstein, as they did through the geographic proximity of northern and continental Europe. *Beaux esprits* such as Louise Stolberg, Julia Reventlow and Caroline Baudissin formed a local circle which compared itself to the one in Weimar and which was also considered to be a local (German!) competitor by Goethe (Scott Sørensen 1998b). However, the most sparkling aristocratic salon hostess was the part Danish, part German Charlotte Schimmelmann (1757–1816), wife of the Danish minister of finance and state affairs. For many years the Schimmelmann pair were at the centre of the social life of the capital – cosmopolitans and great patrons of art and literature. Among others they supported the German poet Friedrich Schiller together with the Duke of Augustenborg to whom Schiller dedicated his *Über die Ästhetische Erziehung des Menschen, in einer Reihe von Briefen* (1793–5). Charlotte Schimmelmann and Charlotte Schiller maintained a regular correspondence from 1797 until the death of the former in 1816, about which she wrote in *Charlotte Schiller und ihre Freunde* (1860) (Scott Sørensen 1998c).

Copenhagen and Stockholm were the two main metropolises of the North around 1800, dominated by the classes whose social standing ranked just beneath that of the court. In Stockholm the salon was very closely connected to the court with a focus on musical events, for instance around Margareta Cronstedt at Karlberg Palace (1763–1816), who was a skilled pianist and became the first female member of the Swedish Academy of Music (Öhrström 1987). Stockholm was also the city most popular with *beaux esprits* from abroad and invested with glamour by the Italian Matilda Orozco (1796–1863), who was married to a Swede. She was a great singer and also a skilled musician (ibid.). Furthermore, Stockholm and the aristocratic salon milieu there were the original inspiration of the partly Finnish Malla Silfverstolpe, who married a middle-class colonel and moved to Uppsala, a city in the ascendant thanks to the draw of its university. Widowed early on, she made her in her view small-scale salon the intimate and intense heart of Swedish Romanticism between the 1820s and 1850s (Holmquist 1998).

Both in Norway and Finland, there was for historical reasons little room for a fashionable aristocratic salon life around 1800. However, one grand *bel esprit*, Aurore Karamzin (1808–1902), used her connections to the Russian court to be able to join the relatively more sophisticated social milieu of the Russian salon. As a young girl, she was lady-in-waiting at the court of the emperor Nikolai I in St Petersburg, and soon became a valued guest in the literary salons of the new capital. During her two Russian marriages, and especially through her second husband, A. Karamzin, the son of a renowned Russian historian, who held a salon much prized by the up-coming intellectual Russian elite, she became a renowned hostess in her own right. She also travelled to Europe, mostly Paris, where she joined the cosmopolitan salon life and contributed to the cultural axis, Helsinki–St Petersburg–Paris. In later years she took up philanthropic causes in Finland (Norrback 1998).

Quite another type of salon developed during the first decades of the nineteenth century among the growing middle classes in all the Nordic countries, still primarily in the metropolises, but now gradually coming to include Oslo and Helsinki as well as, for instance, Uppsala and the smaller forward-looking towns close to the capitals. At least, that is what we know to day. As I shall demonstrate, there is at least one interesting case that contradicts this picture. Two very similar salons grew out of these new trends: those hosted by the Danish Karen Margrethe (Kamma) Rahbek and those of the Swedish Thekla Knös.

The wife of an author, publisher, teacher and professor of aesthetics, Kamma Rahbek (1775–1829) belonged to a new group of intellectuals for whom their involvement with literature gradually became a profession, and to whom the cultivation of Danish language and literature was a necessary counterweight to the influence of French and German culture. Though her home, Bakkehuset, was to be found outside the city, she made it the centre of a literary circle, known as the heart of the Danish Golden Age in the first decades of the nineteenth century. With its humble though delicate simplicity it later became a national and middle-class symbol (Scott Sørensen 1998d).

As a child Thekla Knös (1815–1880) often visited the salon of Malla Silfverstolpe in the company of her mother, the widow of a professor at the university in Uppsala, with whom she later created her own salon. It, too, enjoyed considerable popularity with the famous writers and artists of Swedish Romanticism and was immortalized in a national commemorative literature, in this case due to its atmosphere of the fantastic and exotic created by Knös' facility in arranging plants, figurines and unusual objects from abroad. In difference to Kamma Rahbek, Thekla Knös made her salon activities into the inspiration for authorship in genres such as the lyrical ballad, narrative verse, and the short story and for letters, diaries, etc. She also incorporated the life of the salon into several of her own works, among them her 1862 *roman à clef Elfvornas Qväller* (Mansén 1993).

Thekla Knös marks a transformation of the *bel esprit* and salon culture which had its apotheosis in Norway and Finland. Without an aristocracy or higher official class of any importance during the period of Danish domination, a salon life evolved out of social gatherings held among the wealthy commercial families and officials of the Norwegian middle class. A quite special case was that of the Danish-Norwegian Christiane Koren (1764–1815), married to a local official at Hovind, north of Christiania (Oslo). She created a salon-by-letter, a circulating mixture of a journal and a diary which kept the so-called Hovind circle together in the difficult years of the dissolution from Denmark. However, the closest one comes to a *bel esprit* in a continental sense is Caroline Fougstad who gathered together a circle of ambitious young (male) academics in Christiania in the 1830s. One of the female visitors to her salon was the young Camilla Collett (1813–95) who later became the celebrated author of the novel *Amtmandens døtre* (1854) (*The prefect's daughters*). Usually considered as a monument to the breakthrough of a national Norwegian literature, it was, as Torill Steinfeld (1996) points out, equally influenced by the continental salon. Camilla Collett had visited Paris and stayed in Hamburg where she had been a popular guest in the city's salons and a close friend of the *bel esprit* Therese von Bacheracht. The latter introduced Collett to the new German literature and especially the works of female writers, such as Bettine von Arnim's *Goethes Briefwechsel mit einem Kinde* (1835) and Rahel Varnhagen's *Ein Buch des Andenkens für ihre Freunde* (1834). These works were a palpable and fully acknowledged inspiration for Collett's later journalism, written both at home and abroad, and often considered the beginning of modern feminism.

Also closely connected by posterity to a burgeoning nationalism on the one hand and on the other to a modern feminism among the growing middle class, the Tengström circle became a cultural power-house for three generations in Finland. It produced several educated women, among them Fredrika Runeberg (1807–79), who strove not only to be inspirational host-esses to the famous men of Finnish Romanticism, but also to create careers of their own (Kindstedt & Pelkonen 1998). Runeberg took the initiative to establish an exclusive, women-only, salon in the so-called *Kronhagen*, later to be continued by the younger members in *Kronohagssälskabet*. Out of the ranks of these societies came several women writers as well as contribu-tions to the growing public debate surrounding the *"querelle des femmes"* during the middle of the century. With such activities salon culture was radically changing towards proper participation in the public sphere and professionalism, developments also seen in the cases of Thekla Knös and Camilla Collett.

Let me complete this historical sketch by citing the promised exception and by offering some conclusions on the question of cultural identity. At the end of a fjord in western Norway (Hardanger) in an isolated village Catharine Hermine Kølle (1788–1859) held her local *Ulvik Parliament* for a small community of farm workers and fishermen between the 1830s and 1850s (Ryall 1998). Inspired by the Romantic cult of hiking, she traversed large areas of Norway, but she also walked to Denmark, Sweden, Germany and even Italy, and on each occasion she brought her experiences home in the form of sketches and notes. Thus she laid the ground in her "local centre" for both a sense of national pride and of the specificities and commonalities of northern and southern Europe. In so doing, she personifies the utopian vision, then as now, of establishing a dialogue between the national, the Nordic, and the European identity.

The cultural poetics of the salon and the *bel esprit*

In the following outline of the cultural poetics of the salon, and the role of the *bel esprit*, I shall take inspiration from cultural sociologist Pierre Bourdieu who in his *Distinction. A social critique of the judgement of taste* (1979) utilized the notion of taste as developed in contemporary philosopher Immanuel Kant's *Kritik der Urteilskraft* (1790).

The thesis is that the culture of the salon can be analyzed by means of the category of taste, and that Kant can be said to have conceptualized its basic idea through his theory of taste – even if he offers an empirical criticism of salon life.[6] His central claim in this respect is that one cannot reason about taste or define a criterion of quality, that there is no absolute truth, and no method, only training and manner, and that it is therefore necessary to establish an aesthetically nurtured or educated forum to initiate the ability to make aesthetic judgements. The salon was such a proper forum, even if the salons of his own day did not fulfil the ideal. However, taste was the arbiter by which each individual *bel esprit* strove to qualify, but also to distinguish, herself and her circle, and thus took part in a process in which aesthetic distinctions became social stratifications and a means of social mobility.

This is exactly where Bourdieu comes in. He sees the Kantian notion of taste as a precursor of modernity in its foregrounding of style at the expense of previous formal distinctions. In the Kantian celebration of aesthetic judgement, Bourdieu sees an early tendency to stylize social life: to give priority to form and manner over function and matter, to focus on attitudes instead of essence, and to cultivate the world of objects. It lays the ground for the social differentiation by style that he considers to be one of the basic trends of modernity. From this perspective, the salon can be understood through the interplay of such elements as the physical bearing of the hostess and her surroundings, the conversation and the social rituals of the circle around her, and the performances in her home. Following Bourdieu, there has to be an aesthetic correspondence in the way the elements are presented and put together which points to the basic concept, in order that each *bel esprit* can personify the universal idea of beauty but in so doing also reveal her salon as extraordinary, unique.

The basic distinctions in the Kantian universe of taste run between ordinary and pure taste on the one hand and the sense of beauty and the sublime on the other. The category of the beautiful designates that which is immediately pleasing and which is a common experience, the sublime that which in contrast provokes fear and even horror, but also admiration and which is a highly exclusive experience. Kant judges the sublime to be the most exquisite expression of pure taste that corresponds to a male scale of noble, heroic emotions; the beautiful he considers to be closer to sensual taste and identified with the female and a scale of intimacy – even if in his critique Kant very carefully plays down the sexual element. Bourdieu condemns the distinction in general but stresses the fact that it is carried over into the modern split between high art and popular aesthetics which has been equally linked to the issue of gender.

In his *Anthropologie in pragmatischer Hinsicht* (1798/1800) Kant assigns women a leading though highly ambiguous role in the universe of taste. Deeply influenced by J. J. Rousseau, he elaborates on the different roles of the two sexes in the sphere of taste and social life. He claims that women's sense of beauty is part of their sexual character, which he extends to their bodily performance, their mental attitudes and social arrangements, and furthermore connects to the requisite tendency towards – conventional – virtue in sexual matters. According to Kant, it makes them pleasant associates and gives them a cultivating function in social life. However, it also means that despite their closeness to nature women are equally exposed to the artificial – and lack real virtue. A man is easy to decode, he says; a woman never reveals her secret to the philosopher (Kant 1964:6,652). He admits the fear this provokes, knowing that it might reflect his own inability to decipher woman. In any event, he implicitly puts forward the conclusion that just as nature, a woman can elicit the sublime, but she cannot express it herself. This idea was later fully developed in Romantic philosophy and poetry into the explicit claim that genius is exclusively male while the female personifies beauty as The Beauty. Kant does not deny women intellectual skills but he presages the restoration of high Romanticism in his distinction between wit and judgement – wit reveals the charming (female) talent, judgement the bright (male) genius (Battersby 1989).

Let us explore this whole complex a little further and take a closer look at the theory of *Geselligkeit* developed by contemporary German philosophers and salon guests, among them Friedrich Schleiermacher who in his *Versuch einer Theorie des geselligen Beitragens* (1799) designates it as an art form in itself, including the *ars conversationis* (Schleiermacher 1984:310–25). According to him *Geselligkeit* is only to be found beyond the specific interests of both the private and the public sphere and is without any purpose beyond itself. Thus, it designates an ideal harmony between the individual and the societal, a kind of continuous ebb and flow where the one supports the other and where every specific interest is held back. However, to vitalize this ideal it is necessary for everybody to find a distinct manner in which each can both fulfil and rein in his or her individuality, including its sexual component. Furthermore, it is required that everyone is included and that everyone contributes, in other words that the participants form a consistent circle. Just as Kant and other contemporary philosophers, Schleiermacher expresses the idea that women better than men, who are equally marked by their private and public standing, can afford to give in to the required attitudes of mutual play, partly because they have more to gain in forgetting their personal affairs. However, contrary to Kant, he celebrates the element of masquerade and in so doing both asserts and celebrates the advanced role of women.

Instead of trying to dismiss this whole gender paradigm, I want to suggest here that it is only in late Romanticism that it becomes a very stable, and restraining, gender schema. Until then it leaves open a space for the *beaux esprits* which they utilize and so transform it into what I shall conceptualize as a female sublimity (with Schor 1987 and Jacobus 1995). But to qualify this position, let me expand on two Danish cases, the salons of Charlotte Schimmelmann and Karen Margrethe Rahbek.

The house and the garden

The house and the garden became readable signs of the taste of the hostess herself, even if she often lived in her husband's home, bounded by his social status and position. At least, he was often the one who decided the framework, for example the architecture and the landscape, leaving her the interior design of house and garden.

Such was certainly the case for Charlotte Schimmelmann, born the daughter of a German colonel from the middle class and of a mother from the minor Danish-Norwegian aristocracy, who in 1782 was married to the very rich and most influential minister of finance. During the winter the couple resided in the Schimmelmann mansion in the capital, where Charlotte Schimmelmann had to fulfil official duties. Her grand salon evenings took place in the large banqueting hall and they could sometimes develop into an almost public event, especially when a big concert was given or a dramatic piece was performed by a visiting theatre company. In such cases, she might even open up her home to paying guests. In so doing she took a leading role in the cultural life of the city, often also giving herself a political role – mostly unwelcome in the eyes of her contemporaries. On other occasions she might assemble a more select circle of guests in one of the several salons of the mansion for a more intimate and usually literary event.

Despite the fact that the Schimmelmanns belonged to the country's financial and political elite, during the summer they lived a relatively unostentatious country existence at Sølyst[7] outside the city where Charlotte Schimmelmann could cultivate a kind of society more interested in literature, nature and friendship. Together with members of the aristocratic circle surrounding the state administration the couple devoted themselves to

Figure 7.1 *Sølyst.* Painting by Hans Hansen, *c.* 1805. (L. Bobé, 1938)

132

the projects of Enlightenment and Sensibility. The period between the French Revolution and Denmark's involvement in the Napoleonic Wars in 1808 was a time of prosperity and political reform which gave the aristocratic government behind Crown Prince Frederick VI a fair wind. When Schimmelmann, now also minister of state affairs, could escape from his duties in the city, the pair often went on tours in the woods of North Zealand and on sailing trips to the Swedish archipelago, but most often the landscape garden in the English or Romantic style around Sølyst formed the perfect setting for the celebration of their beliefs in spiritual growth and social progress. "Emiliekilden" (the spring of Emilie) in the hillside of the park, near the sea, was made a memorial grove – a sentimental symbol of loss (in memory of Schimmelmann's first wife), but also opened to passing wanderers and local inhabitants so becoming the first public park in Denmark and thus, too, a symbol of the Enlightenment project.

Unlike her more illustrious contemporaries, Kamma Rahbek had only one home, Bakkehuset,[8] just outside Copenhagen. And when she married the man of letters who later became professor of aesthetics, Knud Lyne Rahbek, it was in to Bakkehuset that she moved. Originally a farm, it became a relatively simple private residence for the married couple, their various lodgers and the varied circle of writers and intellectuals around them. In Bakkehuset there was a miniature salon, facing the garden. However, during the winter it was unheated, so then any visiting friends of the house would gather in Kamma Rahbek's little corner room where the writing table was laid for tea or a simple but delicate meal. Apart from the table, the room contained only a few chairs at the corner windows and a sofa where Kamma Rahbek rested when she was indisposed – or where she seated guests with whom she wished to converse in private. However, the intended simplicity was embellished by a wealth of decorations designed and crafted by the hostess herself. Thus, Kamma Rahbek became a renowned maker of small, refined boxes and highly skilled in the art of flower arrangements.

When Kamma Rahbek moved in, the little piece of land around Bakkehuset lay uncultivated, like a floating boundary between the city and the countryside. She consulted gardeners at home and abroad, and gradually laid out a garden which marked the boundary towards the city on the one side and uncultivated nature on the other. It was divided into a flower garden and a kitchen garden, something which was still unusual and which in itself prompted many visits. Kamma Rahbek became widely known for her horticultural skills and her rare plants, and her advice was even sought by the royal gardeners. More unusually, she also cultivated the many common Danish plants, earlier considered weeds. While the herb garden provided fresh produce for the kitchen, the flower garden delivered delicate blooms with which to decorate the rooms. The flowers were used both

Figure 7.2   *Bakkehuset.* The south wing. Gouache by H. Buntzen, 1826.
(A. Tønnesen, 1995)

fresh-cut and dried, and made into bouquets or garlands, they decorated
the lids of the boxes, or formed the material for Kamma's own flower
arrangements. Thus, Kamma Rahbek created a kind of everyday poetry of
flowers which has formed the background for the massive, Romantic myth
that surrounds her. The connection between flowers and poetry was established in the way she enclosed dried flowers in her letters together with
pieces of poetry and succeeded in making the custom a sign of friendship.
Often she commented on the flowers: their history and possible use, the
significance of the specific flower, and its relevance in relation to the recipi-
ent in a kind of language of flowers known also from contemporary flower
books. However, what really completed this language of flowers was the
way she made language, spoken or written, into "flowers of speech", a
rhetorically bound garland or arabesque. Thus, poetry was made out of
flowers, and vice versa, and we know from her correspondence that in so
doing she identified with the German poet Novalis and his seminal Romantic metaphor, "the blue flower", from his novel *Henrich von Ofterdingen*
(1802).

Bakkehuset achieved a mythical reputation even in its own day. Many of
the men of letters, like the poet Adam Oehlenschläger, visited Charlotte
Schimmelmann and Friederike Brun as well as Kamma Rahbek, but they all
joined in the acclaim for Bakkehuset and praised it as the place where they
felt most at home and most at ease. In all these celebrations, echoed in
many a memorial wreath, the poetry of flowers is central, but it also gradually metamorphosed from Novalis's transcendent blue flower into the clichés
of late Romanticism and a simplistic identification of women with flowers.

Figure 7.3   The garden of Bakkehuset (east). Painting by Chr. Hetsch, 1883.
(A. Tønnesen, 1995)

The meal and the conversation

A salon evening usually started with a meal which was not only meant to satisfy the physical needs but also to be an inspiration for the ensuing brilliant conversation, the "food for thought" so to speak. We can see the association between food and spirit, digestion and contemplation reflected in the Kantian concept of taste, and it has survived in phrases such as "roll the words around your tongue" and "spiritual sustenance". The analogy between physical and mental processes is probably deeply rooted in cultural history – whether of symbolic origin in a metaphoric relation between the sense of taste and the so-called sixth sense, or of more literal origin in a metonymic slippage between different areas of the mouth and oral functions (eating and talking). What is special in this context is the way the meal assumed a ritual significance in the life of the salon.

To both *Charlotte Schimmelmann* and *Kamma Rahbek* the aesthetics of the arrangement of the meal and the synthesis between sight, smell, taste and imagination were of paramount importance. The food, the way in which the table was laid, and the company comprised a sensuous and spiritual whole, an experience of synaesthesia, at its best one of sublimity. However, it could be of a highly different character. Inspired by the French tradition, Charlotte Schimmelmann talked about her "grand *petit dinér*" which might include six or seven spicy dishes, arranged for as many as 100 guests from

135

all over Europe, all over the world in fact. Usually it took place around four o'clock in the afternoon in the banqueting hall and was followed in the evening by a simpler and more informal *"souper"* for a more intimate group of guests in one of the salons, to be completed by tea served in the hostess's private apartment for a few close friends. In Bakkehuset, the guests of the day, no more than three or four individuals, were received with a sweet and generously laden tea table. Sometimes they might stay for a simpler but no less delicious dinner, perhaps comprised of paté de foie gras, fruit and a mild wine. The content of the rest of the evening was entirely comprised of food for the spirit.

In both cases the conversation was concentrated on taste and aesthetic judgement, but it could also concern scientific thinking or political reasoning. What is beautiful and what is sublime? How do you recognize true thoughts and good feelings? These are some of the questions commonly reflected on in both salons, while the content, and the form as well, could be very different, and also vary in each according to circumstance. One of the most striking differences is that in Charlotte Schimmelmann's salon politics and taste were intimately connected, whereas politics in Kamma Rahbek's salon were displaced by – or rather subordinated to the judgements of taste. And while the first salon was highly cosmopolitan in composition and outlook, the latter was confined exclusively to the adherents of a growing patriotism.

Charlotte Schimmelmann stood for what I would call an aristocratic humanism or even radicalism, founded equally on Enlightenment ideas and the cultivation of sensibility. She belonged to a liberal, aristocratic milieu in which the political efforts of the men were complemented by the cultural activities of the women. Thus, she was engaged not only in patronage of the arts and sciences, but also in pedagogics, and was among other things head of the educational projects on her husband's country estates and factories and involved in the establishment of a national scheme for the education of teachers. Considering herself a European or rather a cosmopolitan in a new era of spiritual elevation and social progress, she found Denmark too narrow a sphere of interest. She appreciated the opportunities her social status provided for interaction with people from different countries, cultures and social strata and she talked of her salon as a kind of *Laterna Magica* in which all the world was reflected – and in which she herself was also reflected. Due to these priorities, conversation in her salon was often circumscribed in part by the sheer volume of people and their inevitable subdivision into different groups and agendas, in part by a mixture of competing interests. On the other hand, the conversation could also change when the setting shifted from the city to the countryside, from a more official to a more intimate context. Then, the salon evenings at Sølyst could change from amusing, playful entertainment to embrace deep philosophical discussions.

In her relation to politics and taste, Kamma Rahbek adopted a deliberately ambiguous position. To the extent that literature was a professional ambition in the circle of writers, publishers and teachers around her, one might say that political discourse was made one with the liberation of Danish language and literature from the system of patronage and German – and French – cultural hegemony. Yet Kamma Rahbek often declared herself a freedom-loving citizen of the world, a true cosmopolitan of the spirit. Another paradox was that she maintained herself to be without any knowledge of "the infinitely great" and without any poetic talent, at the same time making claims for the significance of "the infinitely small" and another kind of poetic competence. In this way she managed to make the "infinitely small" an object of taste and, moreover, question the conventional hierarchy of both public spheres and aesthetic categories.

The judicious use of subtle irony became the hallmark of Kamma Rahbek's conversational style. To her, conversation was not only an art form in the sense that it had to create and balance the social interaction of the salon. Conversation was a constant play in and with language itself. It was not only talk about something but speech in its own right; it was not only meant to express oneself but a means of creating oneself, not least the female self. With her sensitivity to the open, democratic nature of language, she developed her own form of romantic irony which made salon evenings in her company such enthralling experiences. Many of the men of letters surrounding her openly admired her conversational skills and she made it her "life's work" to use them.

However, Kamma Rahbek has also been exposed as an example of the degeneration of the art of conversation for the same reasons. Freed from the idealized rules of classical rhetoric, the conversation became intimate in a new way, governed by its own rules and norms, in this case an implicit, code-like and underplayed style. Inspired by the Romantic German poet Jean Paul, Kamma Rahbek gave vent to often incomprehensible displays of wit framed in subtle linguistic ambiguity. She developed a kind of secret language, the so-called Bakkehus-language, only understood by the initiated, among them Oehlenschläger. Often, it escalated into pure nonsense, an almost childish play on sounds and rhythms, its quality even played down by Oehlenschläger himself in his memoirs.

Art and literature

After the meal some kind of artistic event or activity was arranged. A significant feature of the salon was that even though it was dominated mainly by one art form, in this case literature, the fine arts were often combined. A typical salon evening offered a literary feature with a musical accompaniment and a dramatic display, and it was exactly the interaction between genres and senses which was sought after in a kind of multi-media experience. In the literary salon, however, literature was at the heart of the whole event: it was read, performed, accompanied, written – and lived. Reading and writing were closely connected activities, since one frequently commented on what one read and how in letters, diaries, and autobiographies which were, in turn, often read aloud among a group of the initiated. Thus, around 1800 reading and writing formed an integral part of the mutual interchange of ideas, experiences and aesthetic norms in relatively closed circles. But this common trend could take very different forms. When comparing the salons of Charlotte Schimmelmann and Kamma Rahbek, one may imagine a process during which literature becomes partly more public, partly more private – a matter of professionalism.

Charlotte Schimmelmann and her husband gave financial support to a number of contemporary men of letters and artists, first and foremost among them the Danish poet Jens Baggesen and the German poet Schiller. For many years (1797–1816) Charlotte Schimmelmann corresponded with Schiller's wife, and from these letters we know that many salon evenings in the Schimmelmann home were inspired by the two poets.[9] Baggesen himself was often present, when he was not travelling, and he was pleased to contribute by reciting his own works or those of Schiller, accompanied by music or illustrated by attitudes, performed by the foster daughters of the household or members of the inner circle.

The correspondence also gives us a glimpse of how Charlotte Schimmelmann used literature as a kind of guide on the question of how to live her life, and how she identified with her chosen favourites, almost feeling that she lived with them: "Recently have I – often and readily – lived spiritually together with Schiller," she exclaims in a letter to the poet's wife (January 1804). She expresses the idea that literature must convey the ideal of humanity in a time of chaos and thus deliver the ground for hope, and that this is the reason why she feels safe with Schiller, feels insecure about Goethe, and both admires and condemns Germaine de Staël. However, she also admits that the power of literature is the way it speaks to her imagination and her body and kindles her passions, an effect that is not easy to reflect on in writing but which nevertheless runs like an undercurrent through her letters and results in dramatic outbursts such as: "I'm pure expectation, and longing for Schiller's new drama" (October 1799). Later on, she dives into her "images of sorrow", provoked now by the political situation in Europe on the one hand and her despair at not being able to express herself properly on the other. With these sorrowful pictures she, in her own writing, establishes an intimate connection between the personal and the political dramas of the period of the Napoleonic Wars – interpreted by a sensitive and sensuous woman by means of the rhetoric of sensibility.

In Charlotte Schimmelmann's milieu the letter functioned as a bond between relatives and friends, who were spread out all over the monarchy and often all over Europe, and at the same time as a source of information. This is also a motivation for her correspondence with Charlotte Schiller, which simultaneously served to fulfil her ambition to be acquainted with the famous Weimar circle. In the beginning of their correpondence, her letters to the wife of the famous author are rather conventional but gradually she breaks away from sentimental rhetoric. She expresses her longing to meet her penfriend at least once and yet the level of spiritual intimacy is predicated on the premise of distance and absence. The legitimate theme between the correspondents is initially the joint celebration of their two husbands – the poet and educator of the people, Schiller, and the statesman and philanthropist, Schimmelmann, united in their search for truth, morals and beauty. Gradually the perspective evolves into a discussion of the role of the partner, the wife, and muse and the possible transgression of these roles. Charlotte Schimmelmann creates for herself an all-encompassing mission in life as a mediator between the two men, their contemporaries and posterity, while she creates for Charlotte Schiller a corresponding glory as a mother, especially the mother of a new genius – Schiller's son.

In Kamma Rahbek's case the literary involvement looks quite different. Her salon was tightly connected to an expanding literary public. All the authors who are counted among the so-called Danish Golden Age associated with Kamma and Knud Lyne Rahbek, each of whom, in their own way, helped nurture the new generation: Knud Lyne Rahbek as a critic, publisher and professor at the university; Kamma Rahbek as a supportive but also challenging listener to A. Oehlenschläger, N.F.S. Grundvig, B.S. Ingemann, H.C. Andersen, J.L. Heiberg, P.M. Møller and others. In Kamma Rahbek's little corner room the budding poets could put themselves informally to the test, for an evening spent here was more like a gathering of friends of the house who might read extracts from European literature aloud to each other or discuss the affairs and events of the domestic literary world.

From Kamma Rahbeks correspondence[10] we know what she read as well as something about how she read. She also had her favourites, among them the German poets Novalis and Jean Paul. But she also read a lot of Spanish, Italian and even Portuguese literature in the original, and she read a lot of classical literature, too. Although she did not identify with specific texts, authors, or messages as Charlotte Schimmelmann did, in a way she identified with literature as a language. Her reading of Novalis's aesthetic fragments had convinced her that the letter was a genuine poetic genre, and letters certainly were her most intense engagement. In contrast to Charlotte Schimmelmann, she corresponded with the people around her – with many talented women, among them Friederike Brun, but mostly with men of letters, including the archbishop J.P. Mynster and the professor C. Molbech. Particularly in her correspondence with the latter, she hoped to make the romantic utopia of congeniality come true in a kinship of male and female, but she had to give up. Every time they met, they were at odds with one another, and the worldly affairs of each twisted their spiritual community. Though the experience was traumatic for her, this intense though short-lived correspondence also represents the zenith of her letter-writing skills.

In the letters to Molbech, she excels in the delight of words, making chains of words into a linguistic arabesque with much the same – almost erotic – qualities as invested her flower garlands. However, she also gives vent to the subtle irony of her conversational style, an irony which is intimately connected to her simultaneous deprecation and praise for her own letters and talents and the constant twists and turns of the interplay between the small and great, low and high, the commonplace and the outstanding, etc.

Despite their many differences, the two cases have much information to offer about the prerequisites of the modern woman reader and writer. What they reveal is a connection between modern literature and modern femininity of a sublime erotic character – with a shift from the "real" body to the psychic or imaginary body, from "real life" to the realms of reading and writing. Neither Charlotte Schimmelmann nor Kamma Rahbek had any literary ambitions, yet they were both acutely conscious of the eye over their shoulder when they wrote their letters. They often complained that they could not express themselves properly and they continuously struggled to make language a medium for self-expression.

The body and the attitude

A soul of beauty in a beautiful body was one of the gendered maxims of the day, inspired by Rousseau, adapted by Kant and developed in the works of Goethe, Schiller and pre-Romanticism, but also acted out in the salon genre *par excellence* – the attitude or the tableau. The ideal established a powerful relationship between art, nature and woman in the way the female body was conceptualized as the synthesis between nature and art in a unifying form – Beauty. It was inspired by antiquity and transposed into the arts through dancing and acting. The point of contact between sculpture and dance or theatre was the attitude, originally a fundamental classical pose, which came to be cultivated as an art form in the salon in genres such as attitudes and *tableaux vivants*.

The original plastic attitudes, eventually combined into a series, were inspired by the sculptured bodies of antique decoration and the theory of moods as developed by the philosophers of antiquity (Holmström 1967). They were practised by Mme de Genlis (1746–1830) and Lady Hamilton (1761–1815), while Henriette Hendel-Schiötz (1772–1849) developed living tableaux in which attitudes were linked into a sequence with words and music and guided in a dramatic direction. Friederike Brun's daughter, Ida Bombelles (1792–1857), became famous all over Europe for her exposition of this art, and she was both inspired by and was the inspiration for the Danish sculptor B. Thorvaldsen in the way she presented the female body as a classical, light, and upwardly aspiring form in the pattern of the Graces and antique literary sources (Klitgaard Povlsen 1998b).

GREVINDE MAGDALENE CHARLOTTE HEDEVIG SCHIMMELMANN,
FØDT SCHUBART,
f. 10. Aug. 1757 † 2. Decbr. 1816.

Figure 7.4   Charlotte Schimmelmann. Portrait by E. Pauelsen, 1789. (L. Bobé, 1938)

In Charlotte Schimmelmann's salon the influence of this tradition was felt in the way the great female figures from Schiller's historical dramas were brought to life by the foster daughters of the house, especially by the adopted Louison, daughter of a craftsman. In Charlotte Schimmelmann's letters to the poet's wife, she describes the female child in the spirit of J.J. Rousseau: in her complete naturalness, she seems to have been born with many talents, a gift to the arts, only needing to be perfected by the aesthetic educator. Still inspired by Rousseau, Charlotte Schimmelmann reflects on female physicality as an aesthetic norm that more or less hides its own creation and appears as pure nature, and she describes her attempts to create the ideal through the aesthetic education of Louison. Just as Friederike Brun, she is very aware of being the creator and she identifies with the artist, not the artefact. In a way one may say that these mothers sacrificed their daughters on the altar of art, and the project can be understood as a way of handling the dilemma of

The Beauty: to be The Beauty yourself meant that you could not relate to beauty.

However, the reverse of this vibrant, marbled female body was the cold, dead female body which formed another distinct leitmotif in the art and literature of the day (Sanders 1997) and also makes itself felt in Charlotte Schimmelmann's life and letters. Her body has its own speech, she explains, despite her will and efforts and despite her ideals. It is both the sounding board of her soul, as when she devotes herself to reading, and something foreign, something outside herself which turns against her, not least when rheumatism attacks her fingers and stops her from writing. In her letters, the body is doubled up, in a manner of speaking, like a deviation from itself as the site of both pleasure and dejection.

Speaking of the body, there are many similarities between Charlotte Schimmelmann and Kamma Rahbek. Both were almost ethereal in appearance and very much in accordance with the airy, weightless and graceful ideal of the female body expressed in contemporary art, but in completely different ways. Charlotte Schimmelmann chose light garments, wrapping herself in a light shawl which she slung about her as if to play on the tension between stasis and movement, between being wrapped up and being revealing, in the style of Ida Brun and the Graces. Kamma Rahbek dressed in practical and neutral grey with a functional shawl draped around her shoulders, albeit one of light-weight muslin of the best quality.

The other side of this idealized female body was in both cases the weak and sick body. Although neither woman was very old, Charlotte Schimmelmann suffered from severe rheumatism and a generally weak constitution, Kamma Rahbek from the then relatively common weak-chestedness (tuberculosis) which was often identified as a female ailment. Kamma Rahbek was from her early days obsessed with her physical symptoms, describing them in her letters and complaining about them, at the same time making jokes about them with an almost grotesque exaggeration.

Images and myths of the Nordic *bel esprit* and salon

To be a *bel esprit* demanded financial resources which the salon hostess often possessed either through marriage or family. Thus, she was at the same time influential in the sphere of culture while inherently socially dependent. Limitations to her activities were dictated by her sexuality and the demands of motherhood and consequently the *bel esprit* was often childless (as were both Charlotte Schimmelmann and Kamma Rahbek), a widow (Malla Silfverstolpe and Aurore Karamzin), or a spinster (Thekla Knös) – or resided in a platonic *ménage à trois* (Friederike Brun). To be a *bel esprit*, however, meant to overcome precisely such limitations, to create and perform an image of beauty, and in so doing to recreate the classical image, the muse.

Figure 7.5   Karen Margarethe Rahbek. Silhouette by F.L. Schmitz, 1805, decorated by H.P. Hansen. (K. Dreyer, 1993/4).

In this project, and especially in this period, the idea of "the grand couple" played an important part – whether in relation to the husband, the platonic lover, or the admired artist. Ulrike Prokop (1991–2) puts forward the thesis that the idea of the grand couple, which arose at the close of the eighteenth century, was merely a male projection of an idealized self. According to my analysis, however, it was as much a self-image, created by the female aesthete out of her promoting and communicating role in the salon which gave her a voice of her own and legitimized her need to read and write. Only gradually did the ambition to write interrupt the role of the female partner and stimulate the both pleasing and painful dealings with language evidenced in the letters of Charlotte Schimmelmann and Kamma Rahbek. Other Nordic *beaux esprits* such as Friederike Brun, Camilla Collett and Fredrika Runeberg, on the other hand, lived most of their lives in the tension between the self-images of the female partner and the woman writer. This was a tension moving towards a split, caused by the conceptual ambiguity of The Beauty.

None of the Scandinavian *beaux esprits* met Mary Wollstonecraft during her visit in 1795, and described in her *Letters written during a short residence in Sweden, Norway and Denmark* (1796). Maybe she was too radical, maybe she had neither the time nor the inclination to socialize with them. However, according to Jacobus (1995), in her travel journal Mary Wollstonecraft claims female sensitivity to be a necessary, but painful consciousness of the connections between the private and the political dramas of the period of the Napoleonic Wars, the European restoration and the backlash of sexual politics in the aftermath of the French Revolution. Thus, hope is expressed in a subliminal, linguistic sensuality – a kind of eroticized melancholy, perhaps the proper expression of a female sublimity under the circumstances. An analogous assessment is given in a recent, feminist-inspired evaluation of Germaine de Staël's authorship (Amend 1991), just as I have tried to make erotic melancholy a still more significant trait in the Nordic salon culture.

But then again, one has to be very conscious about the dynamics of mythmaking. In the attempt to deconstruct, that is to both acknowledge and refute old myths, one necessarily engages in the construction of new ones that may for a period seem more suitable. This is no less true when one asks the question: do there exist such constructs as a common Nordic salon culture or the Nordic *bel esprit*? Our now completed conducted tour has exposed a permanent influence emanating from continental Europe and a more informal interchange within the Nordic countries, embedded in the paradox that closer relations on the one hand mirror a growing patriotism on the other. When it comes to theory, a similar point can be made. The theory of the salon, developed in European gender and cultural studies, has turned out to be very productive. However, it is also clear that the Nordic salons developed in other directions and contain other themes which in the future will stimulate if not brand new theories, then a shift in interests and evaluations. Still, there is much research to be done to complete the picture. Both inside and outside the contemporary North.

Notes

1. The Schimmelmann mansion was built by A.A. Berckentin in 1751, and formed a part of the large, fashionably laid-out Frederiksstad (City of Frederick) around Amalienborg Castle. The city was planned by Frederik V as a symbol of the alliance between the bourgeoisie and the king in the enlightened autocracy, but it became more of a monument to the new official aristocracy. In 1761 C.H. Schimmelmann, Ernst Schimmelmann's father, bought the mansion. It is owned today by Oddfellow-ordenen (the Odd Fellow Order). The businessman

C. Brun bought the neighbouring Moltke's mansion, today owned by Håndværker-foreningen (the Trade Guild).

2. This chapter is based on the project "Nordic Salon Culture", funded by the Nordic Council of the Humanities (NOS-H) in 1994–7 (Scott Sørensen, 1998), and for the first time presented to an international public. My presentation draws on the studies of the 12 researchers from Denmark (Lisbeth Ahlgren Jensen, Karen Klitgaard Povlsen, Anne Scott Sørensen), Norway (Anka Ryall, Torill Steinfeld), Sweden (Ingrid Holmquist, Elisabeth Mansen, Eva Öhrström), and Finland (Barbro Kindstedt, Maja Pelkonen, Märtha Norrback).

3. The term salon referred originally, in the seventeenth century, to the room in a large house where guests were received. During the eighteenth century it came to describe the room where people met to converse, but it was also used to describe artistic exhibitions or musical performances, and the encyclopaedia's articles on art criticism as well. According to Wilhelmy (1989) it first achieved the meaning given to it here with Germaine de Staël's novel *Corinne* (1807).

4. An early critique of Habermas's ideal bourgeois public was delivered by A. Kluge & O. Negt in their study of the labour movement and its politics of communication in *Proletarisches Öffentlichkeit* (Frankfurt am Main: Suhrkampf, 1972).

5. Privately published in *Frauen zur Goethezeit* by Ilse Foerst-Crato, 1975.

6. His ultimate image of horror is Ninon de Lenclos (1623?–1706), a French courtesan close to the court milieu of the *ancien régime*, but also with a free and already by Voltaire idealized social life. She represents a salon tradition of its own, the salon of the courtesan.

7. Sølyst (the pleasure of the sea) was bought by Schimmelmann as a summer residence, and modernized in the style of the new classicism, while the park was laid out in the so-called English (or Romantic) style. Sølyst is now owned by Det Kongelige Københavnske Skydeselskab (the Royal Copenhagen Rifle Club), and is rented out as reception rooms.

8. Bakkehuset (the house on the hill), originally a royal farm built in 1622 and in 1756 given to the minister, Lord J.L. Holstein-Ledreborg. He built a new sum-mer residence on the land, named Ny Bakkehus (The new house on the hill). It was later bought by the court physician J.J. von Berger, who made it the centre of prominent social gatherings towards the end of the century. He sold the old house which was turned into an inn. One of the guests was K.L. Rahbek. Today the buildings house the museum of the Danish Golden Age.

9. Selections of Charlotte Schimmelmann's letters have been published by Louis Bobé in *Efterladte Papirer fra den Reventlowske Familiekreds 1770–1827* (Post-humous papers from the Reventlow family circle), 10 vols (vol. 5 and 6). Copen-hagen 1895–1931. Her letters to Charlotte Schiller in the period 1797–1816 have been published in German in L. Uhrlichs, *Charlotte von Schiller und ihre Freunde*, vol. 2 (Charlotte Schiller and her friends). Stuttgart 1860.

10. Kamma Rahbek's correspondence was to some extent published just after her death or at the beginning of the twentieth century, but several volumes have been published recently again or for the first time: *Kamma Rahbek's brevveksling med Chr. Molbech* (Kamma Rahbek's correspondence with Chr. Molbech), Kirsten Dreyer (ed.) Copenhagen: Museum Tusculanums Forlag, 1993–4. Peter Brams Valore, *Guldaldertidens kvinder. Omkring Frederikke Brun og Kamma Rahbek* (The Women of the Golden Age. Around Frederikke Brun and Kamma Rahbek), (Copenhagen: Bakkehusmuseet, 1989).

References

Amend, A. 1991. *Zwischen Implosion und Explosion – zur Dynamik der Melancholie im Werk der Germaine de Staël*. Trier: Wissenschaftlicher Verlag Trier.

Bader, R. & D. Fricke (eds) 1979. *Die französische Autorin vom Mittelalter bis zur Gegenwart*. Wiesbaden: Akademische Verlagsgeselleschaft Athenaion.

Battersby, C. 1989. *Gender and genius: towards a feminist Aesthetics*. Bloomington: Indiana University Press.

Behrens, K. (ed.) 1981. *Frauenbriefe der Romantik*. Frankfurt am Main: Insel.

Bourdieu, P. 1986. *Distinction. A social critique of the judgement of taste*. London: Routledge. (*Le Distinction, Critique sociale du jugement*, 1979.)

Drewitz, I. 1965. *Berliner Salons. Gesellschaft und Literatur zwischen Aufklärung und Industriezeitalter*. Berlin: Berlinische Reminiszenzen.

Enzenberger, H.M. 1988. *Requim für eine Romantische Frau: Die Geschichte von Auguste Bussmann und Clemens Brentano*. Berlin: Friedenauer Presse.

Goodman, D. 1989. Enlightened salons: the convergence of female and philosophic ambitions. *Eighteenth Century Studies*, vol. 22, 329–50.

Habermas, J. 1990 (1962). *Strukturwandel der Öffentlichkeit*. Frankfurt am Main: Suhrkamp.

Hertz, D. 1991 (1991/1979). *Die jüdischen Salons im alten Berlin*. Frankfurt am Main: Antoin Hein.

Heyden-Rynsch, V. von der 1992. *Europäische Salons: Höhepunkte einer versunkenen weiblichen Kultur*. Munich: Artemis & Winkler.

Holmquist, I. 1998. Vänskap och kärlek som projekt i salongskulturen: Om Malla Silfverstolpe och Amalia von Helvig som salongskvinnor och skribenter. (Friendship and love as projects in salon culture: About Malla Silfverstolpe and Amalie von Helvig as *beaux esprits* and writers.) In Scott Sørensen 1998a.

Holmström, K. Gram 1967. *Monodrama, attitudes, tableaux vivants. Studies on some trends of theatrical fashion 1770–1815*. Stockholm: University of Stockholm, *Acta Universitatis*.

Humbolt, C. von & F. Brun 1975. *Women in Goethe's time. A correspondence*, ed. Ilse Foerst-Crato. Düsseldorf: Bruns.

Jacobus, M. 1995. *First things*. Ithaca, NY Cornell University Press.

Kant, I. [1798/1800] 1964. *Antrophologie in pragmatischer Hinsicht. Werke*, Wilhelm Weischedel (ed.), vol. VI. Darmstadt: Insel.

Kant, I. [1790] 1992. *Kritik der Urteilskraft*. Frankfurt: Suhrkamp.

Kindstedt, B. & M. Pelkonen 1998. Lördagssällskapet, Kronhagen og Kronohagssällskapet: Litterära saloner inom den tengstömska kretsen (The Saturday Society and the Society of Kronhagen and Kronohagen: Literary salons in the Tengström Circle). In Scott Sørensen (ed.) 1998a.

Klitgaard Poulsen, K. 1998a. Friederike Bruns saloner 1790–1835) (The salons of Friederike Brun 1790–1835). In Scott Sørensen (ed.) 1998a.

Klitgaard Poulsen, K. 1998b. Attituden som æstetisk opdragelse. Ida og Friederike Brun i årene 1795–1816 (The attitude and aesthetic education. Ida and Friederike Brun 1795–1816). In Scott Sørensen (ed.) 1998a.

Lougee, C.C. 1976. *Le Paradis des femmes: women, salons, and social stratification in seventeenth-century France*. Princeton, NJ: Princeton University Press.

Mansén, E. 1993. *Konsten att förgylla vardagen: Thekla Knös och romantikens Uppsala* (The art of everyday life. Thekla Knös and Uppsala Romanticism). Lund: Bokförlaget Nya Doxa.

Myers, S. Harcstark 1990. *The Bluestocking Circle: women, friendship, and the life of the mind in eighteenth-century England*, 2nd edn, 1992. Oxford: Clarendon Press.

Norrback, M. 1998. Aurore Karamzin och det aristokratiske salonlivet i aksen Petersburg, Helsingfors och Paris vid mitten af 1800-tallet (Aurore Karamzin and the aristocratic salon life in the axis St Petersburg/Helsinki/Paris in the middle of the nineteenth century). In Scott Sørensen (ed.) 1998a.

Öhrström, E. 1987. *Borgerliga kvinnors musicerande i 1800–talets Sverige* (The music-making of bourgeois women in nineteenth-century Sweden). Göteborg: Musikvetenskapliga institutionen.

Prokop, U. 1991–2. *Die Illusion vom Grossen Paar: Weibliche Lebenstwürfe im deutschen Bildungsbürgertum 1750–1770* vol. 1–2. Frankfurt am Main: Fischer Taschenbuch Verlag.

Ryall, A. 1998. Dannelse, fotturisme og norskhet: Catharine Kölle og Ulviksparlamentet (Refinement, walking, and Norwegian nationalism). In Scott Sørensen (ed.) 1998a.

Sanders, K. 1997: *Konturer. Skulptur- og dødsbilleder fra guldalderlitteraturen* (Contours. Images of sculptures and death in the literature of the Golden Age). Copenhagen: Museum Tusculanum.

Schleiermacher, F. 1799/1984. Versuch einer Theorie des geselligen Beitragens. In *Kritische Gesamtausgabe* (Critical works), vol. I.2 Hans-Joachim Birkner et al. (eds). Berlin/New York: Walter de Gruyter.

Scholz, H. 1992: *Widersprüche in bürgerlichen Frauenbild: Zur ästhetischen Reflexion und Poetischen Praxis bei Lessing, Friedrich Schlegel und Schiller*. Weinheim: Deutscher Studien Verlag.

Schor, N. 1987: *Reading in detail: aesthetics and the feminine*. New York and London: Methuen.

Scott Sørensen (ed.), A. 1998a. *Nordisk salonkultur: et studie i nordiske salonmiljøer, 1780–1850* (Nordic salon culture: a study in Nordic salon milieux, 1780–1850). Odense: Odense University Press.

Scott Sørensen, A. 1998b. Min magiske Laterne: Charlotte Schimmelmann og Sølyst (My magic lantern: Charlotte Schimmelmann and Sølyst). In Scott Sørensen (ed.) 1998a.

Scott Sørensen, A. 1998c. Den nordiske kreds: En aristokratisk salonkultur (The Nordic circle: an aristocratic salon culture). In Scott Sørensen (ed.) 1998a.

Scott Sørensen, A. 1998d. Blomsterpoesi: Kamma Rahbek og Bakkehuset (Poetry of flowers: Kamma Rahbek and Bakkehuset). In Scott Sørensen (ed.) 1998a.

Seibert, P. 1993. *Der literarische Salon: Literatur und Geselligkeit zwischen Aufkläring und Vormärz*. Stuttgart und Weimar: J.B. Metzler.

Steinfeld, T. 1996. *Den unge Camilla Collett: Et kvindehjertes historie* (The young Camilla Collett: a history of a woman's heart). Oslo: Gyldendal Norsk.

Steinfeld, T. 1998. Valgslektskap og venskabskult: Christiane Koren og Hovindkretsen (Elective affinities and the cult of Friendship: Christiane Koren and the Hovind circle). In Scott Sørensen (ed.) 1998a.

Terrall, M. 1996. Salon, academy, and boudoir. Generation and desire in Maupertius's science of life. *Isis* (History of the Science Society), vol. 87, 217–29.

Weckel, Ulrike 1996. A lost paradise of female culture. Remaining questions for investigating German literary salons in the late eighteenth and early nineteenth century. *The Construction of Gender in the long 19th Century*. Paper presented at the first German Nordic Conference on Gender History, Stockholm.

Wilhelmy, P. 1989. *Der Berliner Salon im 19. Jahrhundert (1780–1914)*. Berlin and New York: Walter de Gruyter.

CHAPTER EIGHT

The dream of reality: a study of a feminine dramatic tradition, the one-act play

Anna Lyngfelt

As in the past, the dramaturgy dominating the Nordic stage today can be said to be one of conflict. This dramaturgy demands that conflicts take place between the actors on stage, and that there be a climax and a conclusion related to the conflicts initiated. It also assumes that performers and audience accept these conditions, thinking and judging on the basis of the limits set in the play. Thus the dramaturgy of conflict also determines what is worth playing and analyzing as drama.

From this point of view the idea of the work of women dramatists being sidelined is reasonable, at least if their dramas are influenced by literary genres other than Aristotelian tragedy.

A study of one-act plays performed during the nineteenth century helps us understand why there are so few established women dramatists. Not until their modern breakthrough is it easy to find any at all, especially in the public sphere. Women were of course interested in theatre before this period (1870–90), but they generally expressed themselves in other genres, for instance by joining literary salons.

By studying one-act plays, which were increasingly staged in theatres during the latter part of the nineteenth century, we can see why women dramatists could be so easily dismissed, a result of the often glaring dramaturgical shortcomings of their work.[1] We also realize that these one-act plays show clearly that women dramatists worked partly from a tradition other than the Aristotelian one that dominated the stages of the period.

In this chapter, I shall discuss how women dramatists were influenced by non-established dramatic traditions when choosing the one-act form during the modern breakthrough. The opportunity for acting afforded by the social life of the nineteenth century, and for putting on plays in literary salons, made the writing of one-act plays an attractive proposition to women. The tradition of women's participation in *tableaux vivants* and of their abiding interest in epic and lyric genres probably grew in importance when they started writing plays for the public.

As examples, I use three one-act plays that were popular at the time but are neglected today: Victoria Benedictsson's *Romeo's Juliet* (*Romeos Julia*) and *On the Telephone* (*I telefon*), and Anne Charlotte Edgren Leffler's *A guardian angel* (*En räddande engel*).[2] They are all, in different ways, representative of the one-act plays written by women during the modern breakthrough in Sweden.

Since, during the modern breakthrough, such plays were subject to diverse influences, they differ from each other dramaturgically. Some of them are more Aristotelian than others, and they are related in various ways to the dramatic device of conflict. It is my impression that, compared with men, when writing one-act plays, women refrain more from writing miniature full-length dramas.[3]

Typical of *Romeo's Juliet*, written by Victoria Benedictsson in 1888, is its intimate tone with seemingly pointless small-talk which permeates the play. The story proceeds more through small actions and reactions than through an all-inclusive conflict.

Two men call on a celebrated actress, "Romeo's Juliet". One of them is there to court her – he was overcome when he saw her playing "Juliet" at the theatre. The other man, using his alleged acquaintance with the actress, only functions as an intermediary, and leaves the stage after introducing his friend.

"Juliet" does not respond to the expectations of the courting "Romeo", so the courting is reduced to the delivery of flowers. In everyday life, "Juliet" turns out to be a mother whose appearance rather encourages respect for her private life than any attempts at courtship.

The play consists of the conversation between this "Romeo" and his everyday "Juliet". In the plot, where "Romeo" is expected to serve as a protagonist, the confrontation with the "antagonist", "Juliet", results in mutual understanding and respect. However, this does not exclude conflict in the conversation; "Juliet's" and "Romeo's" attempts to approach one another lead to incessant collisions between different ways of understanding the world around them, and of the use of language.

The one-act play is filled with linguistic clichés which, when used repeatedly in different situations, appear contradictory and thus increase the tension in the piece. One example of this is the use of associations evoked by the names "Romeo" and "Juliet", for example on page 75.[4] Here Zetterschöld tells Mrs Ramberg (after Mrs Ramberg's hints at her unhappiness): "You look happy – Juliet."[5] Mrs Ramberg answers her suitor, who is put off: "I am happy – Romeo."[6] It is not obvious to Zetterschöld that what he sees on stage ("Juliet") cannot be used for a realistic understanding of Mrs Ramberg, and Benedictsson also plays with an image of the surrounding world which is coherent and without contradictions.

Between the two gentlemen, Mrs Ramberg is spoken of as "decent"[7] but "stupid".[8] The language of the courting Zetterschöld nourishes his imagination and his ideas of conquest: "The way to make a woman yours is to catch her,"[9] Zetterschöld explains, for "You must not know [socially] the women you love".[10] By the end of the play, "decency" and "stupidity" have acquired new meanings, and Mrs Ramberg has been given an opportunity to explain her work as an artist.[11]

Instead of a climax it is possible to see an anti-climax (Zetterschöld's courting), with a number of conflicts as a substitute – clashes between different conceptions of the surrounding world illustrate a conflict between "reality" and "illusion". Perceptions of reality are brought into focus and questioned when Benedictsson shows, indeed highlights, their subjectivity. She points out the limitations of the perceptions, and shows how such perceptions are interrelated because subjects are incessantly confronted with one another. This might be seen as a step away from naturalistic insistence on causal relations and determinism.[12]

Romeo's Julia both violates and uses the conventions of theatre at the same time. Victoria Benedictsson creates tension by playing on the expectations of the audience concerning the suitor as man of action; a focus which leads, however, to a change of perspective when the action shifts to a conversation led by "Juliet", the everyday "Mrs Ramberg" (instead of Zetterschöld). The point of the dialogue is to display the many qualities of the "real" Mrs Ramberg which lie behind the Juliet-figure, and it becomes important to convince the audience that the rumours circulated about her are false. The statements concerning both sides of her ("Juliet"/Mrs Ramberg), are unfolded and investigated in the conversation of the one-act play.

In the one-act play *On the telephone*, also by Benedictsson, which was a success at the Royal Dramatic Theatre in 1887, the situation is similar to that found in a literary salon.[13] Not only is the scene supposed to be salon-like, as in *Romeo's Juliet*, but the small-talk over a glass of wine is interrupted by declamatory pieces.[14] The principal character is also a woman, Siri, who does not hesitate to act and lead the conversation.

The theme of this one-act play has strong echoes of Cinderella: the young girl, Siri, is left alone while the other daughters of the house are at a ball. The fiancé of one of the girls at the ball turns up, and keeps Siri company. The conflict suggested to the audience lies in the break-up between the man and his fiancée, the girl who is out dancing at the ball. The small-talk between Siri and the fiancé gradually develops into a proposal of marriage, a proposal that could mean a decent life for Siri, since it gives her the opportunity of leaving the house where she has been more or less forced to stay, even as a grown woman.

It is characteristic of *On the telephone* that it is narrative and not takes very little account of chronology. A number of rather straightforward "episodes" make up the one-act play. Interruptions and digressions, together with a sense of privacy, make its form reminiscent of an exchange of letters. Benedictsson repeatedly violates the audience's expectations of elaborated conflicts with their conventional progression to a climax.

The beginning of *On the telephone* resembles a monologue. Siri is talking on the telephone with her close friend Karl. She tells him that she is "all alone at home tonight",[15] since she does not have a dress for the ball. She gossips about the girls of the house, especially Ida ("the fiancée"), and the latter's husband-to-be.

It is suggested in the "monologue" that something must be wrong with the engagement. Yet Benedictsson refrains from describing the intimated conflict (between the man and his fiancée). Instead, the small-talk continues after the telephone conversation, but with Birger, Ida's fiancé, since he turns up and is invited to keep Siri company.

Siri turns to Birger and tells him in a friendly, letter-like manner about her dreams for the future. A "letter in reply" follows, since Siri's narration is followed by narration by Birger. Birger, too, talks about his background and his dreams.

An intimate dialogue ensues, where questions of love and life are just as important as the pleasure "of presiding at the table, attending to the tea-pot"[16] and talking about "delicious pastries".[17]

The "turning-point" is unconventionally anti-dramatic[18]:

BIRGER. Do you know what it means to stand in surety for a person?
SIRI. Oh, yes! Yes . . . It is something that makes you a looser. You may lose everything you have. Are you standing in surety for some person?
BIRGER. Yes.
SIRI. And you have lost?
BIRGER. Yes.
SIRI. Everything you have?
BIRGER. Yes.
SIRI. And are you poor now?
BIRGER. Yes. – You seem to be happy about it?
SIRI. No – o, not happy; – that was very unfortunate. But I do like you more.

The conflict between Birger and Ida appears to be used as an excuse for a woman of Siri's position to talk about her social situation on the stage.[19] A confidant is needed to give Siri the opportunity of explaining what it is like to be an unmarried woman without money of her own in the late nineteenth century, and the potential complication with two women and one man involved helps to stimulate interest in the conversation between Siri and Birger.

Generally, the difference between the private, intimate tone of the monologue-like parts (with their letter-like familiarity), and the distanced commenting in between, creates unpredictability and excitement. The small-talk works on the "monologues" as refined, sometimes ironic, comment, and is playful, as in a parlour game. The conversation is also dramatic.[20]

Other means than those of dramatic conflict are, however, used to create tension in *On the telephone*. Benedictsson constructs the lines rather like a collage, which opens up for a dialogue with society at large; the principal characters take steps, one after the other, from the reality sketched out, and give their view of themselves and their situation through their monologue-like parts.[21]

What the female one-act playwrights intend to discuss often comes through indirectly, as in Anne Charlotte Edgren Leffler's *A guardian angel*, in a number of *tableaux vivants*. The one-act play, set on stage for the first time in 1883, seems to have grown out of the tradition of putting on *tableaux vivants* in the literary salons.

In *A guardian angel* a sketched love triangle brings home the message, which concerns gender roles, a message conveyed through examples taken from human situations. This demonstration is parallel to the somewhat simplistic plot of the love triangle, and is in structure more similar to a collage of *tableaux vivants*-like images than to that of classic drama.

Tableaux vivants,[22] as a mode of narration, were important forms of entertainment in the life of the literary salons,[23] and the interest in striking attitudes and portraying human situations (typical of *tableaux vivants*) was easy to transform into the short dramatic form of the one-act play. Presenting an example as a means of persuasion is an important aspect of *tableaux vivants* as well as of one-act plays.

A guardian angel begins with a young lady at a ball, Arla, who expresses her disappointment with the social life at the ball. Another ballroom guest, Eugenie, takes over and, together with her mother, shows how frustration permeates the ball. Evald, Arla's younger brother, helps to highlight the differences between the sexes when it comes to the possibility of controlling one's situation. Gurli, Arla's younger sister who is being courted by the same male guest as Arla at the ball, enters, giving the impression of a naïve and innocent girl. Cecilia, who is imprisoned in her sex role, is introduced.

Lagersköld declares his love for Arla, and this declaration is shown to have nothing to do with the wishes and hope of the young woman. The girls' lack of power is made clear, and their upbringing is cited as an explanation for young women's behaviour and not very realistic expectations.[24]

The setting of *A guardian angel* is a ball where different "examples" are exposed – characters whose thoughts or behaviour turn into arguments in the discussion Edgren Leffler wishes to conduct about young girls entering into marriage. Thus the one-act play contributes to the contemporary debate on love and marriage.

The images, as examples, show the imbalance of power between the sexes. They function as arguments by pointing out how young women are exposed to sophisticated oppression. The examples thus support the critical opening of the play (the disappointment of Arla), and make it clearer.

The development in the play (Lagersköld's courting) does not give a picture of social life in the ballroom as something positive from a young woman's perspective, and the very end of the play is provocative.[25]

The final point, of the type used in the short stories of Guy de Maupassant, is interesting, since it shows an affinity with the short story rather than with dramaturgy, which requires a conclusion after conflicts and a climax.[26] The influence of the short story cannot, however, entirely explain the play's free form. Nor does it contradict the influence of the *tableaux vivants* – both are traditions incorporated by the playwright from the culture of the nineteenth-century literary salon.[27]

In *A guardian angel*, the device of contrast often replaces the plot to create tension. Arla's opinion of a production of *Romeo and Juliet* is contrasted with Gurli's (Arla is critical after her theatre visit, while Gurli is overwhelmed). The possibilities for women as opposed to those available to men are outlined[28] and naïveté is contrasted with experience.[29]

The contrasting of images is another device for creating tension, where the audience is at a distance yet is allowed to see "close-up" pictures. Two of the young women in this one-act play by Edgren Leffler express their innermost feelings which contrast with the distant, almost exhibitionist effect of the stereotypical examples. Arla thinks aloud: "The gentlemen are able to pay one or two compliments, but that's not chivalry in my opinion. And I do not think the dance is beautiful – it lacks rhythm. And the gentlemen look bored and indifferent – and the ladies . . ."[30] "They are heavily powered," she adds in her next line.[31] In the following line she continues: "They are also artificial. I detest affectation. If I were to see only one natural-looking woman here I would run forward and embrace her."[32]

Cecilia's intimate tone illuminates the "image" of her otherwise depressing situation. Proudly she says that she "declines . . . all the house-proud happiness" and instead sings the praises of secret liaisons.[33]

In the questioning of conventions for young women in *A guardian angel*, there is a desire to take part in changing society, outside the theatre. An implicit questioning of the conventions of the theatre can also be seen in the playwright's ingenious way of evading the demand for an intrigue with action (by outlining a love triangle).

Disappointment, frustration and women's lack of power are all demon-strated in the intrigue Lagersköld initiates by courting both Gurli and Arla. *A guardian angel* questions the ball as the way of entry to marriage, and this is illustrated by a number of examples. The criticism of the ball itself also shows, in summarizing example, that something is wrong with the way girls are being taught to behave and handle their parents, their own lives and the idea of marriage.

Accordingly, in Edgren Leffler's one-act play it is possible to trace a *tableaux-vivants* tradition, i.e., the practice of imitating and illustrating famous paintings and sculptures – but in *A guardian angel* the *tableaux vivants* have been filled with a society-oriented, modern content. Instead of famous paintings, clichés are used as examples and arguments in the con-tinuous debate on marriage and gender roles. The various examples in the play illustrate women's circumscribed position and the feelings aroused when women lack power and influence. The method of first displaying an image and then dissolving it makes the examples clear and interesting, yet not too provocative (since they disappear). Impressions from a female world could thus, by reason of their link to the *tableaux-vivants* tradition, be displayed in an entertaining way.

It could be argued, though, that not only women would be influenced by the manners of literary salons, since men visited these salons as well. Traces from the social life of literary salons should then have had an impact on male dramaturgy, too. Since this is not the case, the answer must be a matter of "usefulness": men did not need the games of social life to express themselves, while women realized they could use the art of entertainment to tell what would otherwise be untellable. What the women are able to do with their one-act plays is to employ the games of social life for something more than entertainment. By using an unassuming format they could mark their positions in the contemporary debate on marriage and the status of women.

Female one-act playwrights do not, however, stand outside the tradition of Aristotelian, classical theatre; in fact, women use the interest raised by a not too striking breach of conventions. This is the case in *Romeo's Juliet* when Benedictsson keeps the audience in suspense as to whether the pro-posal will meet with success. In *On the telephone* and *A guardian angel* the interest aroused by the expectations concerning action, after a proposal has been made, is also exploited.[34]

There may be a historical explanation for the fact that women's one-act plays written and staged during the modern breakthrough appear to be unconventional and to correspond to feminist ideas of a more recent date.[35] In a sense, women's one-act plays are conventional, but women develop literary genres where they have a strong position, and not a weak one, as was the case with Aristotelian, classical drama. In literary salons, women were in a position of strength. There, interest focused on reading novels and poetry, diaries and letters were written and *tableaux vivants* performed.[36]

The traditions of the salon culture are discernible in the playful and intimate tone of the one-act play, a tone which is used now and then to make ironic comments and cautiously raise some questions.

The one-act plays can be said to be "dramatizing" rather than showing dramatic action. As illustrated by the discussion of Benedictsson's *On the telephone*, one-act plays may be episodic and narrative in form. Impressions are created through small-talk, apparently aimless, with unpredictability constituting tension and forming the lines in a collage-like fashion. The situation in such plays is also heavily redolent of the salon.

Tension is built up by views being confronted with each other (not really turning into conflicts), repetition, and the method of contrasting images where the audience is at a distance with "close-ups". Focus on the situation of women, in its broadest sense, is alternated with private and personal comments from the characters in the one-act plays. Clichés, often linguistic, are employed. As in *Romeo's Juliet*, climax may be replaced by anti-climax.

One-act plays, as the *tableau vivant* such as *A guardian angel*, often illustrate women's circumscribed social position. First, women's background is outlined, then their dreams and visions for the future are made clear.[37] These plays do not progress chronologically.

Feelings of disappointment and frustration stemming from the women's lack of power and influence break through the surface of the entertainment. The distribution of power between the sexes is depicted – although with a light touch. Personal views on reality are emphasized, since the illumination of women's circumscribed position plays a prominent part in the dramatic structure.

Views on the female sex are articulated in the linguistic clichés which are brought into focus, showing that they are rooted in language and gender. Use of language is investigated and new meanings develop when phrases are repeated in different contexts. (One example of such a play on words is the use of the name "Juliet" in *Romeo's Juliet*.)

The one-act plays from the modern breakthrough reflect a desire to take part in the changing of society. Female one-act playwrights discovered that they could make use of the female interest in epics and lyrics, and the dramatizing of the literary salons; working from the *tableaux-vivants* tradition they could appear unconventional (yet not provocative) as dramatists writing for the theatre, and their plays would be performed. This also meant that they participated in the on-going debate on marriage and the status of women in society.

Notes

1. Below is an example of a puzzled reception. *On the telephone* by Victoria Benedictsson was reviewed in *Dagens Nyheter*, 8 March 1887 (p. 2, under the heading "Theatre and music"):

   > After this followed: "On the telephone", A Bagatelle by Ernst Ahlgren [Her male pseudonym] (Mrs Benedictsson). This was also a rather entertaining play, although it has, as regards the composition, a considerable shortcoming, namely that the actual idea for intrigue is in a telephone call – parenthetically, most excellently performed by Mrs *Hartmann* – right at the start of the play. If you do not follow this conversation with attention, you will not easily understand the final development, which is reasonably consistently effected, however. In addition the authoress' highly praised ability to sketch characters, which is well-known from her novels, does not fail. Our principal interest, however, adheres to the young Siri, whose role is most splendidly captured by Mrs Hartmann. When the curtain fell, the theatre resounded with applause, resulting in no less than three curtain-calls.

2. All titles of and quotations from one-act plays in this chapter, are translated by me. The quotations cited will be found in Swedish in the notes.
3. Twenty-nine one-act plays were produced at the Royal Dramatic Theatre in Stockholm, starting in 1869–70 and up to and including 1889–90. A complete catalogue is given in A. Lyngfelt, "Att förena blidhet med skärpa", in *Det glömda 1800-talet*, Y. Leffler (ed.), 133–52 (Karlstad: Centrum för språk och litteratur – Högskolan i Karlstad, 1983). See also Lyngfelt 1996.
4. Ahlgren 1920. All page references (as regards quotations and examples) in *Romeo's Juliet* and *On the telephone* refer to this volume.
5. Ibid., p. 75: "Ni ser lycklig ut – Julia."
6. Ibid., "Jag är lycklig – Romeo."
7. Ibid., p. 56, "ärbar".
8. Ibid., p. 57, "dum".
9. Ibid., p. 56, "Konsten att vinna en kvinna består i att gripa till."
10. Ibid., p. 57, "Man skall inte känna de kvinnor man älskar."
11. Zetterschöld on his discovery and recently acquired experience: "I went to seek an artist and found a human being. I wanted to make the acquaintance of an actress and got to know a subtle reflecting woman . . .": "Jag gick att söka en konstnärinna och fann en människa. Jag ville bli bekant med en skådespelerska och lärde känna en fint tänkande kvinna . . ." (ibid., p. 83).
12. In this respect *Romeo's Juliet* differs from a contemporary, male playwright's dramatic piece, Bjørnstjerne Bjørnsons *En handske* – see A. Hejlsted, "L'Homme fatal" in this anthology.
13. From the archives of the Royal Dramatic Theatres it is evident that *On the telephone* was produced no less than 26 times, from its opening on 7 March up to and including 31 May 1887.
14. In *Romeo's Juliet* the story takes place in the home of Mrs Ramberg, in an "elegantly furnished room with flowers, foliage plants and luxury articles: a sewing table with a sewing basket and a piece of embroidery in progress; a writing-desk covered with stapled sheets of paper in blue covers; paperweights

and artworks" (see Ahlgren 1920:55). The stage directions for *On the telephone* specify: "a large room, furnished in an old-fashioned way. On the left a large writing-table, close to a telephone. Large windows with small panes and thick, dark woollen curtains. To the right a large old-fashioned tiled stove with a mantelpiece, upon which are placed two large vases without flowers. Near the stove, a small table" (ibid.:7).

15. Ibid., p. 8, "alldeles ensam hemma i kväll".
16. Ibid., p. 40, "att få presidera vid bordet och sköta tekannan".
17. Ibid., "läckra cakes".
18. Ibid., p. 30:

> BIRGER. Vet ni vad det vill säga att gå i borgen?
> SIRI. Om jag vet! Jo–o. Det är något som man förlorar på. Man kan mista allt vad man äger och har. Har ni gått i borgen?
> BIRGER. Ja.
> SIRI. Då har ni förlorat?
> BIRGER. Ja.
> SIRI. Allt vad ni äger och har?
> BIRGER. Ja.
> SIRI. Då är ni fattig nu?
> BIRGER. Ja. – Jag tror ni blev glad för det?
> SIRI. Ne–ej, inte glad; – för det var ju fasligt ledsamt. Men jag tycker bättre om er.

19. The conflict between Birger and Ida consists in the fact that Ida, or rather her step-father Eskilson, a district rural court judge, seems to be interested in Birger as a husband/son-in-law mainly because of his fortune. Birger disapproves of this.
20. It is likely that Siri illustrated through her body language her line on p. 32 (ibid.):

> All of the others were so elegant, so elegant. They swaggered about, and the rustling of their skirts was so dignified. – They were beautiful to see, at any rate. And they had fans, and they waved [them] like this, and then they swaggered about and turned their trains, and then came gentlemen who bowed like this, and you should have seen the condescending looks of the women – they kept so straight and took a glance sideways, like this.

21. Accordingly, the structure of *On the telephone* differs from the Aristotelian conventions, as described by Annemette Hejlsted in "L'Homme fatal".
22. In *Meyers enzyklopädisches Lexikon*, vol. 14, 712, (Mannheim: Bibligrafisches Institut, 1975), the following is written about "lebende Bilder (frz. tableaux vivants)":

> stumme, unbewegte Darstellungen von Szenen aus der antiken Mythologie, christl. Überlieferung und nat. Geschichte durch lebende Personen auf der Bühne, häufig nach dem Vorbild bekannter Werke aus der Malerei und Plastik, v. a. als prunkvolle Einlagen bei festl. Anlässen. – L.B. sind seit der Antike bezeugt (Kaiserin Theodora von Byzanz), bes. beliebt im Spät – M A im Rahmen des geistlichen Spiels, so v. a. bei Prozessionsspielen und Predigtspielen, aber auch sonst

als Einlagen in grösseren dramat. Spielen, häufig als Prefiguration. In der Neuzeit wurde die Tradition der l. n B. durch die Gräfin Stéphanie Félicité von Genlis wieder aufgenommen; an sie knüpfte Lady Emma Hamilton mit ihren, "Attitudes" (l. B. nach antiken Statuen) an. Das 19. Jh. pflegte l. B. v. a. im Rahmen bürgerl. Vereinsfestlichkeiten (Darstellungen aus der vaterländ. Geschichte).

In addition to this, in *Brockhaus Enzyklopädie* (Mannheim 1990), vol. 13, p. 173, "lebende Bilder / Tableaux vivants" are described as an important part of the festivities of the Renaissance: "Bei festl. Einzugen von hohen Persönlichkeiten und festl. Umzugen wurden in der Renaissance l. B. an wichtigen Punkten einer Stadt aufgestellt oder auf Wagen oder Karren mitgefuhrt."

23. See, for example, pp. 86 & 305 in *Malla Montgomery-Silfverstolpes Memoarer*, published by Malla Grandinson (Stockholm: Bonniers, 1910).

24. The reason Arla showed some interest in the undesirable gentleman, Captain Lagersköld, is explained by the cabinet minister to his wife as follows:

> The problem is that your daughter is being brought up to be a goose who does not understand anything. You see, that is the consequence of your convent system. Have I not told you time and again that girls, kept shut up like that, are always ready to fall into the arms of the first man who comes along, with some basic skill in how to handle them (p. 26).

25. Arla asks her mother to read the Bible to her. Earlier in the play Arla has been derogatory about Bible reading. I think the closing point of this one-act play is a provocation. Is this dramatic reversal – the development of Arla from independence to an obedient, well-behaved daughter – really desired by the audience?

26. Many mixed dramatic forms were developed during the nineteenth century. This is clearly shown by Almqvist in "Hvad innebära poesiens två förnämsta konstslag? Hvad är skillnaden emellan ett Epos and Drama?", pp. 395–427 in Almqvist 1844.

27. In addition to the *tableaux-vivants* tradition the one-act playwrights were also influenced by another salon phenomenon, i.e., the staging of *proverbes dramatiques*.

28. The situation of the ballroom guest Eugenie is contrasted with that of Arla and Evald, Gurli's little brother.

29. Also in *Amorina. Den förrykta frökens lefnadslopp och sällsynta bedrifter* (1822), by Almqvist, tension is created by darkness and light in the "portraits" (through "Johannes" and "Amorina", for example).

30. All references to pages for the one-act play *A guardian angel* relate to the type-written manuscript kept at the Kungliga Biblioteket in Stockholm, courtesy of Gustaf Mittag-Leffler (the authoress's brother). The line quoted here is from this manuscript, p. 4: "Herrarne kunna nog säga en och annan artighet, men det är inte hvad jag menar med ridderlighet. Och inte tycker jag heller att dansen är vacker – det är ju ingen rytm uti den. Och så se herrarne så trötta och liknöjda ut – och damerna . . .".

31. Ibid., "De ä så pudrade".

32. Ibid., pp. 4–5: "Och så ä de tillgjorda. Jag afskyr tillgjordhet. Om jag finge se en enda riktigt naturlig blick hos någon här i afton, tror jag att jag skulle springa fram och omfamna henne."
33. Ibid., pp. 15–16, hon "betackar sig", "för all den der husliga lycksaligheten".
34. See also above nn. 12 and 21.
35. Various forms of modern theatre – from a feminist perspective – are studied by G. Austin (1990). S. Case takes an interest in a female dramatic form, based on psychoanalysis (Case 1988). See also Aston 1995.
36. See pp. 54–84 in Lyngfelt 1996.
37. In *Romeo's Juliet* the principal female character describes her desires to leave the environment in which she was raised when she chose the profession of actress. In *On the telephone* Siri ("Cinderella") dreams about leaving her every-day life, and in *A guardian angel* Arla provides a comparison between the courting and balls of real life and those of her dreams.

References

Ahlgren, E. 1920. *Samlade skrifter. Sjätte bandet. Dramatik.* Stockholm: Bonniers.

Almqvist, C.J.L. 1844. Hvad innebära poesiens två förnämsta konstslag? Hvad är skillnaden emellan ett Epos and Drama? In *C.J.L. Almqvist. Monografi. Samlad och utgifven för att lätta öfversigten och bedömandet af vissa bland tidens frågor,* 395–427. Jönköping: J.P. Lundström.

Aston, E. 1995. *An introduction to feminism and theatre.* London: Routledge.

Austin, G. 1990. *Feminist theories for dramatic criticism.* Ann Arbor: University of Michigan Press.

Brockhaus Enzyklopädie 1990. Vol. 13. Mannheim.

Case, S. 1988. *Feminism and theatre.* Basingstoke: Macmillan.

Lyngfelt, A. 1993. Att förena blidhet med skärpa. In *Det glömda 1800-talet.* Y. Leffler (ed.), 133–52. Karlstad: Centrum för språk och litteratur – Högskolan i Karlstad.

Lyngfelt, A. 1996. *Den avväpnande förtroligheten. Enaktare i Sverige 1870–90.* PhD thesis, Department of Literature, University of Gothenburg.

Meyers enzyklopädisches Lexikon. 1975. Vol. 14. Mannheim: Bibligrafisches Institut.

Montgomery-Silfverstolpe, M. 1920. *Malla Montgomery-Silfverstolpes Memoarer.* Stockholm: Bonniers.

CHAPTER NINE

Gender as the dynamo: when public organizations have to change[1]

Hanne Nexø Jensen

The Nordic countries differ from many other countries by virtue of the development of a welfare state. In Scandinavia, the state takes on many tasks – particularly in education, the fields of social policy and health (e.g., childcare and care of the elderly), which other countries tackle in other ways. The state is feminized in the sense that women constitute the majority of all public employees. In Denmark, nearly two thirds of public personnel are women. The percentage of working women in Scandinavia is very high. In Denmark, the figure was 75 per cent in 1995 and for working mothers of young children (women between 20 and 30 years of age) the figure is 79 per cent.[2] In other words, the Scandinavian welfare state is populated by female employees and attends to issues, described as welfare work, which, traditionally, women have performed in the home and in the local community.

In the Nordic countries, the public sector has come under strain due to economic stagnation (though least of all in Norway). This has been one reason for questioning the structure and *modus operandi* of public organizations. Changes in public organizations have been proposed. I have considered it important to investigate the significance of gender for public organizations undergoing change. This is an interesting issue in the Scandinavian context because of the high percentage of working women and because of the heavy burden of welfare work, evidenced in the amount and the cost of the tasks undertaken by the public services.

Mainstream organization theory, in its current state, has problems with capturing gender. Research in the field of women, gender and organizations has, hitherto, mostly focused on women and leadership and on the constraints that prevent women achieving leadership positions.[3] This is a central theme but is not the focus of this chapter. Researchers working on gender and organizations from a post-feminist and deconstructionist perspective consider gender as a construct and that it is the *conceptualization* of gender, the body and sexuality, etc. that is crucial (see, e.g., Hearn et al. 1989, Acker 1992). One goal is to reveal how women are subordinate to men in everyday practice. This is important. But I consider it relevant to adopt a gender perspective on gender and change in organizations by utilizing two specific approaches.[4] One approach involves investigating the potential for change among women and among men and in femininity and masculinity and what this signifies for an organization. Another approach is to investigate the significance of organizational changes for gender, including relationships between genders. The two approaches make it necessary to integrate elements from research on women and gender with research on organizations and public administration.

The main aim of this chapter is to present, deploy and discuss the value of an integrative analytical model which I use in an investigation of changes in the Danish Labour Exchange and job centres (in Danish, Arbejds-formidlingskontorer) in the period 1990–91. The chapter attempts to isolate an answer, first, to what changes in public organizations involve and, secondly, to how to study the significance of gender for changes in public organizations. As an illustrative case study, the chapter contains information taken from a study of gender and change in the Labour Exchange offices in Denmark.

Changes in public organizations

The concept of change is often used without precise definition. In relation to organizations one can – at the general level – distinguish between conscious, planned change and unconscious, unplanned change. Since the political element is important in public organizations, one may ask whether and how politicians conceive of, plan and implement planned changes in organizations. This conception could lead to the construction of a continuum ranging from, at one end, conscious, political attempts to direct changes (such as administrative reforms)[5] to, at the other end, subconscious, everyday changes in which attitudes, norms and behaviour undergo change (see, e.g., Weick 1969, Christensen & Molin 1983).

The Labour Exchange is a public organization whose task it is to find and allocate jobs, exercise control over the unemployed, service private firms, provide advice on training and careers and compile statistics and forecasts on conditions in the labour market. The individual Labour Exchange office is under regional management that, in turn, answers to a central, national management. The Labour Exchange, as presently constituted, was set up by legislation passed in 1968 and, since then, unemployment has increased considerably. Funds directed to the Labour Exchange are increasing, but not in proportion to the number of unemployed, or to the constant stream of new labour market reforms with proposals for training and mobilizing the unemployed as well as providing a service to business. Over time, there has been a tendency to swing from prioritizing the unemployed to prioritizing the companies: a process not without conflicts.

The most recent changes that the Labour Exchange faced when I carried out my investigation in 1990–91, were demands for cuts in expenditure, structural changes, fewer employees and to meet the requirements of a Plan of Action for Equal Opportunities. The cuts were stipulated in the government budget and have to be seen in the light of the government's overall goal of modernizing the public sector and making it more efficient. The regional offices had to decide themselves what form the cuts and the structural changes would take. One requirement was that the Labour Exchange system should function more effectively (i.e., implement a better use of resources). Another requirement was that service to private companies should have higher priority. Cuts and structural changes signify conscious, planned changes.

I have used the Labour Exchange as a case study since the gender composition of office staff varies and, in addition, it varies at different levels in the organization (see Table 9.1). Moreover, all the offices have the same product: in contrast to, for example, the Danish State Railways in which one department works on the actual running of the trains, another with ferries and yet others with administrative tasks: that is to say, an organization in which each unit has a somewhat different product and in which work is often gender-segregated.

The gender distribution in the Labour Exchange district offices that were studied is, *in toto*, 65 per cent women and 35 per cent men and this corresponds to the national average for all Labour Exchanges. In one office there are 75 per cent women. This means an overrepresentation of women which is merely part of an overall pattern which is given in the matrix in Table 9.1. There are no organizations in the investigation which have few women and many men among non-leaders (as in Organizations 3 and 4 in Table 9.1).

Gender and organization under change: an analytical framework

Three questions are imperative in working with gender and organizations under change. First, does gender have any significance for organizational change? The question should be considered *vis-à-vis* mainstream organizational researchers who do not discuss gender (or ethnicity, religion, etc.). Hence it is necessary to document that gender *does have* significance for organizations. This requires the adoption of a gender perspective on the study of gender and organizations under change.

If the answer to this first question is yes, what more precisely does gender signify for organizational change? A second question is what does

Table 9.1 Matrix for choice of organization with different gender distributions at two organizational levels

	Non-Leaders	Leaders
Organization 1	Many women/few men	Few women/many men
Example	Hospital (women as nurses, men as doctors)	
Organization 2	Many women/few men	Many women/few men
Example	Daycare centre (majority of female staff)	
Organization 3	Few women/many men	Few women/many men
Example	Metal-working factory	
Organization 4	Few women/many men	Many women/few men

organizational change mean for gender? The questions are interesting since there are few similar studies, even at a time when (public) organizations are undergoing many changes. I have chosen to illuminate the point by reporting on the results of a case study, the significance of gender for organizations undergoing change and the significance of organizational change for gender.

There remains the third question. How do we study and analyze whether, if anything, and what gender means for changes in organizations? I attempt to answer this last question by developing an analytical framework with inputs from women and gender research together with research on gender and organizations.

The analytical framework

There is a marked trend in gender studies to focus on men's dominance over women (see, e.g., Hartmann 1979, Eisenstein 1979, Halsaa 1987, Hartsock 1983). There are countless empirical examples of men dominating women. Men receive more wages and there is still a striking predominance of male leaders in both public and private organizations. The continued male dominance can be explained by the way in which existing structures (both societal and organizational) are reproduced.

It is, of course, a key research task to investigate which (societal) structures maintain male dominance over women and how they effect this. However, I also consider it important to investigate the strengths of women and femininity in relation, *inter alia*, to change. This presumes that one does not take a specific relationship of domination as given but investigates specific relations between men and women empirically. Thereafter, one can draw conclusions as to the nature of a specific power relationship of gender or as to how it manifests itself.

In this chapter, organizational theories as applied in political science are considered mainstream. Mainstream organization theory examines why public organizations are public, the significance of its environment for an organization and the significance of different institutional norms and values. Of course, mainstream theories also discuss how organizations are defined and under what conditions an organization functions most productively and most efficiently. At first glance, the literature in this field appears to include hardly any references to gender.[6]

One can distinguish two main branches of social science research on "gender and organizations". The one branch is research into women in the labour market where the focus is on the gender distribution of labour, gender segregation, the link between working life and family life and into state policy in this field. Since the subject of this chapter considers the organization as a unit, the field of research on women in the labour market is left out. The other branch is WIM research, Women-in-Management, crucial to which is investigation of the potential and the constraints on women becoming leaders and also a study of the characteristics of women leaders. But I am not interested in a specific group of employees (leaders or potential leaders), but investigate all employee groups.[7]

Within gender research, there are examples of researchers who work on developing and elaborating organization theory in relation to gender (cf., e.g., Hearn & Parkin 1983, Hearn et al. 1989, Calas & Smircich 1989, Mills & Tancred 1992, Acker 1990 & 1992). These authors are influenced by a postmodernist line of thought and some of them by a deconstructive mode of thought. Crucial is the *conceptualization* of gender, the body and sexuality. Joan Acker writes that

> Gender refers to patterned, socially produced, distinctions between female and male, feminine and masculine. Gender is not something that people are, in some inherent sense, although we may consciously think of ourselves in this way. Rather, for the individual and the collective, it is a daily accomplishment that occurs in the course of participation in work organizations as well as in many other locations and relations (Acker 1992:250).

Joan Acker's aim is to develop a gendered organization theory with a point of departure in a depiction of four processes by means of which organizations are gendered (the gender division of labour, the creation of symbols, interaction between individuals and the individual's perception and behaviour in relation to environment).

By focusing on how organizations are gendered, Joan Acker depicts actual conditions. This is, of course, the first step on the road to change. But there is, I think, a certain risk that she does not give sufficient prominence to the potential for change in a given situation. And, further, that the possibilities for structural change and changes in power relations are played down. In an attempt to give priority to the potential for change, my starting point is a discussion and analysis of a number of contributions to research on gender and women. My choice is also related to the fact that the issue of gender is pretty much absent from mainstream organization theory and that the literature on women, gender and organization does not analyze the significance of gender for change.

Analytically, I distinguish between the following three levels in social science research on women and gender: (1) women's situation and men's situation; (2) gender relations; and (3) the structure of gender relations.[8] It is also important to capture the interplay between levels. I will briefly elaborate what I mean by gender and the three levels of analysis.

Gender is, at one and the same time, both something we have and something we are. One can distinguish between such different analytical gender categories as the biological, the psychological, the sexual and the cultural. In my context, the key distinction is between the biological and the social categories, i.e., and in order to simplify the description, between sex and gender.[9] In addition, it can be argued that the social gender sets the framework for the other categories.

I assume that gender is a biological fact but one which is given different social interpretations, depending on the historical context. Women and men do exist as genders and play dissimilar roles in procreation, pregnancy and nurturing. We are born either as a girl or as a boy, i.e., we have a particular sex. But we are also born into a structure in which gender already has a special meaning, i.e., we are gendered even though we – as human beings – can also affect the structure, even change it. As such, the concept "gender" refers to a social process.

Gender is neither exclusively a biological fact nor exclusively a social construct; gender is both/and. We must try to understand the nature of the link between sex and gender and we must understand that gender, and the differences between men and women, change, due to changes in social, cultural, political and economic conditions. One can make the actual circumstances of women (and men) visible and analyze them by focusing on *women's situation and men's situation*. Gender is a variable and hence organizations have a gender. This can, for example, be assessed by quantifying the number of women and men at different levels of an organization.

Gender relations are the way(s) women and men, women or men interrelate in a given societal context. This can involve, for example, investigating what happens between women and men in connection with solving a specific task in an organization.

The structure of gender relations focuses on how gender already *is* encapsulated in a given structure or process, for example, in an organizational structure or in organizational processes. The concept of the structure of gender relations further indicates that gender is not just something we carry around with us as a biological fact. Gender is also evident in our practice and in the existing structures such as organizations, the family, the school and in society, too. Organizations *are* gendered (Acker 1990) when we seek to grasp how gender is encapsulated in organizations' structures and processes. One consequence of a structure of gender relations is that gender is of significance even where only one gender is present, for example, in a group of soldiers (men) in a barracks or a group of women shelling prawns in a factory in Greenland. If the other (biological) gender enters this space, one can investigate empirically a given gender relationship between women and men. Such a relationship can show that there are differences between men and women and can reveal an actual relationship of dominance.

An analytical framework that can reveal circumstances in an organization must relate to several features. Even though I do not build explicitly on "Women-and-the-labour-market" research or on WIM research, I have found inspiration particularly in WIM research and other literature on women, gender and organizations. It is, for example, important to make one's analytical level explicit. I distinguish between the level of organization and the level of society (see Table 9.2). I further distinguish between the individual and the structure. One can capture different relations of dominance by, *inter alia*, differentiating between employees at different levels of an organization. Gender is not only a variable and a biological fact. Gender is a social process and gender is encapsulated in existing structures. Hence one must distinguish between the fact that organizations have and are gendered and capture the interplay between "have" and "are". That is, we must see how many women and men are employed in an organization, at what level and in what jobs (organizations have a gender). We can operationalize this by looking at the situation of women and men. The study of gender relations focuses on the interactions between women and men.

Organizations are gendered since a specific interpretation of gender is encapsulated in the organization's structures and processes: in, for example, the form of norms about who, traditionally, occupies a particular type of job (e.g., management). It can also be a matter of which norms and values (effectiveness, decisiveness, or empathy and nurturing) are expected in a given job. One can operationalize this aspect with the help of the concept of the gender relation of structures.

I have emphasized the study of the interrelationship between the fact that organizations have and are a gender in different contexts. I have investigated the daily life of a Labour Exchange; changes (structural changes, dismissals/firings and the Labour Exchange's Plan of Action for Equal Opportunities); and the life of employees outside the organization together with their visions about work and life as well (see Table 9.2).

Table 9.2 An analytical framework for organizations under change. Visions are drawn outside the frame since they are concerned with imagining something else than that which is *in* the frame

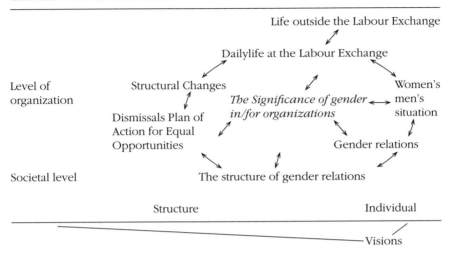

A case study – the significance of gender in the Labour Exchange

What remains is to answer the questions as to whether gender does have importance for organizations and change and, if so, exactly what gender does mean. The answers are based on the results of the project Gender and organizations under change (Jensen 1993). I carried out a study of a number of selected Labour Exchange offices and job centres where I observed, interviewed and sent out questionnaires. To the degree that the answers to the questionnaire survey substantiated the findings of the interviews I have ascribed the results of my analysis greater significance. As to the results, the focus of this article concerns gender's significance for change in the Labour Exchange.

On the basis of my investigations and analyses of conditions at five selected Labour Exchange offices I have concluded that gender is of significance in and for organizations. In the Labour Exchange, gender seems to have particular importance for the working climate, professionalism and change. The presence of both sexes (preferably an equal distribution) gives the best atmosphere: the working climate is most congenial when the proportion of women and men is roughly equal. The worst rough edges of each sex get worn off when the opposite sex is present. The job, too, is more fun and this contributes to an increase in the organization's productivity. Professionalism, and the qualifications necessary to perform the tasks of the exchange, seem to be enriched by an interplay between feminine and masculine values and qualities. As to the results that concern change in the Labour Exchange, I will elaborate them on the basis of the following: women's and men's situation, gender relations and the structure of gender relations.

The situation of women and men in Labour Exchanges is, at one and the same time, identical and different. Different in that there is a gender division of labour based on differences in education and, in addition, as to what posts women and men attain. It is significant that, far more often than men, women have an office training and a social worker/teacher training education, while men more frequently have a technical/craftsman background. As a consequence, both a vertical gender division of labour is built up (the office staff are women and the managers men), and there is a horizontal division of labour in that female and male counsellors have different tasks. Roughly speaking, the women work with the unemployed, as women do the housework jobs like cleaning, washing and preparing food. The men take care of the jobs outside the office – job assignment and contact with companies – just as, at home, men take charge of the outside jobs: the garden and the car. In this respect, the Labour Exchange mirrors a general societal structuring of gender.

To a certain degree, the situation of the sexes is the same since, particularly among one group of employees (job advisers), there seems to be little difference as to what women and men work on. In relation to change it turned out that, generally, women are more satisfied than men that changes in the Labour Exchange are to occur. Women think that, as an organization, the Labour Exchange needs a shake up. Some of the men also think that changes are necessary, but many men are sceptical about change. Seemingly, men would rather themselves suggest what is to be changed than change themselves (or have others do it to them).

Gender relations – defined as interaction between women and men, between women and between men – I have examined by looking at participation in group work, social relations at the workplace and influence in the organization. Many Labour Exchange employees are in work groups. There are, however, more men than women who do not meet with their own professional group. Thus, women, to a higher degree than men, appear to have professional relationships with other women and men. A significant finding is that, compared to women, men feel that their opportunities for exercising influence are greater. But there is a difference between women: the office staff to a greater degree than the counsellors feel that they do not have influence.

As to *the structure of gender relations*, I will briefly describe how I have operationalized the concept. I relate the answers to the interviews to *ideal types* – in the Weberian sense – of feminine and masculine values.[10] The idea of using ideal types of feminine and masculine values is to have, in unadulterated form, certain existing gender characteristics of an organization as these are expressed in interviews. The existing *structure of gender*

Table 9.3   Categories of feminine and masculine values

Feminine values			Masculine values		
Used by	Women	Men	Used by	Women	Men
Intuition	+	+	Logic	+	+
Emotion	+		Rationality	+	+
Submissive			Aggressivity		
Empathy			Exploitative		
Spontaneity	+		Strategic		
Nurturing	+		Independent		
Co-operative	+	+	Competitive		

Note: Both women and men can be carriers of/express, e.g., feminine values. The table is filled out according to what changes the interviewees thought were required in the Labour Exchange.

relations is part of the framework for what is permissible for an employee (woman or man), for which values are given priority (feminine or masculine). The structure of gender relations contains both elements that promote change and elements that hinder change.

The so-called feminine values are (inspired by Morgan 1986) intuition, emotion, submissiveness, empathy, spontaneity, nurturing and co-operation. The so-called masculine values are logic, rationality, aggression, exploitation, strategy, independence and competition (see Table 9.3).

It is important to avoid rank ordering the values. We can separate the biological and the social gender. I have done so by emphasizing that it is not only women who are the carriers of feminine values and not only men who are the carriers of masculine values; women can express masculine values, and vice versa. However, ideal-typically, we can expect that feminine values are, *ceteris paribus*, linked to the biological female gender and that masculine values are linked to the biological male gender.

A crucial result of the case study is the finding that women and men use masculine values in arguing about why change is necessary. The Labour Exchange is regarded as an organization that must function rationally (one of the masculine value elements). A measure of efficiency is whether the Labour Exchange finds sufficient job placements. In this regard, the Labour Exchange is an inefficient organization as it currently functions. Masculine values are also used to characterize *goals* for changes in the Labour Exchange. The exchange must become an effective and productive organization in which technical-economic and rational elements have a prominent role. This is true, for example, of the service to companies, including prioritizing the "product" (the product package) while at the same time giving lower priority to job seekers: giving information and counselling to groups rather than to individuals.

The feminine values are emphasized as necessary *means*, if the goals of a more effective and productive organization are to be achieved. Many employees – both women and men – do not think the changes will succeed without co-operation, empathy and nurturing.

Hence it is not feminine values that hinder organizational change, but rather masculine values. In the organizations I investigated, a group of women employees served as the dynamo of change while the men were, generally, more critical of changes at the Labour Exchange. This also emerges in that when women were asked about their preferences for future job situations, they claimed they would accept a post at the same career level but wanted a more challenging job. These results are in radical contrast to the myth of women as brakes on organizational change.[11]

It is one thing to chart, via interviews, feminine and masculine values in a process of change. What is interesting is whether feminine values do, in fact, play a role or whether the existing structure of gender relations, including a relation of subordination between women and men, together with feminine and masculine values will block fundamental changes in the existing power structure.

The significance of gender for change in public organizations

What prospects can be traced on the basis of my investigation and analysis in which I interpret the results from an organizational and a gender perspective? An *organizational research perspective* focuses on structures, cultures, processes and production as such: all of which are important and key elements in organizational analysis. In the Labour Exchange example, significant structural changes are occurring in one area and, generally, the emphasis is on a production-and-efficiency profile in the Labour Exchange.

Incorporating a *women and gender research approach* in the analysis of changes in the Labour Exchange throws light on new features and perspectives in the process of change, features that an organizational approach does not capture. There are certain obvious and interesting trends that suggest that changes can occur in gender relations and in the structure of gender relations.

First, a struggle is going on as to the gender identity of company contact work. It has been the pattern in the Labour Exchange that men take charge of contact with companies. This is a task that is thought to require special knowledge of the companies which male Labour Exchange consultants often have by virtue of their previous occupations. During the process of change that was going on in the Labour Exchange while I carried out my investigation, the work with companies was restructured. Several women fought to take part in deciding how this was to be done. A battle over the gender identity of this job took place since the changing practice shook up the conventional ideas about the combination of gender and job (company contact = male work).

Secondly, there was a struggle in the Labour Exchange about to what extent feminine values should have a prominent role in the work of the exchange: that is, about whether counselling of individual clients should have high priority or whether the prevailing masculine values should be dominant in the work norms of the Labour Exchange, i.e., whether a fixation on product, production and efficiency should have a prominent role. Thirdly, it proved to be the case that feminine values were viewed as a necessary instrument in the process of change.

It is an open question whether the trends mentioned above will actually lead to changes in power relations between the genders. Would women's appropriation of the work with companies merely leave the Labour Exchange as a whole with even greater difficulty in attracting a male workforce? However, the results of my study indicate that it is not a matter of either/or. Both men and women can work with companies and both feminine and masculine values are necessary in an organization. It is not sufficient to focus on single aspects in the study of organizations and this is a well-known phenomenon within organization research. Allison (1969) analyzed the Cuban Missile Crisis from three different perspectives and it is today quite common for researchers to plead for the use of several perspectives in the study of organizations.[12]

One explanation as to why different perspectives are necessary is that reality is so complex that it is impossible to capture everything important from only one perspective. Another reason is that all organizations are constantly in the situation of tackling dilemmas: conceived of as insoluble conflicts (see, *inter alia*, Beck Jørgensen 1992:56). An organization must produce, a Labour Exchange must procure jobs and service companies. But an organization has to be reproduced *qua* organization, too. A Labour Exchange must legitimize itself in relation to the outside world: it can do so by its acts, i.e., by delivering the product expected of it. It has been difficult for the Labour Exchange to fill a large number of assigned jobs (at the time of the investigation, the Labour Exchange assigned 6–9 per cent of all jobs throughout the country). Hence the Labour Exchange has had to legitimize itself politically: that is, produce explanations for the rationale of the organization.[13] In many ways, the Labour Exchange has a public image in which, culturally, the organization has been associated with a heavy, dusty, public bureaucracy. At the same time, the wave of modernizations whose image is that of service has also hit the Labour Exchange. And, further, the exchange must find a balance between feminine and masculine values professionally, in its work climate and in its products.

Since I carried out my investigation, an interesting Labour Exchange organization has grown up in Copenhagen: the Labour Market Service. Two characteristics of the new organization should be emphasized. One feature is that the new body is a service organization that gives priority to servicing both companies and their users. The service element is crucial and can be compared with feminine values. The other feature is that they work, partly, targeting those with higher educational and/or professional qualifications and co-operate with private employment agencies. These features can be considered a product improvement, as more efficient. An attempt is made to give equal weight to both feminine and masculine values in one and the same organization. This is also an organization that has to tackle the dilemma of embodying at one and the same time the traditional conception of a Labour Exchange office (control, signing on) and the ambition of the public sector to be similar to the private sector (service and efficiency).

A both/and perspective on this new organization, in which gender is present at every level, can give us an insight into and an understanding of how this Labour Exchange organization is distinguished from others and also into the kinds of dilemma this new organization faces: dilemmas that the more traditional Labour Exchanges often manage by separating the solution of tasks in time and space.

One cannot generalize the results of my investigation of selected Labour Exchange offices to the significance of gender for change in and of all public organizations. The public sector is far too heterogeneous for that. Public organizations tackle very different types of task which are often quite different from those of the Labour Exchange. But at a time when public organizations are bombarded with demands for change – or are subject to change – it stands to reason that this is the time to investigate. There are, in fact, research results that suggest that it is easier to carry out fundamental changes, e.g., in the structure of gender relations, when there are signs of change in an organization. One Norwegian study indicated that an increase in the number of women in government departments promotes innovative behaviour, i.e., that more employees actually suggest changes. The author is of the view that this phenomenon is related to the fact that women are less adjusted to the norms and procedures of public organizations, they are more conflict and change-oriented (Christensen 1989).

Since the 1980s, the local councils in Scandinavia have undergone and are undergoing a process of change in which administrations are amalgamated so that educational, social and cultural briefs become one administration area instead of three. The priorities are, in a nutshell: anti-hierarchy, total solutions and cross-sectoral work (see, e.g., Sehested et al. 1992). Is this tantamount to prioritizing feminine values? Is it possible to influence the balance between feminine and masculine values in the process of local council change and hence contribute to a change in the structure of gender relations? To answer these questions requires analysis of the processes of change that are taking place by drawing on a gender perspective.

A gender perspective on organizational changes which builds on insights from *both* organization and administration research *and* women and gender research can generate new insights and knowledge about the way in which the organizations in the Nordic welfare states function. This is true of the significance of organizational change for gender at a time when it appears to be possible to change existing power relations. It is also true of the significance of gender for organizational change where my own investigation shows that women can be the dynamo of change.

Notes

1. This chapter is a revised version of a paper delivered at the Nordic conference entitled "What are Nordic feminist thoughts?". I wish to thank the editors, the workshop participants, Lis Højgaard and Torben Beck Jørgensen for their constructive critiques of an earlier draft of this chapter.
2. The figures are from the Statistiske Efterretninger (Statistical Information), 1996:26.
3. For example, Højgaard 1990, 1991, Kvande & Rasmussen 1990, Billing & Alvesson 1989, Blum & Smith 1988, Hale & Kelly (eds) 1989, and Guy (ed.) 1992.
4. I define *gender research* as research that produces knowledge about gender (see Widerberg 1989) in which *women's research* is defined as research that produces knowledge about women. Organization research produces similar knowledge about organizations.
5. In Denmark, the Modernization Programmes are examples of administrative reforms. In England, the Next Step Agency reforms are comparable examples.
6. For a more extensive discussion of results as to gender in mainstream organization research, see Jensen 1990, 1993, 1994.
7. In Jensen 1993:78ff there is a more extensive discussion of the arguments concerning "Women-in-the-labour-market" research and WIM research.
8. The analytical levels are inspired by Dahlerup (1989a, 1989b) and Connell (1987). For an elaboration see Jensen (1993:43ff).
9. In the Danish language, there are no separate words for sex and gender.
10. Ideal types can be considered as ahistorical stereotypes. Ahistoricity can be avoided by developing new value sets. This is, however, a huge task. Hence, one must bear in mind that these are ideal types which are not necessarily relevant in every societal (historical) context or applicable to all social groups.
11. But I have not argued that there are no women who act conservatively. What is new, and what this study indicates, is that women, too, can be the motive force for change, the dynamo.
12. For example, see Morgan 1986, Christensen 1991, Schultz 1990.
13. The concept of politics/action is taken from Brunsson 1986.

References

Acker, J. 1990. Hierarchies, jobs, bodies: a theory of gendered organizations. *Gender & Society* 4 (2), 139–58.
Acker, J. 1992. Gendering organizational theory. In *Gendering organizational analysis*. A.J. Mills & P. Tancred (eds), 248–60. London: Sage.

Allison, G.T. 1969. Conceptual models and the Cuban Missile Crisis. *American Political Science Review* (3).

Beck Jørgensen, T. 1992. Politik og produktion (Politics and production). In *Livet i offentlige organisationer. Institutionsdrift i spændingsfeltet mellem stat, profession og marked* (Life in public organizations. Institutions in the tension between state, profession and the market). T. Beck Jørgensen & P. Melander (eds), 45–63. Copenhagen: Jurist- & Økonomforbundets Forlag.

Billing, Y.D. & M. Alvesson 1989. *Køn – ledelse – organisation. Et studium af tre forskellige organisationer* (Gender – management – organization. A study of three different organizations). Copenhagen: Jurist – & Økonomforbundets Forlag.

Blum, L. & V. Smith 1988. Women's mobility in the corporation: a critique of the politics of optimism. *Signs: Journal of Women in Culture and Society* **13** (3), 528–45.

Brunsson, N. 1986. Politik och handling (Politics and action). In *Politik och ekonomi. En kritik av rationalitet som samhällsföreställning* (Politics and economics. A critique of rationality) N. Brunsson (ed.), 19–49. Lund: Doxa.

Calás, M.B. & L. Smircich 1989. Using the 'F' word: feminist theories and the social consequences of organizational research. Paper presented at the August 1989 Academy of Management Meeting. Washington D.C.

Christensen, T. 1989. Innovasjonsatferd i sentralforvaltningen: Strukturelle og demografiske forklaringer på variasjon (Innovative behaviour in central administration: structural and demographic explanations of variations). In *Institusjonspolitikk og forvaltningsutvikling. Bidrag til anvendt statsvitenskap* (Institutional politics and administrative development. A contribution to political science in use). M. Egeberg (ed.), 165–85. Oslo: Tano.

Christensen, T. 1991. *Virksomhetsplanlegging – myteskaping eller instrumentell problemløsning?* (Company planning – building myths or instrumental problem solving?) Oslo: Tano.

Christensen, S. & J. Molin 1983. *Organisationskulturer. (Organizational culture)*. Copenhagen: Akademisk Forlag.

Connell, R.W. 1987. *Gender and power. Society, the person, and sexual politics.* Standford, Calif.: Standford University Press.

Dahlerup, D. 1989a. Findes der en særlig kvindevidenskab? (Is there a special science of women?). In *Kvindeforskningsseminar. Videnskabshistorie og -teori* (Women's research seminar. History and theory of science). A.M. Berg et al. (eds), 31–9. Copenhagen.

Dahlerup, D. 1989b. Når man ikke kan se skoven for bare træer. Kvinder og køn i forskningen (When you cannot see the wood for the trees. Women and gender in science). In *Dømmekraft. Objektivitet, subjektivitet og videnskab* (Judgment. Objectivity, subjectivity and science), S. Brock & P. Pedersen (eds), 11–47. Århus: Aarhus Universitetsforlag.

Eisenstein, Z. (ed.) 1979. *Capitalist patriarchy and the case for socialist feminism.* New York: Monthly Review Press.

Guy, M.E. (ed.) 1992. *Women and men of the states. Public administration at the state level.* New York: M.E. Sharpe.

Hale, M. & R.M. Kelly (eds) 1989. *Gender and bureaucracy, and democracy.* Westport, Conn.: Greenwood Press.

Halsaa, B. 1987. Har kvinnor gemensamma interessen? (Do women have interests in common?). *Kvinnovetenskaplig tidskrift* (4), 42–56.

Hartmann, H. 1979. The unhappy marriage of Marxism and feminism. Towards a more progressive union. *Capital & Class* (8), 1–33.

Hartsock, N. 1983. *Money, sex and power. Toward a feminist historical materialism.* New York: London: Longman.

Hearn, J. & W.P. Parkin 1983. Gender and organizations: a selective review and a critique of a neglected area. *Organizations Studies* **4** (3), 219–42.

Hearn, J. et al. (eds) 1989. *The sexuality of organization.* London: Sage.

Højgaard, L. 1990. *Vil kvinder lede? Et spørgsmål om fornyelse* (Do women want to become leaders?). Copenhagen: Ligestillingsrådet.

Højgaard, L. 1991. *Vil mænd lede? Et spørgsmål om loyalitet* (Do men want to become leaders?). Copenhagen: Ligestillingsrådet.

Jensen, H.N. 1990. En kønnere organisationsteori (A gendered theory of organizations). In *Nyere tendenser i politologien. Stat og forvaltning* (New trends in political science. State and public administration). P. Bogason (ed.), 81–104. Copenhagen: Forlaget Politiske Studier.

Jensen, H.N. 1993. *Køn og organisationer under forandring* (Gender and organizations under change). PhD thesis, Institute of Political Science, Series of PhD Reports, no. 1, Copenhagen.

Jensen, H.N. 1994. Gendered theories of organizations. In *Gender and organizations – changing perspectives. Theoretical considerations and empirical findings.* J. de Bruijn & E. Cyba (eds), 21–51. Amsterdam: VU University Press.

Kvande, E. & B. Rasmussen 1990. *Nye kvinneliv. Kvinner i menns organisasjoner* (New life for women: women in men's organizations). Oslo: Ad Notam.

Mills, A.J. & P. Tancred (eds) 1992. *Gendering organizational analysis.* London: Sage.

Morgan, G. 1986. *Images of organization.* London: Sage.

Schultz, M. 1990. *Kultur i organisationer. Funktion eller symbol?* (Culture in organizations. Function or symbol?). Copenhagen: Handelshøjskolens Forlag.

Sehested, K. et al. 1992. *Effekter af strukturændringer i kommuner* (Effects of structural changes in local government). Copenhagen: AKF.

Weick, K. 1969/1979. *The social psychology of organizing*, 2nd edn. Reading, Mass.: Addison-Wesley.

Widerberg, K. 1989. Korsväger innom samhällsvetenskaplig kvinnoforskning (Crossroads in social science women's research). *Nytt om kvinneforskning* (1), 35–42.

CHAPTER TEN

Sexual harassment and the genderization of work

Kjersti Ericsson

The mushroom and the mycelium

When feminists and the women's movement made wife-battering visible, this was considered provocative. It was perhaps not the exposure of the phenomenon itself that was most provocative. In addition to making it visible, feminist researchers placed violence against women within a larger framework: the study of power relations between the sexes. This power relation emerged as the main theme in analyses of domestic violence. We can borrow a metaphor from mycology: one would not understand very much about the mushroom if one were to concentrate exclusively on the conspicuous hat. The important part is the widespread subterranean mycelium.

Sexual harassment in the workplace has also become a hot topic among feminist researchers in the Nordic countries. In 1992, the theme was taken up in a Danish book *Seksuel Chikane (Sexual harassment)* by the Danish psychologist Liby Tata Arcel, and in a Norwegian book *Sex i arbeid(et) (Sex at work)*, edited by sociologists Marianne C. Brantsæter and Karin Widerberg, both of whom work at the University of Oslo. Sexual harassment can also be seen as a mushroom with an extensive underground mycelium. Hearn & Parkin (1987) point out that making sexual harassment visible provides an important empirical contribution to the study of organizations. These studies are examples of how the understanding of organizations is undergoing change through feminist research. They have opened the door to a broader study of gender and its influences in work organizations. Gender differences at work have most often been treated as something coming from the outside, as the English sociologist Humphrey summarizes:

> Sexual differentiation is seen as largely determined outside the labour market in the sexual division of labour in the household.

However, it has become increasingly obvious that gender, or power relations between the sexes, permeates all social institutions, and that the supposedly objective economic laws and market competition work through and within gendered structures (Humphrey 1985:219).

Holter (1992) makes a similar point with respect to organizations in general. Both in everyday speech and in theoretical presentations, an organization is often understood as an empty form, a gender-neutral framework. This framework is filled up with people who act within the limits defined by the organization. "Gender" is seen as something the participants bring with them from the outside world.

Various "mushrooms" may serve as a point of departure for studying "the mycelium": that which is genderized in the organizations of work. Humphrey's point of departure are studies showing the connection between the workers' gender and what is understood to be skilled and unskilled work. The sexual segregation of the labour market, the manner in which it is created and re-created, can also serve as an entrance (see, among others, Dahlerup 1989). Women and leadership could be a third angle. "From women and leadership to gender and organizations", is the evocative title of Kvande & Rasmussen's (1992) summarization, from a feminist perspective, of Norwegian leadership and organizational research. The organization is understood as an arena where social structures of meaning are constructed with reference to gender. Within this perspective, it is demonstrated that gender is not something that women carry with them into organizations. Gender, here understood as masculinity, is important as an interpretive framework for organization and leadership. From focusing on women as being problematic with respect to leadership and activity in organizations, one focuses now on the organization as being a male construct.

Sexual harassment at work is my "mushroom". Sexuality has been chosen because it emphasizes that the genderization of work organizations is woven together with the intimate, personal sides of sexual identity. When genderization of work is negotiated or contested, sexual identity as experienced is also at stake. My point of departure will be two forms of sexual harassment that are described as typical for different parts of the sex-segregated labour market. On this basis, I will reflect on the question of gender as a qualification in work. What do masculinity and femininity respectively represent as qualifications? The two forms of sexual harassment lead up to two themes: the defence of masculinity as a qualification and the exploitation of femininity.

Sexual harassment and gender as qualification

Arcel (1992) distinguishes between two types of sexual harassment which she labels "the sexually harassing milieu" and "something-for-something harassment", respectively. In the sexually harassing milieu, sexual behaviour is an expression of enmity towards women, and the aim is to frighten them. Here, it is not one woman who is harassed by one man, rather it is a collective undertaking by all the men. This form of sexual harassment is most common in male-dominated work environments. Something-for-something harassment happens when a man demands sexual services from a woman in return for promises of reward, or against threats of punishment if the demands are not fulfilled. This form of harassment occurs most often in workplaces where women work in traditionally female jobs, while the managerial functions are carried out by men.

The difference between these two forms of sexual harassment is not absolute. However, this difference can provide the angle for the study of masculinity and femininity as qualifications at the workplace. The first type points to the defence of masculinity as a qualification, the other to the exploitation of femininity.

While Arcel sticks to the descriptive level in her treatment of the two forms of sexual harassment, Gutek (1985) tries to explain the occurrence of sexual harassment in various work situations. For her, the concept of "sex-role spillover" is central. By "sex-role spillover", she means a transferring to the workplace of sexually based roles that are usually irrelevant or inappropriate with respect to the job. Many sides of the gender roles can be transferred to work. The most relevant aspect with respect to "sex at work" has to do with being a sex-object. To be a sex-object is central to the female sex-role. It is unclear if the masculine sex-role has an equally strong sexual aspect, says Gutek. If it does, it has probably to do with sexual aggression and assertion. "Sex-role spillover" as the explanation for sexual harassment is based on role theory with the concepts of work-role and sex-role. Gutek defines work-role as a set of expectations attached to the task that has to be carried out in a given job.

"Sex-role spillover" springs from the quantitative composition of the labour force. When one sex dominates in number at a workplace, sex roles spill over into the work-role. The sex that is in the minority will then experience a lack of concordance between sex and work roles:

> The person of the numerically subordinate gender is essentially a role deviate, and these deviating aspects become salient. Hence, a non-traditionally employed woman is a "woman in a man's job". She is perceived and treated differently. Because her gender is salient to herself as well as to others, she perceives this differential treatment to be discriminatory (in general) and harassment (when the content is sexual) . . . A second type of sex role spillover is to the job itself. Most workers are treated similarly. In the case of women, this sets up a condition under which they generally will be

unaware of sexual harassment. If harassment happens to other workers in the same job, it is viewed as part of the job and therefore acceptable (or at least expected) (Gutek 1985:150).

The problem with the term "sex-role spillover" is that gender and sexuality can easily be understood as something that comes from the outside and "gushes into" work when the numerical composition of the workplace allows for it. That sex and sexuality come from "without" is in agreement with the organizations' own self-image, says Gutek, a self-image which she criticizes. However, she wants a concept that makes action at the workplace feasible. This may be the reason why she, despite herself, chooses a term that conjures up a picture of sex as something coming from "outside". If gender comes from outside, it can perhaps also be driven out again:

> Sex-role spillover focuses on the workplace and its environment rather than on either individual differences or broad cultural themes. One advantage of focusing on the workplace is that it can serve as an arena for handling problems explicated by the inter-group and sex-role models. The workplace may be a more manageable arena for change than society at large (Gutek 1985:18).

It is perhaps easier to change the workplace than to change society, says Gutek. I wonder. Gender seems actively to contribute towards the formation and re-formation of structures in the work situation. Technological, economic and social changes can break down the old sexual divisions of work. But sexual hierarchy and sexual segregation is re-created in new forms (see Hagemann 1994, Wikander 1989). Besides, the organization of work is so central in the formation of our society as a whole that it has little meaning to differentiate too sharply between work and society. Sexual segregation in the labour market has long historical roots, summarizes Dahlerup (1989), introducing a collection of articles on sexual segregation in the labour market in the Nordic countries. Nevertheless, sexual segregation is not merely a historical lag. It is an actively working process even today. The separation of the sexes into occupations, work functions and wage categories is maintained in many companies despite societal changes. In other companies, changes can lead to a temporary breakdown of old sexual divisions, before they are re-created into new forms. Moreover, sexual segregation at the workplace does not merely mirror the sexual divisions in the family. Sexual segregation is also a dynamically active factor in the companies themselves. Thus the companies contribute actively to the maintenance of male dominance in society, both within and without their four walls.

The genderization of work does not come exclusively from without, and yet neither does it arise exclusively from within. Economic, political and cultural relations have formed the sexual structures of modern workplaces, produced new knowledge of gender and changed the concrete formulation of the sexual contract. In their turn, the modern institutions of work have become important anchors for a modern sexual order (Hagemann 1994).

I have chosen the expression "sex as qualification" in dealing with some aspects of "the mycelium" of "the mushroom" that is sexual harassment. This choice has many reasons. First, qualification can be wide-ranging, from formal knowledge and skills to more implicit demands on behaviour and attitudes. Such implicit demands are sometimes referred to as "the hidden curriculum" in research on socialization. For example, the Danish psychologists Bauer & Borg (1976) claim to have identified the following "hidden" socializing requirements in the Danish classroom: the requirement to work individually, to be attentive to the teacher and to control motor and verbal expression; the demand to adapt oneself to the school's divisions of time and space; the requirement to conform to the wishes of an invisible authority. Similarly, requirements of qualification in the workplace will include both well-defined knowledge and skills and more implicit expectations. Secondly, the term qualification connects several societal institutions. Qualification for work (in the broad sense) is created in many arenas: in the family, the school, in organizational life and in leisure. The organizing and functioning of work again have their repercussions on the other institutions in society in the form of demands for qualification, both formal and informal. The term qualification, viewed thus, points to a relation (many-sided and contradictory) between "without" and "within". Thirdly, as Holmer & Karlsson (1991) point out, the term implies something acquired, something that has been brought about. They trace the word back to its Latin origin, *qualis* (such as) and *facere* (to do). The use of the term is in accordance with its Latin roots. Qualification, then, means that somebody does something that makes him or her fit (qualified) for a job. Conversely, it can point to something that happens in the employment market which influences other societal institutions, for example the education system. Fourthly, and finally, qualification is an arena for struggle between various interests. Holmer & Karlsson (1994) summarize qualification as a struggle of interests independent of terminology and theoretical perspectives. It is the main and common theme in a collection of articles by Sweden's foremost researchers in the area of which they are the editors (ibid.). One of the contributors presents this formulation:

> That which in a given society and in a given point of time, is accounted for as qualification and is regarded as such, is the result of a struggle of interests between social forces with varying power and influence. Power also decides over the knowledge/expertise that can be expressed in the work process, and what should be counted as in or out of a competence level at school (Berner 1991:123).

To summarize: when I use the expression "gender as qualification" in the workplace, I am thinking of skills, ways of being and attitudes that are ascribed to the sexes and are put to use at work; of something that originates from an interaction between work and other societal institutions; of something that is socially constructed; of something that is a result of interest struggles and power relations. Sex as qualification is formed in a struggle of interests. Behind the two types of sexual harassment identified and labelled by Arcel, one glimpses two different struggles. "The sexually harassing milieu" may be seen as expressive of the struggle to defend masculinity as a qualification. In this struggle the combatants belong to the same class – they are all workers – but are divided by sex. "Something-for-something harassment" may be linked to the struggle to exploit femininity, a struggle that is often fought out between subordinate women and men who hold senior positions. The "mushroom" that is sexual harassment leads into a mycelium where gender and class are interwoven in intricate ways. Two sections of this chapter, "The archetypical proletarians" and "Masculinity as counter-power" treat the defence of masculinity as qualification, while the section "Femininity without boundaries" treats the exploitation of femininity as qualification.

As mentioned, the mycelium, that which is genderized in the organizations of working life, can be studied with the help of different "mushrooms". Which "mushroom" one chooses is perhaps not of consequence. By choosing sexual harassment, one comes close to the emotionally loaded character of the struggle of gender as qualification. One approaches the links between the personal and the political. The struggle is not just about power and economy, it also concerns the vulnerable sides of sexual identity as it is experienced. This makes it easier to understand why the defence of masculinity as qualification is so important, and why the exploitation of femininity as qualification is so difficult to defend oneself against.

The norm of "objectified masculinity"

Worker and employer in the capitalist labour market face each other in a relationship of exchange. They enter into a contract, and are exchangeable in principle. Their relationship is not personal, the limits are clear-cut, and they have no obligations towards each other beyond the limits of the contract. The market demands that people relate to one another in an objectified manner. This manner contrasts both feudalism's patriarchal traditional bonds between master and servant, and the personal bonds within the family. What is personal, the feelings, the subjective, has been banished to the private sphere.

With the growth of capitalism, a sharp distinction was also created between production and housework. This distinction has played an important role for the definition of what is feminine and what is masculine, also in wage work. Division of work between the sexes was nothing new. Neither was the combination of sexual division of work with male superiority. The new development was that these two forms of work, production and reproduction, became separated in time and space, and were placed within different institutional frames. The result of this separation was that production and the market with their wages and regulation through contracts assumed a masculine character, while reproduction and the home with their unpaid work and unlimited obligations assumed a feminine character. When a connection is established between the masculine and market production, the market's objectified manner of relating becomes associated with masculinity. The norm for human relations in market production becomes what I will refer to as objectified masculinity. This objectified masculinity will, because it is the norm, appear as neutral, genderless. Holter (1992) summarizes that the underlying and unspoken premises for the arrangement of organizations are far from gender-neutral. They consist of conceptions of masculinity and femininity, in relation to work, qualifications and power. According to these conceptions, what men do and think are the norm, a neutral standard for the employee.

Waring (1988) gives a funny example of how men's activities are seen as the use of valuable time and hence are wage-worthy, while women's activities are seen as something they ought to do out of the goodness of their hearts, without time and wage coming into the picture. She quotes Singer & Wells (1984), who refer to women as egg-donors and men as sperm-donors for childless people:

> There is every reason to expect an adequate supply of eggs for reproductive technology from voluntary donations as long as there are patients in IVF (in vitro fertilization) programs producing surplus eggs. A woman donating an egg can do so without inconvenience and without harming her own chances of becoming pregnant. We would expect most of these women to be very willing to donate surplus eggs to other infertile women. There would be no need to offer monetary incentive . . . The weight of argument by the abstract and practical, is clearly in favour of setting up a voluntary system for egg donation. As long as IVF patients produce surplus eggs, it should be a purely voluntary system, for the patients do not suffer any inconvenience as a result of the donation. Sperm donors, on the other hand, do have to give up their time to make donations, and they have to put up with some inconvenience (quoted in Waring 1988:192).

To be a sperm-donor is thus work that ought to be paid for, to be an egg-donor is charity or caring for others. The distinction between the "masculine" market production and the "feminine" reproduction lurks in the background. Even when a woman is in paid work, her work can be defined as a form of housework, which thus is less valuable in monetary terms. Thompson (1983) mentions an example from 1978 where a representative of the employer justified the low salary paid to a woman who washed toilets compared to that of a man who did the same job with the argument that one expected a housekeeping approach from a (female) charwoman and a labouring orientation from her male counterpart.

It is not just the conceptions of how people in work organizations conduct themselves (or ought to conduct themselves) that are in agreement with the norm of objectified masculinity. Also, notions of how the *organizations themselves* function (or ought to function) have a striking resemblance to this norm. Gutek (1985) points out that the frequent occurrence of expressions of sexuality at the workplace is in contradiction to rational models for the functioning of organizations. Organization theory, whether it is based on Weber's concept of bureaucratic rationalizing, or on more recent motivation theories at the individual level that underline goals and relations between behaviour at work and expected rewards, does not leave much room for the expression of sexuality. Sexuality is emotional, not rational. An organization that has a self-image as rational can react to expressions of sexuality by ignoring, overlooking, suppressing or denying them.

In an evaluation of mainstream perspectives on organization theory, Thompson & McHugh (1990) point out that rationality and efficiency have been important themes. These concepts have most often been presented in mainstream theory in neutral terms as if rationality were a simple determinant for the structures, processes and goals of organizations. An image of a functional relation between rational organizations and a rational society is projected. This perspective removes questions of politics, power and control from the study of the choices of organizations. Further, traditional theories underestimate the role rationality and effectivity play as ideological constructions that contribute to the legitimation of the positions, rewards and actions of the dominant groups. Both organizations and the people in them are subjected to a seemingly neutral norm, into which masculinity is woven. The distinction between production/market/man and reproduction/home/woman has never been absolute. It is also in part created through struggle, not least by working-class men, as the next section will show. This struggle shows that even "class" is not neutral and genderless. The time has come to take a look at the type of workplaces that, according to Arcel, can develop sexually harassing milieux.

The archetypical proletarians

"Miners have a special place in the cult of the working class, they're the archetypical proletarians" (Campbell 1984:114). It may therefore be of special interest to look at the archetypical proletarians' attitudes to females of the same class. Marx gives an exciting glimpse into this relationship in the very early days of industrialization in *Das Kapital*. He quotes from a "bluebook" on the running of mines, "Report from the Select Committee on Mines, 23, July 1866", where miners are interviewed about their working conditions. Also included were questions about their views on women workers (work under the earth was already forbidden to women at this point). Marx quotes (there are many different miners who answer):

What do miners think of women being employed in the mines?
It is largely condemned.
Why?
They consider it humiliating for women . . . They use a kind of male clothing. In many cases all decency is suppressed. Many women smoke. The work is as dirty as the work in the mines themselves. There are many married women among them who are unable to fulfill their wifely duties.
Would widows be able to find such paying jobs in other areas?
I cannot answer that.
And in any case, you will take away from them this livelihood?
Yes.
Why this attitude?
We the miners, have much too much respect for the fair sex, to allow them to go into the coal mines . . . This work is for the most part very heavy. Many of these girls lift 10 tons each day.
Do you think that the women workers who are employed in the mines are more immoral than those who are employed in factories?
In percentage there are more "loose women" here than in the factories.
But neither are you satisfied with the moral condition in the factories?
No.
Would you not also forbid women from working in the factories?
No, I would not do that.
Why not?
Because it is more decent and suitable for the female sex.
But in any case you mean that it is harmful to their morals – is it not?
No, not anywhere as close as it is when they work in the mines. Besides, I am speaking not just of the moral, but also of the physical and social conditions. Social decadence among girls is extreme and very regrettable. If these girls become wives of miners, the husbands suffer greatly from this decadence, it drives them out of their homes and into drunkenness . . .
Would you rather not forbid women from working everywhere, where it is degrading?
Yes . . . The best qualities in children come out through the upbringing the mother is responsible for.

But this applies also for the women who work in agriculture – right? This work is carried out only in the summer months, but here with us, they work through all the seasons, often day and night, wet to the bone, with weakened constitution and broken down health. You have not studied this question so thoroughly? I have looked around, and I can say this much, that nowhere have I seen any work that women do that can be compared to work in the mines. It is men's work, and in addition, a job for strong men. The most conscious class of miners who try to come up socially and get a more human life, get no support from their wives, but instead get dragged down by them (Marx 1983:157, Norwegian edition).

Marx informs us that the women workers received between 1 shilling and 1 shilling and 6 pence per day, while a male worker would have to be paid 2 shillings and 6 pence per day. It is not difficult to understand why the employers used women workers. The low cost of female labour was also one important reason why male miners wanted the women *out*. The quotation from Marx also shows that the male workers looked upon the presence of their female counterparts in the mines as something that both threatened the women's femininity and their own masculinity. They express the Victorian notion that the woman's task is to rescue the man morally.

The fight to get women out of mining went on over a long period in Wigan Pier, the mining town that Campbell (1984) describes. Both in the 1880s and in 1911, during campaigns run by miners and some mine owners to keep women workers out of mining work, deputations of women mine workers went to parliament to present their case. The women in Wigan Pier wore trousers and were strong as horses, says Campbell. Yet, both their strength and their androgynous uniform were used against them. And just as the women mine workers in the quotation from Marx, they were seen as a moral threat.

Masculinity as counter-power

The labour movement's demands for the special protection of women indicate that male interests were woven together with class interests. Women ought to be protected from the hardest forms of work, such as work down in the mines and nightwork. The demand for special protection had many sides to it. One aspect had to do with concern for women's reproductive functions. One wished to protect them from work that could be dangerous to their health. Besides, working conditions for women workers were inhuman, and it was therefore not all that strange if one wished to get rid of the worst excesses, even if this applied only to women. Also, the demand to prohibit nightwork for women can be seen, over a greater time perspective, as a step in the struggle for a normal working day for all workers.

In Norway, the female labour unions fought for special protection (although there were a number of important exceptions). What was important to them was to limit the terrible exploitation they experienced (see Hagemann 1982). The struggle for special protection was undoubtedly used by male workers as a means of getting women out of their trade. The male workers' efforts to get the women out are usually understood as an attempt to prevent the undermining of their pay scales, and to secure the best paid jobs for themselves. These arguments are certainly correct. But I believe that this struggle also had another objective: to defend the male character of work. For the archetypical proletarian, this became even more important as their struggle as a class drew strength from their identity as a sex. I quote a poem written by my father who worked as an iron and metal industry worker for many years (Ericsson 1963):

Sad to be an engineer
getting a thrashing
from the workers
in negotiation after
negotiation.

But in any case
he can display his women.
He brings them to the factory and
points to where the women should look.

Till he realizes
that they are peeping secretly
at the workers' naked shoulders
shining with soot and sweat.

The poem has the suggestive title "Class struggle". Here, the worker through his masculinity triumphs over his class superiors.

In the poem, the male workers are conspicuously sexual. As Hearn & Parkin (1987) point out, men who are leaders and managers may be seen as "asexual", and yet charged with male sexuality on the basis of their power and strength. An influential model of masculinity is the boss who is "married to the job". An even stronger asexual model comes from the professions, especially the Church, medicine, economics and the law. Male professionals working in these fields are particularly "asexualized" in accordance with their assumed neutral competence, which is a part of the masculinity they present. This assumed asexuality co-exists with its seeming contradiction, where success and career become a symbol of men's masculinity and sexuality.

The situation is different for men in subordinate positions. For such men, positioned as they are in the class hierarchy, sexually charged masculinity is not a result of being dominant at the place of work. Masculinity, in order to be affirmed, and in order to serve as a symbol of strength that counters the weakness their subordinate position in the hierarchy signals, needs to be more open. While power implies masculinity and sexuality in the upper classes, masculinity and sexuality imply power in the lower classes.

To be conspicuously male is an alternative to possessing economic power as a source of strength. This does not serve merely as an affirmation that one possesses the main characteristics of masculinity, despite one's subordinate position in a class hierarchy. Masculinity may also, as in the poem quoted above, be mobilized as a source of strength in the class struggle, that is, masculinity as counter-power. This type of masculinity exceeds the basic norm of objectified masculinity. When masculinity serves as counter-power, it is demonstrative – I will call it "strutting masculinity". To hold on to masculinity as qualification may therefore become just as important to the workers as to employers in such workplaces. If one views masculinity as counter-power, it also becomes easier to understand why "the men's club" in labour unions is so unbelievably enduring. And it becomes easier to understand why the union leader whom Campbell interviews in Sheffield refers to union work as "macho":

> I was very aggressive, I was the most aggressive person I knew. So the job I was in was beautiful for letting all that out. I felt I could say anything I wanted. The trade union world is macho and brazen and it is all about wearing your credentials on your sleeve. You rise to it, you try to outdo in smartness or militancy the speaker before you (Campbell 1984:139).

As late as the 1990s, the Swedish labour union leader called the Social Democratic Women's Movement in the country "a swarm of cunts". This was not merely a pointed vulgarity, but a clear message referring to the male character of the union, formulated in the most provocative terminology of "strutting masculinity".

The fact that subordination is related to femininity and dominance to masculinity can also be seen in the relation between Blacks and Whites. In the history of racism, Black is often associated with the feminine. Bernal (1987) refers to Gobineau, "the father of European racism", who was extremely explicit in his sexualized presentation of race – Whites were "masculine" while Blacks were "fundamentally feminine". He was not alone. Around the same period, 1860, the well-known American scientist Louis Agassiz was concerned that a "mixing of races" could lead to a "feminization" of the population (Gould 1981). It is, therefore, not surprising that one can find examples of the use of masculinity as counter-power in the struggle against racism. According to the Black feminist Bell Hooks (1981), the struggle for the civil rights and human dignity of Blacks in the USA, also in part became a struggle for strengthening Black men's power over "their" women. She illustrates this through the example of Amiri Baraka, one of the black movement's foremost poets, who in a section of the play *Madheart* glorifies violence against women as a means of strengthening the Black man's greatness and worth. Black men's struggle against racism is woven together with the struggle to strengthen their identity as a sex. Thus it becomes, as in the case of the miners, a struggle that is fought partially at the cost of women.

An important concept in the workers' movement's political terminology is that of the "nuclear proletariat". Campbell's archetypical proletarian is part of the nuclear proletariat, along with workers in the large, traditional industrial workplaces. The nuclear proletariat is "the vanguard of the working class" – they are best organized, have the strongest class consciousness and the greatest clout in the class struggle. They are the model that others, the more peripheral sections of the working class, must try to emulate. The nuclear proletariat places its stamp on the whole culture of the workers' movement, and their leaders are the only ones who can put themselves forward as real representatives of the unions.

The images that the nuclear proletariat invoke are masculine – "the man with the helmet", "the boys on the floor". It is in the nuclear proletariat that the masculine character of the class projects itself most clearly. The traditionally strongest section of the working class, politically and organizationally, they are also the most manly. Should the connections between class and masculinity be dissolved, this culture would lose an important source of its strength in the class struggle.

Women find it problematic to adjust to the "strutting masculine" culture in such workplaces. Skinhøj (1989:149) found that Danish girls often discontinued their training in traditionally male trades as early as the first year. One of the reasons for this was the prevailing social tone and culture: "The atmosphere may, as some of the women say, be described by catch words such as 'beer, horn music, – and horror films'."

What Arcel describes as the sexually harassing milieu can be seen as a rejection mechanism, a reaction to a possible feminization of work and the working-class culture, which is seen as a threat to the strength of this culture.

Femininity without borders

What Arcel refers to as the sexually harassing milieu may develop in workplaces where it is important, not least for the workers, to maintain masculinity as qualification. Something-for-something harassment is more characteristic of workplaces where femininity is a qualification; femininity as qualification breaks with the norm of objectified masculinity.

According to Arcel, the woman's work-functions in such jobs consist of many services that resemble the functions a wife carries out at home, like caring and support. The distinction between the professional role and the personal is not so sharp. The Norwegian nurse and sociologist Torun Hamran describes the nursing culture in a modern hospital:

> "To do good work" and "to have a good department" become more extensive terms than [achieving] a *good result* in a more technical sense. The distinction between profession and person – who you are and what you do – is not so clear-cut. The individual employee will not be so easy to replace. It is not of "no consequence" who you work with (Hamran 1992:87).

The personal and the professional are woven together in caring and service occupations. Men disappear rapidly from these jobs. If they stay on, for example in nursing, they often disappear upwards towards administrative, leadership positions. The fact that men disappear has of course something to do with salary scales. However, I believe that it can also be explained by the kind of work and the diffuse borders between the personal and the professional that characterize many female-dominated service occupations. Men may choose to stay away from occupations that do not have just that "objective", impersonal stamp. In a magazine interview a male nurse expresses himself thus:

> Women have greater difficulties in assuming a strictly professional attitude. Just now both Richard and I work in the psychiatric ward where it becomes especially evident, since it is so important to set definite limits. On the positive side, one can of course point out that women in the health sector provide a caring that is absolutely necessary, something we men are not always aware of as being essential (*Kvinnejournalen* 1986).

The male nurse draws a distinction between "the purely professional" and "care" – a distinction that is perhaps not as self-evident to female nurses. The non-contract-regulated, limitless obligations that characterize women's work in the home, sticks to women, at least partly, when they are employed. Widerberg describes femininity as a qualification for work in the following terms:

> Women are expected to be *available and caring* (like mother, "who is always there") and these expectations are laid down as both formal and informal job qualifications in typically female professions. A woman can be interrupted in her work (e.g., the secretary), and she should accept the interruption with a smile . . .

To subordinate oneself to men becomes in itself an expression of femininity. Beyond this, the feminine also often consists of honouring the above mentioned expectations (of availability and caring), expectations that we associate with the roles of mother and mistress. While the "expectations associated with mother" are seen as more or less "legitimate" and are therefore quite easy to address, the "expectations associated with the mistress" are more enshrouded in taboos. The heterosexual woman of today is expected to be available, obliging and attractive. At the same time we obviously expect the woman at the workplace to be "sexy" or "motherly" towards all men and women, and not just towards one man. In other words, she ought to be professionally sexy and motherly, *professionally feminine* (Brantsæter 1990). If not she will be perceived as mother or mistress, and not as an employee (Widerberg 1992:127).

Sexual harassment takes place when men exploit these feminine qualifications beyond the limits that are seen as legitimate. The demand for availability with respect to providing care is extended constantly and eventually includes the demand for sexual availability. In the old days, the master of the house or the son of the house regularly got the maids pregnant. The sexual harassment of subordinate women in the service occupations by their male superiors or bosses can partially be seen as a continuation of this tradition.

Femininity as a qualification is in many ways a paradox. It is taken for granted and exploited, both in forms that are considered legitimate and in forms that are considered illegitimate (sexual harassment). At the same time, this femininity is a deviance from the basic norm of objectified masculinity, and is therefore downgraded. The word qualification is in this connection singularly ill-chosen. As femininity is associated with the "personal", women's activities are *not* considered a result of qualifications. Since both (presumptive gender-neutral) employees and many work organizations as such are subjected to the norm of objectified masculinity, femininity as qualification is made invisible and invalid. The importance of women's caring qualities and availability, not only in many occupations, but also for the internal functioning of organizations themselves, is hidden by the organizations' rational and effective self-image. In contrast, women's behaviour is understood to be "personal" and "emotional", and is thus seen as belonging to another sphere. In this manner essential female qualifications become non-qualifications.

Women's work in the service sector in some way resembles, and can be seen as a continuation of, women's role in the home. Industrial work carried out by women does not have this particular feature. All the same, femininity often is a paradoxical qualification, in industrial work as well. For example, women's skills are seen as part of their "natural" femininity – and consequently, the work they do is considered unskilled. Women's dexterity is presented by many industrial leaders as an argument for the employment of women in certain types of industrial work (see Humphrey 1985). The jobs that women most often get require dexterity, accuracy, patience and the capacity to sit still, as summarized by Fürst from a Swedish survey (1989). All the job-recruiters whom Fürst interviewed believed these qualifications to be feminine. But qualifications of this kind are rather used as arguments for bringing down the pay scales than as arguments supporting extra wages. Thompson (1983:197) mentions an official brochure published by the authorities in Malaysia, where "the oriental woman's" dexterity is praised, saying: "Who, therefore, could be better qualified by nature and inheritance to contribute to the efficiency of a bench-assembly production line?" Even specialized skills such as tobacco spinning are not seen as being equal in value to masculine skills, says Thompson. Job evaluations are used as a means to discriminate against women. Systems of evaluation that are assumed to be objective, define qualities that are valued in men's work, such as accuracy, good concentration and dexterity, as being "natural" untrained skills in women's work.

"Man does, woman is", says the poet Robert Frost. This applies also to the workplace. The man's activities are perceived as skilled or professional, as something he *does*. The woman's activities on the other hand, are extensions of femininity, something that she *is*. In industrial work, too, one may observe how organizations make use of women's qualifications, while at the same time making them invisible by defining them as expressions of femininity, as a part of women's nature.

To be subordinate to men is in itself an expression of femininity, claims Widerberg (1992). This aspect of femininity is put to use as a disciplining mechanism in working life. Susan Joekes (1985) has studied the male and female workforce in Morocco where labour is very strongly divided on the basis of sex. However, there is a demand for a certain number of male workers, even in the female-dominated sectors. Joekes explains why owners of companies want to keep a small number of male workers at strategic points in the production process, even if they cost more. They are valuable because the owners can use power relations between the sexes as a means of strengthening discipline among the workers.

One such method is the use of male workers to set the pace on the assembly line. Assembly line work is most often carried out as piece-work in order to keep the pace up. But many factory owners have chosen another method: they place a couple of workers who are on piece-work in each assembly line. The others are paid by the hour. Since all the workers in a line are dependent on each other, the tempo of work is accelerated, for all the workers. As the "pace setters" are men, and women are used to subordinating themselves to men, it is difficult for them to raise any protests, whether it be against the tempo or against the higher salaries that men receive for the same job. In this manner, company owners ensure a higher work tempo from the women without having to pay them extra. In the printing industries in Norway, even as late as the 1970s, it was common practice that when skilled bookbinders (men) and bookbinding assistants (women) worked together, the skilled bookbinders were on piece-work. The assistants who put things in order and worked with some parts of the operation, and who therefore had to follow the tempo set by the skilled workers, were paid by the hour. It is common that men are supervisors over the female workers: Male methods of control are woven together with methods of disciplining work subordinates. Foged & Marcussen describe conditions in a Danish office:

> At the same time, there is a male leader who sits in a little room right next to the typing room and is separated from them by a thin wall. In this manner he has an ear in the typing room all the time without actually being there. The noise from the machines, as well as the women's chatting reach him through the walls . . . "It is best to do things in the manner in which we have always done them," is the leadership's answer when the women come with other suggestions. The tradition that is followed here is that women shall have a male leader and be supervised, otherwise they will chat (Foged & Marcussen 1984:88).

Cultural concepts of propriety may also be used. The norms for what is "troublemaking" and "insubordination" are often quite different in female workplaces than in male workplaces. "Why are we afraid to go to the toilet during work hours if the foreman or the boss is present? And if we do, we consider ourselves the bravest women in the world!" writes Palmer (1986:74), a worker in a Norwegian fish packing factory.

Norway and several other Nordic countries combine (on a global scale) a very high female participation in employment and politics with a sexually divided labour market. A parliamentary report on equal opportunity in Norway (Parliamentary Report no. 70, 1991–2) found that only 6 per cent of employed people were in occupations with a relatively even (40 per cent – 60 per cent) sexual division of labour. About half of all employed women were in occupations where more than 90 per cent of the employees were women. Women made up over 70 per cent of the workforce in the public sector, most of them at the local and district/municipal level. More than 80 per cent of these women worked in one of the following six occupations: cleaning, home help, nursing aides, nurses assistants at institutions, clerical assistants and teaching. In all these occupations, except teaching, there were less than 5 per cent men. In 1995, women formed 65 per cent of the labour force in the public, social and private services sector, but only 11 per cent in the oil, mining, electricity and construction sectors. Of the total number of employees, women constituted 46 per cent, but only 27 per cent of employees in leadership positions (mostly on lower or middle levels) (Norwegian Council of Equal Opportunity 1996). The sexually divided employment market is also wage-divided: wage levels in female-dominated branches are lower than wage-levels where men predominate. In an analysis of the concept of qualification, Berner argues: "It is perhaps not worth the trouble to try to find out what qualification is really about. Instead one should see it as a litmus paper for something else: What is one fighting about apropos qualification?" (1989:16). What emerges on my litmus paper is a process where society's struggle for sexual order, companies' struggles to survive in the market, the class struggle and the struggle for hegemony in the unions are woven together. Gender as qualification in the workplace points right at central, social contradictions. This is so, even in the Nordic countries, the paragons of "equal opportunity" for women.

A fruitful foreign element?

The "personal" and limitless qualities that adhere to women, also as employees, may be exploited by their superiors in innumerable ways. But from the point of view of the unions, these characteristics can be regarded as a threat. The following example is extreme, yet very illustrative (it is from a Norwegian factory in 1989). The woman working in the canteen served very good, home-made food in the lunch break. Then the company decided to cut down on the canteen worker's work hours by two hours, with a corresponding reduction in pay. She no longer had time to make the food herself, and had to switch to serving ready-made food. The other workers were disappointed when the home-made food disappeared. The canteen worker accordingly went back to working her old work hours, without getting back her old salary, to make good, home-made food as before, to satisfy the workers.

From the point of view of the unions, the canteen worker's behaviour is not just irrational; it is also dangerous and may undermine negotiated deals and tariffs. The personal and limitless side of femininity, that the husband enjoys in the home, is transformed into a threatening foreign element when it invades the workplace. Limiting exploitation has been the main objective of the unions' struggle from the beginnings of capitalism. The canteen worker's break with objectified masculinity seen in this light signals a lack of class-consciousness.

In a similar way, the so-called subjective, in the shape of feminist research, is seen as a threatening foreign element when it invades science. I have used sexual harassment as an angle from which to understand the gendered deep-structures in the seemingly neutral labour market with its economic rationality. The study of the genderized deep-structures of work may be seen as a parallel to the problematizing of the Western scientific tradition's objectivity and rationality, carried out by feminist theoreticians. On closer scrutiny, scientific objectivity and rationality can be seen as enmeshed with hegemonic masculinity. Several writers have drawn connections between the mode of production and thought forms in society: ". . . the positivist tradition of the autonomy of scientific knowledge is itself part of the general objectification of social relations that accompanied the transition from feudal to modern capitalist societies (Rose et al. 1990:33).

In science, too, the norm is objectified masculinity, which is therefore perceived as neutral. Perhaps the contents of objectified science contribute to attract men, just as the contents of the "personal" service occupations contribute in keeping men away?

Evelyn Fox Keller describes science as an area where men's psychological need for a special kind of autonomy and clear-cut boundaries between themselves and others, is satisfied through the prevailing views on objectivity and rationality: "Would not a characterisation of science which appears to gratify particular emotional needs give rise to a self-selection of scientists – a self-selection that would, in turn, lead to the perpetuation of that same characterisation?" (Fox Keller 1985:90).

It is also interesting to look at the position of the nuclear proletariat within the workers' movement. Perhaps one can compare the nuclear proletariat's standing in the working class as a whole to the standing of physics in the world of science. Just as male-dominated physics reigns supreme at the top of a hierarchy, as the "real", hard science, the model that all the other "softer" ones should try to imitate, so the nuclear proletariat tops the hierarchy of the working class, where nursing assistants and other similar groups represent the "soft", bottom level.

Today, jobs in traditional industry are rapidly vanishing, and the remnants of the nuclear proletariat is fighting with its back to the wall. Women in the "peripheral" sections now account for about half the employed members of the working class. In this situation, traditional class-consciousness, the culture and way of organizing, is in crisis. Here we can see another vague parallel to Western, mainstream science. Both traditional working-class culture and mainstream science are in need of a new foundation where masculinity is not an implicit part of the basic assumptions.

Masculine working-class organizations can, just as objective, male-dominated science, point to impressive results. Women in the caring occupations as well have had to learn how to make demands and draw up limits in their struggle for better wages and working conditions. However, along with impressive results come great problems. And some important issues have disappeared from view. The canteen worker referred to above acted as if the important thing was to satisfy the needs of people, not to sell her labour as expensively as possible. But the male-dominated labour movement has often acted as if the working capacity of living human beings should, as a matter of course, be sold as a thing, a commodity. The male working-class movement's relations to women and children produced a historical compromise with capital that brought to an end the workers' socialist fantasy (Campbell 1984). The class struggle was fought exclusively within the framework of the prevailing system: capitalism and patriarchy.

I started with a "mushroom": sexual harassment. The mycelium of this mushroom is the gendered character of work, which lives in an inseparable symbiosis with the seemingly neutral, economic rationality governing the labour market. Female employees are also a sex. This makes it possible for employers to exploit and discipline them in gendered ways. Their qualifications are translated into "female nature", and so extra pay is unnecessary. In the eyes of their male union comrades, women do not seem to be "real" workers, because masculinity is woven into class culture and class-consciousness. In this manner, female employees become doubly vulnerable: they are exploited in gendered ways and at the same time alienated from the organization that should be championing their interests.

References

Afshar, H. (ed.), 1985. *Women, work and ideology in the Third World*. London: Tavistock.

Arcel, L.T. 1992. *Seksuel Chikane* (Sexual harassment). Copenhagen: Hans Reitzel.

Bauer, M. & K. Borg 1976. Den skjulte læreplan (The hidden curriculum). *Unge pædagoger* **A**, **16**.

Bernal, M. 1987. *Black Athena*. London: Free Association Books.

Berner, B. 1989. *Kunskapens vägar. Teknik och lärande i skola och arbetsliv* (The paths of knowledge. Technique and teaching at school and work). Lund: Arkiv.

Berner, B. 1991. Kvalifikationens sociala sammanhang. Eller: Vad betyder en utbildning? (The social context of qualification. Or: what is the meaning of an education?). In *Kvalifikation. Hur kompetens och meriter värderas i det moderna sämhallet* (Qualification. How competence and merits are evaluated in modern society). J. Holmer & J.C. Karlsson (eds), 123–36. Stockholm: Konsultförlaget AB.

Brantsæter, M.C. 1990. *Om kjønnets logikk – i et lesbisk perspektiv: intervjuer med lesbiske kvinner og deres erfaringer i arbeidslivet* (On the logic of gender – in a lesbian perspective: interviews with lesbian women on their experiences in the labour market). Oslo: Department of sociology, University of Oslo.

Brantsæter, M.C. & K. Widerberg. 1992. *Sex i Arbeid(et)*. (Sex at work). Oslo: Tiden Norsk Forlag.

Campbell, B. 1984. *Wigan Pier revisited*. London: Virago.

Dahlerup, D. 1989. Kan arbeidsmarkedets kønsopdeling brydes? (Can sexual division in the labour market be dismantled?). In *Køn sorterer. Kønsopdeling på arbejdspladsen* (Sex sorts. Sexual division at the workplace), Drude Dahlerup (ed.), 2–43. Copenhagen: Nordisk Ministerråd.

Ericsson, H. 1963. *Hendenes hærskarer* (The multitude of hands). Oslo: Aschehoug.

Foged, B. & R. Marcussen 1984. *Det fleksible køn* (The flexible sex). Copenhagen: Tiderne Skifter.

Fox Keller, E. 1985. *Reflections on gender and science.* New York: Yale University Press.

Fürst, G. 1989. Konkurrens, kvalifikation och könssegregation – arbetskraftsefterfrågan i fokus (Competition, qualification and sexual segregation – the demands for a workforce in focus). See Dahlerup (ed.), 45–56.

Gould, S.J. 1981.*The mismeasure of man.* London: Penguin.

Gutek, B.A. 1985. *Sex and the workplace.* San Francisco: Jossey-Bass.

Hagemann, G. 1982. Særvern av kvinner – arbeidervern eller diskriminering? (The special protection of women – a protection for workers or discrimination?). In *Kvinner selv . . . sju bidrag til norsk kvinnehistorie* (Even women . . . seven contributions to Norwegian women's history). I. Blom & G. Hagemann (eds), 95–21. Oslo: H. Aschehoug.

Hagemann, G. 1994. *Kjønn og industrialisering* (Sex and industrialization). Oslo: Universitetsforlaget.

Hamran, T. 1992. *Pleiekulturen – en utfordring til den teknologiske tenkemåten* (The care-culture – a challenge to the technological manner of thinking). Oslo: Gyldendal norsk Forlag.

Hearn, J. & W. Parkin 1987. *"Sex" at "work". The power and paradox of organization sexuality.* New York: St. Martin's Press.

Holmer, J. & J.C. Karlsson (eds) 1991. *Kvalifikation. Hur kompetens och meriter värderas i det moderna samhället* (Qualification. How competence and merits are evaluated in modern society). Stockholm: Konsultförlaget AB.

Holter, H. 1992. Motstand og avverge i organisasjoner: fremdeles et aktuelt tema? (Resistance and barriers in organizations: still a topic of current interest?). *Nytt om kvinneforskning* **2**, 74–86.

Hooks, B. 1981. *Ain't I a woman?* Boston, Mass.: South End Press.

Humphrey, J. 1985. Gender, pay and skill: manual workers in Brazilian industry. In Afshar (ed.), 214–31.

Joekes, S. 1985. Working for lipstick? Male and female labour in the clothing industry in Morocco. See Afshar (ed.), 183–213.

Kvande, E. & B. Rasmussen 1992. *Fra kvinner og ledelse til kjønn og organisasjoner. Kvinneperspektiv på LOS-forskningen* (From women and leadership to gender and organizations. A woman's perspective). Trondheim: Department of Sociology and Political Sciences, University of Trondheim.

Kvinnejournalen (Women's Journal) 1986. **2**, 18–23.

Likestillingsrådet 1996. *Mini-fakta om likestilling (Mini-facts on equal opportunity).* Oslo: Likestillingsrådet.

Marx, K. 1983. *Kapitalen.* Første bok. Del 3. (*Das Kapital,* Bk 1, Pt 3). Norwegian edn. Oslo: Oktober.

Palmer, M. 1986. Vi tøffe damer i kvinnfolkjobber. (Us tough women in women's work.) In *Kvinnekamp: Vi eier morgendagen!* (The struggle for women's rights: Tomorrow is ours!), K. Ericsson (ed.), 69–79. Oslo: Oktober.

Rose, S., R. Lewontin, L.J. Kamin 1990. *Not in our genes.* London: Penguin.

Singer, P. & D. Wells 1984. *The reproductive revolution: new ways of making babies.* Oxford: Oxford University Press.

Skinhøj, K.T. 1989. Kan "mandefagsstrategien" nedbryde arbejdsmarkedets kønsopdeling? (Can male-strategy dismantle sexual division in the employment market?). See Dahlerup (ed.), 145–62.

Stortingsmelding nr. 70(1991–92): Likestillingspolitikk for 90-åra. (Parliamentary Report no. 70 (1991–2): Equal rights politics for the 1990s)

Thompson, P. 1983. *The nature of work. An introduction to debates on the labour process.* London: Macmillan.

Thompson, P. & D. McHugh 1990. *Work organisations. A critical introduction.* Basingstoke: Macmillan Educational.

Waring. M. 1988. *If women counted.* London: Macmillan.

Widerberg, K. 1992. Kjønn og sex – problematiske selfølgeligheter (Gender and sex – problematic and self-evident). See Brantsæter & Widerberg (eds), 120–9.

Wikander, U. 1989. Genusarbetsdelning: Könssegregering i arbetslivet under hundra år. Fallet Gustavsberg (The genderized division of labour: sexual segregation in work-life over the last hundred years. The Gustavsberg case). See Dahlerup (ed.), 163–77. Copenhagen: Nordisk Ministerråd.

CHAPTER ELEVEN

Attraction and love at work

Elina Haavio-Mannila*

The spectrum of erotic and sexual relations in the workplace

Women and men are bound to each other through erotic attraction, work relations, political relations, as students, parents, confidants, through sport, and in artistic creation. Nevertheless, the feminist theoretical analysis of activities involving women and men as partners in discord and harmony is incomplete (Jónasdóttir 1991, 1994). Jónasdóttir imagines that the specific realities of sexual life (eroticism) entail a particular strength/power development in human beings and a transference of power between people that has great significance for how we behave to each other and how we organize our societies.

The neglect of research in cross-gender relations outside the family derives from the belief held by many classical sociologists, e.g., Max Weber and Talcott Parsons, who saw work and family as totally separate life spheres: work was considered as emotionally neutral, family as an emotional area. Nevertheless, it is difficult to exclude one's emotions while at work. This was shown, for example, by the sociologist George C. Homans (1951) who studied informal interaction and sentiments of liking in the workplace.

Homans paid attention neither to gender nor cross-gender relations in the workplace. Erotic and sexual attraction was first acknowledged as part of the sociology and psychology of the workplace in the 1970s and 1980s (Quinn 1977, MacKinnon 1979, Crull 1982, Collins 1983, Tangri et al. 1982, Hearn & Parkin 1995, Hearn et al. 1989, Haavio-Mannila et al. 1984, Haavio-Mannila 1988, Gruber 1990, Brantsaeter & Widerberg 1992, Arcel 1992, Kauppinen-Toropainen & Gruber 1993). As more and more women have entered the labour force, it has become evident that the workplace is a setting

* The author would like to thank Professor J.P. Roos at the Department of Social Policy, University of Helsinki, for helpful comments and useful references.

where men and women often share the same work, interact informally and have feelings of attraction, or aversion, towards each other. According to Quinn (1977), organizational environments provide potential for romantic relationships, even though this is not prescribed by bureaucratic rules. An organization maintains routine interaction over time and allows people to discover attractive aspects of one other.

Erotically and sexually charged interaction ranges from voluntary, reciprocated love and sex relations to involuntary, non-symmetrical sexual attention. *Being attracted to or falling in love with* a co-worker or someone met at work is common at least in the Nordic countries, the USA and the former Soviet Union where studies on their incidence and prevalence have been conducted: almost every second respondent to different surveys has during their lifetime fallen in love with a co-worker or someone else met at work (Haavio-Mannila 1989, 1992, 1993, Haavio-Mannila et al. 1984, 1988).

I have earlier analyzed the love process using Reiss's *wheel theory of love* (1976:93–7) as a conceptual tool. He distinguishes four steps in the development of love: rapport, self-revelation, mutual dependency and personality need fulfilment. These aspects of love development can be observed in cross-gender work relations. In Finland in 1981, 28 per cent of employed men and 26 per cent of women had close friends among opposite sex co-workers (rapport), 13 per cent of men and 11 per cent of women discussed personal problems with them (self-revelation), 17 per cent of men and 13 per cent of women had lunch with them (mutual dependency), and 8 per cent of men and 16 per cent of women had received help with personal problems from opposite sex co-workers (personality need fulfilment). Nevertheless, only 4 per cent were in love with a co-worker at the time of the interview. But during their entire lifetime, as many as 36 per cent of employed urban men (N=281) and 38 per cent of women (N=296) had fallen in love with a co-worker or someone else met at work (Haavio-Mannila et al. 1984:27,159). In 1992, in a representative sample of Finns aged 18 to 74 (including those who had never worked), lifetime workplace romances were reported by 46 per cent of men (N=1 104) and 39 per cent of women (N=1 145) (Kontula & Haavio-Mannila 1995). In 1996, in St Petersburg in Russia where a representative sample of people aged 18 to 74 were questioned, 47 per cent of men (N=791) and 50 per cent of women (N=1 121) admitted that during their lifetime they had been infatuated or fallen in love with a co-worker or someone whom they had met at work (Gronow et al. 1997).

Societies and work organizations have developed structural and cultural barriers against intimate relations at work, partly because they are seen as a threat to the family, partly because they may interfere with the formal communication in the work organization. For example, cross-gender interaction at work is heavily restricted by the sexual segregation of occupations and work tasks, and by the physical separation of men and women into different places of work. Cultural norms and taboos as well as the informal social control exercised by co-workers and superiors often limit cross-gender interaction at work. Feminists have raised questions about the exploitative nature of cross-gender contacts in work settings.

Another type of cross-gender interaction at work, *sexual harassment,* was "discovered" in the United States in the mid-1970s. According to Gutek (1992), this "discovery" was somewhat counter-intuitive, since some women were believed to benefit from practising seductive and sexual behaviours at work, gaining unfair advantage and acquiring perks and privileges through their flirtatious behaviour. MacKinnon (1979) contended that sexual harassment was primarily a problem for women, that it rarely happened to men, and therefore that it should be viewed as a form of sex discrimination. Nevertheless, men are also objects of uninvited and unwanted sexual harassment at work (Tangri et al. 1982, Högbacka et al. 1987). Men more often than women consider work-related incidents of sexual activity or approach, which they have not themselves initiated, as positive whereas women consider them offensive (Kontula & Haavio-Mannila 1995).

Romances and sexual harassment are not the only types of erotic and sexual interaction at work. *Worker flirting* was studied in Poland by Konecki (1990). His observations revealed the frequent occurrence of para-sexual interaction between men and women workers, most frequently in the production units, but also among clerks in certain Polish factories. Its non-verbal aspect consisted of the pinching of women workers by men, mutual embracing between men and women, flirtatious self-exposure by women, the simulation of sexual behaviour or of sexual intercourse in close contacts, and the undressing of women by men, with the women's passive or active consent. Worker flirting also included a verbal element. Both men and women were initiators of flirting, irrespective of their age and the age differences between sexes. The author concludes that relations within this ritual interaction were, for the most part, symmetrical. There were three social rules followed by workers who were flirting: (a) the rule of observability by others – workers flirting away from the group in dyads were negatively sanctioned by their co-workers; (b) the rule that flirting cannot continue outside the workplace – if it does, it is sharply branded with humorous comment and malicious gossip; and (c) worker flirting has its limits – it does not lead to sexual consummation.

In North America and Europe people are more sensitive when interpreting certain behaviour as sexual harassment than in Eastern Europe. In the Nordic countries, the Protestant ethic and the feminist movement have contributed to a relative erotic peace in the workplace, and romantic attachments between co-workers are permissible. In the Estonian and Russian workplace there is more eroticization of male–female friendships; flirtation and sexual harassment are more common among co-workers, but there are fewer romances (Haavio-Mannila 1992).

Gender composition of the workplace is the most important structural factor explaining cross-gender interaction at work (Kanter 1977a, 1977b, Gruber & Bjorn 1982, Högbacka et al. 1987, Haavio-Mannila et al. 1988, Gutek et al. 1990). Demographic and other social characteristics such as gender, age, marital status, education, occupation and income have all been found to have an impact on love and sexual harassment at work (e.g., US Merit Systems Protection Board 1981, Holm-Löfgren 1980, Tangri et al. 1982, Collins 1983, Gutek 1985, Gutek et al. 1990, Högbacka et al. 1987, Haavio-Mannila 1988, 1992, 1993a, Gruber 1990, Kauppinen-Toropainen & Gruber 1993, Varsa 1993). Even lifestyle, for example, the use of alcohol and number of sexual partners are factors that have an effect on cross-gender relations at work (Haavio-Mannila 1988, Kontula & Haavio-Mannila 1993).

Study design and data

Most of the previous research on sex at work has either been based on small or unrepresentative samples or has included only a few questions related to different types of sexuality in the workplace (cf. Hearn & Parkin 1987, Quinn et al. 1984, 1990, Hagman 1988). Here, incidence, antecedents and consequences of becoming attracted or falling in love at work will be studied on the basis of large surveys conducted in four northern European capitals and in Finland.

Attraction at work will be analyzed from a gender perspective. Feminist studies have shown the greater vulnerability of women in the sexual inter-action at work. Marxist-feminist theory states that women are exploited as sexual objects by men who have power over their working conditions (Hagman 1987, Varsa 1993). According to Jónasdóttir, men exploit women's loving capacities. It is the man who decides the prerequisites or conditions for living together. Here, she refers not only to intimate couple relationships in a marriage or cohabitation, but also to a similar unequal exchange of care and pleasure which takes place between men and women at work, in politics, etc., viz individuals and groups. Men not only have the right to women's love, care and devotion, but also the right to give vent to their need for women and the freedom to take for themselves. Women, on the other hand, have the right freely to give of themselves, but a very limited legitimate freedom to take for themselves (Jónasdóttir 1991:35,36).

In this chapter, in addition to studying gender differences, incidences of falling in love at work will be related to other structural and individual factors. Finally, consequences of workplace infatuations will be studied in the light of two typologies constructed on the basis of (a) the awareness of and reaction to the feelings of the lover by the love object; and (b) the sexual consummation of the relationship and its institutionalization as a marriage or cohabitation.

The study is based on three data sets. (a) Postal surveys of representative samples of trade union members in Copenhagen, Helsinki and Stockholm, enhanced by personal interviews in Helsinki, and questionnaires filled in by employees in Tallinn in selected places of work between 1986 and 1988. Four occupational groups, engineers, teachers, nurses and industrial workers were studied. The number of respondents was 1 241. (b) Personal interviews (where the intimate questions were filled in by the respondents themselves) of a representative sample of Finns aged 18 to 74 conducted in 1992. The number of respondents was 2 250 and the response rate 76 per cent. Of the respondents, 1 694 had been working during the past two years and were included in this study. (c) Personal interviews of people belonging to a representative population sample aged 18 to 74 registered for voting in St Petersburg, Russia, conducted in spring 1996. The total number of interviewees was 2 081; 1 912 had work-life experience. In this survey, too, the respondents themselves filled in the answers to the questions on workplace romances.

Results

Falling in love at work

In Copenhagen, Stockholm, Helsinki and Tallinn, 12 per cent of the engineers, teachers, nurses, and industrial workers studied were, on average, in love with a co-worker at the time of the survey, 43 per cent had been in love earlier, and 45 per cent had never experienced any workplace attraction. Love at work was most common in those occupational groups in which people had daily contact with the opposite sex, i.e., among female engineers and male nurses and teachers. The proportion of persons ever having been attracted to a co-worker was 58 per cent for men and 52 per cent for women. Workplace attractions were reported more often in Stockholm and Helsinki than in Copenhagen and Tallinn.

In Finland in 1992, 48 per cent of men currently at work and 44 per cent of corresponding women had during their lifetime "been attracted to or fallen in love with a co-worker or a person met at work". Only 4 per cent of both genders were attracted to or in love at the time of the interview. The incidence of workplace love affairs is thus quite high, but their duration is short.

The social background of people falling in love at work is studied by using as independent variables gender composition of the workplace, age, education, self-evaluated sexual assertiveness (whether one considers oneself sexually active, adept and attractive), having at present a steady sexual relationship, and the lifetime number of sexual partners. According to Multiple Classification Analyses (MCA), these six variables explain 11 per cent of the variation of experiences of love at work for men and 8 per cent for women. For men the following four variables were statistically significant determinants of love at work: sharing the same work tasks with women, high level of education, many lifetime sexual partners, and sexual assertiveness. Age and having a steady sexual partner did not explain men's infatuations at work.

For women, three of the significant variables connected with love at work were the same as for men: sharing the same work tasks with men, high level of education, and many sexual partners. In addition, not having a steady sexual partner at present increased the likelihood of women becoming infatuated at work. Age and sexual assertiveness were not related to the incidence of women's falling in love at work when the influence of the other variables was controlled.

Workplace romances are sometimes frowned upon as a threat to marriage. In order to find out to what extent these relations take place simultaneously or parallel to family relations, the Finnish sex survey inquired if people had "been attracted or fallen in love at work while being married or cohabiting with someone else". Of the people ever having fallen in love at work, 48 per cent of men and 47 per cent of women said that they had feelings of love towards a co-worker or someone else met at work while married or cohabiting with someone else, while 34 per cent of men and 45 per cent of women said that they had not fallen in love at work while married or living with someone else. The rest of the interviewees had never been married or cohabited.

Workplace romances are thus often conducted in parallel to permanent marital or cohabitation relationships. One may wonder if they endanger the participants' peace of mind or marital relationship, yet neither seems to be the case. According to a Finnish study, men and women enjoying simultaneous "close and important" relationships with their spouse and an opposite-sex co-worker were happier in their daily life than were people having a close relationship with the spouse only, with an opposite sex co-worker only, or with neither. People with two parallel opposite-gender relationships also were happier than non-married people. Having two close relationships was also associated with high self-esteem, particularly among women. In regard to marital cohesion, it was found that those respondents who had a fairly (not very) close relationship with their best cross-gender co-worker were most happy in their marriage (Haavio-Mannila 1988:151,152,207). This indicates that it is possible to maintain simultaneous close relations with the spouse and an opposite gender co-worker. Only a very close relationship with an opposite-gender co-worker endangers marriage; it may also be a symptom of a problematic marital relationship.

Consequences of love at work

Consequences of love at work are mostly positive but there are also some negative ones: distress, jealousy and envy are encountered. However, the

Table 11.1   Consequences of love at work in Finland in 1992 and in St Petersburg in 1996, by gender (%)

	Men		Women	
Consequences	Finland	St Petersburg	Finland	St Petersburg
Pleasant friendship	86	66	83	66
Happiness and joy	67	27	76	36
Sexual relationship	35	45	39	36
Marriage or moving in together	9	14	15	11
Heartache and distress/sorrow	16	30	25	45
Jealousy	16	20	14	24
Envy and resentment at work	9	7	11	9
N	(417)	(312)	(359)	(481)

positive consequences were much more common than the negative ones (Tables 11.1 & 11.2).

Women more often than men reported happiness and joy and marriage as a consequence of their last romance at work. But women also told of more heartache and distress than did men. Women thus frequently experience both positive and negative emotions in connection with erotic involvements at work. Men and women equally often said that their attraction was followed by a pleasant friendship, jealousy, envy and resentment at work. In Finland there was no gender difference in reports of a sexual relationship as a consequence of falling in love at work whereas in St Petersburg men more often than women told of that type of consequence.

It is worth noting that 76 per cent of Finnish women and 67 per cent of men, but only 36 per cent of Russian women and 27 per cent of men, derive joy from workplace romances. In Finland 25 per cent of women (16 per cent of men) derive distress, in St Petersburg 45 per cent (of men, 30 per cent). The positive consequences outweigh the negative ones in Finland, but this is not as clearly the case in St Petersburg. The official ideology in the communist era condemned sexual relations at work and this negative perspective on love in the workplace may continue by being reflected in the answers given by the Russian respondents.

In feminist discussions, the positive aspects of erotic and sexual interaction in the workplace have been neglected. For women, male friends at work are a resource as men still occupy the higher positions in paid work. If women avoid getting involved with male co-workers in order to escape sexual harassment or disappointment in love, the gender groups will stay separate. This is not advantageous for women's careers nor for their enjoyment of work. However, in my opinion it is unnecessary for women to use sexuality as a means of getting ahead in the work organization. Nor is that

Table 11.2   Consequences of love at work in four occupational groups
(engineers, teachers, nurses, and workers) in Copenhagen, Stockholm,
Helsinki, and Tallinn in 1988, by gender (%)

Consequences	Men	Women	Average
Positive			
Joy and stimulation	87	92	89
A pleasant friendship	83	86	85
Happiness and pleasure	72	73	73
A sexual relationship	56	54	55
Improved work performance	40	55	47
We got married	18	14	16
Negative			
Heartache and suffering	23	28	25
Jealousy	12	14	13
Problems in my friend's marriage	13	14	13
Problems in my marriage	10	14	12
Mental health problems	8	14	11
Envy and resentment at work	9	12	11
She/he got divorced	5	8	6
I got a divorce	3	6	4
Improved status at work	3	4	3
(N)	(300)	(247)	(547)

traditional in northern Europe. Only 3 or 4 per cent of male and female
engineers, teachers, nurses, and industrial workers in Copenhagen, Helsinki, Stockholm and Tallinn have improved their status at work through a
workplace romance (Table 11.2). It would be interesting to assemble data
in respect of these norms and practices for Eastern Europe.

In the four occupational groups studied in the four Nordic capitals, gender differences in reported consequences of workplace affairs are small.
Women more often than men had experienced improved work performance, mental health problems, and divorce as consequences of love at work.
Table 11.2 confirms the Finnish results shown in Table 11.1: women both
gain and lose more in workplace relationships than do men.

Unrequited, hidden and reciprocal love

Consequences of workplace romances vary according to the type of love
relationship. For the engineers, teachers, nurses and industrial workers in
Copenhagen, Stockholm and Tallinn, love at work could be classified into
three types: (a) *one-sided* or *unrequited* love, indicating that the loved one

ELINA HAAVIO-MANNILA

Table 11.3 Consequences of love at work in four occupational groups (engineers, teachers, nurses, and service workers) in Copenhagen, Stockholm, and Tallinn in 1988, by openness to romance and gender (M = men, W = women) (%)

Consequences	Gender	Rejected love	Hidden love	Reciprocal love
			Openness to romance	
Positive				
Joy and stimulation	M	69	77	95
	W	(83)	85	93
Pleasant friendship	M	50	60	89
	W	(83)	78	85
Happiness and pleasure	M	44	50	73
	W	(50)	49	73
Sexual relationship	M	6	5	76
	W	(–)	7	71
Improved work	M	39	47	37
performance	W	(83)	56	49
Negative				
Heartache and suffering	M	37	12	22
	W	(33)	7	29
Mental health problems	M	6	5	10
	W	(–)	10	19
Jealousy	M	12	5	11
	W	(17)	2	13
Envy and resentment	M	–	–	11
at work	W	(17)	5	12
(N)	M	(16)	(40)	(175)
	W	(6)	(41)	(140)

did not respond to the feelings of the lover; (b) *hidden* love, meaning that the object of attachment was not aware of the feelings of attraction or love entertained by the respondent; and (c) *reciprocal* love, which includes a positive response by the love object to the feelings of the lover.

Unrequited love was reported by 7 per cent of respondents, while 19 per cent had not revealed their feelings towards the object of attraction. Men were more often rejected as lovers (10 per cent) than women (3 per cent), whereas women hid their feelings more (23 per cent) than did men (18 per cent).

The consequences of unrequited love were the most disastrous (Table 11.3). Unrequited lovers most often reported heartache and suffering. They least often found joy and stimulation, friendship, happiness and pleasure, and a sexual relationship as a result of love at work. Nevertheless, none of them reported mental health problems.

206

Reciprocated love was found to be most rewarding. It brought joy and stimulation, happiness and pleasure, friendship, sex and, for women, it improved their work performance. Hidden love was in most cases better than rejected love, but not as good as symmetrical love.

Hidden love conveyed more positive consequences than unrequited and reciprocated love in one respect: it improved the work performance of both sexes. When a person does not dare openly reveal his or her affections to their object, he or she can engage in work with heightened intensity. This may be a compensatory mechanism from the point of view of the individual, but it may benefit one's career and the employer gets more work done.

Negative consequences of workplace affairs include heartache and suffering, mental health problems, jealousy, and envy and resentment at work which were more common in reciprocated love affairs than in hidden ones; they were almost as common as in one-sided affairs. Reciprocated love is more engaging and visible than secret fancying. Moreover, women became more mentally perturbed by both hidden and reciprocated love affairs than did men.

Sexual and non-sexual relationships

Consequences of workplace attractions will be analyzed next on the basis of whether they lead to sexual intercourse and marriage or cohabitation. Three types of attraction will be compared: (a) *getting married or moving in together*; (b) *having sex without marriage or cohabitation ensuing*; and (c) *having a non-sexual (Platonic) relationship.*

Getting married to or having sex with a co-worker brought more joy, friendship and happiness than having a non-sexual Platonic relationship (Table 11.4). Joy and friendship were achieved in sexual relations even without marriage. Happiness derived most often from marriage. For women, improved work performance and status at work were associated with marriage to a co-worker.

Women derived joy, friendship and happiness from non-sexual erotic relations slightly more than did men. This may be related to the traditional idealization of women's chastity. Women may also have non-sexual aspirations in their affective contacts with men since women gain from interaction with men because men still occupy positions of power in the workplace.

The negative consequences of love at work were most pronounced for people having sex with a co-worker without getting married. This applies to heartache and distress, mental health problems, jealousy, and problems in their own marriage. Getting married leads to envy at work. Problems in the co-worker's marriage were equally common in marital and non-marital sexual relationships. Non-sexual relations brought relatively few problems, except heartache and suffering.

Table 11.4   Consequences of work romance in four occupational groups (engineers, teachers, nurses, and service workers) in Helsinki, Stockholm and Copenhagen in 1988, by type of relationship and gender (M = men, W = women) (%)

| Consequences | Gender | Type of relationship | | | Significance[1] |
		Marriage	Sex	No sex	
Positive					
Joy and stimulation	M	95	96	75	Type***
	W	96	96	86	
Pleasant friendship	M	95	91	83	Type***
	W	100	81	86	
Happiness and pleasure	M	92	80	52	Type***
	W	96	76	59	
Improved work performance	M	34	36	36	Gender*
	W	68	41	48	
Improved status at work	M	–	3	3	Interaction***
	W	20	–	4	
Negative					
Heartache and suffering	M	5	31	18	Type***
	W	14	31	19	
Mental health problems	M	5	4	3	Type** and
	W	–	17	1	interaction**
Jealousy	M	8	10	7	Type*
	W	14	18	5	
Envy and resentment at work	M	13	9	3	Type***
	W	18	11	2	
Problems in my marriage	M	8	11	9	Type**
	W	9	22	4	
Problems in my friend's marriage	M	15	22	5	Type***
	W	20	18	5	
I got a divorce	M	11	2	–	Type***
	W	14	9	1	
She/he got divorced	M	11	7	–	Type***
	W	14	10	1	
(N)	M	(40)	(91)	(105)	
	W	(24)	(82)	(85)	

[1] Statistically significant differences between types of relationship (type: marriage, sex, and no sex) and genders (men and women).
Note: Asterisks indicate level of significance: 1 asterisk = p < 0.05; 2 asterisks = p < 0.01; 3 asterisks = p < 0.001.

Table 11.5   Consequences of last workplace romance in Finland in 1992, by type of relationship and gender (M = men, W = women) (%)

Consequences	Gender	Type of relationship			Significance[1]
		Marriage	Sex	No sex	
Pleasant friendship	M	85	91	81	ns
	W	84	81	83	
Happiness and joy	M	92	81	55	Type*** and
	W	93	91	67	gender***
Heartache and distress	M	19	31	9	Type*** and
	W	33	48	14	gender***
Jealousy	M	17	24	8	Type***
	W	32	28	8	
Envy and resentment at work	M	12	16	6	Type*
	W	12	12	11	
(N)	M	(59)	(140)	(104)	
	W	(132)	(87)	(277)	

[1] See Table 11.4, p. 208.
Note: See Table 11.4, p. 208.

In the Finnish survey, only five consequences of workplace affairs were examined (Table 11.5). The relationships between the type of romance and their consequences resemble those found in the surveys conducted in the Nordic capitals. A pleasant friendship was as likely to develop irrespective of whether the romance included sex or led to marriage. Happiness and joy increased when the relationship progressed from a non-sexual to a sexual one, and finally to marriage. Sexual relations which did not lead to marriage brought most heartache and distress.

Gender differences in happiness and joy were relatively large in non-sexual and non-marital sexual relationships. Women found the factor of attraction at work as such, not as a means of finding a spouse, more appealing than did men. The negative consequences of non-marital sexual relationships were more common among women than among men. While 48 per cent of the women reported heartache and distress as consequences of such relationships, only 31 per cent of the men did so. One third of the women but only every fifth man who married a co-worker reported heartache and distress as a consequence of their work romance. This is related to the jealousy encountered by 32 per cent of the women (17 per cent of men) married to a co-worker.

Envy and resentment at work accompanied men's marital and other sexual relationships with co-workers more often (12–16 per cent) than their non-sexual affairs (6 per cent). The type of relationship did not affect envy in the workplace as perceived by women.

Summary and discussion

Love at work is symmetrical with respect to gender: men and women as often report having been attracted to or having fallen in love with a co-worker or someone else met at work. Almost every second person in selected occupational groups in Northern and Eastern European capitals and in the whole working population of Finland had experienced a workplace romance during his or her lifetime. Most of these infatuations developed into pleasant friendships. They brought more happiness and joy than heartache, jealousy, or mental health problems. However, women more often than men reported both positive and negative consequences of workplace attractions. Love at work seems to be emotionally more dramatic for women than for men. This supports Jónasdóttir's (1991:36) assumption that men can continually appropriate significantly more of women's life force and capacity than they themselves give back to women, even though women enjoy men's company.

The results can also be tied to *feminist policies* concerning cross-gender relations at work. In the United States these policies are strongly directed against sexual harassment, a development which is criticized by the American "anti-feminist feminist" Camilla Paglia:

> The sexual revolution of my Sixties generation broke the ancient codes of decorum that protected respectable ladies from profanation by foul language. We demanded an end to the double standard. What troubles me about the "hostile workplace" category of sexual harassment policy is that women are being returned to their old status of delicate flowers who must be protected from assault by male lechers. It is anti-feminist to ask for special treatment for women (Paglia 1992:47).

According to Paglia, we should teach general ethics to both men and women, but sexual relationships themselves must not be policed. Sex, just as city streets, would be risk-free only in a totalitarian regime, she writes (ibid.:vii–viii). "It's up to the woman to give clear signals of what her wishes are" (ibid.:64). But one wonders what happens if these clear signals are not respected or are misinterpreted.

Another US feminist, Naomi Wolfe (1993) also criticizes the feminist movement for its intolerance and unnecessary hatred of men. She demands a more positive perspective and believes that the position of women has greatly improved. When discussing the recent backlash against women she points out that in frustration at moving ahead so slowly and even sliding back, women tend to misunderstand how grave a threat to men's real power their claims pose. The backlash is an eminently rational, if intolerable, reaction to a massive and real threat.

We are not simply experiencing a "war against women" in which women are unthreatening victims. We are in the midst of a *civil war over gender* [my italics], in which there is not one side waging battle but two, unevenly matched though they may be. It is also a war against men (Wolfe 1993:14).

It is, in my opinion, fairly clear that part of the civil war over gender, when it manifests itself as sexual harassment, has to be controlled in the workplace by official policies and educational programmes. But should one intervene in the more or less symmetrical and voluntary romances between co-workers? The Swedish sociologist Rita Liljeström has criticized the promiscuous sexual behaviour in the Swedish workplace at the end of the 1970s. She saw that the free-floating sexuality lead to *erotic war* (Liljeström 1981:276). In the erotic war sexual stimulation is present everywhere. The opposite of erotic war is *erotic peace* which, according to Liljeström, should prevail in work settings. This is my opinion, too.

Fear of unbridled sexuality leading to disruption of official channels of communication in the work organization has been one reason why employers in the USA have tried to discourage love between managers (Collins 1983). But it is difficult to *control human emotions.*

Both organisations and sexuality are patterns of feelings and emotions; both rest on emotional presence and involvement to survive. Though the instrumentality of organisations may be contrasted with the expressiveness of sexuality, the reality is that organisations are places of emotion, ranging from anger to joy to sorrow, from love to hate, with characteristic emotional climates and cultures . . . [The] patterning of affect is perhaps illustrated most clearly in the possibility of sexual attraction, liaison and fantasy between members of organisations (Hearn & Parkin 1987:135–6).

The present study shows that there is plenty of emotional activity in work organizations, as was proposed by Hearn & Parkin.

Falling in love at work means *a change in the work situation* of the person in love. "Given that the routines of life are comfortable and important to us, a break with ordinary routines – such as occurs when we fall in love with a new partner – could be a problem. Surely, it is a pleasant experience to be in love and it heightens self-esteem" (Hendrick & Hendrick 1988). Being infatuated means that we have to restructure our lives, accommodate ourselves to the lifestyle of someone else, adopt new routines, and bring our new partner into our own daily pattern of activities (Duck 1992:44). In the work setting it may not be appropriate to get caught up in the general intensity of feeling that leaves other concerns in the background such as is characteristic of "limerence" (intensive infatuation) (Tennov 1989:24).

The strong emotional involvement of people in love enhances work performance. In northern European capitals 55 per cent of women and 40 per cent of men in four occupational groups reported improved work performance as a consequence of love at work. As many as 85 per cent of erotic relationships developed into pleasant friendships. When love is going well, people report *feeling good both in mind and in body* (Hendrick & Hendrick 1988). The results of our surveys show that a very large majority of the north Europeans and North Americans who fell in love at work felt positive about the experience.

Infatuation, particularly limerence (cf. Tennov 1989) does not last for ever. Those whose partners have broken off with them typically report sleep disturbance, headaches and loss of emotional control. Those who caused the break-up suffered less, except that females reported stomach upsets (Duck 1992:45). These *health problems* resemble the heartache and suffering which was reported by 20–25 per cent of respondents who fell in love at work. Fortunately, mental health problems were reported by only a few.

There are also negative emotions experienced as a consequence of loving relationships, for instance *jealousy*. They affect our self-esteem or our sense of competence in social interactions or as partners (Bringle 1991). People attempt to suppress and control jealousy, partly because it may be socially frowned upon, partly because they may feel that it reveals too much of a dependency on the relationship, and partly because it creates an unpleasant degree of restrictive possessiveness with respect to the partner (Duck 1992:50). It is probable that a considerable degree of control of jealousy takes place in the workplace as it is not considered proper to be dependent or possessive of one's co-workers.

Jealousy as well as *envy* may destroy even same-gender co-worker relations. According to Bringle (1991), one is jealous of what is one's own, but envious of that which is other people's. Thus one is jealous – or possessive – of one's own partner, but envious of – or covetous of – someone else's. Even though most workplace attractions are symmetrical, there are also unrequited lovers and hidden feelings of love. It may be confusing to unburden oneself to co-workers who have similar feelings toward the same love object. However, hidden feelings of jealousy and envy are not common consequences of workplace romances: jealousy was reported by 15 per cent, envy and resentment at work by 10 per cent of our respondents.

The *negative attitude toward heterosexual love and sex* among some feminists irritates Naomi Wolfe (1993). She criticizes Adrienne Rich for provoking anti-sexual attitudes among women.

> While Adrienne Rich's main theory – that we can't know if our sexuality is chosen until we account for everything coercing us toward it – is perfectly sound, her arguments trickled down into,

"All men get love from women only through coercion"; "All female closeness is lesbian"; and . . . "Straight women are deluding themselves." As the influence of these theories spread, it became noticeably *démodé* for a feminist to admit out loud to wanting intercourse (Wolfe 1993:134).

According to Wolfe, "victim-feminist anxiety over robust female heterosexuality has led to a situation in which there is an elaborate vocabulary with which to describe sexual harm done by men, but almost no vocabulary in which a woman can celebrate sex with men" (ibid.:199). In her mind, there has to be room "for a radical heterosexuality, an eros between men and women that does not diminish female power, but affirms it" (ibid.:201). This is an empirical question which can be studied.

The results of my study confirm Wolfe's statements about the positive side of sexuality in interpersonal relations. Workplace romances including those leading to sexual intercourse brought happiness and joy to women more than to men and more than non-sexual relations, even though they also had more negative consequences. Sexual relations are thus not as threatening for women as they were earlier, before adequate contraception was available. This conclusion is supported by the fact that, in Finland, women's satisfaction with sexual intercourse significantly increased from 1971 to 1992 (Kontula & Haavio-Mannila 1995).

In accordance with feminist arguments, sexual relations also have more negative consequences for women than for men. The situation for women is ambivalent. Which is better: to gain a great deal of pleasure but suffer to some extent as a result of a sexual relationship or to have less fun and less distress by keeping the relationship non-sexual?

Naomi Wolfe asks us to be kinder to ourselves. "Let's be less afraid of our animal nature – even when it leads those of us who are heterosexual to feel the greater knowledge of self in the arms of a man" (Wolfe 1993:202). It is uncertain to what extent her advice suits people falling in love at work. Informal norms in the Nordic countries leave the decision-making and handling of work romances to the lovers. Our interviews show that a great majority of people are of the opinion that outsiders should not interfere (Haavio-Mannila 1992).

A distinction made by Wolfe helps analyze attraction and love at work. She separates two traditions of feminism: *power feminism* and *victim feminism*.

> Over the last twenty years, the old belief in a tolerant assertiveness, a claim to human participation and human rights – power feminism – was embattled by the rise of a set of beliefs that cast women as beleaguered, fragile, intuitive angels: victim feminism . . . This [victim] feminism has slowed women's progress, impeded their

self-knowledge, and been responsible for most of the inconsistent, negative, even chauvinistic spots of regressive thinking that are alienating many women and men (Wolfe 1993:147).

In the field of sexuality, victim feminism is anti-sexual whereas power feminism believes that what every woman does with her body and in her bed is her own business (ibid.:148–50). Power feminism may (or may not) be another name for "liberal feminism" which has prevailed in the Nordic countries. A majority of Nordic women and men believe that attraction, love and sex at work is up to the lovers, not the business of other people. On the basis of the opinions and experiences of the working people in the Nordic countries it is possible to conclude that there is a risk that feminists may miss the positive aspects of love and sexuality.

References

Arcel, L.T. 1992. *Seksuel chikane – Ufrivillig sex på arbejdspladsen. Hvad kan gore ved det?* (Sexual harassment). Copenhagen: Hans Reitzel.

Brantsaeter, M.C. & K. Widerberg 1992. *Sex i arbeid(et) i Norge* (Sex at work in Norway). Oslo: Tiden Norsk.

Bringle, R.G. 1991. Psychosocial aspects of jealousy: a transactional model. In *The psychology of jealousy and envy*, P. Salovey (ed.). New York: Guildford.

Collins, E.G.C. 1983. Managers and lovers. *Harvard Business Review*, September–October.

Crull, P. 1982. Stress effects of sexual harassment on the job. *American Journal of Orthopsychiatry* **52**, 539–44.

Duck, S. 1992. *Human relationships*. London: Sage.

Gronow, J., E. Haavio-Mannila, M. Kivinen, M. Lonkila, A. Rotkirch 1997. Cultural inertia and social change in Russia. Distributions by gender and age group. University of Helsinki, Department of Sociology. Stencil.

Gruber, J.E. 1990. Methodological problems and policy implications in sexual harassment research. *Population Research and Policy Review* **9**, 235–54.

Gruber, J. & L. Bjorn 1982. Blue-collar blues: the sexual harassment of women autoworkers. *Work and Occupation* **9**, 271–98.

Gutek, B.A. 1985. *Sex and the workplace. The impact of sexual behavior and harassment on women, men, and organizations*. San Francisco: Jossey-Bass.

Gutek, B.A. 1992. Responses to sexual harassment. Stencil. Tucson: Department of Management and Policy, College of Business and Public Administration, University of Arizona.

Gutek, B.A., A.G. Cohen, A.M. Konrad 1990. Predicting social-sexual behavior at work: a contact hypothesis. *Academy of Management Journal* **33**, 560–77.

Haavio-Mannila, E. 1988. *Työpaikan rakkaussuhteet* (Love relations in the workplace). Helsinki: WSOY.

Haavio-Mannila, E. 1989. Formell aktivitet och informell interaktion mellan kvinnor och män på arbetsplatsen (Formal activity and informal interaction between men and women in the workplace). In *Kon sorterer – Konsopdeling på arbejdspladsen*, D. Dahlerup (ed.), 91–102. Copenhagen: Nordisk Ministerråd.

Haavio-Mannila, E. 1992. *Work, family and well-being in five North- and East-European capitals.* Helsinki: Academia Scientiarum Fennica, Series B, 255.

Haavio-Mannila, E. 1993a. *Women in the workplace in three types of societies.* Ann Arbor, Michigan: University of Michigan, Center for the Education of Women.

Haavio-Mannila, E. 1993b. Love and sexual attention in the workplace. Paper presented at the symposium Women, men and cross-gender interaction at work, Third European Congress of Psychology, 4–9 July, Tampere, Finland.

Haavio-Mannila, E., R. Jallinoja, H. Strandell 1984. *Perhe, työ ja tunteet (Family, work and emotions).* Juva: WSOY.

Haavio-Mannila, E., K. Kauppinen-Toropainen, I. Kandolin 1988. The effect of sex composition of the workplace on friendship, romance, and sex at work. In *Women and Work – An Annual Review* **3**, B.A. Gutek, A.H. Stromberg, L. Larwood (eds), 123–37. Newbury Park: Sage.

Hagman, N. 1987. *Sextrakasserier pa jobbet (Sexual harassment in the workplace).* Helsingborg: Schmidts.

Hearn, Jeff & W. Parkin 1995. *"Sex" at "work": the power and paradox of organisation sexuality.* Hemel Hempstead: Harvester Wheatsheaf/Prentice Hall. Rev. edn.

Hearn, J., D.L. Sheppard, P. Tancred-Sheriff, G. Burrell (eds) 1989. *The sexuality of organization.* London: Sage.

Hendrick, C. & S.S. Hendrick 1988. Lovers wear rose colored glasses. *Journal of Social and Personal Relationships* **5**, 161–83.

Högbacka, R., I. Kandolin, E. Haavio-Mannila, K. Kauppinen-Toropainen 1987. *Sexual harassment in the workplace: results of a survey of Finns.* Helsinki: Ministry of Social Affairs and Health, Finland, Equality Publications, Series E: Abstract 2.

Holm-Löfgren, B. 1980. *Ansvar, avund, arbetsglädje – En folklivsstudie av människan i kontorskulturen.* Responsibility, envy, joy of work. Stockholm: Askild & Kärnekull.

Homans, George C. 1951. *The human group.* New York: Routledge & Kegan Paul.

Jónasdóttir, A.G. 1991. *Love power and political interests.* Ørebro Studies 7. Kumla: University of Ørebro.

Jónasdóttir, A.G. 1994. *Why women are oppressed.* Philadelphia: Temple University Press.

Kanter, R.M. 1977a. *Men and women of the corporation,* New York: Basic Books.

Kanter, R.M. 1977b. Some effects of proportions in group life: skewed sex ratios and responses to token women. *American Journal of Sociology* **82**, 965–90.

Kauppinen-Toropainen, K., I. Kandolin, E. Haavio-Mannila 1988. Sex segregation of work in Finland and the quality of women's work. *Journal of Organizational Behavior* **9**, 15–27.

Kauppinen-Toropainen, K. & J.E. Gruber 1993. Antecedents and outcomes of woman-unfriendly experiences: a study of Scandinavian, former Soviet, and American women. *Psychology of Women Quarterly* **17**, 431–56.

Konecki, K. 1990. Dependency and worker flirting. In *Organizational symbolism*, B.A. Turner (ed.), 55–66. Berlin/New York: Walter de Gruyter.

Kontula, O. & E. Haavio-Mannila 1995. *Sexual pleasures – the enhancement of sex life in Finland, 1971–1992.* Aldershot: Dartmouth.

Lehto, A.-M. 1991. *Työelämän laatu ja tasa-arvo (Quality of work life and equality).* Helsinki: Statistics Finland, Research Reports 189.

Liljeström, R. 1981. Könsroller och sexualitet (Gender roles and sexuality). In *Prostitution.* Stockholm: Liber.

MacKinnon, C.A. 1979. *Sexual harassment of working women. A case of sex discrimination,* New Haven, Conn. Yale University Press.

Paglia, C. 1992. *Sex, art, and American culture.* New York: Vintage.

Quinn, R.E. 1977. Coping with cupid – the formation, impact, and management of romantic relationships in organizations. *Administrative Science Quarterly* **22**, 30–45.

Quinn, R.E. & P.L. Lees 1984. Attraction and harassment: dynamics of sexual politics in the workplace. *Organizational Dynamics* **13**, 35–46.

Quinn, R.E., S. Lobel, A. Warfield 1990. The dynamics of non-sexual love – an exploration of psychological intimacy in cross-gender work relationships. University of Michigan, School of Business Administration. Manuscript.

Reiss, I.L. 1976. *Family systems in America.* Hinsdale, Illinois: Dryden Press.

Tangri, S.S., M.R. Burt, L.B. Johnson 1982. Sexual harassment at work: three explanatory models. *Journal of Social Issues* **38**, 33–54.

Tennov, D. 1989. *Love and limerence – the experience of being in love* (4th edn; original 1979). Chelsea, Michigan: Scarborough House.

U.S. Merit Systems Protection Board 1981. *Sexual harassment in the federal workplace. Is it a problem?* Washington D.C.: U.S. Government Printing Office.

Varsa, H. 1993. *Sukupuolinen häirintä ja ahdistelu työelämässä.* (*Sexual harassment in working life*). Helsinki: Sosiaali- ja Terveysministeriö. Tasa-arvojulkaisuja, Sarja A: Tutkimuksia 1.

Wolfe, N. 1993. *Fire with fire – the female power and how it will change the 21st century.* London: Chatto & Windus.

CHAPTER TWELVE

The gender relation and professionalism in the postmodern world – social brotherhood and beyond

Karen Sjørup

Introduction

In this chapter it is argued that the concept of patriarchy is not a suitable one to describe power relations between the genders. The concept "brother-hood" far more precisely encapsulates the dynamics of the relationship between men, and between the genders in modern society. At the same time it is this very brotherhood which, in these postmodern times, is under-going great changes as women move into the traditionally male professions.

Brotherhoods and women's advances within these communities are analyzed here with regard to the power/gender relation in the medical area of gynaecology. The study is of a local Danish public hospital, with an equal number of male and female doctors. The analysis is inspired by Foucault's discourse analysis and by Max Weber's analysis of power and forms of rationality. In addition, Talcott Parsons' functionalist theory of systems will be drawn upon in order to examine the metaphoric in the expression of the legitimate power of the scientific discourse in the expression of "objective", positivist knowledge as power. This is expressed not least in postwar, strongly American influenced, Western "value free" science. This chapter works on the assumption that the objectifying power metaphoric of science affects other power discourses in modern society. However, power can also be changed by new expressions, and thus power relations and gender construction can change in some discourses without necessarily changing in others.

The analysis of the dynamics of power in the gender relationship takes its point of departure in that power, which is produced in modern scientific discourses and so by its agents and social institutions, is associated with these expressions of discourse. Therefore, I do not write about a single aspect of male power. Rather, I write about a series of representations of power which together make up the power game in which genders act and react in a series of broader generalizations. At the same time, the analysis of this production of power presupposes a tangible empirical analysis, as it is important in a discourse-analytical context that the production of knowledge-power is dynamic, since it occurs in leaps and bounds, from above and below, rather than in agreement with a broader frame of development.

Modern brotherhoods

What do these brotherhoods consist of, and how do they differ from a patriarchal organization? According to the American literary theorist Juliet Flower MacCannell (1991), modern society is, at the symbolic level, a post-Oedipal society, because the patriarchal power of premodern society was replaced by the value-laden triumvirate, "liberty, equality and brotherhood". Freedom thus conceived is freedom from parental power or, in MacCannell's understanding, a showdown with the parent as the bearer of culture. The brotherly super-ego replaces the father-ego's function as the social "it", so becoming the collective link between "you" and "I", a joint will, which, however, in our society is considered to be fundamentally genderless, precisely because the "it" expresses the shared ability to ignore differences. In this way the "it" invokes itself as the seat of truth. As knowledge in objectified form.

According to MacCannell, the "it" has become a new tyrant based on brotherhood and the absence of the parental relation. The brother has committed symbolic patricide against his tyrannical patriarchal father and now among his equals acts as the patriarchal metaphor in the modern artificial collective. He is, however, no Oedipus, his patricide is not based on love for his mother, but, on the contrary, on the demand for equality. The ego enjoys severing all family ties; his connection to the social is homosexual, because – according to MacCannell – the "it" is homosexual, rooted in infantile homosexuality. Thus, the instinct is directed neither towards the mother nor towards the father. Modern society at the most general level does not allow the sister function in the same way as patriarchal society did not allow the mother function.

Brotherhood is an egalitarian form of power based on the idea of the social citizen and on a rationalistic power of knowledge anchored in scientific discourse. With a point of departure in French family history dating from the middle of the eighteenth century, Jacques Donzelot has described how the scientific societies took over the control of children's and families' lives and health (Donzelot 1979). This was accomplished through what Foucault has termed the growth of the modern bio-political discourses, such as pedagogy, medicine, psychology. The term governmentality is used by Foucault to describe the governing of modern welfare states relying on the self-control of individuals and bio-political control.

The transition to a new form of power is implicit in the modern social brotherhood. Two primary forms of control (power) can be distinguished with reference to Weber. These are traditional power and legal power. *Traditional power*, to which Weber attributes patriarchy, is based on inherited power, power in the form of parenthood and inheritance and where the rules for its exercise are arbitrary and based on tradition. On the other hand *legal power* is based on law, profession and limited competence. It is exercised in agreement with formally correct limitations on itself (Weber 1971:91f).

In this way the regime of the modern brotherhood is expressed within the rules for the exercise of legal power. The discourse production which occurs in scientific regimes of the professions creates the point of departure for the exercise of "the law", for what is perceived as right and proper. Thus, it produces a truth which is legal and depersonalized, not one bound to a traditional relationship of control. On the contrary, it is produced relationally. In the same way social brotherhood encourages a new form of rationality.

Weber (1971) distinguishes between four forms of rationality, namely, the object rational: (1) the technical-economic and (2) the value rational rationality (the political conviction); and the non-object rational: (3) the affective-caring (emotions) and (4) the traditional rationality (custom, kinship). The technical-economic rationality is that sense of reason which is considered progressive and consistent with scientific principle in modern society and also with the construction of professionalism. While on the other hand affective-caring rationality represents the care and concern for the weak, which does not always allow itself to conform to the modern scientific order.

With a point of departure in Foucault's concept of bio-power, however, one has to talk of a certain mixing of the two rationalities. This is not least because of the scientific discourse of childcare, nursing and the work of housewives (Donzelot 1979), which is also part of the modern episteme, a fusion that becomes even more relevant in postmodern society with its erosion of the private/public dichotomy.

However, it is my point that the modern brotherhoods construct an egalitarian form of power based upon the notion of legal power and technical economic rationality. Therefore, they entail a rejection of the father, of power based on inherited knowledge and tradition, and the preference for scientific reason over emotions. In this way the generalized brother is the discourse-bearing young man, while older men and women are subsumed under the generalization.

The new professionals in Denmark today

The modus operandi of the modern scientific professions is an important key to understanding the production of power in modern society. At the same time, however, the basis for this production of power is undergoing radical change in the society I will characterize as postmodern. One of the most important changes is the increasing number of women in the professions.

In Denmark towards the close of the 1990s men and women basically perform an equal amount of paid work. This situation may be unique; it may be an expression of the fact that Danish society is to a high degree a culturally and ethnically homogeneous, enlightened modern society. Geographically, politically and historically it is placed halfway between the East and the West, between extreme capitalism to the West and defunct state socialism to the East. The difference between men and women's employment is quantitatively about the same in the younger generation today, where approximately 90 per cent of both men and women are employed. In contrast to the southern European countries, their rate of paid employment outside the home does not mean that Danish women do not have children. On the contrary, there is a baby-boom in Denmark in the late 1990s after a period between 1967 and 1983 which saw rapidly declining birth rates.[1]

The generation which is over 45 years of age in the late 1990s sought to solve the dilemma between family and paid work with part-time work. However, this model is far less common in the younger generation, where the number of part-time workers is falling rapidly.

Throughout the 1970s and 1980s there has been a dramatic increase in the provision of daycare facilities for children. In 1991 half of all children under the age of three and two thirds of children between the ages of three and six were cared for in public nurseries. In recent years a guarantee of care has been given designed to ensure that children who previously would have had to wait up to 18 months for a place may now start daycare just after the end of their mother's maternity leave. At the same time and in relation to the other EU countries (but not to the other Nordic countries) Denmark has far more advantageous terms governing paid maternity and parental leave. There are 26 weeks paid maternity leave – half of which may be shared with the father – and a year's paid parental leave per child. In the dominantly Marxist-inspired feminist research of the 1970s many researchers[2] saw women's transition to paid work in the 1960s as a temporary expression of women fulfilling a reserve function, and in the main acting as unskilled workers during an industrial boom with rapidly increasing production. History, however, has proved this feminist research wrong. Women worked predominantly in the service sector, primarily as semi-professionals, and they continued to seek employment with renewed vigour in the recession of the 1970s.

In the 1980s and 1990s this tendency increased further. In the main in the 1960s women sought semi-professional training – as helpers for male professionals – as office assistants, secretaries, nurses, shop assistants, etc. They often left the workplace while their children were small, many later returning to work part-time. The tendency today is for many young women – to a greater degree than young men – to seek professional training. Thus, the number of female students at Danish universities in 1991 exceeded the number of males.[3] That women studied at university was not something new. Already in the 1930s, one third of all university students in Denmark were women. The difference is that only a small minority of the female students of the 1930s completed their studies, and of those who actually graduated only a few practised their profession. Today there is not a markedly greater number of women than men who do not finish their studies, and they and their peers are expected to use their degrees. University studies may be said to have gradually gone from being a "finishing school" for women, who were expected to become housewives, to being a "career" move and, thus, a real mode of entry into the professions.

Despite the fact that there is still a clear segregation of the genders in the choice of studies, including at the professional level, there are a series of formerly exclusively male bastions which are on the way to being quantitatively dominated by women. One of these is medicine where 63 per cent of the students and about half of the new graduates today are women, and it is from here that I shall take my point of departure in the analysis of the change in the bastions of brotherhood.

Case study: the change of gender construction in gynaecology

According to Foucault the areas of knowledge that have to do with the control of the mind and body are important elements in the modern episteme, that is to say in the expression of modern scientific discourse. The development of this control of the mind ("subjectification") can, according to Foucault, be characterized as a dual process whereby the individual becomes the subject in an active understanding (agent) and in a passive understanding (subjected). This is because bio-power is a form of power which is practised on people as living beings in a population where individual reproductive and sexual behaviour are associated with national power and policies (Foucault 1991). It refers to a form of power that is practised on people as free individuals and, thus, a form which presupposes their capacity as active agents. Hence, new forms of oppositional policies still arise, because individuals have begun to formulate needs and demands as a basis for political counter-demands.

This theory of the basis of power is a repudiation of a one-sided conception which sees the discourse of power only as something which is practised upon the dominated. At the same time it contains a theory of the inclusion of the body and of the soul in the power relationship. Similarly, the power relationship between the genders is, thus, seen as a mutual relationship where "power" is productively expressed through both a discoursive articulation of gender and through the individual's placement of themselves in this gender construction.

Viewed in this light, gynaecology can be seen as an area of bio-power where the patients (women) cannot just be described as dominated, but where an exchange of power constantly occurs between doctor and patient, between women and men and between women and women. The field of gynaecology is an especially important one for analysis because it has a special role – namely, in historical feminist research – as a central link in the patriarchal control of women's bodies and sexuality. This is partly ascribed to the male-dominated sphere of gynaecology's power struggle with female midwives for the right to control births; partly to the scientific creation of a specific pathology of women's reproductive functions (Rosenbeck 1987, 1992, Ehrenreich & English 1979, Shorter 1983, Daly 1979); and partly to the fact that women's reproductive functions in the area between psychoanalysis and gynaecology have been seen as strongly linked to female hysteria. In this light it is important to analyze what happens when women move into the area of gynaecology as experts.

Historically gynaecology has subsumed a large part of the work of midwives. For much of the twentieth century midwives worked primarily on the basis of experience, and in the homes of women giving birth.

As a profession for women nursing has in a higher degree developed as a function of the hospitalization of the sick through medical practice. The rationale of care in nursing was originally – by contrast to the profession of midwifery – based on a religious calling (though less so in Denmark). It was connected with a life of celibacy and, to a certain extent, seen as a contrast to a worldly, scientific basis for medicine. This rationale of caring might be said to have been old-fashioned from its inception because of its religious roots, and, to some extent, in conflict with the rationale of the professionals.

In the twentieth century, nursing has become a secular activity associated with a socialization of women to motherhood as a real and symbolic function in modern society. Nursing training became a training for "motherhood". It was, therefore, formerly primarily younger women who practised the profession until they married. At the same time nursing as a profession created a scientific discourse of motherhood, among other things visible in the customary Danish practice of "quietness, cleanliness and regularity" in the care of children (Donzelot 1979, Kristensen & Schmidt 1987). The rationale of femininity in the definition of care has, then, not only restricted femininity – to what Weber has called the non-object rationale: the religious, the emotional and the physical – but has also functioned as a condition for the male rationale's successful definition of it. At the same time the rationale of care has been incorporated as a lesser function in scientific treatment, subjugated to male professionalism. In nursing there has not been the same struggle for professional authority with doctors as there has been between doctors and midwives. The two professions (nursing and medicine) have entered into an unambiguous attribution of gender and of professionalism, where gender alone has had the ability to signal the individual's function in the division of labour.

The case study is of a gynaecology ward at a Danish provincial hospital. All the doctors involved were interviewed[4] twice, partly in groups and partly individually. The interviews were conducted qualitatively, each interview lasting about an hour and concentrating on the questions: How do doctors perceive the relationship between themselves and their colleagues as professionals and as gendered? Do they think that they work differently and do some have higher status than others and is this associated with gender? From whom do they seek advice, and with whom do they work best? With whom do they associate – both at the hospital and outside?

On the gynaecological ward there was both a female and a male consultant, five senior registrars, two of whom were women, and finally a rapidly changing group of registrars with a roughly equal number of men and women; the female consultant in particular stressed that equality between the genders was departmental policy. In addition a number of midwives and nurses worked on the ward who were exclusively female. Further, nursing auxiliaries and cleaning staff worked on the ward together with a number of male porters. These latter groups, however, were seemingly not a part of and did not have much interaction with the professional community of doctors. It might be said that the professional top was far more gender-equal than the semi-professionals lower down the hierarchy, a trend which is by no means specific to this area and one that holds true equally of public administration, education, the social services sector and, to a certain extent, private sector employees.

Professionality, brotherhood and female doctors

The male-defined technical-economic professional culture sees itself and its basis of knowledge as objective and impersonal. Both the male and the female doctors in the case study stress this idealized picture of the profession. Correspondingly, it is important for joint professional understanding that gender is unimportant for the professional. The doctors studied believed that all doctors act in the same way as professionals – though with individual variations that are only expected to affect professional practice marginally.

In a group interview with a female senior registrar and two female registrars, where one of the young registrars at first claimed that female doctors are more caring and try to inform the patients more than their male counterparts, she was quickly put in her place by the senior registrar. The latter stressed that this is only the expression of individual rather than gender-specific differences. Correspondingly, the three male senior registrars claimed that there are no differences between male and female doctors. They were actually slightly offended that the interviewers should suggest something of this nature. Implicit in their reaction was the belief that being a professional presupposes that one's gender is not allowed to affect one's professional practice.

Co-operation between doctors was anchored in a solidarity based on confidence in each other's professional knowledge and the simultaneous requirement not to "go it alone", but all the time to secure professional cover, i.e., support. The three male senior registrars asserted that it was standard, accepted and expected practice to consult each other, and that one has another doctor see a patient and give their opinion before any important decision on treatment is taken. The female doctors had, thus, natural access to the brotherhood, because their training and function were the same. The community I have chosen to describe as a brotherhood was defined not by gender, but by education and function.

For the doctors interviewed it was obvious that there is no difference between the qualifications and actual practice of male and female doctors. The male doctors almost saw it as an attack on the whole profession, and on the professionalism of female doctors, when something of the sort was hinted at. One is qualified because of one's education and the tour of duty one undergoes. At the same time one should respect one's place in the hierarchy of qualifications if one does not want one's professionalism to be questioned.

Even though at the start of the interviews the male doctors denied harbouring any doubts about female doctors being as professional as themselves, a slightly different picture later emerged from the interviews. They spoke of female "insufficiency", which makes the female doctors far too painstaking in the writing of reports, and that they take too much time in their duties because they are overly conscientious. In short, they argued that women's feelings of insecurity make them over-conform to professional discipline. At the same time, an impression might be given that the male doctors were less likely to accept a lesser offence against the hierarchic pattern by a female doctor than they might if it were perpetrated by a male colleague. Thus, on one occasion a female registrar was criticized for having forgotten to inform the duty senior registrar before she started a Caesarean section. Not because she could not do it on her own, but because the professional code set this as standard practice and as a guarantee of objectivity in the decision-making process. There was a break in solidarity; she set herself apart from the brotherhood.

The brotherhood is also bureaucratic. It contains a hierarchy which is not based on patriarchal paternal power, but where promotion in the system is dependent on education and professional results. According to Weber (1971) that hegemony, of which patriarchy is an expression, has been replaced by a legal hegemony based on rules and professional competence. "Patricide" – the repudiation of the father's power as it is exercised through property rights, paternity and seniority – is, thus, completely central to modern brotherhood-oriented male dominance, which is dominant in the formerly male-dominated professions.

The symbolic meaning of the scientific, technical rationale in professional practice means that both male and female doctors are blinded to the obvious elements of the traditional patriarchal hegemony, which have none the less survived in the brotherhood. The conflict in the expressions comes not least when, on the one hand, it is asserted that there is no difference, yet on the other a series of events is described where female doctors – as individuals – have not lived up to professional standards.

Scientific standards – the clinical gaze

The gynaecologists in the case study claimed that, first and foremost, they use scientific methods based on observation and clinical examination with a background in objective, representative scientific trials. As such, they confirm a practice in healthcare which is based on the doctor's "clinical gaze".

According to Foucault's analysis it is exactly this clinical gaze which is fundamental for the history of the modern hospital service:

> The medical gaze embraces more than is said by the word "gaze" alone. It contains within a single structure different sensorial fields. The sight/touch/hearing trinity defines a perceptual configuration in which the inaccessible illness is tracked down by markers, gauged in depth, drawn to the surface, and projected virtually on the dispersed organs of the corpse. The "glance" has become a complex organization with a view to a spatial assignation of the invisible (Foucault 1991:164).

Hospitalization of the sick formed the objective material for medicine's observation and collection of knowledge. Therefore, the patient had to stay in hospital for long periods in the early days of modern medicine, which in turn resulted in the establishment of nursing as a profession. The inclusion of pregnancy, birth and gynaecological illnesses into clinical practice led to an assessment of their pathology and was a prerequisite for their discoursive articulation. The development of obstetrics as a science was in marked contrast to the "silent" continuity of transmission of bodily experience from woman to woman. According to Foucault, this human activity of making oneself into the object of one's own science is an important element in the rise of modern science. The invisible is made visible, is observed and is classified so that truth can be gleaned from nature.

The male consultant in the case study stressed the importance of maintaining scientific standards at work. In his view, the profession only seriously established such standards in the 1950s and 1960s, when hospital observation and experiments in the treatment of patients developed into a positivist practice, with scientific examination of new methods of treatment through random experiment using control groups. He and the other doctors in the case study distanced themselves from earlier types of pathological assessment of women's bodies, and from the opinion that psychological illnesses in women could be understood in relation to their reproductive function.

In this way, confrontation with patriarchal forms of practice in the profession can also be seen as a confrontation with the ideologically bounded elements in the oppression of women, especially in gynaecology. The professionally correct doctor views illness and the reproductive function from a technical standpoint and is professionally "ignorant" of the associated social or psychological problems. A few of the female doctors holding the opposite view, one which prioritizes personal freedom, overstep professional objectivity and distance. This happened, for example, when a young female registrar with roots in the 1970s women's movement suggested that the department take the initiative to form self-help groups among patients who had undergone surgery to their wombs. This was rejected and characterized as unprofessional by the consultant, because it would go beyond the professionally agreed methods of treatment and the area of gynaecology.

The interviews showed that the scientific norms applied at work were specially negotiated at the morning meeting, where the male consultant decided the tone and had the last word. This was also where the male senior registrars demonstrated their knowledge of the latest scientific advances.

The professional consensus that characterizes all the interviewed gynaecologists agrees with Talcott Parsons' formulation of medical practice as a link in a harmonious and conflict-free functionalist system, one in which human behaviour can be analyzed rationally because of a series of system variables and their combinations. According to Talcott Parsons (1964) the right to practice the calling is based on "achievement", that is to say, it is appropriated by personal effort such as education and promotion. The criterion for practice is technical competence. The construction of professionalism in medicine presupposes, as it does for other professions, functional specificity, affective neutrality, collective orientation and universality.

Functional specificity – affective neutrality

The doctor is not a "wise man" who can speak on all of life's questions, but a person who has attained specific, technical abilities and who relates specifically to the areas in which his speciality is expressed. The idea that one's status as a doctor is attained by "achievement" – through "learning by doing" – means that the doctor accepts his role as a technician, skilled in a functionally specific area. He or she is thus a person who has achieved skills in one area and thereby renounced the right to know anything about other specialities.

The young female gynaecologists in the case study stated that there was too little time (20 minutes) for the examination of patients during out-patient clinics, because such brief appointments did not allow them to talk to the patients and follow up earlier examinations. The male doctors, on the other hand, thought that 10 minutes was enough, seeing no reason for the doctor to talk to the patient, who in most cases was not seeing the same doctor again. They thought that the doctor might encroach upon the mid-wives' field of expertise and that anyway it was the latters' job to monitor the patient.

If one accepts Talcott Parsons' analysis of functional specificity – that one does not go beyond the bounds of that area for which one's scientific objectivity is adequate – this difference of approach precisely constitutes a break in it. The most important tool in scientific diagnosis is in harmony with the rules for positivist scientific practice of the clinical gaze, that is to say the doctor's observation of the patient and, in this case, of the female sexual organs.

In this sense conversation with the patient is only a tool to enhance observation, while the interjection of the patient's evaluation of her own situation is viewed as a disturbance to that process. Positivist science pre-supposes that the object of knowledge can be studied as a thing which does not involve itself as a joint interpreting subject in the analysis of its own case.

It is, then, a break in scientific standards in the opinion of the male senior registrars when the young female gynaecologists in the case study would prefer to talk to the patients more, advise them and hear their opin-ion of their physical condition. In this preference, they are perceived as straying from the principle of "the clinical gaze" (Foucault 1973), a gaze which is specifically focused on the clinical situation. However, the male doctors' evaluation of their female colleagues' more feminine, interactive approach is ambiguous: it makes the women into potentially poorer clini-cians from a scientific perspective, but in practice the female gynaecologists often have a better relationship with the patients and the male doctors recognize that the patients prefer female gynaecologists to male.

The doctor as a practitioner of science acts on objectively and scientific-ally founded norms which predicate a demand for emotional neutrality. His sympathies or antipathies for the specific patient are irrelevant. In the same way he is obliged not to allow himself to be affected emotionally by the very emotional events he sees every day. The male doctors express the ambiguity that, on the one hand, they see it as important not to become emotionally involved, while, on the other hand, they feel this as a loss. In their opinion the female gynaecologists are better at comforting and talking to patients in a crisis, even if they themselves do not know how they should tackle the situation. However, they stress that the practice of gynaecology in particular demands an emotional and physical distance, because a comforting touch can easily be misinterpreted and given a sexual nuance.

According to the English sociologist Jeff Hearn (1987) the selective control of emotions in oneself and others, co-workers and patients, is an important part of the masculine construction of professions such as medicine. Control is a part of the hierarchical pattern where patients and subordinates are allowed to express emotions within certain limits, but the doctor must be unemotional:

> They may display "affective neutrality", even talk about emotions, become "experts" of emotions, yet not be seen as emotional. A degree of controlled friendliness may conjoin with this denial of emotion. In effect, the problem of emotional control of such professionals is primarily located through others – subordinate staff and "clients" – in the form of an institutionalised defence structured in interpersonal relations and other persons. These professions and their masculinities are havens of occupational extroversion and projection (Hearn 1987:140).

According to Hearn the doctors' position of power is, among other things, defined by their ability to delegate the emotional work to subordinate staff. Thus, one might claim that the male gynaecologists in the case, in stressing the female gynaecologists' special ability to comfort and to communicate, relegate them to the professional level of the subordinate staff, even though this is definitely not explicitly expressed.

However, it looks as if the professional control of emotion did not imply a taboo against expressing more emotional and not least sexual feelings between professional equals – the male and female gynaecologists. I will return to this later. According to Parsons, orientation to the collective entails the doctor's responsibility to treat all patients by the same norms, not to pursue commercial interests and, most importantly, to be concerned for the patient's welfare. A patriarchal or nepotistic attitude is, thus, unprofessional according to the professional norms, which demand that personal involvement is played down.

Universalism entails the doctor's responsibility to treat the patient in accordance with universal rules, that is, according to existing practice for treatment of the illness in question, and, in principle, to ensure that any doctor at any hospital follows the same treatment. At the same time professional practice presupposes that the doctor keeps him- or herself up to date with the latest scientific advances, and that the methods of treatment used are those recognized as best, seen through positivist scientific spectacles. This means that the methods of treatment have been thoroughly tested according to scientific principles, or that the treatment is part of a trial – which it frequently is as a consequence of the individual doctor's need to carry out scientific research to gain further qualifications and so advance their career within the system.

Parsons stresses that precisely the break with traditional hegemony – patriarchal power – entails a democratization of the relationship between colleagues and between doctor and patient. The relationship is technical in nature and includes not a personal relationship of dependency, but one between the doctor who diagnoses and treats and the carrier of his object, namely the specific physical ailment. The ethic of professional conduct is stipulated by the scientific regulations which require the doctor to keep personal involvement out of the doctor–patient relationship. It is striking that, among the doctors interviewed, the male senior registrars and the male consultant strongly emphasized these ethical regulations governing contact with patients. They described the ability to make the relationship a purely clinical, professional one as ethically correct, as advanced and progressive.

Sexuality in professional brotherhood

It is characteristic of the case study that it was important for the professional ethic to dismiss any hint of sexual relations with the patients. The male doctors saw the maintenance of professional distance precisely as a safeguard for the patients' personal boundaries of intimacy, while a sexually nuanced language between male and female doctors and a flirtatious tone in social contact between doctors was, conversely, perfectly acceptable. In the opinion of the female consultant, having as many female as male gynaecologists was an important element in maintaining a friendly and flirtatious atmosphere between the genders.

As far as sexual overtones in relationships with the nurses went, the doctors described how, when the male chief registrar did his rounds, the nurses did their hair, put on make-up and were eager to help him, while the female chief registrar did not receive the same attention from the nurses. On the contrary, she said that sometimes she had to take a bedpan to prove that she too had value. The doctors perceived this difference as a form of "cultural lag" from earlier power relations, a situation maintained mainly by the nurses, and, thus, connected to an earlier pattern for the distribution of power and sexuality. The male consultant's status was, therefore, emphasized through the subordinate group's gender-specific sexual signals, while the female consultant's status was not really emphasized. At the same time, in the case study (and possibly specific to this department), there was a clear trend to relegate the sexualization of the doctor–nurse relationship to the background in favour of a sexualization of the relationship between female and male doctors. As the male registrars mentioned, it used to be the nurses who created an atmosphere of fun and familiarity. They were now matronly and boring, while the young female doctors were lively and willing to have fun.

Such a development, among other things, expresses the fact that the doctor–nurse myth is bound up with the idea of the young nurse and the older doctor. At the close of the twentieth century, developments are moving in the direction of women staying in the workplace throughout their working lives, creating a higher average age among nurses. The relatively recent entry of women into the medical profession as doctors thus explains the lower average age for this group.

It was clear from the interviews that the male doctors were enthusiastic about the young female doctors on the ward. They described them as lively and fun, flirtatious and pretty, without this seeming to affect the male doctors' opinion of their professional expertise. On the contrary, the male doctors thought that the female patients preferred the young female doctors. At the same time, it struck the interviewers that this group of young women doctors did not radiate much power, but, on the contrary, typically related flirtatiously and considerately to their male colleagues. They brought in wine on Friday afternoons, arranged parties and outings and adopted a kindly and flirtatious tone. One of them commented: "When I phone and wake a male colleague who is on call, I usually say, 'I can no longer do without you, my darling!'"

As described, emotional control is central to the doctors' professional ideals. Hearn states that controlling his own emotions makes it possible for the male doctor to control the affect and emotional articulation of the patients. Among the subordinate semi-professional groups other forms of affect are permissible conduct. Thus, it was characteristic for the case study that the male doctors were very careful not to send signals of sexual attraction to the female patients, while such conduct was permissible *vis-à-vis* the female doctors.

It is probably also true (though not overtly expressed) that the public debate on "sexual harassment" has made it unacceptable to send sexual signals to subordinate groups, even though the male doctor–female nurse relation may still function as a sexual stereotype for a sexuality based on male power and female subjugation (and probably also on the idea that they marry, and afterwards she leaves the public scene to concentrate on the private sphere). One can, therefore, also state that the public/private sphere dichotomy, as it relates to sexuality, no longer exists. Elina Haavio-Mannila (see Chapter 11, Attraction and love at work, above pp. 198–217) has noted that half of all adults have experienced infatuations with a colleague and this often ends in marriage. In the cases where it does not end in marriage but in a more casual sexual relationship, the woman is more prone to experience psychological problems. It is also true of the doctors in our case study that there have been different instances of sexual attraction and that marriages have broken up as a result. At the same time, the situation for most of the female doctors in the case study was that they lived alone.

New postmodern tones in the brotherhood and the profession

There is, then, in the medical profession of doctor, a high degree of consistency between the norms for the practice of legal power with professional and bureaucratic standards. This demands particularism, control of affect, collectivism and universality. Furthermore, it includes recognition of educational level and professionally founded promotion as a background for the hierarchy of power. It demands a distancing between the person and the professional, between private and public life, between brotherhood-oriented life, forms of contact with colleagues and sexuality. This presupposes that the object of knowledge accepts its object status or, to be more precise, lays its organs open for the doctor's clinical gaze, accepts the object status of its body and the right of medicine to judge its treatment. It also presupposes that subjective life, private life and sexuality allow themselves to be outside professional expression. It is precisely these premises that no longer hold true and which I will now describe.

Ordinary popular knowledge has undergone a revolution in recent decades, not least with respect to gynaecology. The ordinary level of knowledge in the younger generation has increased dramatically, particularly in the area of health and sickness, which is an important topic in women's magazines. Alternative forms of treatment have mushroomed as a way of coping with one's own body and illness. Furthermore, an important element in the women's movement of the 1970s was the recapture of giving birth. Ante-natal classes were started in the women's house in Copenhagen, a practice which soon spread to the rest of the country, and women were shown how to write lists of their wishes with demands for how the birth should proceed. At the same time movements such as the association dedicated to parents and birth were created. These sought knowledge of alternative forms of childbirth – water births, home births – and of the care of infants. Together these developments have contributed to an increase in popular knowledge and have put the female patient in a position of partnership, whether in consultation, or as a person who makes their own informed demands regarding gynaecological treatment. The doctor's position of power is anchored primarily in the monopoly of knowledge, and when this is challenged a dramatic change in the doctor–patient relationship occurs.

This new relationship of negotiation is probably easier for the female doctors to cope with. Suddenly it has become necessary to incorporate elements other than the purely professional, if one is to meet the demand for negotiation. Personal evaluation, the inclusion of personal physical experience and birth, become a basis for a negotiation between equal partners, a relationship which is not based on a one-sided objectification.

On the other hand when she divests herself of her object status the patient loses her personal "immunity" in relation to the system. The system or profession no longer orients itself to single functions or "faults in the equipment" with which she visits the doctor, but presupposes that she can participate as a partner in the consultation – that she exposes a far larger part of herself. She must be herself and not just put on the mask of "patient". Therefore, one might claim that what was initially a revolt of the object is now diffused into what one could call a revolt internalizing the discourse. The discourse is thereby internalized as a subjective strategy.

However, there is also a series of new trends operating within gynaecology which will not be detailed here. Among other things, there is the growing internationally and commercially oriented technology of *in vitro* fertilization, which can be seen variously as medicine's need to become master of life and death, as a commercial interest to trade freely with human life or as women's desire, whatever their age, to have the perfect child.

There is also a general trend towards taking medicine outside the hospital, as long hospital stays are an ever increasing socio-economic burden, and the need for hospitals as an experimental base for the study of common diseases is receding in importance. Technological developments, both in the pharmaceutical industry and in clinical practice, have made the patient less a patient and more someone who demands a specific treatment, a consumer who, as far as obstetrics is concerned, can buy a variety of medicinal products in the marketplace. Such products include pregnancy tests, fertility tests, semen packs, etc. and by going straight to the shop rather than the doctor they avoid medicine's direct objectification and bodily control.

Another difference which illustrates the new postmodern trends in the relationship between gender and professionalism is the schism in the relationship between public and private in the personal lives of individual doctors. It was characteristic of the case study that the male doctors were far more family-oriented than their female colleagues. Several were married for the second or third time and had a second family of young children and a wife with a semi-professional background. In contrast, the female doctors were much less family-minded. Several of them lived alone, or alone with a child after a divorce. Hence, the community of colleagues often spread into the women's private lives. They took the initiative in involving the male doctors by arranging parties and outings, bringing in wine on Friday evenings, etc. But it was perfectly clear that there was a difference in the men and women's level of commitment. It was based on the pattern discernible among the highly educated, which has also been noted in other studies, that women often live alone and have only one child, while men live in a series of monogamous relationships with several sets of children.

When one considers that an increasing part of everyday life is spent at the workplace or in job and day centres, then one can speak of women more than men as having transferred their daily lives there. The men can still differentiate meaningfully between life at work and life at home. However, for the female doctors in the case study it was far truer that family life had diminished and, correspondingly, that personal life (emotional life, close interpersonal relations, leisure pursuits) were connected with their work. There is, thus, a tendency for women to transfer "female" ideals of "the good life" to the workplace.

Another aspect of postmodern development is that in recent decades, not least at the national administrative level, there has been a general move away from professionally exclusive and bureaucratic forms of organization towards more *ad hoc* organizational forms. In the hospital, an organization based on group control of projects, holistics, equality, and co-operation across professional boundaries, a correspondingly marked change has not occurred. However, the rapid recruitment of women into the medical profession as doctors creates a new scenario where the doctor's position of power is less important.

Even though neither the female nor the male gynaecologists would entertain the idea of gender-specific professional practices, there is much to indicate that the female doctors oriented themselves towards the subordinate semi-professions. They oriented themselves towards dialogue with the patients, while the male doctors to a higher degree oriented themselves to the professional community and to the career ladder. Furthermore, it was characteristic that the male doctors more than their female colleagues stressed the conflict of professional boundaries with midwives.

If one equates the new postmodern forms of organization in public institutions with forms that are more service-minded, organized in an *ad hoc* manner across professional boundaries in project groups, and oriented towards the users and towards an integrated care approach, then one can say that the female doctors far better than the male implement these new ideas in medicine. Correspondingly, they are probably less likely to be promoted than the men.

The feminization of the public sector – mother love as a social matter

Even though one may be correct in claiming that the female doctors in the case study do not change professional practice very markedly, they are, nevertheless, part of a larger change, which purely quantitatively finds expression in the women's entry into the public discourse and in particular the discourse of bio-power (medicine, education, psychology). It is precisely these discourses which, according to Foucault, are very important in the modern episteme, and for the expression and discipline of the subject with which it is associated. The change consists not least in the abolition of the division between private and public space established in early modern society. This division was emphasized by the early sociologists as a prerequisite for the development of modern, specialized, industrial culture based on organic solidarity. According to Simmel (1911) love is part of objective culture; the objectification of culture is, thus, connected to special-ization, while female culture is outside this specialization.

Specialization is seen by Simmel as one of the most important roots of the dynamic of modern culture and as out of step with female loyalty towards values and things. According to Simmel, men are less loyal and this forms the background for the dynamic in specialization and differentiation in modern culture. Women lack objective cultural goals but not human productivity. It is exactly this that is connected to a way of life where all life is mediated through an indivisible subjective centre.

However, female culture in postmodern society has actually been objectified. It has become part of the same differentiation and specialization as male culture. And in their guise as a foundation for modern industrial culture, the female forms of production are not, as Simmel assumes, bound to an indivisible motherly centre. The control of feelings has become part of specialization.

Practitioners of gynaecology can be compared with the social-worker or the nursery nurse who practises some of the functions of work that express this shift. Their work may involve getting so close to a small child for many hours each day that they almost act as its mother. But at the same time the nurse must not form so close a relationship with the child that the child cannot, without causing lasting psychological damage, be moved up to join the next age group in the nursery when it reaches the appropriate age. Similar controls operate in work functions where the professional comes so close to people's disintegration, loneliness or despair that they are keenly aware that the only real comfort is to give the person a lover, a best friend, a spouse or a mother. However, entering into a discourse of the profession forces one to choose between the system's replacements for closeness which embrace such alternative provision as an old people's home, supplement-ary benefit, the taking of children into care, or drug rehabilitation. What is new is not that such work can be found, but that an ever increasing part of all work is saturated with it, and that a larger part of human contacts, of the satisfaction of human needs, is met by professionals in the public sphere. It means that today both women and men must learn techniques for conduct-ing emotional work in a publicly acceptable and, at the same time, personal and impersonal way.

The American cultural critic Richard Sennet sees this shift as an expres-sion of the decline of public life in our time. According to Sennet, in the eighteenth century one sought to retain a segregation between the public and the private, where the public sector first and foremost distinguished itself from the private and private manners. "This principle of community [the modern tyranny of intimacy] is the very opposite of the 'sociable' com-munity of the 18th century in which the acts of disguise, the masks, were what people shared" (Sennet 1977:222). The public sphere was considered immoral, a place where one could break the rules of respectability, while the intimate sphere was idealized as a refuge against the dangers of the public sphere. This distinction between the public and the private meant, however, something different for women and for men. For women public life was connected with disgrace, for men it was the realm of freedom seen in relation to the virtuous life of the home.

Sennet claims that the public sphere has now become subjected to the norms of privacy:

> The western societies are moving from a state of being directed towards others, to an introvert state of being, with the provision, that in the midst of the self-centredness no-one can say what is *inside*. As a consequence of this there is confusion between public and private life. People conduct public tasks with a point of departure in the norms of private/intimate life, tasks which can possibly only be conducted with the norms for an impersonal connection (Sennet 1977:5).

Thus, one can also claim that as women come to live the same lives as men, and as men have been unable to maintain the specific character of the public sphere, the distinction between the intimate and the public, the respectable and the dishonourable has also dissolved and it is seemingly the norms of privacy clad in public garb which come to form the new life.

Sexuality in a state of flux

It holds true for sexuality as for mother love that these matters are seen as belonging to the subjective, private and non-professional sphere within professional understanding and ethics. The professional is, thus, expected to relate as a brother/colleague to other doctors and as objective/distancing to patients. Specifically, in gynaecology, where the arena for the expression of the speciality are the reproductive functions and the functions associated with sexual practice, it is characteristic that the professional does not involve themself in the sexual practices of the patients, and is careful that the clinical situation between doctor and patient does not have sexual overtones. Gynaecology as a profession contains an important factor that is directly connected with femininity, the specific female biology and at the same time the locus of sexuality, which Foucault located in the Victorian period (Foucault 1978). This confirmed the legitimate breeding couple as the normal configuration for sexual desire and associated female sexuality with motherhood, and with the private sphere.

The circumstances for the practice of gynaecology in the postmodern world indicate a new shift in the administration of sexual desire. Femininity is identified less with motherhood and more with an active sexual role (among other things where an important part of the gynaecologist's work consists in performing abortions and also has to do with keeping women functioning sexually throughout their lives). Thus, gynaecology may be said to have moved beyond the pan-optical observation, beyond the heavily discoursive bio-power, where the doctor is seen as an active carrier of the discourse. There the doctor functions as the discourse-generating subject in a dichotomous relationship to the objectified female body, which just happens to be the receptacle for the subject of his professional, objective and scientifically based professional display. Gynaecological practice has moved on to a level where, on the one hand, there is an ever increasing demarcation between gynaecological technical scientific development towards rendering the female body redundant as the locus of the creation of life, and the local gynaecological practice around pregnancy, abortion, birth and illness. At the same time more and more gynaecologists are women, carriers of the same organs and the same physical experience as their patients, and therefore unable to maintain the same subject/object relation. It also means that in patient relation there is no longer the gender-specific and identifiable difference between female care and comfort and male authority.

The dynamic of the relationship is no longer between the women's love and the men's authority, but a dynamic where there is more negotiation without previously fixed positions. In this way the gender-based division of labour's professional, dynamic and sexually based position – such as the sensitive nurse and the powerful male doctor – has lost its foundation.

The administration of desire has left the private space in the postmodern world and has become visible in the public space. Already in modern society the nurse, precisely because she was forbidden according to the requirement for chastity, became a target for sexual fantasy and the creation of myth. Today in the postmodern world the doctor–patient relation as a sexual relation is still the object of taboos and therefore also an object of sexual fascination.

From the case study it is clear that both male and female gynaecologists, at the same time as they stress their relations as colleagues and their professional distance, display an erotic undercurrent between them; the young female gynaecologists dress provocatively and use body language of an erotic nature: their white coats are short and unbuttoned revealing their tanned legs. This does not provoke any professional criticism – on the contrary these women are stressed as the ideal. At the same time they function as "professional seductresses" because they live alone and often arrange parties and small get-togethers, whereas the male doctors live in a far more marital sexual pattern.

Conclusion

As the case study illustrates, there is currently a departure from the rationalities that have their background in a gender-specific division of labour, where male professionalism emphasizes objective scientific practice and female professionalism emphasizes care.

However, the departure is not unambiguous: female doctors can, to a much lesser extent than male doctors, simply allow themselves to be social-ized into a gender construction and a professional identity based on an identification with older colleagues. For them there is no unity between gender and professionalism. To a much higher degree they have to live up to other standards, which in the example of the female doctors in the case study implies that femininity – including that which is perceived as sexually attractive – is measured by how caring, convivial and socially integrated they are, not only in relation to colleagues and the other staff, but also to the patients.

At the same time they are expected to be loyal towards the scientific-medical discourse, which presupposes a form of loyalty based on object-ively and scientifically oriented uniform behaviour on the part of the doctors, "a clinical gaze" which does not allow itself to be disturbed by the patients' co-operation during treatment.

The discourse is not only under attack from alternative forms of treat-ment, from the patients' demands to be heard and from active insight in treatment, but from within the medical establishment there is a very power-ful emphasis on upholding internally prescribed professional standards, which allows the discourse to develop its own power-knowledge regime on its own terms.

In the public debate it has often been said that a series of foreign and Danish research projects has shown a higher frequency of suicide among female doctors. And the above case clearly illustrates the dilemma currently confronting female doctors. To put it bluntly, the female doctor must assim-ilate the male rationale to prove that she is professional, and the female rationale to prove that she is a woman. A number of these conditions can probably be transferred to other groups of female professionals, who must also fight a tough battle in order to retain an identity that at the same time is both female and professional.

On the one hand the demand that the women adjust themselves to the professional standards of brotherhood is clearly expressed. Transgressions are more severely punished, despite the fact that the rules of brotherhood are not always clear to the women, as they are learned in a boys' fellowship to which the women have not had access, and which is based on a struc-tural delimitation of the female rationale whereby knowledge-power is main-tained by delegation of the most emotionally charged and care-oriented functions to subordinate personnel.

On the other hand the general "feminization of the public sphere" cre-ates a norm for public life which Sennet (1979) claims is based on the rules of intimacy. The claim is that the professional is not allowed to hide behind the neutralizing uniform of the bureaucrat, but on the contrary is expected to treat the patient/client as a good friend. Thus, the more caring-rationale way of relating to medicine is much more in harmony with the demands which the postmodern patients – the confident consumers of medical services – make. The demand of the medical discourse for exclusivity unavoidably becomes outdated at a time when public knowledge of medical subjects and the popular consumption of alternative forms of treatment are actually breaking down the professional monopoly of medicine and its discoursive unity.

One can probably speak of a series of competing discourses today, in which each in its own way articulates the treatment of illness. Rather than the scientific principle of "the clinical gaze", one can say that the principle, which, according to Foucault (1978), characterizes the development of sexual science and psychiatry, namely the dogma of confession (the opinion that a cure must be expressed by the patient's therapeutic admissions), has evolved into a more dialogue-based and self-treating ideal. It can, to a much higher degree, be said to form the background for postmodern conceptions of health and illness. The male gynaecologists in the case study stressed that the female doctors were far better at dealing with the patients than they were themselves – an admission in complete harmony with the feminization of the public sphere, which spreads female "private forms of contact" to the public sector. Such forms of contact deny the reification and distance of professionalism and instead favour a view of the doctor–patient relationship as a relationship between best friends.

Notes

1. In 1968, 74 543 children were born in Denmark; in 1983, 50 822; in 1991, 64 358. (source: Denmark's statistics. Statistisk Årbog in the relevant years/Statistic notes).
2. There was a longer debate on this subject with a point of departure in Brita Fogeds book, *Kvindearbejde* 1950–71.
3. Thus, in 1991 there were 24 819 male students at university and 25 052 female. Naturally, it should not be glossed over that there are still gender-specific differences in the choice of degree. Thus, at Denmark's technical university there were 6 203 male and 1 851 female students. On the other hand this clearly also expresses a growth in the number of female students (source: Denmark's statistics. Statistisk Årbog in the relevant years/Statistic notes).
4. The interviews were conducted together with Henriette Christrup in 1990.

References

Andersen, L. et al. 1990. *Livsmagt* (Power over/of life). Yearbook for feminist research, no. 2. Aarhus: Aarhus University Press.
Baudrillard, J. 1982. *At glemme Foucault* (Forgetting Foucault). Copenhagen: Rhodos.
Baudrillard, J. 1984. *Forførelsen* (Seduction). Copenhagen: Sjakalen.

Borchorst, A. & Birte Siim 1984. *Kvinder I velfærdsstaten* (Women and the welfare state). Aalborg: Aalborg University Press.

Brown, C. 1981. Mothers, fathers and children: from private to public patriarchy. In L. Sargent, *The unhappy marriage of Marxism and feminism.* London: Pluto Press.

Carlsson, C.W. 1992. Vad kommer efter genussystemet (What after the gender system). *Kvinnovetenskapligt tidskrift* **3**, 92.

Daly, M. 1978. *Gyn/ecology: the metaethics of radical feminism.* Boston: Beacon Press.

Donzelot, J. 1979. *The policing of families.* New York: Pantheon.

Ehrenreich, B. & D. English 1979. *For her own good.* New York: Doubleday.

Eisenstein, Z. 1979. *Capitalist patriarchy and the case for socialist feminism.* New York: Monthly Review Press.

Foucault, M. 1972. *The archaeology of knowledge.* London: Tavistock.

Foucault, M. 1973. *The birth of the clinic.* London: Tavistock.

Foucault, M. 1978. *Viljen til viden* (The will to knowledge). Seksualitetens historie 1. Copenhagen: Rhodos. (Originally *La volonté de savoir.* Paris: Gallimar, 1976.)

Foucault, M. 1984a. *Le souci de soi.* Paris: Gallimar.

Foucault, M. 1984b. *L'usage de plaisirs.* Paris: Gallimar.

Foucault, M. 1991. Governmentality. In *The Foucault effect,* Burchell et al. (eds). London: Wheatsheaf/Harvester.

Giddens, A. 1992. *The transformation of intimacy.* London: Polity Press.

Hartmann, H. 1981. The unhappy marriage of Marxism and feminism. In L. Sargent Lydia (ed.). London: Pluto Press.

Hartmann, H. 1983. Capitalism and patriarchy: an overview. In *Capitalism and patriarchy,* A.-B. Ravn (ed.). Aalborg: Aalborg University Press.

Hearn, J. 1987. *The gender of oppression.* Brighton: Wheatsheaf/Harvester.

Hirdmann, Y. 1992a. Genussytemet – reflexioner kring kvinnors sociala underordning (The system of gender). *Kvinnovetenskapligt tidskrift* **3**, 92.

Hirdmann, Y. 1992b. Skevläsning – till debatten om genussystem (Cross-readings). *Kvinnovetenskapligt tidskrift* **3**, 92.

Holt, B. et al. 1984. *Kvinder mellem mæslinger, mænd og magt, en analyse af kønsrelationen blandt DJØF'ere* (An analysis of gender relations among professionals). Copenhagen: Sociologisk Institut.

Jónasdóttir, A. 1991. *Love, power and political interest.* Örebo: Örebo University Press.

Kristensen, J.E. & L.H. Schmidt 1987. *Lys, luft og renlighed* (Light, air and cleanliness). Århus: Modtryk.

Kristeva, J. 1983. *Histoires d'amour.* Paris: Denoël.

MacCannell, J. 1991. *The regime of the brother – after patriarchy.* London: Routledge.

Parsons, T. 1964. *The social system.* New York: Free Press of Glencoe.

Rosenbeck, B. 1987. *Kvindekøn* (The female gender). Copenhagen: Gyldendal.

Rosenbeck, B. 1992. *Kroppens politik* (The politics of the body). Copenhagen: Museum Tusculanum.

Sennet, R. 1977. *The fall of public man.* Cambridge: Cambridge University Press.

Shorter, E. 1983. *A history of women's bodies.* London:

Simmel, G. 1984. *On women, sexuality and love.* New York: Yale University Press. (Originally *Weibliche Kultur,* 1911.)

Walby, S. 1991. *Theorizing patriarchy.* Oxford: Basil Blackwell.

Wärness, K. 1980. *Omsorg som lønarbejde* – en begrebsdiskussion (Care as wage work). *Kvinnovetenskapligt tidskrift* **3**, 80.

Weber, M. 1971. *Wissenschaft als Beruf. Gesammelte Aufsätze zur Wissenschafts-lehre* (Science as profession). In Max Weber, *Makt og Byråkrati* (Power and bureaucracy), trans. E. Fivelsdal. Norwegian edn. Oslo: Gyldendals Studiefakler.

Young, I. 1981. Beyond the unhappy marriage. A critique of dual systems theory. In *The unhappy marriage of Marxism and feminism*, L. Sargent (ed.). London: Pluto Press.

PART THREE

Identity/subjectivity – between equality and difference

CHAPTER THIRTEEN

Understanding women in the psychological mode: the challenge from the experiences of Nordic women

Hanne Haavind

Introduction

Within the discipline of psychology there is a well-known debate going on as to how psychological modes of understanding are sexist. Countless criticisms have pointed to how psychological concepts and theories act to establish general norms of behaviour that implicitly follow masculinity (Weisstein 1971, Haavind 1978, Tavris 1992, Marecek 1995). Other criticisms directed attention to how the experiences of women could so easily be misrepresented by implicit valorization of how well the activities of women fitted into the satisfaction of the needs of others with regard to priority and support (Chesler 1972, Haavind 1973; Chodorow & Contratto 1982). Among the contributions along these lines is the deconstruction of the position of women in heterosexual relationships (Millett 1970; Kitzinger et al. 1992). According to both types of criticism, the possible subjectivities of women would be transformed by psychological concepts into a degrading and oppressive representation of their intentions. Instead of revealing the psychological aspects of the social subordination of women, psychology as a mode of understanding the female self contributed to legitimizing the oppression of women through normalization and valorization of femininity (Haavind 1978, Ethelberg 1983).

Feminist psychology originated in these criticisms and has been nurtured by them for close to three decades. Many women psychologists have taken up the challenge and developed alternative modes of understanding which they claim to be more sensitive to the experiences of women, and to give more adequate theoretical representations of their subjectivities (Miller 1976, Jordan et al. 1991, Miller 1994, Gilligan 1982, Brown & Gilligan 1992,

Chodorow 1978, 1995). This was achieved through a simple but significant change of the research questions away from what characterizes the woman as a person to inquire what these women are doing, and what they are trying to achieve for themselves and others (Haavind 1987a, 1992). The modes of understanding that will be presented here belong to this critical effort. To present new pictures of what women may have on their minds has proved to be more acceptable than to change the modes of understanding within psychology (Henriques et al. 1984, Morawski 1994). Feminist psychology has taught the interested audience a great deal about women's appropriation of their life experiences, without having any recognizable effect on the basic procedures within psychology for conceptualizing the processes of person-formation. For the specialist audience there is much to learn about women's suffering and survival, about their self-limitations and their development – mostly in specialist journals and books. However, for the research psychology that claims to be just "normal science", there is business as usual. An assumed gender neutrality is the norm (Haavind 1988, 1989). More recently feminist psychology has joined forces with other forms of critical psychology, whether social-constructionist, socio-cultural, discursive or narrative (Gergen 1991, Wertsch 1991, Potter & Wetherell 1987, Polkinghorne 1993).

The feminist enterprise to rehabilitate the understanding of women in the psychological mode ran into new types of conceptual difficulties. The debates on sexism were replaced by debates about essentialism and reverse discrimination following from the efforts to give women voice and dignity (e.g., *Feminism & Psychology* 1994). Did a feminist psychology necessarily claim that all women were the same in the psychological sense, and should the content of this essence be drawn in from the margin because it represented a positive alternative to prevailing modes of understanding human activities (Gilligan 1982, Miller 1976, *Feminism & Psychology* 1994)? Or, conversely, if increased sensitivity towards the diversity of women was needed, then femininity was just a local fiction and should be avoided as an analytical concept. What, then, was left of the feminist enterprise within psychology (Butler 1990)? This chapter will not proclaim feminist psychology as a campaign for women or for femininity, but as a campaign for revealing negotiations of male dominance and female subordination as inseparable from the countless personal expressions of gender (West & Zimmerman 1987, Deaux & Major 1987, Haavind 1992, 1994a). Or, as one may as well put it, the countless gendered expressions of people (Kaschak 1992, Chodorow 1995).

The rise of feminist critiques within psychology follows similar paths in Western psychology: inspired by the new women's liberation, taken up by women psychologists, brought to special areas of knowledge in clinical and social psychology, and left outside whatever is defined as core or basic to the discipline. This is in part because whatever a feminist psychology brings to fruition, it will be more local, textualized and contextualized than the proclaimed "general" study of human behaviour and mind. It is also partly because feminist psychologists will take separate paths depending on the cultural contexts and the characteristics of the gendered codes they relate to; what characterizes the transformation of experiences into people will, of necessity, be marked by the very stuff the actual women do process. To mention one example, in Anglo-American feminist psychology gender diversity and contrast that relate to race are accentuated (West & Fenstermaker 1995, Frankenberg 1993). A corresponding salience cannot be found in Nordic projects (Ålund 1997). Nordic projects have, however, more clearly covered diversity according to social changes in the public and private distribution of preconditions and resources for living life as a woman person (Haavind 1992, 1994a, Bjerrum Nielsen 1988; Bjerrum Nielsen & Rudberg 1994, Leira 1992).

The basic assumption in feminist research on psychological processes is not the essential character of femininity, but the potential capacity of the feminist researcher to collect, share and present the experiences of others in a way that points to their psychological significance. Ways of mediating between situations and persons, between experiences and intentions, are the unit of knowledge accretion and generalization. To put it differently, when all women do not equal each other in the psychological sense, empirical studies are worthwhile, and it is within the reach of the researcher to relate to and improve the understanding of women whose experiences deviate from her own and from those of other women (Haavind 1992). What women do share is suppression through gender, and the transformation of the many forms of making women secondary in relationships, into the personal characteristics identified as femininity. Personal gender is formed when relational experiences are aggregated and interpreted as personal capacities and preferences (Haavind 1984a, 1985). It is a process from selection through mastery to appropriation (Wertsch 1997).

The arguments presented here are based on experiences gleaned from studying women in Norway, Denmark and Sweden. The project to generate psychological interpretations of the life-experiences of women in the Nordic countries poses some limitations and some possibilities for the researchers. These limitations and possibilities correspond to the cultural and social preconditions for living as a woman that will be covered in each specific study as well as through all of them taken together.

These studies concern different groups of women sampled according to certain experiences they have in common. General interest is attached to experiences that many women suffer from, such as forms of sexual violence or the development of eating disorders (Dahl 1993, Hydén 1994, Nilsson 1994), or accomplish, such as professional status (Johannessen 1994, Magnusson 1996); experiences that are closely related to the fate or the preferences of women, such as being a mother (Haavind 1987b, Hansen & Trana 1994, Andenæs 1989a, 1989b), as well as experiences that are not easily accessible to women on demand, such as being a researcher or a professional manager (Haavind 1989, Johannessen 1994, Søndergaard 1993). The kinds of experience are strategically selected by the researcher to facilitate study of the psychological processes of connecting events as experienced and agency as expressed. Of special interest are studies of women who have entered positions that were earlier reserved for men, and which have been made into gender-neutral positions, albeit retaining a distinct flavour of masculinity to the capacities (skills) that are asked for in those who occupy them. These studies analyze the experiences of women as leaders in large corporations, as students at universities, and as qualified and unskilled workers in public services (Johannessen 1994, Søndergaard 1994, Magnusson 1998). The studies that concern women who have suffered the very harsh experiences of degradation and abuse which are incompatible with the prevailing standards of humanity, will delve into the tensions between personal suffering and resistance. The analysis will reveal the tensions and search for subjective answers in the experiences of women who have been battered by a man who is their husband – in a relationship where the use of violence is a questionable marital act. And this will also be the case with the experiences of women who have been sexually abused by a man who will both have the strength to do so and the guts to deny the event and so throw doubt on the woman's credibility. The answers to such tensions will highlight some of the general issues around the construction of the person within psychology, namely, how to account for the ambiguities in human existence that relate to power. Two such important ambiguities intimately connected to the female condition are presented; the balancing act of being influenced by others and acting on their views and the existential doubt as to whether one will attain credibility and have one's own subjectivity confirmed (Hydén 1994, Dahl 1993, Anstorp & Clasen 1988a, 1988b).

Limitations of space do not allow for inclusion of the specific results of research into such different types of experience. Each study will present an analysis of *the state of affairs* in women's ways of becoming women as well as a reflective stance on the *modes of understanding* these processes (Polkinghorne 1993). The purpose here is not to identify and describe personalized self-constructions among groups of women in Norway as compared to groups or categories of women in other countries. Rather it is to create a reflective stance towards some of the questionable characteristics of the prevailing modes of understanding women within psychology. The first characteristic of conventional analyses is to model psychological processes with just vague and general references to the social changes that actual women participate in (Ethelberg 1983). Contrary to this convention in psychological methodology, the studies mentioned above have deliberately inscribed the significance of personal changes and developments as these relate to social changes that confront actual women (Haavind 1994a).

The twofold changes

The Nordic challenge in feminist psychology relates to grasping and generalizing the formative social changes that develop into self-constructions here. Nordic women are not what they used to be. That is the case in most locations, in most social and cultural systems. But what is the horizon of available meanings presented so far? The most important characteristic is the cultural questioning of social regulation through gender. This leaves no woman untouched, and opens up for many possible individual positions (Rudie 1984). The changes in social opportunities according to gender can be described from different historical perspectives. One perspective follows the postwar period and the change away from the way of life of the urban housewife as the canonical form of female existence. This is a generational set of changes. They are offered to as well as accomplished by women, in roughly two waves. The first wave was stirred up by some women reaching young adulthood in the 1970s, when they claimed for themselves the opportunity to live a life less restricted and less deferential than that of their housewife-mothers. The next wave is the present one, where some young women in transition to adulthood are claiming that they want to break away from the overly controlled life of the new feminists. As they see it, some of the women who nurtured a desire to transcend the boundaries of gender and create gender equality were simply overstating their case. The present generation consider that their mothers – now in middle age – have ended up living in ways that are too rigid and too burdensome. Even though the daughter generation tends to see the traps which ensnared their mothers' generation as inseparable from their success in becoming the sort of women who have never existed before – the followers are not intent on copying them. The idea of self-creation as a basic female task is passed over and strengthened by these waves, but the material that is taken up and moulded is seemingly new.

Another perspective of historical changes follows the transition from a predominantly agricultural society to a society where production is increasingly industrial (a transition which in the Nordic countries took place rather late), into a modern society based on education and the processing of information in the production of goods and services. Parallel to these transitions, the concept of person is broadened to include women and promote their access to individual rights, to political representation, to work, to money, to education. And what is perhaps even more important for the identification of the female subject is the demand for security and responsibility in the personal choices of love partners and whether to have children. For Nordic women individual rights are secured not only through competition with males on "equal terms", but through the development of a welfare state directed at the distribution of health and care (Leira 1992).

Taken together, both perspectives of societal change make every new cohort of women capable of seeing themselves as progressing along a pathway of greater access to social arenas. The personal appropriation of this collective move is to make their social participation broader and more influential. Their subjective intentions are characterized and acknowledged by themselves as expanding self-control and increasing personal responsibility. However, these personal ideas of advancement do not necessarily accord with the evidence of historians. The point here is that these concepts of change are the story lines used by women to present and characterize themselves as social actors. They inscribe themselves in history as women breaking away from the social destiny of women (Hansen & Trana 1994, Thorsen 1996). They follow cultural trends in a way that is personalized and experienced as going against traditional influences and forms of controlling women (Andenæs 1989a, 1989b).

These are not just stories about personal change, they are stories about women as initiators of social change, and stories about women as the targets of changes initiated by other women. They are utilizing preconditions secured by earlier generations of women, and they are creating themselves in new ways. The present generation of women will often describe their own development with explicit reference to their self-invention – a creation without models of continuity (Bengtsson 1990, Hansen & Trana 1994). As one woman put it when she characterized how far she had moved in her realization of reciprocal marital interaction, "We should have changed that – for real! But I think this will be a little better among the younger ones" (Magnusson 1998).

Every woman, then, could be said to handle a two-fold set of changes in the monitoring of her personal development. The societal preconditions for living life as a woman have changed, and the individual woman is undergoing personal changes throughout her lifetime. Psychological modes of understanding will adapt to this duality by giving up the prevailing effort to establish a psychological standard for proper, adequate or mature femininity, and a recommended trajectory to reach it. In doing so, models for understanding personal development in women may use conceptualizations of personal narratives and of self-monitoring (Thorsen 1996, Magnusson 1998).

Studies of Nordic women can adopt an empirical stance vis-à-vis the question of the possible psychological meanings of these social changes. In a society where inequality and social injustice related to the relations between men and women are weighted for, does gender as a social code vanish? The observations tell us that the meanings of gender are transformed rather than disappear. The self-monitoring of personal development is definitely gender-specific. The demand taken up by everyone is to "be your gender" (Johannessen 1994, Søndergaard 1994). The task can be undertaken in many ways, but it is still related to a version of handling femininity, since they all end up by describing how women became women.

There is general agreement that cohorts of women are changing in ways that could be summarized as creating new perspectives for observing and accounting for social differences among women. Women who are well educated and hold jobs requiring qualifications do relate to less well-educated women who are paid for taking on the female tasks of service and care in new organizational settings. And all the positions and capacities some women acquire thanks to reduced gender segregation make them more like men in some social settings, yet still distinctively different from the men in a manner that has made gender more difficult to grasp. A new psychology of women should have the capacity to make gender-specific statements not just about women and men, but rather about personal appropriation of on-going social affairs. The concepts and models of how femininity and masculinity are related should have the capacity to steer clear of universalist claims to truth and from establishing a normative content of femininity (Haavind 1988).

The psychological challenge is to follow how women come to be women when there is less social pressure put on them – or when the social forces are actively and purposefully moulded by women who see themselves as "new" women. Just to fulfil a set of prescriptions for a traditional female role-model is taken as a point of departure. When the resulting self is accounted for, it is a solution similar to that of many other women, but still me. Accountability has replaced adaptation or fit as explanation of the self. The major changes in women's self-constructions have put the context at risk (Modell 1996). Self-monitoring is both a psychological and a political issue for women here. What the first generation of female gender-benders have done to transform institutional practices and to move and reinterpret the horizon of possible meanings attached to living as a woman, has now been taken by the next generation as both a starting point and a point of departure (Bjerrum Nielsen 1988).

These interrelated changes in female subjectivities and in preconditions for having a life that can be accounted for as the life of a woman, leave the conventional conceptualizations of gender in a paradoxical puzzle. Feminine-identification in women is gone yet still there, gendered meanings in culture are operating yet have no force (Bjerrum Nielsen & Rudberg 1994, Søndergaard 1996). The personal accounts merge with the accounts offered from psychology and other scientific discourses to explain where the new expressions of female gender are coming from. Sometimes gender is inscribed in the process as a hidden and unruly force of (hetero)sexual attraction, operating behind our backs and against our will. More sophisticated analyses point to how efforts to counteract some meanings of gender will create new ones (Søndergaard 1996).

Gender is inscribed in the organization of culture in many ways, and not just in one universal way or not at all. The question is not whether gender changes are just superficial cosmetic operations, or whether gender as two kinds of natural substance is hiding in the deepest and unknown recesses of our minds. The question is what is happening in the minds of women when they observe social participants who are transforming interactional practices that have been strongly correlated with gender segregation and gendered power. Most women practise a generative mixture of joining in and staying outside – in the service of finding themselves. The result can be seen not just as new debates, but as new personal tensions and traps. The question of what is on women's minds in the Nordic countries is of general interest to psychology also outside this locality. The case of women in the Nordic countries is one of strategic importance. Nordic women change gendered meanings by changing themselves within a culture where the consensus to do so is broader than anywhere else, and where some of the results of attitudes favouring gender equality are implemented more effectively than anywhere else (Bjørklund 1985).

Integration as an ideal and male dominance as illegitimate

The social project to do away with gender on the one hand, and to give a stronger influence to women and a wider recognition of their interests on the other, will take place both simultaneously and interchangeably. The Nordic countries have women as politicians in government and in parliament. And, what is more, everyone expects to have them there. Any reduction in the proportion of women in political bodies would be seriously questioned, and taken as a political defeat for those held responsible. The definition of women as targets of political concern has given rise to new political issues. Compared to other European countries and North America, the participation of the state in the creation and support of child welfare arrangements, and of other care and health provision as well, has had a great impact on the expectations and the responsibilities of women. The conflicting views in the political debates about public support for childcare concern the competing preferences for increased availability of public daycare as opposed to preferences for cash benefits for women taking care of their own children. The question of whether this is a legitimate political issue is superseded.

The social situation of women and its cultural interpretations could be described and evaluated in a variety of ways. What concerns us here is their description as a characterization of the established conditions that women will encounter when they are making themselves into just that – women. The conditions met by women will differ according to their social status and their success in transforming them. Still, an aggregated description capable of encapsulating the important individual challenges might go as follows. Societal preconditions are undergoing changes that are telling women how social integration of the two genders in all social arenas is becoming a realizable goal, and how any instances of male dominance can be questioned as illegitimate.

Studies of enduring heterosexual relationships show that younger women are increasing the demands they put on their male partners compared to the demands set by older women. Staying in a relationship is not just the fate and the only respectable option for a woman, but an on-going personal choice (Hansen & Trana 1994, Haavind 1984a, Ødegård 1991). Women's expectations and demands relate to reciprocity and shared participation in the day-to-day creation of family life (Haavind 1984b). Voluntary involvement and respectful and considerate love are becoming increasingly important as prerequisites for staying together in a relationship. Parallel to that, arguments of duty and necessity are losing ground.

In tandem with the changed discourses about reciprocity in heterosexual couples, the ways of life of single mothers have also changed. Their state has become an unattractive, but accessible way out of suffering personal defeat in marriage. Women living alone with their children are guaranteed public support. The simultaneous *right to choose* and the *right to reject* living as heterosexual women with children in a stable relationship with a man is demanded by most women. And women have used every opportunity to pursue their interest along these two lines. For example, the Nordic women are among the most careful users of female-controlled contraceptives in the world. This is a not a device for rejecting children, but one that enables them to make their own decisions, paying careful attention to the fostering of appropriate personal wishes and to ensuring a prepared and suitable social situation. Nordic women have a fertility rate that is among the highest in Europe (Blom et al. 1993).

There are some striking parallels in the efforts of individual women over the twentieth century. From different positions and in different ways they have worked systematically and continuously to unravel what tradition and habit have combined to create as women's destiny (Rudie 1984). The female life-model adopted a rather rigid format consisting of monogamous life-long marriage, heterosexual practice, continuous exposure to childbearing, together with family-oriented work and care. Irrespective of how many women fell short of this model, it was the canonical way of being a woman. Any deviation provoked a negative reaction, which could lead to increased control, or rejection. Women's modes of breaking away from this model developed incrementally, through inventive ways of deconstructing their activities and responsibilities and reconstituting them in new ways, according to personal choice. Through these efforts and the achievements that followed, women have created themselves as social subjects. Modern women do not accept a fixed package, but choose their life responsibilities according to their preferences. Each woman decides for herself whether she will have sex without the risk of pregnancy, and children without the protection of marriage. Living in an enduring monogamous relationship without childbearing can be a personal decision, and it can be realized in a relationship with a man or with a woman. Indeed, some people are trying to make shared parenting a constituent of same-sex love relationships. Work and access to money may be organized inside or apart from family relationships, and so on.

A general process of women creating themselves through responsible choices ends up with a variety of possible trajectories and outcomes. The shared value here is that all of these possibilities are worthy of respect (Hansen & Trana 1994). However, demographic data indicate that the increased opportunity to arrange their lives according to their own preferences has led the majority of women to adopt a common model: early sex and cohabitation within heterosexual relationships, followed by shared parenting at a mature age, with two children close in age: and all the while the women maintain paid employment outside the home interspersed with adaptations – in the form of leave of absence or a reduced work schedule – to enable them to care (i.e., work) for their own families (Blom et al. 1993, Skrede 1986, Skrede & Tornes 1986, Magnusson 1996). To tolerate lesbian relationships, to respect the voluntarily childless, and to accept separation as a not too difficult way out of a failed relationship are all important ingredients in constructing the trajectories of the majority of women who are guided by personal choice. Free access to options that are taken up by the few functions psychologically as a guarantee for the freedom of everyone, and for a conception of freedom that is not incompatible with responsibilities and dependencies. Such a freedom is valued as an expression of a feminine self because it is constituted with due attention to the actual dependencies and responsibilities of women (Ødegård 1991).

As an ideology gender segregation is flawed, and what is left of traditional forms as well as what is new in the creations of gender boundaries, will be accounted for in new ways. Social arrangements cannot easily be justified by reference to their capacity to separate people according to gender – except for public lavatories. The reproduction of actual segregation of men and women is seen as simply accidental, as following on from certain practical considerations, or as the aggregated effects of individual choice.

The close association between masculinity and dominance as essential to social order has also lost ground. On the one hand, leadership is more easily valued when it is construed in a gender-neutral fashion and made available to women. On the other hand, effective leadership will automatically add something to the masculinity of a man in a way that perpetuates unified acknowledgement of his personal and professional self. Any personal evaluation of a woman as a leader will just as automatically lead to possible doubts about either the professional capacities or the femininity of that woman. It is common among female top-managers to claim a self-understanding that is beyond gender in professionalism and true to gender in body-performance (Johannessen 1994). As a complimentary gesture it has become common for influential men who are somewhat set apart from the everyday chores and the responsibilities for care within their families, to say that they regret it for their own sake. Men's somewhat ambiguous efforts to take on more of the household chores and care duties are explained by psychological causes: men tend to think that women enjoy keeping the dominant position within the family and are not allowing them in (Holter & Aarseth 1993).

Gender segregation and male dominance are losing ground in social structuring as well as in social discourse. The new social arrangements and the new social justifications are established first of all by women operating in social contexts where the discredited principles of regulating gender still operate. This leaves an enormous gap for ambiguity of interpretation in the person/situation matrix, and for different subjective solutions to the dilemmas in personal development as to what could possibly be achieved by whom and preferred by whom (Søndergaard 1996). The conditions that are expanding opportunities for some women could equally create new ways of societal control and limitation for other women.

A cultural contextual method in the psychological study of gender

The interconnections between societal changes and personal development are based on subjective transformations of meanings. Deeply personal as such transformations may be felt, they are still not just an individual affair. Identity-formation in the psychological sense is more about identifying with one person in the service of separating from someone else. Gender acts as an important demarcation line, still without implementing any connecting identification between all women at all times. The imperative is "what kind of woman?" Each "answer" is evaluated according to what this "does" to other women comparatively as well as to men complementarily. Gender is not the matrix of meanings that make all women the same and different from all men, but rather the matrix of meanings that make each woman different from all other women and still a reasonable example of the kind (Haavind 1994a).

The reduction of gender segregation and the questionable status of male dominance should not be taken as a societal change that is already accomplished and unanimously approved by everyone. It is in itself an issue that is highly contested between women and men. Still it is presented here as a fruitful idea or guideline for looking into series of subjective interview recordings in an effort to understand what the subject as agent must confront. The concept of individual development relies heavily on the aims of each person as they encounter and transform actual conditions as social participants.

A general statement about the necessary intrinsic relationship between the individual and their surroundings could achieve a high level of consensus within the discipline of psychology. However, when it comes to methodological conventions for carrying out empirical studies, they are easily abandoned. At best they are replaced by a set of background factors possibly "influencing" individuals in a general way (Modell 1996). Methodological conventions within psychology select background factors according to a quasi-experimental design, as if they existed independently of the persons who relate to them. Then personal development may be taken as an effect that could be described by an independent observer using a general standard for developmental progress. The psychological models on the intermediate level of abstraction will tend to construct the characteristics of persons independently of their social context, as an on-going process within the individual. These presuppositions are actually adaptations to the claims made by models for statistical analysis of data from large groups of people. Such models search for interdependence in aspects that have to be registered independently. The demands for using a quantitative model replace any judgement as to whether this is an adequate modelling of the psychological processes involved. In the psychological interpretations of the results, the connections between the person and their experiences taken to represent a general relationship of a certain strength between individuals and influencing factors.

This way of modelling usually predetermines any study of the impact of gender. Societal preconditions are thereby construed as causes that influence people, and all preconditions are seen as neutral in the sense that they carry no gendered meanings. The significance of gender is placed exclusively as an intermediate device that may shape the effect according to the gendered characteristics that a person seems to carry. Gender, then, is modelled as something that resides with the individual. This mode of modelling and analyzing has reached a kind of scientific hegemony within the methodology of psychology, even though it is well known in theory that the "same" preconditions do not necessarily represent the same environment for men and for women.

The perspective of the twofold change offered here represents an alternative perspective. Women do not relate to preconditions that are equal to or comparable with those of men; they act on preconditions that vary just in the meanings applicable to women and to men and therefore represent different possibilities for them. The contexts are mindful. The meaning-making process is not unidirectional. Rather, the meanings are confirmed by the ways women relate to them and are utilizing them – and the women are possibly changing them further by changing themselves.

The psychological possibilities and limitations are construed differently not just between men and women, but also between groups of women. The personal impact of a specific social opportunity or its availability is perceived according to the horizon of possibilities that is associated with the actual category of person and the possible construction of a viable self. Any gender-specific modelling of personal development will have to reflect the fact that the person is situated in his or her context in a way that creates a set of intrinsic connections. If the context of living in a marriage is registered independently as the "same" condition for men as for women, the question of what a heterosexual marriage means to the development of women will be omitted. The results, whether they indicate that women are more, less or just as satisfied with their marriages as are men, use men as the yardstick and the implicit norm. If the idea is to understand how women inscribe marital possibilities and experiences in their own developmental efforts, it might turn out that sometimes they do so by comparing themselves to their male partner, and sometimes they don't. The comparisons are purposive manipulations of the connections between persons and situations. It is an effort by the women to initiate change or to justify the status quo.

However, the comparison of a female self to groups of men is not the only possible hypothetical manipulation women may make to judge the state of affairs. They may as well compare themselves to images of femininity, or to particular groups of women when assessing their on-going experiences. It is the social idealization of gender integration and the shrinking legitimacy of male dominance that has paved the way for self-references across gender for some women. For other women the comparison of their position in marriage to that of men in general simply does not make sense. If the researchers are relying on a specific convention for comparison of male and female individuals in their analyses, they ignore the empirical variation in how men and women are positioned. A methodological requirement is to set the record straight and not mistake hypothetical comparisons for equal or comparable positions in what a man and a woman is up against. Men and women are not situated in parallel positions when they encounter societal preconditions. When married to each other, they do not experience the same marriage. They experience the actual social condition of marriage as they present it to each other – as men and as women – two different kinds (Haavind 1984a).

To generate empirical data suitable for investigating the interdependency of societal preconditions and personal intentions and accomplishments as a twofold change, qualitative descriptions of the life experiences of women are needed. Each study may collect the stories from a set of women that relate to parallel conditions or who have gone through a certain type of experience. The sample may be composed strategically to balance common features as well as variations. The interviews offer principles for organizing experiences into personal knowledge, chronologically as a life history or episodically as aggregations of certain types of experience. The script or the format is established throughout the interview.

What is collected through an interview is not just the content of the experiences, but access to a recording self. Each narrator relates to the events in her life in the way she records them and accounts for them. By paying attention to them she assigns their significance for her assumptions of who she is and could possibly be (Haavind 1992, Magnusson 1998). The interviewer is shaping the recordings, supporting them and expanding them according to his or her capacity to understand what the protagonist is doing and trying to achieve. This is the first step in the gradual transformation of the unique interdependence of social experiences and personal development created by a specific person into conceptualizations of interdependencies that are relatively more shared and general. Psychological understanding is congruent with sets of self-understanding, but does not correspond exactly to any single example of such understanding.

Analysis of sets of recordings from interviews is carried out in a search for connections within stories, and they are tested for generality and variation across stories. The focus for connections between societal preconditions and personal intentions is through participation in social relationships as mutually defined. The search in the analysis is an interpretive oscillation between four steps or aspects contained in any fully-fledged story. These are:

- *societal and cultural preconditions* as they are made relevant by being directed at or being within reach of the subject;
- *actual social relationships* to other men and women with focus on how the subject and the other are involved in patterned interactions;
- *subjective agency* as expressed in intentions originating within and directed at someone or something – as utilization, counteraction, avoidance, achievement, resignation, enjoyment, etc. – and thereby identified as one's own;
- *possibilities and limitations* as perceived by the subject for reflecting and presenting herself as a person, and the actual inventive performance that is both *unique and reasonable* to others.

In the analysis gender is presupposed in all steps or aspects. The social and cultural preconditions carry gendered meanings. Actual social relationships are established and developed into gendered patterns, and the participants in social interaction pay continuous attention to gender. The personal agency is doing something about gender, thereby providing an answer to how this person is gendering herself. The performance is validated or questioned as expressions of this personal gender. The question that is answered through the analysis is not whether gender works, but how. And further, the answer is not to point to just one set of possible meanings associated with gender, but to a whole array of potential meanings which can be realized in repetitive or shifting ways.

Negotiating meanings of gender into a gendered self

If the methodological perspective in developing psychological understanding of men and women is established as comparisons between selected groups, the results will be restricted in form and content to gender differences (or equalities) in behaviour and capacities. To make valid comparisons, the groups will have to be comparable, which means that they have the same kind of experiences except for gender, and that their social positioning is parallel so that they are facing similar preconditions. In the actual relationships between men and women the fulfilment of these two assumptions is the exception rather than the rule. The methodology of comparisons has to be expanded with a methodology for interactions. The comparison model construes gender as something people *have*; an interactive model construes gender as something people *do* (Deaux & Major 1987, West & Zimmerman 1987, West & Fenstermaker 1995).

In an interactive model gender is an on-going affair, an issue of negotiation in social relationships. The distinction between male and female is made relevant for everyone as the basic question of who you are. The ascribed gender functions as a framework for interpretations of the actions. Every interaction immediately establishes reciprocal agreement concerning the sex of the participants, and every action would have been understood differently if it had been the reaction of an actor belonging to the other sex. This naturalization of the link between body and category is self-evident to the social actors. Socially constructed as given by nature, it can be seen as something that precedes social life. This illustrates the puzzling character of the conceptual distinction between sex and gender. The concept of gender was presented to produce a model of men and women as socially created. It worked to reduce sex into something else that was not. The pertinent task in modern construction of gendered selves has been to find your way between the two kinds of material or building blocks that you work with, namely what is given to you as something you will have to accept as you, and what you can foresee and appropriate as you. Self-construction is an on-going task, implying that no one can fully know what is already there and what must follow. Through this mode of understanding personal gender is socially constructed as made of two kinds of material, one kind deriving from nature and one kind deriving from culture. This fragmentation of gender is an adaptation to the twofold changes and a way of handling the unresolved cultural tensions between gender segregation and integration and male dominance and gender justice.

In Nordic culture the debates about which part or how large a proportion of womanliness is created by nature, and which part or how large a proportion is culturally developed are not just a matter of what can be proven, but a question of what can be done individually and collectively to influence the meanings of gender. The answer is seen as important for what kind of gender justice can be achieved. And every women can find information that may assist her in finding her "true self", and in eventually separating it from the self that has been socially "imposed" on her. This will in turn facilitate her judgement of which part of herself can be directed by herself according to her own wishes. Psychologically gendered selves, then, are split up into three aspects or fragments in the same person: gender as given by nature, gender as imposed by others, and the gender which feels comfortable or which one would like to achieve for oneself.

Identity work involves splitting oneself into parts and putting them together again, separating and uniting them to understand and validate an agentic and reflective self. Everyone is obliged to do identity work on a continuous basis. The issue of what kind of a woman an individual is, is negotiated in social interaction as a side-issue to the other issues that are developed in dialogues. Whether desired or not, women are constantly involved in negotiations concerning what their actions prove about the kind of women they are or could possibly be (Rudie 1984, Haavind 1985). This question has no ultimate answer. Gendered meanings are predetermined as well as capable of change.

The construction of an oppositional distinction between male and female gender leads to the assumption that there exist several components within every person that could be checked against meanings associated with either masculinity or femininity. Or to put it the other way around, the social changes that are questioning the social segregation of women from men as a sign of social order, and throwing doubt on the legitimacy of the subordination of women to men, will result in ideas of fragmented and moveable personal genderization. What is negotiated, then, is not the individual's fate as a woman, nor their gender as a whole, but their parts as gendered and themselves as responsible for their own future achievements (Bengtsson 1990, Søndergaard 1996).

Discourses about gender establish such parts or fragments by referring to them and accounting for their significance in the composition of identity. The references are reflexive, one part relates to the other. The basic distinction concerns bodies. Bodies are perceived as having a sex and therefore as being sexed accordingly. The essence of the feminine body is to be what the other is not, and of the masculine body to have what the other lacks.

As already mentioned, the presumed nature of one gender being what the other is not makes the genderization of bodies into a process that takes place independently of individual human action. Hence it becomes a process that precedes the genderization of any other aspect of the person. In the next step this makes the body a place where everything else that is attributed to the person has to be attached and related to what is already said to be there (Søndergaard 1996). Sexual orientation is one such aspect that attaches to the person in a way that is important for him or her to enact, and therefore to accept, to hide, to defend . . . By relating to "it", it becomes mine.

As everyone knows, sexual desire is presumed to be gendered according to the body, by being directed mainly and consistently at persons of the opposite sex and reciprocal desire. If this is not the case, it is a personal and not a cultural choice. Anyone who discovers stronger erotic attractions towards a person of the same sex could possibly perceive himself or herself as having an incorrect or unsuitable body, and really as having a self that was gendered in accordance with the desire and not with the body. However, if a woman likes to be and prefers to love a body with female attributes, she will rather construe herself as a lesbian in a world not so well suited to lesbians, than as a man in an unfit body.

As several historical studies of changes in mentality have shown, the idea of different sexual orientations was gradually developed in acknowledgement of the separation of body, desire and self (Rosenbeck 1987). The conceptualization of hetero- and homosexuality was "discovered" as inhering to some people as a trick of nature. The demand for social acceptance was based on the idea that same-sex desire was impossible to resist for some people, because it accorded with their individual nature. They were not fighting the heterosexual order, they just could not fit in themselves. The negotiated result, a separate kind of nature, based on the possibility of creating body and desire in fragmentation, was accepted because it fulfilled some demands for creative invention raised by the prevailing cultural discourse of the nature of man. The "scientific" discovery of homosexuality helped the establishment of the last scientific discipline, sexology. The helplessness and the suffering of the identified cases made homosexuals innocent; they claimed no capacity to seduce those without the same nature inside. As a result heterosexuality was reconstructed as well, as a force originating in men and women. It was released from the inside of the body and directed outwards, searching for someone – "opposite" – on the outside. Heterosexual desire became the basis for a certain kind of personal relationship, accounting for a marriage that should bring something more to the couple than organization of reproductive and productive tasks according to gender.

When sexuality was made into a personal preference, as well as a personal responsibility, it paved the way for further development of systems for reciprocal confirmation of gender opposites as mutually attractive. All individuals are not heterosexual, but as soon as they realize what they are, they will seek to satisfy the desire originating within and aroused from outside. Sexual desire is accepted as a *part* of self because it is inevitable and cannot be fully controlled. A recognized desire brings into play other parts of the self to balance resistance or to give in. It could be called *my sexuality*, or hetero-sexuality possessing *me*. To accept irrationality as a part of oneself, becomes a new task in proper identity work.

The result of the campaigns of the first homosexual activists was that their existence was acknowledged, and their homosexuality was accepted as having been caused by the diversity of nature as it had fallen on the individual. However, this result is challenged by some lesbians who claim that their preference for female lovers is a deliberate choice of lifestyle and personal identification. Their desire is rational, they resist male company, not because of feelings of bodily and sexual repulsion for males, but because of social and personal choices. The campaigns are on-going. People participate in order to bear witnesses to what they believe to be the truth.

Through endless negotiation the meanings of gender are made more diverse. The simple stereotypes are known to everyone, but there is no need to follow them. When young Danish students in different disciplines within the social sciences were asked what they considered to be the impact of gender on themselves and their friends, they tended to think that nobody paid any special attention to gender norms (Søndergaard 1994). They had difficulties in accounting for what it meant to them, considering it to be personal and endlessly varied. As students they perceived their task to be to look away from gender. With respect to off-campus activities, they tended to think that gender played its game with them in ways they could not themselves control. When they recorded their experiences of episodes in different social milieux where they were involved in social activities in a more or less ordinary way, gender was present. Their very recordings were a form of suggestion in the negotiations as to what gender may possibly mean (Søndergaard 1996).

An analysis of the very varied statements from students concerning gender, and the difficulties of the same students in trying to explain their own use of gender as a system for choosing and accounting for their personal preferences with reference to a gender ideology with a fixed and shared content, presented another kind of pattern. The person is compartmentalized into parts or fragments, and all parts can be seen on a continuum ranging from the overtly masculine to the overtly feminine. Everything the individual wishes for or actually does can be inscribed in the matrix as expressing something associated with femininity or masculinity from a specific aspect that takes on a certain position in the construction of self.

In her analysis of Danish students, Dorte Marie Søndergaard (1996) distinguished seven components that seemed to be embedded in the descriptions of their every-day activities and how they accounted for them. The exact number of components and the distinctions drawn between them may vary between cultures and sub-cultures. The point here is to show that sensitivity to these aspects of identity work increases the capacity of the researcher to understand the women in the psychological mode; the possible operating principles used by individuals to make sense of their behaviour and that of others in ways that cover the actual observed variation within and across individuals. The seven components are:

- signification of the body;
- orientation of desire;
- position in the sexual encounter;
- repertoire of qualifications and capacities;
- inclusion and involvement in socially organized activities;
- bodily performance and presentation;
- self-reflection.

The "rating" of the different aspects of the person as feminine and masculine, and how these aspects are singled out and then combined to be unified into a person, constitutes the possibilities for creating new and unique individuals as variations of well-known and conventionally gendered themes. Such is the task of female students entering an academic arena that until recently was nearly exclusively male, but has adapted to the ideal of gender integration by claiming to be gender-neutral (Søndergaard 1994). If a female student prefers, she may select what she considers to be the masculine rather than the feminine part of any component, and still include it in her feminine self that resides within her female body. Thereby she is satisfying the requirement to be her gender in a personalized way. But most commonly she will break with the conventional and stereotypical connections in just a few aspects. Every break unleashes a potential question, and more conventional scoring on other aspects will compensate, and act as an answer. In this way no doubt is cast on what she really is – a natural woman self. Each negotiator has to balance the intentions that carry a danger of being associated with the opposite gender by herself or by others, with the possibilities of gaining validation from significant others as properly gendered.

Negotiations are carried out with others and reflectively with oneself. The actual form is selected by identification; how must I act in order to be accepted as one of the girls in fourth grade, a professor yet still one of the mothers, a female long-distance runner, etc? Negotiations take place when the interactional partners adjust to each other. Gender is usually not the explicit subject of the conversation, but it might be. The explicit rules for handling gender are different in different social arenas. Behaviour that is seen as seductive in a woman may thus be highly valued on a date, but viewed as highly suspicious in the office. On most occasions women do not set the rules for how or when one should pay any attention to gender. This is particularly the case for the new social arenas from which women were previously excluded. The rule of no woman or no womanliness admitted, has been replaced by rules claimed to be gender-neutral. These rules secure the old rulers of the domain a meta-control instead of direct control. They are the ones to decide how and when being different as a woman represents something that is acceptable or something that is to be blamed on the "owner" of the womanliness (Haavind 1985, Johannessen 1994).

The conceptualization of the (gender)negotiating (gendered)subject is proposed to replace the conceptualization of a person with a core or essence that is consistent and continuous. Structural theories of personality have been intentionally avoided here. This is not to say that individuals do not consider themselves to be continuous and consistent, and do not refer to their core identity as located inside and therefore observable directly by themselves but only indirectly by others. The imagination of an interior room that houses oneself, is a collective set of linguistic references in the culture under discussion here. The scientific psychological understanding of man has paralleled that of the culture (Butler 1990). The psychological being is split up into psychological part processes that may be analyzed as such, and all of them are seen as belonging together and being integrated in the body by the operation of a self to create and sustain an identity.

Self, then, is a phenomenon – psychologically designed as the subjective reflections about connections or relations within oneself, and also as the connections and the belongingness to other people. Identity as a phenomenon will be defined as the presented result of what is subjectively experienced as an integration of different experiences into a continuous search for coherence. Negotiations will converge into reflections of self in relation to others, or they may be conflicting and confusing and create doubt and discomfort. Consistency is neither self-evident nor necessary – just something that is continuously searched for and evaluated. The result could be *I am changing* or *I am staying the same*. The shared illusion of the body as a gendered pre-existence giving space for a gendered self is the prerequisite for making all kinds of diverse experiences into a governing idea that they belong together because they represent the same in the deepest sense – the psychological woman. A woman who is speaking about herself, may therefore do so with many voices that could all still be identified as hers.

Human activity gives gender to everything

In the conceptualization of psychological gender as a matrix, the two characteristics of the observed results of gender negotiations are united; on the one hand, the unavoidable solidity that goes with the two mutually exclusive kinds, and on the other hand generativity that goes with the different and still linked fragments. This dual character of gender operates as a shared set of presuppositions that constitutes a code and acts as a forestructure of experiences. Gender is not just created through experiences, experiences are created through gender. Individuals are not just created gendered, they are created as individuals through gender (Shotter 1993, Haavind 1987a, Haavind 1994b). Gender acts through language and resides in language. A further exploration of gender as meaning-making will have to inquire into the dual character of fixation and flux.

In accordance with the aspect of *fixation* are the following four capacities of the code.

- Gender is *strongly and rigorously enforced*. The creation of every person into a man or a woman is virtually indispensable. The social imperative is to be your gender.
- Gender is *widely applied*. All kinds of substance and forms may be said to carry feminine or masculine characteristics. It is not just bodies that acquire a flavour of gender, it might as well be taken on by inanimate objects, acts and skills, structures and places. In the metaphorical sense gender will create sentiments and abstractions, like the relationship between nature and culture, or between reason and emotion. Gender is a possible consideration and a resulting assessment of any experience.
- Gender is *signified through the presences of bodies*. Even when gender is left out of the conversation, it is still present through every speaker.
- Gender is *structuring social relationships*. All combinations or connections of speaker and speech are positioning every person in relationships; as opposites or similar, as included or left out by each other.

In accordance with the *flux* are the following four capacities of the code:

- Gender has no fixed substance, *no essence*, no core – neither on the masculine nor on the feminine side. All efforts to specify a core meaning end up with registrations of series of overlaps, exceptions and changes.
- Gender is a potential for meaning-making. Through on-going negotiations it *can be left out or made into an issue*. The search for core meanings is one way of explicitly negotiating gender. To look away from gender – bracketing gender – is another way of handling it. Negotiations relate to the actual meanings of femininity and masculinity, and to how and when gender is relevant or irrelevant, a blessing or a nuisance.
- Notions of gender may be *accepted or counteracted*. Recognizable as well as inventive expressions of gender may be acknowledged. Gender does not make all women the same, but makes each example of woman unique and reasonable. Social change as well as social stability may be explained by reference to gender. People in similar positions in the negotiations may unite to form value systems, and they may inscribe their stance as relevant to their identity work.
- Gendered meanings are *transferred from one phenomenon to another*. Gender accounts for fragmentation and combinations of phenomena. Gender is formatting.

Just think of what is happening when one views Marlene Dietrich wearing a top hat and tuxedo jacket with net stockings and high-heeled shoes. In this case the distinct masculine parts or aspects are compartmentalizing gender, and are making it somewhat ambiguous whether gender is on the surface or inside. In this case it is formatting her as even more feminine. And depending on the gender of the viewer, it renders a he even more masculine and a she less feminine, if they both operate with the assumption that the arena is heterosexual.

The actions of any woman could be interpreted as utterances in the language that is established through the operation of the gendered code. Gender is a code that frames the histories of all women, which is different from claiming that all women end up with the same history. Understanding women in the psychological mode is therefore not to look for what is regularly characteristic of women, but to look for the ways actual women have related to the distinctions of gender as such distinctions have been presented to them in their lives.

To say that gender is a code is to say that in the most general sense it is not the content that is identified as masculine or feminine, it is a kind of regulation through making distinctions. Social codes are used as shared commitment to regulations, and the regulations of the gender code have two distinctive features. First, the regulation within language that positions phenomena as either feminine or masculine is necessarily and always (dis)connection as opposites. The one is defined by not being what the other is. Masculine is the binary opposite of feminine. *Distinctions are made, and a kind of separation is achieved.* Secondly, the regulation or ordering within language of whatever is identified at the masculine and the feminine pole of opposition, is simultaneously and automatically ranked. *The masculine aspects will be relatively ranked above as more dominant, general or relevant than the feminine aspect of the same opposition.* It is any combination of *dichotomization* and *hierarchization* that is gender because it makes gender. Dichotomization together with hierarchization is generally undertaken with gender – the relationship of masculine to feminine – as the guiding metaphor (Haavind 1992).

The relative subordination of femininity to masculinity

This description of the general capacities of the gendered code does not imply that actual women never equal men in what they do and how they think about it. The impact of the gendered code is just that this equality is not establishing gender, but easily makes it into an issue. Correspondingly, it does not follow from the code that actual men always have all the power over the women they relate to, but just that the dominance of men could be seen as an expression of masculinity. When actual women are positioned as dominant in relation to men, they easily experience lack of confidence in their "femininity" (Johannessen 1995). If they act dominant without being so positioned, they are in danger of attracting evaluations of negative femininity (Haavind 1985). However, neither follows in itself; it can be and will be counteracted in certain circumstances. Actual research may find out more about how.

The awareness of the gendered code has to be incorporated into the analytical perspective of the researcher trying to understand the psychological dynamics of the female subjects. This is a recommendation. What is offered here is a set of lenses for viewing the variety of developing and monitoring selves and identities as women – for understanding them in the psychological mode. It is not an a priori definition of gender; it is a generalization of knowledge based on research. The relevance of the capacities and the impact of the gendered code are transformed into guidelines for analyses of new recorded experiences.

With such a recommendation I counteract the ruling convention within psychology for the study of women and men – that the researcher should have no presuppositions as to what gender is about, but leave that entirely to the empirical material to tell. As has been argued here, the idea of neutrality will actually restrict the community of researchers within a set of presuppositions about gender. Since they are just taken for granted, they cannot be reflected upon and scrutinized, nor changed in the analytical encounters with the presuppositions about gender in the women who are studied. Conventional analytical procedures will act as modes of understanding that are not scrutinized for the limitations and distortions they create in the results. The interior relationship between perspective and possible results should be made movable, and this is best done by reflecting on the dual character of the gendered code in *fixation* and *flux* and the two regulative features of gender as *dichotomization* and *hierarchization*.

Power is rendered invisible when men and women acknowledge each other. The result is a fit that creates love, or reason or practicalities. In cultural contexts where integration is idealized and male dominance is made less legitimate, gender as a reason for social arrangements is concealed. The results are still gendered, but without a cause. Any woman increases the probability that she will be valued positively as a woman if she herself co-operates so that her subordination looks like something else – something she desires. Mutual conformation of identity cannot be achieved by realizing gender stereotypes, but through being individual and unique. The reciprocal positive message between the male and the female is a double bind: both are dependent on having the other co-operate in having her submissiveness and his dominance appear as something else. The modern world as it is represented in the studies we have conducted is full of examples of interaction between men and women that are explained as personally chosen or agreed upon for practical reasons, out of necessity, as a result of different personal preferences or out of love (Andenæs 1989a, 1989b, Ulvik 1993, Hvistendahl 1994). When the cases are aggregated into patterns the conse-quences are gender specific, and the woman is rendered relatively more dependent or isolated or restricted or burdened, etc. His state of mind is given precedence and her state of mind is adjusted to fit in with his (Haavind 1993, Hansen & Trana 1994). A modern woman can do everything as long as she does it in relative subordination to a man (Haavind 1984a).

It is now more difficult than previously to make passivity and submis-siveness into a virtue for women as expressions of their femininity. The horizon of possible meanings has been transformed. Dependent women are pitied or even despised. A woman has to improve her self-confidence – in being a woman. An ambiguous message from a culture showing her that she should preferably value herself in a capacity that may be devalued within the social system to which she belongs (Ethelberg 1983). In any case there are some aspects of the social reality that women are supposed not to pay attention to, or not to take personally. To be a reasonable person in general, is dependent on the capacity to look away from being what she is – a woman (Johannessen 1994).

Psychological understanding of the handling of power in the relationship between women and men is regularly based on analyses of the conflicts that arise between them. It is, however, more important to learn from how the agreements are reached and sustained. The contributions from men and women in reaching agreement are not the same – her contribution cannot be replaced by his. If episodes are taken one by one, it is difficult to see the tracks of male dominance. However, the pattern is revealed when several couples are compared, or when one couple is followed through a course of events over a period of time (Haavind 1994a, Holmberg 1993).

The conceptualization of the twofold changes as it is subjectively reacted to and reflected upon among women in the Nordic countries represents a fruitful challenge to the psychological understanding of personal develop-ment in women. Psychologists carrying out research seeking for the subject-ivity of women, will constantly encounter personal recordings that contradict the standards developed within psychology to judge the adequacy of their development.

Understanding women in the psychological mode equates to how power and disconnection are handled in personal relationships, and what is actu-ally given as the possibilities and aspirations of specific women. The level of generalization in such studies is not how women are, but what they can possibly do and what they are learning about themselves. How do they account for their competencies and deficiencies? How are their social inte-gration and vulnerability constructed? What are the terms of discrepancies and coherence in how they are experienced and understood by themselves and others? Their answers will form a model that acknowledges subjectiv-ity, organizes experiences as agent-driven and negotiable, and opens up the discourse to a multiplicity of developmental changes. The model is based on the assumption that all women have to handle the imperative to monitor themselves as women, and that this task inevitably concerns a handling of male dominance in one way or another. Which is also to say that it is male identities that act as context and are therefore put at risk (Modell 1996, Conell 1995).

Studying women's subjectivities as expressed in their stories helps deconstruct gender-neutral models of personal development, and set up gender specifications that are neither a return to the double standard, nor the introduction of new stereotypes. The end of the developmental traject-ories is as open to the researcher as it is to women handling the twofold change. The recommendation for psychology, then, is not to turn to the inside or to the past in a search for a fresh and undistorted look at what is really or naturally feminine or masculine, but to follow the new inventions in lives not yet lived. A cultural contextual psychology assumes that there have never lived women – or men – like us, engaged in a mutual effort to change and expand the restrictions and the rationale constructed by gender. It is an effort to lift ourselves up by the hair.

References

Andenæs, A. 1989a. Identitet og sosial endring. Del I [Identity and social change. Part I]. *Tidsskrift for Norsk psykologforening* **26**, 603–16.

Andenæs, A. 1989b. Identitet og sosial endring. Del II [Identity and social change. Part II]. *Tidsskrift for Norsk psykologforening* **26**, 683–95.

Anstorp, T. & A.K. Clasen 1988a. Når terapi gjør livet enda vanskeligere [When psychotherapy makes life even more difficult]. *Materialisten* **16** (3), 31–45.

Anstorp, T. & A.K. Clasen 1988b. Kvinneterapi [Feminist therapy]. *Materialisten* **16** (3), 46–55.

Bengtsson, M. 1990. *Könssocialization och social förändring – om brott och kontinuitet i ungdomars identitetsutveckling från 1950 til 1970/80 tal* [Gender socialization and social changes – about discontinuity and continuity in identity development in young people from 1950 to 1970/80]. Psykologi i tillämpning 8 (1). Lund University, Sweden.

Bjerrum Nielsen, H. (ed.) 1988. *Jenteliv og likestillingslære* [Girl's lives and education for sex-equality]. Oslo: Cappelen.

Bjerrum Nielsen, H. 1994. Den magiske blokk – om kjønn og identitetsarbeid [The magic block – on gender and identity work]. *Psyke & Logos* **15** (1), 30–47.

Bjerrum Nielsen, H. & M. Rudberg 1994. Girls in change. In *Psychological gender and modernity*, H. Bjerrum Nielsen & M. Rudberg (eds), 137–49. Oslo: Scandinavian University Press.

Bjørklund, T. 1985. *Holdninger til likestilling* [Attitudes towards gender equality]. Arbeidsnotat 5. Institute for Social Research, Oslo, Norway.

Blom, S., T. Noack, L. Østby 1993. *Giftemål og barn – bedre sent enn aldri* [Marriage and childbirth – better late than never]. Sosiale og økonomiske studier. Statistical Bureau of the Census, Oslo, Norway.

Brown, L.M. & C. Gilligan (eds) 1992. *Meeting at the crossroads: women's psychology and girls' development.* New York: Ballantine.

Butler, J. 1990. *Gender trouble. Feminism and the subversion of identity.* New York: Routledge.

Chesler, P. 1972. *Women and madness.* New York: Avon.

Chodorow, N. 1978. *The reproduction of mothering. Psychoanalysis and the sociology of gender.* Berkeley: University of California Press.

Chodorow, N. 1995. Gender as a personal and cultural construction. *Sign* **20**, 516–44.

Chodorow, N. & S. Contratto 1982. The phantasy of the perfect mother. In *Rethinking the family*, B. Thorne & M. Yalom (eds), 191–215. New York: Longman.

Conell, R.W. 1995. *Masculinities.* Berkeley: University of California Press.

Dahl, S. 1993. *Rape – a hazard to women's health.* Oslo: Scandinavian University Press.

Deaux, K. & B. Major 1987. Putting gender into context: an interactive model of gender-related behaviour. *Psychological Review* **94**, 369–89.

Ethelberg, E. 1983. *Kvindelighedens modsigelse – om kvinders personlighedsstrategier overfor mandlig dominans* [The contradictions of femininity – the personal strategies of women towards male dominance]. Copenhagen: Anthropos.

Frankenberg, R. 1993. *White women, race matters. The social construction of whiteness.* Minneapolis: University of Minnesota Press.

Feminism & Psychology 1994. *Special Feature: Critical connections. The Harvard project on Women's psychology and girls' development,* **4** (3).

Gergen, K. 1991. *The saturated self.* New York: Basic Books.

Gilligan, C. 1982. *In a different voice. Psychological theory and women's development.* Cambridge, Mass.: Harvard University Press.

Haavind, H. 1973. Myten om den gode mor [The myth of the good mother]. In *Myten om den gode mor.* H. Haavind et al. (eds), 35–99. Oslo: Pax.

Haavind, H. 1978. Psykologisk forskning om kvinner [Psychological research on women]. In *Sosialpsykologi*, vol.I [Social psychology], L. Hem & H. Holter (eds), 297–326. Oslo: Scandinavian University Press.

Haavind, H. 1984a. Love and power in marriage. In *Patriarchy in a welfare society.* H. Holter (ed.), 136–68. Oslo: Scandinavian University Press.

Haavind, H. 1984b. Fordeling av omsorgsfunksjoner i småbarnsfamilier [Negotiations on sharing of work and caring in families with small children]. In *Myk start – hard landing* [Soft take-off – crash landing], I. Rudie (ed.), 161–91. Oslo: Scandinavian University Press.

Haavind, H. 1985. Förendringar i förhållandet mellan kvinnor och män [Changes in relationships between men and women]. *Kvinnovetenskaplig tidskrift* (3), 17–28.

Haavind, H. 1987a. Kvinners utviklingsmuligheter [Developmental possibilities for women]. *Nytt om kvinneforskning* (4), 65–72.

Haavind, H. 1987b. *Liten og stor. Mødres omsorg og barns utviklingsmuligheter* [The big one and the little one. The organization of care by mothers and the possibilities for development in children]. Oslo: Scandinavian University Press.

Haavind, H. 1988. Er et kjønnsnøytralt menneskesyn et vitenskapelig ideal [Should a gender-neutral view of man be counted as a scientific ideal?]. *Nordisk Psykologi* **40**, 309–24.

Haavind, H. 1989. Makt, følelser og rasjonalitet? [Is rationality possible without the recognition of power and emotion?]. *Nytt norsk tidsskrift* **6**, 248–62.

Haavind, H. 1992. Vi måste söka efter könets förändrade betydelse [We will have to search for the changing meanings of gender]. *Kvinnovetenskaplig tidskrift* (3), 16–34.

Haavind, H. 1993. Analyse av kvinners historier – bearbeiding av makt og splittelse [Analysis of the stories of women – assuming gender as the handling of power and disconnection]. In *Køn i forandring. Ny forskning om køn, socialisering og identitet* [Gender and change. New research on gender, socialization and identity]. A.M. Nielsen et al. (eds), 12–45. Copenhagen: Forlaget Hyldespjæt.

Haavind, H. 1994a. Kjønn i forandring som fenomen og som forståelsesmåte [The changing meanings of gender – as phenomena and as modes of understanding]. *Tidsskrift for Norsk Psykologforening* **31**, 767–84.

Haavind, H. 1994b. Kjønn og klinisk forståelse [Gender and clinical understanding]. In *Psykologi i forandring* [Psychology changing], S. Reichelt (ed.), 81–107. Oslo: Norwegian Psychological Association.

Hansen, B. & H. Trana 1994. Det verdige moderskap i etterkrigstiden. En sosiapsykologisk studie av forbindelseslinjene mellom kulturelle endringer og kvinnelig identitet [The dignified motherhood in the post war period. A social-psychological study of the connections between cultural changes and female identity]. *Tidsskrift for Norsk Psykologforening* **31**, 797–817.

Henriques, J., C. Holloway, C. Urwin, C. Venn, V. Walkerdine (eds) 1984. *Changing the subject.* London: Methuen.

Holmberg, C. 1993. *Det kallas kärlek* [It is called love]. Göteborg: Anamma.

Holter, Ø.G. & H. Aarseth 1993. *Menns livssammenheng* [Men's lives]. Oslo: Ad Notam.

Hvistendahl, M. 1994. Menn som medforeldre. En kvalitativ intervjuundersøkelse av småbarnsfedre [Men as co-parents. A qualitative interview-based study of fathers of pre-school children]. *Tidsskrift for Norsk Psykologforening* **31**, 784–97.

Hydén, M. 1994. *Woman battering as a marital act. The construction of a violent marriage.* Oslo: Scandinavian University Press.

Johannessen, B.F. 1994. *Det flytende kjønnet* [The flotating gender]. Doctoral dissertation, Department of Psychology, University of Bergen, Norway.

Jordan, J.V., A.G. Kaplan, J.B. Miller, I.P. Stiver, J.L. Surrey 1991. *Women's growth in connection. Writings from the Stone Center.* New York: Guilford Press.

Kaschak, E. 1992. *Engendered lives. A new psychology of women's experience.* New York: Basic Books.

Kitzinger, C., S. Wilkinson, R. Perkins (eds) 1992. Heterosexuality. Special Issue. *Feminism & Psychology* **2** (3).

Leira, A. 1992. *Welfare states and working mothers. The Scandinavian experience.* Cambridge: Cambridge University Press.

Magnusson, E. 1996. *Att hålla balansen och passa in. Kvinnoliv i flagnande statsbyråkratier* [To maintain the balance and to fit in. Women's lives in state bureaucracies]. Rapportserie (6). Kvnnovetenskapligt forum, Umeå University, Sweden.

Magnusson, E. 1998. *Vardagens Könsinnebörder under förhandling – om arbete, familj och produktion av Kvinnlighet* [Negociating gender in everyday lives – on work, family and the production of femininity]. Doctoral dissertation. Department of Applied Psychology, University of Umeå, Sweden.

Marecek, J. 1995. Psychology and feminism: can this discipline be saved? In *Feminisms in the academy.* D.C. Stanton & A.J. Stewart (eds), 101–33. Ann Arbor: University of Michigan Press.

Miller, J.B. 1976. *Toward a new psychology of women.* Boston, Mass.: Beacon Press.

Miller, J.B. 1994. Women's psychological development: connections, disconnections and violations. In *Women beyond Freud*, M.M. Berger (ed.), 79–97. New York: Brunner/Mazel.

Millett, K. 1970. *Sexual politics.* New York: Doubleday.

Modell, J. 1996. The uneasy engagement of human development and ethnography. In *Ethnography and human development. Context and meaning in social inquiry,* R. Jessor, A. Colby, R.A. Shweder (eds), 479–505. Chicago: University of Chicago Press.

Morawski, J.G. 1994. *Practicing feminisms, reconstructing psychology.* Ann Arbor: University of Michigan Press.

Nilsson, M. 1994. En tilstand hun går inn i og ikke kommer ut av [A state she approaches and then gets stuck in]. *Tidsskrift for Norsk Psykologforening* **31**, 817–37.

Ødegård, T. 1991. Den elsk-verdige kvinnen. Mønstre og mangfold [The lovable woman. Patterns and varieties]. In *Nye kvinner – nye menn* [New women – new men], R. Haukaa (ed.), 41–61. Oslo: Ad Notam.

Polkinghorne, D.E. 1993. *Narrative knowing and the human sciences.* Albany, NY: State University Press.

Polkinghorne, D.E. 1995. Narrative configuration in qualitative analysis. *International Journal of Qualitative Studies in Education* **8**, 200–33.

Potter, J. & M. Wetherell 1987. *Discourse and social psychology. Beyond attitudes and behaviour.* London: Sage.

Rosenbeck, B. 1987. Kvindekøn. Den moderne kvindeligheds historie, 1880–1980 [Female gender. The history of the modern femininity, 1880–1980]. Copenhagen: Gyldendal.

Rudie, I. 1984. Innledning [Introduction], In *Myk start – hard landing* [Soft start – crash landing], I. Rudie (ed.), 13–37. Oslo: Scandinavian University Press.

Shotter, J. 1993. *Conversational realities. Constructing life through language.* London: Sage.

Skrede, K. 1986. Hvor langt er vi kommet på vei mot likestilling? [How far have we progressed on a road to gender equality?]. In *Kan vi planlegge oss til likestilling i 2010?* [Is it possible to plan for gender equality in 2010?], K. Skrede & K. Tornes (eds), 13–35. Oslo: Scandinavian University Press.

Skrede, K. & K. Tornes 1986 (eds). *Den norske kvinnerevolusjonen* [The women's revolution in Norway]. Oslo: Scandinavian University Press.

Søndergaard, D.M. 1993. Køn på universitetet – kvalifisering til et maskulint handlerum [Gender at the university – qualifying for a masculine social setting]. In *Køn i forandring. Ny forskning om køn, socialisering og identitet* [Changing gender. New research on gender, socialization and identity], T.R. Eriksen et al. (eds), 195–213. Copenhagen: Hyldespjæt.

Søndergaard, D.M. 1994. Køn i formidlingsproces mellem kultur og individ: Nogle analytiske grep [Gender mediated between culture and individual: Some analytical grasps]. *Psyche & Logos* **15**, 47–69.

Søndergaard, D.M. 1996. *Tegnet på kroppen. Køn, koder og konstruksjoner blandt unge voksne i akademia* [The sign on the body. Gender, codes and constructions among young adults in academia]. University of Copenhagen: Museum Tusculanum Press.

Tavris, C. 1992. *The mismeasure of women.* New York: Simon & Schuster.

Thorsen, K. 1996. *Kjønn, livsløp og alderdom* [Gender, life-course and aging]. Doctoral dissertation, Department of Sociology, University of Bergen, Norway.

Ulvik, O.S. 1993. Barn saman – kvinner og menn forhandlar [Having children together – men and women negotiate]. *Tidsskrift for Norsk psykologforening* **30**, 1069–1080.

Weisstein, N. 1971. Psychology constructs the female. In *Woman in sexist society,* V. Gornick & B.K. Moran (eds), 207–25. New York: Basic Books.

Wertsch, J.V. 1997. Narrative tools of history and identity. *Culture and Psychology.* **3**, 5–20.

West, C. & D.H. Zimmerman, 1987. Doing gender. *Gender and Society* **1**, 125–51.

West, C. & S. Fenstermaker 1995. Doing difference. *Gender and Society* **9**, 8–37.

Ålund, A. 1997. Feminism and multiculturalism: recognition of difference and beyond. *Sosiologisk tidsskrift/Journal of Sociology* **5**, 127–45.

CHAPTER FOURTEEN

Reflections on the rationality of emotions and feelings

Sara Heinämaa & Martina Reuter

Western philosophy has often placed emotions in opposition to reason and argued that a person cannot be both emotional and fully rational at the same time. This tradition has also associated women with emotionality; the claim that women are more emotional than men is a recurring theme in discussions of women's capabilities. Moreover, these two traditional claims about emotions often appear intertwined. The consequence is problematic for feminists. If women are more emotional than men, and if emotionality conflicts with reason, then women are less qualified than men for tasks requiring rational capacities, e.g., politics, scholarship, economics, etc.

In this chapter we will study how the argument that women's emotionality leads to defective rationality can be dismantled. Our main concern is with feminist strategies that challenge the opposition between emotion and reason. This means that we are not going to take a stand on women's emotionality.[1] Instead, we shall follow the defenders of emotional rationality and criticize the presumptions that underlie the opposition of reason to emotions.

We are going to study how the relation between emotion and reason is analyzed in specific philosophical texts. We wish to argue that the opposition cannot be resolved in a satisfactory way unless it is placed in a wider conceptual context, related, in particular, to the dualism between mind and body. We shall show that the arguments against women's rational capacities will re-emerge – only in a new form – if we ignore the concerns about mind–body dualism. Simply put, the arguments cannot be dismantled without questioning dichotomous thinking in general.

1   The historical relation of the reason – emotion opposition to the mind–body distinction

Emotions – the so-called passions of the soul – have traditionally been seen as phenomena that mediate the mental and the physical: they appear in the soul or belong to the mind, but have their origin in the body. Aristotle, for example, argued that passions are connected to the lower, "bodily" part of the soul – the so-called animal soul – and should be governed by the rational part of the soul, the intellect.[2]

In the seventeenth century, René Descartes criticized Aristotle's division of the soul. According to Descartes, the human mind is one unified whole. Passions are not its parts but its states – they are thoughts, similar to reflections, perceptions or volitions. Descartes argued that the *origin*, not location, bore the distinguishing mark of the passions: passions are thoughts actively caused by the body and passively received by the mind (Descartes [1649] 1990:328–46). The term "passion" expresses the problematic idea that the passions – emotions – are states in which the rational capacity of the soul is passive. In this respect they are opposed to pure thoughts and volitions which are actively caused by the rational mind (ibid.:328–9, 335).

The tradition to which both Aristotle and Descartes belong has conceived reason and the passions as inherently conflicting faculties. They are supposed to incline or pull the human being in different, possibly opposite, directions. Most Western philosophers have agreed: reason and the passions cannot rule simultaneously.[3] This tradition has also claimed that women are more often ruled by their passions than are men. Women are inclined to receive passively, not to master actively.[4] Aristotle, for example, argued that the rational soul of woman – although it has an intellectual capacity comparable to that of man – still has a weak authoritative component. From this it follows that women are less capable than men of ruling the passions. Because women are so easily influenced, they should be governed by men.[5]

Arguments that women are emotional have been presented many times, and in many different disciplines, since the days of Aristotle, in the philosophy of mind, in psychology as well as in political theory. They still appear in discussions concerning the relation between the sexes. In the quasi-scientific literature of the 1980s the argument took the following form:

> Four or five days before menstruation, the levels of both progesterone and oestrogen plummet. Withdrawal symptoms can be dramatic. In this premenstrual state, with suddenly much less progesterone to calm mood, and much less oestrogen to promote feelings of well-being, behaviour can swing between hostility, aggression (hitherto suppressed by the soothing effect of progesterone), and severe depression occasionally spilling over into the psychotic (Moir & Jessel 1989:73).

2   A feminist argument for the rationality of emotions

The first obstacle that a defender of emotional rationality stumbles upon is conceptual: the concept of rationality has been understood and defined in many different ways. When focusing on emotions, it is important to distinguish between two basic meanings of the term: "rationality" means both the capacity to think, and the capacity to think *well* (in an epistemic or moral sense). In the former case the word is used in a purely descriptive sense; in the latter it is used normatively, in an evaluative sense. It is also important to note that normative rationality presupposes descriptive rationality: you cannot think well if you cannot think.

Thus, the claim that women's actions and ideas are not rational may be grounded in two different ideas. First, it can be claimed that women's capacity to think is defective or insufficient, that is, that their minds lack some crucial faculty.[6] According to this view, women are *arational*. Secondly, it can be claimed that although women have the same mental capacities as men, they use these capacities badly. The idea is that women are *irrational* rather than arational.[7] This ambiguity compels feminists to present two different counter-arguments: one against the idea that emotions are arational and another against the idea that emotions are irrational.

The philosopher Martha Nussbaum tries to do both. Her work is one of the most interesting attempts to defend the view that emotionality does not make people either arational or irrational. Nor is Nussbaum by any means the only feminist thinker to have developed this line of argument. However, her work is among the philosophically most sophisticated.

Despite the merits of Nussbaum's arguments, we are going to question some of their implications. We intend to show that Nussbaum's strategy is problematic, both politically and theoretically. We shall present an alternative that is based on the phenomenological theory of Maurice Merleau-Ponty.

Our criticism focuses on the way Nussbaum defends the rationality of emotions at the descriptive, non-normative level. That is to say, we challenge her argument against the claim that emotions are arational. Her basic idea is that emotions are *essentially* similar to beliefs, and therefore rational in the same sense as beliefs. This line of argument leads Nussbaum to juxtapose emotions to bodily feelings and sensations. In her argument, feelings belong to the realm of non-human nature. They are mere "bodily states" (Nussbaum 1995:372).[8]

The problems with such an approach are twofold. First, Nussbaum's arguments are powerless against the claim that women are less rational than men *because they are controlled by their bodily feelings*. In other words, her distinction between feelings and cognitive emotions leaves room for the argument that feelings distort or even pose a threat to rationality.

This is a problem for feminist politics because bodily sensations and feelings, just as often as emotions, are used as evidence for the supposed non-rationality of women. For example, it is claimed that women are unsuitable for tasks and duties that demand rational deliberation because of the hormonal changes in their bodies: menstruation, pregnancy, etc.[9] Furthermore, women in labour are treated as incapable of making judgements and decisions concerning themselves and their children (Martin 1987, Bergum 1989, Young 1990). In many anti-feminist arguments the ideas of women's emotionality and of their sensibility are intertwined. Because of this, feminist theorists cannot pass over the association between sensations and arationality in silence.

This political difficulty can be seen as a symptom of a fundamental philosophical problem in Nussbaum's conception of emotions. The solution she offers reproduces the dichotomy between the rational mind and the arational body, now as an emotion–feeling distinction. Emotions are associated with the rational mind; feelings get tagged as arational, as is customary with bodily attributes. And these two areas are separated sharply from each other: the difference is an essential one.

The mind–body dichotomy may pose a more serious problem for feminism than do anti-feminist political arguments. This is because the dichotomy tends to take a sexual character: the mind is associated with men and masculinity, and the body with women and femininity. Feminist historians and philosophers have shown that although the Western tradition contains radically different conceptions of the mind–body relation, it has repeated these sexual associations. Because of them, women are seen as unreasonable – however they behave or act (Lloyd 1984, 1993).

3   The cognitivist theory of emotions

Emotions are usually conceived as having two different aspects. On the one hand, they are supposed to be felt: they involve bodily or somatic agitation. Anger, for example, may be felt as blushing and a quickening pulse. On the other hand, emotions share a common property with mental states: they are directed towards the world and its objects. For example, love may be directed towards a person, a country or even an idea. Philosophically, this "directedness" is conceptualized as *intentionality*: emotions, and mental states in general, are said to be intentional and to have intentional objects. The basic problem that theories of emotions face is the question of how these two aspects can be combined, i.e., how to explain what emotions are and how they can possess, or seem to possess, these two features.[10]

Nussbaum's solution is based on the idea that there is an essential connection between emotions and beliefs. This may sound like an exaggeration at first, but Nussbaum's examples render her view more plausible. First, emotions often seem to presuppose cognitive elements, such as perceptions, beliefs, and even knowledge. Love, for example, is connected to beliefs about the value and uniqueness of the beloved. Emotions also seem to change when beliefs connected to them change. Anger disappears when we realize that we have not been wronged.

Nussbaum's theory belongs to the philosophical tradition that takes beliefs to be the paradigmatic mental phenomena. Emotions are modelled on beliefs: their intentionality is conceived of as belief-intentionality, and their felt character is explained as a dependent feature. This tradition can be called *cognitivist* because of the privileged position it gives to cognitive states.[11]

The rationality of emotions is relatively unproblematic in cognitivist theories. It follows from the essential connection that is said to prevail between emotions and beliefs: if emotions are essentially like beliefs or closely connected to them, then they are as rational as beliefs are and in the same sense. Nussbaum's argument proceeds along these lines: she claims that emotions are rational because they are essentially directed towards objects, and intimately connected to beliefs about their objects (Nussbaum 1995:371–73). Moreover, it seems that Nussbaum derives the intentionality of emotions from the intentionality of the relevant beliefs. Intentionality is not intrinsic in the affective state itself, but belongs originally to the belief connected to it (ibid.:372–6).[12]

One important consequence of these cognitivist assumptions is the above-mentioned sharp separation of emotions from bodily feelings. Love, jealousy and hatred all fall under the category of mental states. Hunger, thirst and pain, in turn, are explained as purely non-mental, physical states. They cannot be intentional, because they lack the structure of beliefs that is, according to the cognitivist, necessary for intentionality.

The distinction between feelings and emotions characteristic of cognitivist theories is central also in Nussbaum's argument. She joins the Stoic tradition which emphasizes that it is "very important to distinguish emotions . . . from bodily impulses and drives such as hunger and thirst" (ibid.:372).[13] These states have only causal relations to the world. They are not about anything, they do not intend anything.

In the following pages, we shall discuss the shortcomings and problems of the cognitivist approach. Our intention is to show that the conception of bodily feelings that the theory implies is unsatisfactory. We shall concentrate on Nussbaum's feminist approach, but the counter-examples and alternatives presented will apply to other versions of cognitivism as well.

We are going to study separately the two aspects that Nussbaum lists as the conditions of real emotions: intentionality and the connection to beliefs. They are conflated in Nussbaum's treatment: intentionality presupposes a connection to beliefs. However, our goal is to show that the intentionality – and rationality – of emotions can be defended without supposing that emotions are essentially similar to beliefs.

The benefit of the approach we are going to outline is the unity of mind and body. Emotions are not pitted against bodily feelings; both belong to a *continuum* of intentionality. This approach, however, requires a new understanding of rationality. We shall return to the question of rationality below and introduce, with the help of Amélie Rorty, forms of rationality that are different from belief-rationality.

4 Intentionality

The basic idea of intentionality is relatively clear: a state is intentional if it is directed towards an object. Thus, for example, sentences and words of a language are intentional in *referring* to states of affairs and objects of the world. Knowledge, beliefs and other kinds of mental states are also *about* the world. And finally, all kinds of bodily acts, for example hunting, building and nursing, are *directed* towards objects.

The modern philosophical discussion of intentionality has its roots in Franz Brentano's famous passage which defines all mental states by their specific relation to the world:

> Every mental phenomenon includes something as object within itself, although they do not all do so in the same way. In presentation something is presented, in judgement something is affirmed or denied, in love loved, in hate hated, in desire desired and so on . . . This intentional inexistence is characteristic exclusively of mental phenomena. No physical phenomenon exhibits anything like it (Brentano [1874] 1973:88–9).

Despite the seeming transparency of Brentano's description, there has been a long-standing debate on how it ought to be interpreted.[14]

In the cognitivist paradigm, intentionality is defined through the concepts of *representation*. Cognitivists use linguistic representations, especially declarative sentences, as a model for all intentional phenomena.[15] The intentionality of declarative sentences is defined with the notion of truth value. The definition presupposes a universe with objects that can be identified independently of each other and in univocal terms. An important condition for this model is that all intentional objects are supposed to be determinate and, consequently, fully specifiable.[16]

In the case of emotions, the problem of *indeterminate* objects is eliminated as follows. For example, a person may have a sense of foreboding without being able to say what exactly it is that she is anxious about. The cognitivist points out that this does not mean that the object of her anxiousness is indeterminate. All it shows is that the person's knowledge of the intentional object is imperfect or incomplete. The idea is that although the person intending an object may not be able to specify it exactly, exact specification is nevertheless possible, at least in principle. The object – in itself – is determinate.[17]

This conception of intentionality leaves two families of phenomena outside emotions. Both moods and bodily feelings fall by the wayside because neither meets the cognitivist criteria, viz. that emotions have a determinate object. The relationship of a depressed person to the world, just as that of a person in pain, is undifferentiated and diffuse.[18] Nussbaum follows this line of thinking. According to her, feelings are non-intentional because they do not have particular or determinate objects. Thus they must be separated from beliefs and emotions.

5 Bodily intentions

The cognitivist theory of intentionality has long dominated the analytical philosophy of mind. Though critical views have also been put forward in the Anglo-American tradition, the most promising alternative can be found in a different tradition. The continental phenomenological tradition has focused on indeterminate intentional objects, and thus offers a possible means of conceptualizing intentionality in a way that does not put emotions in opposition to feelings.

Several factors account for the difference. First, phenomenology does not take the relation between declarative language and the world as the model for intentional phenomena. Acts, not sentences, constitute the paradigm of intentionality. Secondly, ambiguous intentional objects are not treated as anomalies. On the contrary, phenomenologists have emphasized everyday experiences in which intentional objects are not specifiable in clear univocal terms.

These points of departure allowed Maurice Merleau-Ponty to develop his theory of the intentional body. To Merleau-Ponty, intentionality is the subject's fundamental attitude towards her world, i.e., her way of being. But here the word "attitude" does not denote a conscious cognitive state. It must be taken in its bodily, corporeal sense: the attitude is a posture taken in the world. The body is directed towards the world in the same way as a hand reaches out towards people and things (Merleau-Ponty [1945] 1992:100, 123).[19]

Thus the body subject that is at the centre of Merleau-Ponty's philosophy is not to be understood as an organism described by physio-chemical and biological sciences. Merleau-Ponty is true to the phenomenological tradition in that he does not try to adjust intentional mental phenomena to fit the scientific image of the world.[20] Instead, he tries to describe the experiences and the phenomena prior to all scientific knowledge.[21]

However, Merleau-Ponty does not accept the conception of the traditional phenomenological ego, either. According to him, Kant and Husserl's conception of the subject as a constructor of the world of experience is an illusion. The world experienced is not posited but encountered as real. It is not a creation of the subject but fundamentally strange and paradoxical (ibid.:129). So Merleau-Ponty's bodily subject is a part of the world. The subject reaches towards the world – not from outside, but from within – in all its activities: by moving, touching, perceiving and speaking.

When intentionality is understood as the body's mode of being, the strict dichotomy between emotions and bodily feelings collapses. Here feelings are as intentional as proper emotions. All are attitudes or postures taken towards the world. The difference is not in the directedness but in the nature of the object directed towards. In some cases the object is determinate and specifiable in clear univocal terms, as is usually the case with love, hatred and jealousy. In other cases the object is obscure, vague or indeterminate, i.e., "ambiguous" in Merleau-Ponty's words (ibid.:81).

The ambiguity is not just a feature of a confused mind, it characterizes the world itself.[22] Merleau-Ponty resolutely argues against all psychologies and philosophies that assume that the world encountered in experience is determinate. He accuses these theorists of replacing the real lived world with an abstraction required by the sciences. In such an "objective world" everything is clear and stable. In the world that is lived and experienced many phenomena are, by their very nature, ambiguous:

> Psychologists have for a long time taken great care to overlook these phenomena . . . There are many unclear sights, as for example a landscape on a misty day, but then we always say that no real landscape is in itself unclear. It is so only for us. The object, psychologists would assert, is never ambiguous, but becomes so only through inattention . . . But the notion of attention, as we shall show more fully, is supported by no evidence provided by consciousness. It is no more than an auxiliary hypothesis, evolved to save the prejudice in favour of an objective world. We must recognize the indeterminacy as a positive phenomenon (ibid.:6).

Intentional objects are neither sharply determinate nor totally indeterminate, but allow for grades of determinacy. Consequently, feelings, moods and emotions do not fall into two distinct classes, but form a continuum: emotions with determinate objects change gradually to less articulated emotions and to moods which do not have specific objects.

Feelings also belong to this continuum. Some of them, hunger for example, have objects (food), although not as specific objects as more fine-grained emotions. Others, for example pain, are directed towards the world as a whole. So an affective attitude may not have a specifiable object, but this does not mean that it is non-intentional. As Heidegger put it: all affective states may ultimately be about the world and never simply about something particular (Heidegger [1927] 1992:§138–40, §172–9).[23]

So far, we have argued, with the help of Merleau-Ponty, that intentionality does not require a connection to beliefs. Thus, bodily feelings and other non-cognitive states can be fully intentional. It remains, however, to be studied what consequences our argument has for the rationality of emotions and feelings.

In Nussbaum's view, feelings and sensations fall outside the realm of rationality because they lack intentionality and are only contingently connected to beliefs. In what follows, we shall study more closely Nussbaum's theory of emotions as beliefs. We shall show that her solution reproduces the mind–body dualism problematic for feminist thinking. This leads us to argue against Nussbaum's theory. Our criticism is based on Amélie Rorty's discussion of rationality. We shall claim that different forms of intentionality are connected to different modes of rationality. If this is accepted, then defending the rationality of emotions does not require that emotions be conceived as radically different from bodily feelings. Our final aim is to make conceptual room for rational bodily feelings, and this leads us back to Merleau-Ponty's theory of the intentional body.

6   The connection to beliefs

Nussbaum's main idea is that emotions are intimately connected with relevant beliefs about their objects, and that this makes them rational in the descriptive sense. Examples make the point clear: anger seems to require, for example, the belief that somebody or something important to me has been harmed by another's deliberate action. If, for some reason, that belief were to change, then the anger could be expected to abate or to change its course accordingly (Nussbaum 1995:373).[24] Feelings, in contrast, are not affected by cognitive changes in the same way. They may occasionally change according to beliefs but the connection is not necessary as in the case of emotions.[25]

There are many different views about the exact nature of the connection between emotions and beliefs. Some philosophers have argued that certain relevant beliefs are necessary conditions for emotions. Others have held that they are both necessary and sufficient. It has been suggested both that beliefs are constituent parts of emotions and that they are causal antecedents of emotions.[26]

Nussbaum follows the ancient Stoics in maintaining that emotions are not only connected to beliefs, or similar to beliefs, but that they *are* a special kind of beliefs (Nussbaum 1990:292, 1995:375).[27] This may sound unintuitive, but becomes more plausible with further elaboration. Emotions are not viewed as beliefs about states of affairs, but as beliefs about *values*. Love, for example, is a belief about the uniqueness and special worth of the beloved. Similarly, grief is a belief that something valuable has been lost (Nussbaum 1987:141, 159).

Although Nussbaum herself rejects any position weaker than the Stoic one, she emphasizes that any cognitivist position will suffice for an argument against the alleged arationality of emotions (Nussbaum 1990:41, 1995:375–6). Any theory in which emotional changes follow on from or adapt to cognitive ones will suffice for questioning the opposition between emotions and reason.

As has been said, the basic problem with cognitivist approaches is that they manage to resolve the reason/emotion opposition only at the cost of establishing the reason/feeling dichotomy. This follows from the dominance of beliefs in the theory. If we claim that the rationality of emotions is based on their connection to beliefs, then we end up accepting the arationality of moods and bodily feelings, because their connection to beliefs is at most contingent.

The arationality of feelings is problematic for feminists who emphasize the specificity of women's bodies. If women have different bodily feelings and perhaps even more of them than men (because of menstruation, pregnancy, childbirth and breast-feeding), and if feelings are arational, then it follows that the life of a woman is less rational than that of a man.

Such implications are what we have set out to undermine in this chapter. Obviously, this could also be done by arguing that women's feelings do not differ from men's. This is the line taken by many feminists. It has been argued that there are no universal differences between women and men.[28] Some have also remarked that all generalizations concerning sexual difference are either trivial, or are valid only during short historical periods and with regard to small groups of people.[29]

Our intention is not to ignore these arguments or to make unwarranted generalizations about the differences between women and men. What we want to do is to make room for the view that *some* women, *some* of the time, may have stronger bodily feelings than human beings have in general, and that this does not make them arational. Our intention is to defend the rationality of emotions in a way that does not conceive feelings to be natural forces, outside human understanding and discourse.

As already noted, the possibility of empirical differences is not the only reason to question the belief-centred assumptions of cognitivist theories. What is philosophically more problematic is that cognitivism reproduces the classical mind–body dichotomy as a distinction between emotions and feelings. Humans are once again split into two: one part is composed of rational non-corporeal beliefs and the other of arational bodily changes, independent of beliefs.

Mind–body dichotomies are especially problematic for feminists because they are not neutral to sex: bodily states are associated with women and femininity, and mental states with men and masculinity. These sexual associations can – at least in principle – be undone without questioning the dichotomous structure itself. However, feminist studies have shown that such undertakings usually fail (Irigaray [1974] 1986, [1984] 1993, Lloyd 1984, 1993). The sexual images disappear from one part of the theory or discourse, only to pop up somewhere else. In the light of these findings, it seems that the sexual dichotomy is not a coincidental appendage of the mind–body distinction, but a structural part of it. A feminist theory of emotions must therefore question all sharp distinctions between rational emotions and arational feelings. This can be done only by questioning whether the rationality of emotions requires a connection to beliefs. We will turn next to Amélie Rorty's argument, which shows that the cognitivist view of rationality as truth is insufficient in the case of emotions.

7 Emotions versus beliefs

Rorty has presented an illuminating counter-example to all theories that are based on the emotion–belief connection. Rorty's example is a story about Jonah, a journalist, who resents his female editor, Esther. Rorty describes an initial situation in which Jonah's affects are in congruity with his beliefs: Jonah thinks Esther is dominating, even tyrannical (Rorty 1988:105). Rorty then describes a process in which Jonah's beliefs gradually change: his colleagues manage to convince him that Esther's assignments are not demanding and that her requests are not arbitrary. However – and this is the point of the counter-example – Jonah's emotions will not adapt to his new beliefs. The change in belief is not followed by a change in emotions:

> After a time of working with Esther, Jonah realizes that she is not a petty tyrant, but he still receives her assignments with a dull resentful ache; and when Anita, the new editor, arrives, he is seething with hostility even before she has had time to settle in and put her family photographs on her desk (ibid.:105).

Rorty argues that although Jonah's emotions conflict with his beliefs they are not arational. She constructs a past for Jonah, a collection of childhood experiences that make his responses understandable (ibid.:108–10). Rorty's idea is that we can make sense of Jonah's behaviour by studying his life as a whole. We do not have to accept the way he feels, but we can see why he feels that way. Jonah's emotions are rational in the sense of being sensible. Thus Rorty claims that emotions do not have to be connected to beliefs in order to be intentional and rational. She does not deny that emotions often are related to beliefs, but this is not always so.

"If the intentional component of an emotion is always a belief, then the conservation of an emotion after a change of belief would always involve a conflict of beliefs" (ibid.:114). This would be absurd, Rorty claims. Her argument is based on the so-called principle of charity.[30] The question is how to understand others' behaviour and how to regard the behaviour as speech, or as human action, in the first place. The principle of charity circumscribes these interpretive projects. According to the principle, it is more probable that we misinterpret another, rather than that she is internally incoherent. Thus it is better to change our interpretation than to cling to one that renders the other inconsistent.

On these grounds, Rorty rejects the idea of a necessary connection between emotions and beliefs: the cognitivist violates the principle of charity in insisting that the failure of emotions to reflect changes in beliefs always involves a contradiction. However, this does not mean that Rorty's analysis would render emotions arational. She argues that the rationality of emotions is not (always) similar to that of beliefs. Rorty is sceptical about the possibility of a general theory of emotions. She claims that emotions do not "form a natural class, as distinct from (say) desires or motives, or some sorts of beliefs and judgments" (ibid.:122). This scepticism has two consequences.

First, Rorty does not think that all emotions are intentional in the same way or to the same degree. Emotions take different places on a continuum of intentionality. Only a fraction of them have belief-intentionality. The rationality of emotions varies depending on the type of intentionality. Some emotions resemble declarative sentences and beliefs, and have truth conditions; they are rational when they are true (or likely to be true). Other emotions are not so determinate. They are more like patterns of attention, and their rationality must be seen as hanging on their *appropriateness* in different situations and in the context of a person's life as a whole. The rationality of an emotion does not always contrast with falsity; sometimes it is more fruitful to evaluate emotions as *inappropriate or harmful* (ibid.:113–14).

Rorty's scepticism has a second consequence. Emotions are not opposed to bodily sensations, feelings or moods. Emotions, moods and feelings all belong to the same continuum of intentionality. Sensations are not natural forces, but forms of human activity, characterized by the same type of ambiguous intentionality and appropriateness that is typical of many emotions.

8 The physiological body and the body subject

We have presented Amélie Rorty's view on emotions as a critique of the cognitivist theory of rationality. Despite its merits, Rorty's analysis also contains a problem which even our brief summary brings to light. She, too, ends up reproducing dualistic thinking. In her case, at issue are not two distinct types of states, as in Nussbaum's theory. Instead, Rorty's dualism is explanatory: emotional states can be understood either intentionally or physiologically.

The basic difficulty is that Rorty formulates her critical views in instrumentalist terms. She speaks of intentionality and physiology as two different *ways of explaining* human behaviour, as two complementary *modes of explanation* (ibid.:112, 116). This begs the following questions: if it is possible to describe and explain emotions and feelings in two different ways, which of the ways is more successful, why, and in what sense?

The problem is not just that the cognitivist can employ questions such as these to pull the rug from under Rorty's criticism. The problem is rather that Rorty herself is forced to choose one explanatory strategy over the other. She refuses to make a choice that would cover affective states in general, but she does have to choose between these two options in specific cases.

However, it is an illusion to think of these two kinds of explanation as being complementary as can be seen from Rorty's treatment of emotions with indeterminate objects. Although Rorty formulates her position in a way that seemingly leaves room for both the physiological and intentional explanation, a closer look will show that only one of the explanations applies to emotions.

Rorty analyzes indeterminate emotions by saying that the physiological theory explains why someone is in a given state, and the intentional explanation accounts for why the state has the particular intentional object that it has (ibid.: 116). The ambiguity in the term *state* leads one to believe that the explanations refer to one and the same state; in this way, the physiological and intentional explanations seem to be complementary.

Actually, there are *two* different states. This is because emotions can be individuated only on the basis of their directedness and object. The physiological explanation does not provide – at least not yet – a way of distinguishing fear from anger. Both involve the same hormonal state.[31]

Thus the state whose origin or cause the physiological explanation illuminates is not an emotional state (e.g., anger), but a related, physiological state (e.g., a high adrenalin level). For the physiological explanation to account for the actual emotional state, there would have to be a specific theory of the connections between hormonal changes and emotions. So far, such a theory has not been forthcoming. So Rorty's two alternative explanations have to do with different things. How they may be related remains to be seen.

Rorty falls back on (explanatory) dualisms because she lacks the concepts of the body subject. To her, the human body is a physiochemical object among other objects. Its activity can, at least in principle, be explained by the same concepts of effective causality as that of non-human organisms and inanimate things.

These problems are overcome in the phenomenological theory of the body. Merleau-Ponty's attempt is to dissolve the dualism of the physical and the intentional for good. He does not see these explanatory models as complementary, but as manifestations of one and the same mistake. Both involve attempts to shoehorn human experience into a scientific worldview. Merleau-Ponty argues that the living human body and its activities and feelings become incomprehensible in such a framework (Merleau-Ponty [1945] 1992:77).

9   Bodily feelings

In his work *Phenomenology of Perception*, Merleau-Ponty studies different types of feeling: sexual arousal, numbness and touch. His remarks on pain are the most useful for our current purpose of outlining the relation between feelings and emotions.

Merleau-Ponty analyzes pain by studying so-called phantom limbs. He focuses on cases in which somebody still feels sensations in a limb that has been amputated. According to him, pain in a physically non-existent limb is a result of the limb still being a part of the person's bodily relation to her world. This relation is in itself intentional, but intentionality does not consist of representations:

> The phantom arm is not a representation of the arm, but the ambivalent presence of an arm. The refusal of mutilation in the case of the phantom limb . . . [is] not a deliberate decision and [does] not take place at the level of positing consciousness which takes up its position explicitly after considering various possibilities (ibid.:81).

Here, refusal means that the limb is, as Merleau-Ponty puts it, kept on the horizon of one's life *through the sensations it gives*. It is maintained as a possibility of moving and acting. In this way pain itself is intentional and part of the special relationship to the world through which humans go beyond the given and direct themselves towards the possible and the imaginary.

Merleau-Ponty elaborates his conception of embodied intentionality with pathological cases. His rationale is to illuminate the normal through the pathological. He wants to bring up phenomena which are so common and habitual that we do not recognize them.[32] The intentionality of pain becomes visible in cases where the pain has no physical referent.

Thus normal cases of pain must also be understood in an analogous way. Let us take a case with special feminist interest: women's labour pains analyzed as postures towards the world. Sociological studies of women's labour experiences have shown that the pain felt by women in labour and delivery varies significantly. These differences cannot always be explained physiologically. It seems that women who stay passive – as objects of other people's acts – experience more intense pain than those who approach childbirth as active subjects (Martin 1987:139–55, Bergum 1989:64–83).[33]

The developers of the active-birth movement have drawn attention to this phenomenon, and have connected it to the medicalization of childbirth. They claim that the modern hospital environment contributes to experiences of pain in delivery. The practices at hospitals are often developed more in accordance with what is convenient for the staff than with the women's needs in mind. According to the active-birth view, the hospital routines prevent women from adopting "natural" positions and movements. This makes labour and delivery unnecessarily painful (Odent [1984] 1986).

The active-birth movement correctly emphasizes the connection between bodily posture and the experience of pain. However, this approach is often too voluntaristic in claiming that the woman consciously chooses her attitude in labour and delivery. Bodily feelings are seen as determined by the conception women have of giving birth and being a mother.[34] The idea of the conscious mind controlling the body is effective even here.

The discourse about active or, as it is often called, *natural* birth also presupposes that there are natural states or positions of the body which predate cultural childbirth practices. Women are thought to be able to return to what is "natural" by acquiring the right views and by doing the right exercises.

This view tends to focus on certain techniques and postures during the act of giving birth, and it promises too much about women's possibilities of controlling their pain. The feeling of pain does not depend primarily on conscious attitudes or postures taken during labour, or on short periods of training, but on the posture and the position the body has grown into in taking in the world. The posture cannot be chosen in one simple conscious act, but it is not a natural state, either. It is a set of practices that develops in experiences and activities throughout the person's whole life. The question is not only about how the body posits itself in space, but also how both space and the body are constituted.[35]

Labour and delivery pains cannot be controlled by decisions or short practice, but only through slow, integrated and persistent adjustment, training and movement. Bodily feelings are not natural states, but part of our intentional relation to the world.

> It is impossible to superimpose on man a lower layer of behaviour which one chooses to call "natural", followed by a manufactured cultural or spiritual level. Everything is both manufactured and natural in man (Merleau-Ponty [1945] 1992:189).

Conclusions

We have argued that the defence of the rationality of emotions should not be purchased at the cost of being forced to accept bodily feelings and sensations as arational. Such a solution reproduces the sexed[36] dichotomy between the rational mind and the irrational body, and leaves room for arguments against women's mental capacities.

This is the basic problem with Martha Nussbaum's proposal. By conforming all forms of intentionality and rationality to the belief model, Nussbaum ends up by placing emotions in opposition to feelings and condemning the latter to non-intentionality and arationality. Amélie Rorty avoids this problem. She develops promising concepts for discussing the different intentionalities and rationalities of emotions, moods and feelings. Despite her complex view of intentionality, she presumes a bodily level "that can, in principle, be fully specified in physical or extensional descriptions" (Rorty 1988:112).

Merleau-Ponty's phenomenology of body offers an alternative. It dismantles – or deconstructs – all mind–body dichotomies by presenting the body as the seat of intentionality. By employing the concept of the intentional body it becomes possible to question both the reason–emotion and the emotion–feeling dichotomies. When we take Merleau-Ponty's conception of intentionality as a starting point, we can say that the difference between beliefs, on the one hand, and feelings, on the other, is not that they fall into two distinct classes, viz. into intentional and non-intentional states. Instead, the difference is in the nature of their intentionality.

Beliefs have particular objects; feelings are directed towards the world as a less differentiated whole. Emotions seem to fall somewhere between them on the continuum of intentionality. But all of them – beliefs, emotions and feelings – are intentional in the broad sense: they are directed towards the world as a whole. This means that they are all also descriptively rational, which means, in turn, that it becomes possible, at least in principle, to evaluate their normative rationality.

However, this approach requires that rationality has to be considered anew. It must be understood in a broader sense than just as belief-rationality. Truth-aptness is clearly not what makes sensations and feelings rational: they simply cannot be true or false. But this does not mean that they are arational. Truth is just one of the standards we can use to evaluate the success of different mental and bodily states. Recall that in his *Passions of the soul*, Descartes presents two different functions for emotions. He declares that they "may serve to preserve the body or render it in some way more perfect" ([1649] 1990:§137:376).[37]

It has been argued that true beliefs are necessary for survival,[38] but this is not sufficient to claim that truth is the only – or even the primary – goal for human beings. The perfection of the body may require other ends as well: community, beauty, pleasure, even *jouissance*.

We are grateful to Lilli Alanen, Ilpo Helén, Lars Hertzberg, Anne Holli, Maisa Honkasalo, Timo Kaitaro, Marja-Liisa Kakkuri-Knuuttila, Simo Knuuttila, Martha Nussbaum, Amélie Rorty and Juha Sihvola for discussions and comments. We are particularly indebted to Mika Mänty for helping us with the English language.

Notes

1. Several feminist theorists accept the idea that women are more emotional, more sensitive to emotions and/or better at expressing them than men – at least in our culture. This view is defended, for example, by feminists who base their views on the so-called object–relation theory. According to them, women's emotional capacities are socially acquired, not biologically determined. See, e.g., Chodorow 1984, Gilligan 1982.

2. See, Aristotle, *Nicomachean ethics*, Book I, 13: 1102a5–1103a10, 1103a10–1109b25 (Aristotle 1984:1741–52).

3. David Hume is the exception here. He argued that passions and reason belong to different realms of human experience. They cannot counter each other at the same level (Hume [1739] 1964:193–7).

    Descartes believed that passions are useful or even necessary for the human being as a mind–body composite. However, he argued that passions should be controlled by reason, and he thought that it is difficult to use the capacity of reason while experiencing an exuberant passion (Descartes [1649] 1990:345, 404).

4. Passivity and femininity were almost synonymous in ancient Greece. See, e.g., Halperin 1990, Reuter 1994. This identification reappears even as late as in the writings of Sigmund Freud. See, e.g., Freud [1932] 1979, cf. Irigaray [1974] 1986.

5. See, Aristotle *Politics*, Book I, 13: 1260a1–1260b20 (Aristotle 1984:1999–2000).

6. See, e.g., Aristotle 1984:1260a1–1300, Weininger 1906, cf. Moir & Jessel 1989.

7. According to Nussbaum, variants of this view can be found in Plato, Epicurus and Lucretius, the Greek and Roman Stoics, and in Spinoza (Nussbaum 1990: 387–388; 1995:366).

8. Cf. Nussbaum 1990:41, 269, 299, 387–8.

9. Cf. Rothman 1979.

10. Some philosophers suspect that there are no essential properties shared by all phenomena called "emotions". If even the paradigmatic basic emotions such as love, hatred, jealousy, delight and generosity do not have a common core, then a theory of emotions seems to be a false hope. For such a position, see, e.g., Wittgenstein 1953, [1958] 1964, Rorty 1988; cf. also Dennett 1979.

11. See, e.g., Nussbaum 1995:375–6; cf. also, Green 1992:28, Rey 1980:170.

12. Actually Nussbaum provides two positions for defenders of emotional rationality. She starts by describing a weak claim according to which emotions are connected to beliefs. Here the intentionality of emotions is derived from that of beliefs (Nussbaum 1995:373–4; cf. Green 1992:45). But after this Nussbaum presents her own theory which is stronger. According to her theory, emotions are not only connected to beliefs, they *are* beliefs. In this case emotions are intrinsically intentional but only because they are nothing but beliefs (Nussbaum 1995:375–6; cf. Nussbaum 1990:41, 292; cf. Green 1992:61). In both cases intentionality is essentially only a feature of beliefs. Cf. section 6 above.

13. Cf. Nussbaum 1987:153.

14. The basic dispute concerns the nature of the intentional object: Is it in the world, outside the mind, or is it inside the mind, as some of Brentano's phrases, for example "includes within itself", suggest? For this dispute, see, e.g., McAlister 1976.

15. See, e.g., Green 1992:16–18.

16. See, e.g., ibid.:16, 38–41.

17. Cf. ibid.:33–4.
18. The indeterminacy is not (just) in the knowledge that the person has of the world, it seems to characterize the affective state itself, including its object.
    The diffuse nature of moods is somewhat different from the indeterminacy of bodily feelings. Moods, such as melancholy and nostalgia, do not have particular, clearly specifiable objects (cf. Solomon 1980:252). The objects of bodily feelings, on the other hand, seem to be either too general, as in the case of hunger and thirst (food, drink), or not separable from the body, as in the case of pain.
19. Cf. Wittgenstein [1958] 1964:6; see also Kwant 1963:26ff., Hammond et al. 1991:168, Heinämaa 1996a:71–86.
20. This is the fundamental difference between Merleau-Ponty's notion of intentionality and the analytic tradition, see, e.g., Searle 1984:13–14, Fodor 1988:ix–xiii.
21. Cf. Husserl [1950] 1982:1–7, [1954] 1978:135–7. See also Kwant 1963:179ff; Hammond et al. 1991:152ff.
22. Cf. Kwant 1963:9ff., Hammond et al. 1991:133–6.
23. Cf. Solomon 1980:252; see also Honkasalo 1995.
24. Nussbaum also argues that the unpleasant feeling that may remain even though the belief is changed cannot be emotional anger, but is some irrational (and arational?) irritation (Nussbaum 1990:292).
25. Against this distinction, one can introduce examples in which bodily feelings seem to depend on beliefs. I might, for example, lose my appetite when finding out that the stew is made from ants and other insects.
    The cognitivist has two possible ways to counter this: He can distinguish the *appetite* directed towards the stew from the *hunger* connected to food or nourishment in general. Even though the new information about the stew may prevent me from eating, it does not stop my hunger: my stomach is still rumbling.
    Secondly, the cognitivist can say that he has been misunderstood: he has not claimed that feelings *never* depend on beliefs, only that this connection is contingent. Even though beliefs sometimes affect bodily feelings, this is not necessary, but happens only in special cases.
    The case of emotions is different: love always subsides when beliefs about the beloved change enough. It might not be replaced by total indifference, but the love will at least change into something else: hate, contempt, jealousy or pity.
26. Cf. Nussbaum 1995:373–5.
27. Cf. Nussbaum 1987; cf. also, Solomon 1980, Green 1992:61ff. Nussbaum does not usually specify how emotional beliefs are acquired or adopted. However, in one context she remarks that emotions cannot be compared to scientific beliefs. Emotional beliefs are "habitual", they are learned through social interaction and especially through stories (Nussbaum 1990:293). But the problem remains: If emotions are beliefs, then they must have truth conditions and objects that are specifiable in a language, at least in principle. This excludes moods and other indeterminate affective states. Conversely, if emotions do not have such truth conditions and clearly specifiable objects, why call them beliefs?
28. This view appears often in early feminist thought. Cf. Mill, [1869] 1971, Beauvoir [1949] 1987.

29. This view is developed to its extreme in postmodern feminism, cf. Butler 1990, Haraway 1991.
30. Cf. Quine 1960:57–61, Davidson 1985:27, 136–7.
31. Cf. Sousa 1990:47–79.
32. Cf. Kwant 1963:37–42, Hammond et al. 1991:181, Heinämaa 1996a:77–86, 93–5.
33. What we have in mind are situations before the administration of pain relief, which may eliminate the pain entirely. It is possible to compare the experiences of women with different attitudes because the analgesic can be used only after the uteral sphincter has opened enough. Before that, all mothers experience pain, but it seems that the quality and intensity of the pain reflects the woman's attitude during delivery.
34. Postures are seen as mediating factors between conscious conceptions of the birth process and bodily sensations. Postures are supposed to be adapted to one's conscious idea of childbirth through various exercises. The idea is that if prenatal training teaches the woman the practices of a hospital, she will experience extra pain. If, on the other hand, the woman lets her "natural body" determine the process, the pain will be less intense. The mental and bodily exercises of active birth aim at returning the woman to "natural practices".
35. Cf. Heinämaa 1996a, Reuter 1996.
36. We prefer the concept *sexed* to the concept *gendered* typical in Anglo-American discussions; cf. Irigaray 1989. This is because *gender* tends to presuppose and bind the argument to the sex-gender distinction which has been shown to be problematic in several respects. See, e.g., Lauretis 1987, Butler 1990, Gatens 1991, Chanter 1993, Heinämaa 1996a, 1996b.
37. Cf. Rorty 1992.
38. For such arguments, see, e.g., Fodor 1990:21, 227; cf. Baier 1985.

References

Aristotle 1984. *The complete works*, vol. II, J. Barnes (ed.). Princeton, NJ: Princeton University Press.

Baier, A. 1985. *Postures of the mind: essays on mind and morals*. Minneapolis: University of Minnesota Press.

Beauvoir, S. de [1949] 1987. *The second sex*, H.M. Parshley (trans.). Harmondsworth, Middlesex: Penguin.

Bergum, V. 1989. *Woman to mother: a transformation*. Grandby, Mass.: Bergin & Garvey.

Bordo, S. 1993. *Unbearable weight: feminism, Western culture, and the body*. Berkeley, Calif.: University of California Press.

Brentano, F. [1874] 1973. *Psychology from an empirical standpoint*, L.L. McAlister (ed.), D.B. Terrell, A.C. Rancurelloand, L.L. McAlister (trans.). London: Routledge & Kegan Paul.

Butler, J. 1990. *Gender trouble*. New York: Routledge.

Butler, J. 1993. *Bodies that matter: on the discursive limits of "sex"*. New York: Routledge.

Chanter, T. 1993. Kristeva's politics of change: tracking essentialism with the help of a sex/gender map. In *Ethics, politics, and Difference in Julia Kriseva's Writing*, K. Oliver (ed.). New York, London: Routledge.

Chodorow, N. 1984. *The reproduction of mothering: psychoanalysis and the sociology of gender.* Berkeley, Calif.: University of California Press.

Cixous, H. 1988. Sorties: out and out: attacks/ways out/forays. In *The newly born woman*, H. Cixous & C. Clément (eds), B. Wing (trans.), 63–132. Minneapolis: University of Minnesota Press.

Davidson, D. 1985. *Inquiries into truth and interpretation.* Oxford: Clarendon Press.

Dennett, D. 1979. *Brainstorms: philosophical essays of mind and psychology.* Hassocks, Sussex: Harvester Press.

Descartes, R. [1649] 1990. The passions of the soul. In *The philosophical writings of Descartes*, vol. I, J. Cottingham, R. Stoothoff, D. Murdoch (trans.), 326–404. Cambridge: Cambridge University Press.

Firestone, S. [1979] 1988. *The dialectic of sex: the case for feminist revolution.* London: Women's Press.

Fodor, J. 1988. *Psychosemantics: the problem of meaning in the philosophy of mind.* Cambridge, Mass.: MIT Press.

Fodor, J. 1990. *A theory of content and other essays.* Cambridge, Mass.: MIT Press.

Freud, S. [1932] 1979. Femininity. In *New introductory lectures on psychoanalysis.* Harmondsworth, Middlesex: Penguin.

Gatens, M. [1983] 1991. A critique of the sex/gender distinction. In *A reader in feminist knowledge*, S. Gunew (ed.), 139–57. London: Routledge.

Gilligan, C. 1982. *In a different voice: psychological theory and women's development.* Cambridge, Mass.: Harvard University Press.

Green, O.H. 1992. *The emotions: a philosophical theory.* Dordrecht: Kluwer Academy Publishers.

Greenspan, P.S. 1988. *Emotions & reasons: an inquiry into emotional justification.* New York: Routledge.

Griffin, S. 1978. *Women and nature: the roaring inside her.* New York: Harper & Row.

Griffin, S. 1982. *Made from this earth.* London: Women's Press.

Griffiths, M. 1988. Feminism, feelings and philosophy. In *Feminist perspectives in philosophy*, M. Griffiths & M. Whitford (eds), 131–51. London: Macmillan.

Halperin, D.M. 1990. Why is Diotima a woman? Platonic *Eros* and the figuration of gender. In *Before sexuality: the construction of erotic experience in the ancient Greek world*, D. Halperin, J. Winker, F. Zeithin (eds), 257–308. Princeton, NJ: Princeton University Press.

Hammond, M., J. Howarth, R. Keat 1991. *Understanding phenomenology.* Cambridge, Mass.: Basil Blackwell.

Haraway, D. 1991. *Simians, cyborgs, and women.* New York: Routledge.

Heidegger, M. [1927] 1992. *Being and time*, J. Macquarrie & E. Robinson (trans.). Oxford: Basil Blackwell.

Heinämaa, S. 1996a. *Ele, tyyli ja sukupuoli: Merleau-Pontyn ja Beauvoirin ruumiinfenomenologia ja sen merkitys sukupuolikysymykselle* (Gesture, style and sex: Merleau-Ponty's and Simone de Beauvoir's phenomenology of the body and its relevance to the question of sexual difference). Helsinki: Gaudemus.

Heinämaa, S. 1996b. Woman – nature, product, style? Rethinking the foundations of feminist philosophy of science. In *Feminism, science, and the philosophy of science*, L.H. Nelson & J. Nelson (eds), 289–308. Dordrecht: Kluwer Academic Publishers.

Honkasalo, M.-L. 1995. Spatiality and pain experience – sketches for (an anthropological) study of pain as an embodied experience. Paper presented at Professor M.C. Dillon's seminar in Helsinki, 14–15 August.

Hume, D. [1739] 1964. *A treatise of human nature*, vol. II. Aalen: Scientia.

Husserl, E. [1950] 1982. *Cartesian meditations*, D. Cairns (trans.). Dordrecht: Martinus Nijhoff.

Husserl, E. [1954] 1978. *The crisis of European sciences and transcendental phenomenology*, D. Carr (trans.). Evanston, Ill.: Northwestern University Press.

Irigaray, L. [1974] 1986. *The speculum of the other woman*, G.C. Gill (trans.). Ithaca, New York: Cornell University Press.

Irigaray, L. 1989. Is the subject of science sexed? In *Feminism and science*, N. Tuana (ed.), C.M. Bové (trans.), 58–68. Bloomington: Indiana University Press.

Irigaray, L. [1984] 1993. *An ethics of sexual difference*, C. Burke & G.C. Gill (trans.). Ithaca, New York: Cornell University Press.

Keller, E.F. 1985. *Reflections on gender and science*. New Haven, Conn.: Yale University Press.

Kwant, R.C. 1963. *The phenomenological philosophy of Merleau-Ponty*. Pittsburgh: Duquesne University Press.

Lauretis, T. de 1987. *The technologies of gender: essays on theory, film, and fiction*. Bloomington: Indiana University Press.

Lloyd, G. 1984. *The man of reason: "Male" and "Female" in Western philosophy*. London: Methuen.

Lloyd, G. 1993. Maleness, metaphor, and the "Crisis" of reason. In *A mind of one's own: feminist essays on reason and objectivity*, L.M. Anthony & C. Witt (eds), 69–83. Boulder, Col.: Westview Press.

McAlister, L.L. 1976. Chisholm and Brentano on intentionality. In *The philosophy of Brentano*, L. McAlister (ed.), 151–9. London: Duckworth.

Martin, E. 1987. *The woman in the body: a cultural analysis of reproduction*. Milton Keynes: Open University Press.

Merleau-Ponty, M. [1945] 1992. *Phenomenology of perception*, C. Smith (trans.). London: Routledge.

Mill, J.S. [1869] 1971. The subjection of women. In *On liberty etc.*, M.G. Fewcett (ed.), Oxford: Oxford University Press.

Moir, A. & D. Jessel 1989. *Brainsex*. London: Mandarin.

Nussbaum, M. 1987. The Stoics on the extirpation of the passions. *Apeiron* **20**, 129–77.

Nussbaum, M. 1990. *Love's knowledge: essays on philosophy and literature*. Oxford: Oxford University Press.

Nussbaum, M. 1995. Emotions and women's capabilities. In *Women, culture and development*, M. Nussbaum & J. Glover (eds), 360–95. Oxford: Clarendon Press.

Odent, M. [1984] 1986. *Birth reborn*. J. Pincus & J. Levin (trans.). Glasgow: Fontana.

Quine, W.V.O. 1960. *Word and object*. Cambridge, Mass.: MIT Press.

Reuter, M. 1994. Feministiska synpunkter på Platons dualismer (Feminist perspectives on Plato's dualisms). *Naistutkimus/Kvinnoforskning* **7**:3, 15–35.

Reuter, M. 1996. Philosophy embodied: Merleau-Ponty and a feminist approach to eating "disorders". In *Feminism, epistemology, and ethics*, I.N. Preus, A.J. Vetlesen, T. Kleven, I. Iversen, D. van der Fehr (eds), 51–66. Oslo: Department of Philosophy, University of Oslo & Unipub.

Rey, G. 1980. Functionalism and emotions. In *Explaining emotions*, A.O. Rorty (ed.), 163–95. Berkeley, Calif.: University of California Press.

Rorty, A.O. 1988. *Mind in action: essays on the philosophy of mind*. Boston: Beacon Press.

Rorty, A.O. 1992. Descartes on thinking with the body. In *The Cambridge companion to Descartes*, J. Cottingham (ed.), 371–92. Cambridge: Cambridge University Press.

Rothman, B.K. 1979. Women, health, and medicine. In *Women: a feminist perspective*, J. Freeman (ed.), 27–40. Palo Alto, Calif.: Mayfield.

Schott, R. 1988. *Cognition and Eros: a critique of the Kantian paradigm.* Boston: Beacon Press.

Searle, J. 1984. *Minds, brains and science.* Cambridge, Mass.: Harvard University Press.

Solomon, R.C. 1980. Emotions and choice. In *Explaining emotions*, A.O. Rorty (ed.), 251–81. Berkeley, Calif.: University of California Press.

Sousa, R. de 1990. *The rationality of emotion.* Cambridge, Mass.: MIT Press.

Weininger, O. 1906. *Sex and character.* London: Heinemann.

Wittgenstein, L. 1953. *Philosophical investigations*, G.E.M. Anscombe (trans.). Oxford: Basil Blackwell.

Wittgenstein, L. [1958] 1964. *The blue and brown books.* Oxford: Basil Blackwell.

Young, I.M. 1990. *Throwing like a girl and other essays in feminist philosophy and social theory.* Bloomington: Indiana University Press.

CHAPTER FIFTEEN

Asta Nielsen: a modern woman before her time?

Kirsten Drotner

"In the visual interpretation, and the abilities of expression and transformation, I'm a nobody compared to her."

Greta Garbo (quoted in Seidel & Hagedorff 1981:221)

"Dip the colours for her for she is unique and unattainable . . ."

Béla Belázs (ibid.:174)

"I shall never forget this face. With her face, Asta Nielsen revealed the wonder of film. No pantomime, no expression – but the language of the soul telling us about the agonies and afflictions of a living being. Greta Garbo has long been called the 'godlike', for me Asta Nielsen was and remains to be the 'human' . . ."

Georg Wilhelm Pabst (ibid.:222)

Asta Nielsen (1881–1972) was one of the earliest and one of the greatest film stars of the silent screen. Until very recently, she has also been one of the least known. Her first film *The Abyss* (*Afgrunden*) dating from 1910 immediately propelled the 29-year-old Danish actress into the orbit of international film-making. Based in Berlin, she made a total of 74 films over the next 22 years, founded her own film company, Art-Film in 1920, and worked with directors ranging from her first husband, Urban Gad, to Ernst Lubitsch, Leopold Jessner and G. W. Pabst. Her fame was made in romantic film melodrama, but like most stars she appeared in several other genres embodying characters as diverse as the suffragette (*Die Suffragette*, 1913), the eskimo (*Das Eskimobaby*, 1917), Prince Hamlet (in *Hamlet*, 1920) – her first independent film) – and Maria Magdalena (*I.N.R.I.*, 1923). Before the First World War, a director of her German production company, Internationalen Film-Vertriebs-Gesellschaft (founded 1911), estimated that Asta Nielsen was seen by 2.5 million cinema-goers every day in about 600 cinemas (Diaz quoted in Seydel & Hagedorff 1981:50).

What made this little-known actress an overnight celebrity? What constitute her unique star qualities? These are complex questions, the answers to which I can only hope to sketch within the space of this chapter. My main contention is this: Asta Nielsen's fame rests on her being one of the first to create a filmic language of eroticism that fuses the expressiveness of theatrical melodrama with the introspection of naturalism in acting. On theoretical grounds of genre, she was fundamental in transforming the nineteenth-century melodrama of the theatre into contemporary modes of narration. On historical grounds of popular culture, she was seminal in offering new forms of cinematic pleasure to both sexes, if for different reasons.

In this chapter I hope to demonstrate the above claims through an analysis of Nielsen's first film, *The abyss*. This film is chosen for two reasons: first, it is even less known than her German productions, being one of only four films made by Asta Nielsen in Denmark – the other three are *The black dream* (*Den sorte drøm*) and *The ballerina* (*Balletdanserinden*) both filmed in 1911, and *Towards the light* (*Mod lyset*) from 1918. Secondly, and more importantly, the film reveals how her stardom was created. By analyzing the filmic aspects of narration, characterization, posture and body movement, and by combining these with the extra-filmic, or cinematic, circumstances of the production and reception of the film, we can glimpse the charisma that subsequently sold Asta Nielsen as a star image to the world. Naturally, such an analysis is inevitably coloured by my knowledge of her later career: possibly I see only those facets that fit her later star image, so to speak. I lay no claim to unearthing the undiluted truth of Asta Nielsen's immediate reception. Even so, I find it fruitful to approach her career, not as a historical fact (the star as filmic and cinematic sign), but as a signifying process that involves both selection and combination of available narrative codes and social conventions. This complex process unfolds within specific historical and personal circumstances, making Asta Nielsen's development into a star a social as much as a symbolic form of meaning production.

A star is made

Danish society around 1910 reflected a period of rapid economic and technological modernization. Between 1870 and 1914, the population almost doubled (to 2.9 million), while another 150,000 emigrated to North America. Unlike in Britain, for example, urbanization in Denmark was very unevenly distributed, with Copenhagen housing more than 25 per cent of the entire population at the outbreak of the First World War. And in contrast to Germany, the industrial middle classes formed a noticeable segment of social and cultural life, although small-scale industries and firms were still the order of the day. While workers' and women's movements were extremely influential in the cities and towns, just as in the other countries of Northern Europe, rural society in Denmark was unique in two respects: the first was the development of farmers' co-operatives, which promulgated self-education and communal independence, and the second the emergence of so-called high schools, i.e., non-vocational training centres that served as social and cultural sites of national enlightenment, particularly for young people of both sexes. Thus, the social experiences and cultural expressions of modernity were shaped by the dual development of an urban modernity favouring individualism and a rural modernity of collectivism, which for both sexes served to underline the dynamics of social and cultural exist-ence, while drawing on divergent strands of cultural expression.

Within these changeable circumstances, Danish film studios mushroomed from 1906, when the Nordic Film Company (Nordisk Film Kompagni) was founded, and by 1914 there were at least 24 studios in more or less perman-ent existence. Nordic Film, however, was the undisputed giant, and soon became the second largest production company in Europe (it is still the world's oldest film studio in operation): during its golden years, 1911–16, the firm produced more than 700 films, of which its director claimed 98 per cent were exported. In 1915 the company employed 1,700 people, actors not included (Neergaard 1957:53, 54, 17). The phenomenal economic suc-cess of Nordic Film rested largely on its early export of multiple-reel films, initiated in 1910 by a rival company, Fotorama, with *The white slave traffic* (*Den hvide slavehandel*), which the German sociologist Emilie Altenloh termed "the first modern sensational drama" (Altenloh 1914:12). Longer films set new technical standards and demanded novel forms of narration. While it was Nordic Film that first reaped the profits of these innovations, it neither invented the feature-length film nor initiated its form of narration.

Significant for this early era of film production, narrative innovation came from an independent group of personal acquaintances, consisting of a young painter-cum-author, an actress and a cinema owner: the author wrote a script with a specific lead in mind, the cinema owner provided Dkr 8 000 to cover production costs, and the entire film was shot within two weeks. The photographer was the only person in the team with some previous experi-ence of film-making and he over-exposed the shots. Under these circum-stances, *The abyss* was born.

The film is a contemporary social melodrama of "female innocence betrayed", set in a narrative framework of country versus city, middle class versus lower class, Christian reticence versus bohemian permissiveness. The young music teacher, Magda Vang (Asta Nielsen), encounters an engineer, Knud Svane, while riding a tram. They have tea in a park and a month later she receives an invitation to spend her summer holiday with Knud and his parents in their country parsonage. Gladly she accepts, only to find herself rather bored by rural life. Declining to accompany Knud and his parents to the Sunday sermon, she follows them to the garden gates. Here, she sees a troupe of circus artists led by a young riding cowboy, Rudolph Stern. Entranced, she later pursuades Knud to take her to the circus, where she makes a feeble attempt to mime one of the dancers in front of the two men. Later the same night, she elopes from her room with Mr Rudolph.

Next, we see Magda in an artists' boarding-house together with Rudolph Stern. Being a womanizer, her lover ignores Magda's entreaties to be true to her and insists that she rehearses her variety dance number for him. He then leaves with another woman. By coincidence, Knud finds Magda in her depressed state and implores her to go with him. Going to her room to pack, Magda meets Rudolph and falls to her feet in front of him. Unobserved by the other two, Knud witnesses the scene and leaves. Magda and Rudolph now go from bad to worse. During a variety performance, Magda sees her lover making advances to a young dancer (dressed in white) as the couple go on stage to perform their dance number (the famous Gaucho dance), a drama of jealousy, in which Magda slowly dances around Mr Rudolph, tieing him up with his lasso. Rudolph's kissing of the young ballerina on leaving the stage enrages Magda who whips and hits her rival. In the final scene of the film, Magda has become the breadwinner, playing the piano in a lowly restaurant. Here Knud and Rudolph meet in a fight. Realizing that Rudolph wants her to sell herself as a prostitute, Magda kills him in desperation and is taken away by the police while Knud looks on.

The structure of the plot resembles those of the contemporary social dramas that were becoming increasingly popular in Danish film at the time, most successfully, as we noted, in *The white slave traffic* which opened just five weeks before *The abyss*. More unconventional is the professional casting in all major parts of the film. For its first screening on 12 September, the cinema owner-cum-producer invited to his cinema, Kosmorama, among others the staff of the Royal Theatre, who were very impressed by the film. So were ordinary people: police had to be called out to restrain queues, and after the film had its premiere in Düsseldorf in December, its lead, Asta Nielsen became a household name on the Continent.

The circumstances of the film's production and reception offer important clues to its success: the film's producer was a well-educated and much-travelled translator. With his experience of writing and painting, Urban Gad, the script-writer and director, had an advanced notion of narrative structure and continuity, as well as a keen eye for visual effect. In addition, he had a solid upper middle-class background (his father was an admiral and his mother a well-known playwright and socialite in Copenhagen), a status that undoubtedly helped pave the way for the film's acceptance as art, first within the circle of colleagues and journalists, then within the wider group of middle-class audiences.

The Danish press hailed the film as "great and genuine art", and the reviews resembled theatre journalism more than the usual brief film notices of the day. Two aspects were emphasized in particular: the unusual celebrity opening ("in Parisian fashion"), and the powerful acting of well-known actors, whom the journalists assumed were familiar to the public. The so-called Gaucho dance and the final scene were remarked on: "the death scene in particular was played with great 'cinematic power'. A dance scene featuring Miss Nielsen and Mr Poul Reumert was unusually suggestive" (*Socialdemokraten*). The leading daily *Politiken* stressed Asta Nielsen's performance as unique: "in the scene where she is being led down the stairs by the policeman's arm, her dull, almost somnambulistic gaze, endows her with a tragic stature that is totally enthralling . . . A Gaucho dance created by Reumert and Miss Asta Nielsen is a must for everybody." According to *Ekstrabladet*, a new mass-circulation newspaper, the film showed "colourful and lively pictures of artistic and suburban life, burning love and burning hate, temperament and storms of the soul and, in addition, the Gaucho dance, that will be seen and discussed as intensely as the Apache dance used to be." In short, *The abyss* served fundamentally to assert the respectability of cinema and to secure a more well-heeled middle-class audience for contemporary film melodrama.

Internationally, *The abyss* became by far the most popular of Danish films prior to the First World War (Neergaard 1957:61). In Germany alone, it played for eight years and was instrumental in ousting Italian films from their second place on the list of imports (France topped the list). The film also catapulted Asta Nielsen to immediate stardom: in the years 1911–14, she made eight films in eight weeks in Germany each year, all of them directed, and most of them scripted, by Urban Gad. By 1914, she was the undisputed queen of German cinema, earning DM 85 000 a year (Altenloh 1914:31, 32) – most of which she lost during the war. Yet the tremendous foreign success of the film cannot be attributed solely to external factors of length, well-timed publicity and well-known actors (they were not credited in the film). A closer look at the production process is revealing, however. First, the actors were all professionals who knew one another from the stage. Secondly, they all put their "every ability and sincerity" into the film, as Asta Nielsen was later to write in her autobiography *The silent muse* (*Den tiende muse*, 1945–46). Thirdly, Asta Nielsen's own work process was essential. Born of poor parents, by a combination of pluck and luck she was trained as an actress at the Royal Theatre of Copenhagen, which had recently taken up the plays of Ibsen and Strindberg with their more naturalistic style of performance. Subsequently, during her eight years of engagement at other theatres, Nielsen widened her range of acting techniques by often playing comic old hags and spinsters, and on at least one occasion a young man (Fønss 1930:117) – her lean figure and alto voice were regarded by her managers as beyond the pale for leading ladies of the stage. In her autobiography she states that she wanted no rehearsal for her first shot in *The abyss*, which is also its final scene:

I was led downstairs past the humming of the camera, which I immediately felt to be highly enticing, and I sort of woke up standing among my colleagues. It was clear to me that, in order to really express an essential scene in a dramatic film, one must harbour the capability of withdrawing from one's surroundings. The difficulty for film actors to develop the character and moods of a part can only be overcome by a form of self-suggestion. Here, abilities and technique are of no avail, only the absolute gift for empathy [*indlevelse*] with the fragments, collected in the imagination, which demands an authenticity of expression in front of the revealing lens.

As I came to myself, I felt a strange silence around me; it was broken by the famous actor Stribolt who came to me and said: "In two months you will be world-famous" (Nielsen 1945:129).

It is evident that Nielsen's ideal acting mode was expression through introspection. And it remained that way. On a personal level this mode was a result of her combined training in classical and lighter (if not boulevard) theatre. But in more general terms, her acting may be seen as a fusion of the naturalistic acting style learned at the Royal Theatre, and a more melodramatic rhetoric of impersonation that was needed if a woman in her mid-twenties was to "cover", in the literal sense of the word, female characters who were 50 years her senior.

The Gaucho dance: body and movement

The central dance scene of *The abyss* demonstrates important elements in the acting style that subsequently came to distinguish Nielsen. On a filmic level of analysis, in narrative terms the scene is a fundamental *mise en abyme* of the entire film: here Magda enacts her passion and power for the first time, with the aim of securing her love. The second time she acts with similar physical force is in the final scene when she kills her lover. This scene emblematically signifies the duality of passion as sensuality and suffering (cf. the Latin *passio* that denotes both aspects). The importance of the scene is further underlined by numbers: it is the third and last time that Magda dances in the film. (In the opening and closing scenes, Magda is seen playing the piano, a more sedate and approved form of feminine expression and employment, but also a marker of her loss of social status.) Furthermore, the symbolism of colour is important: in the initial dance scene outside the circus Magda is dressed with decorum in white; during her dance rehearsal she gradually undresses, revealing a white bodice underneath a black skirt. In the Gaucho dance, her rival wears white, while Magda's skin-tight black silk dress serves to heighten the effect of her body movements. In her autobiography, Nielsen describes the scene as follows:

Figure 15.1   Danish actors Asta Nielsen and Poul Reumert in the famous Gaucho-scene in *Afgrunden* (*The abyss*). The scene became a favourite focus for censors and an equally favoured attraction for audiences across boundaries of nation and gender. (Courtesy Danish Film Archive)

> Tightly pressing myself to him, I performed my amorous writhings around the poor victim, and being ignorant of the restraint demanded by film, this to me as yet unknown profession, I put all I could muster of longing, unrequited love and burning passion into my rhythmic endeavour (Nielsen 1945:131).

More than any other single scene, it is possibly her rendition of the Gaucho dance that destined Nielsen for stardom. Her posture is passion condensed, her dance is power in movement. Through her slow-moving body, Nielsen unites intensified image and dynamic change in a way that creates a character of contradictory female eroticism. In an analysis of Asta Nielsen's special erotic attraction, the Hungarian author and film theorist, Béla Belázs, was to remark later that eroticsim was the "*Filmstoff an sich*":

> First, because it is always also a bodily experience, and hence visible. Secondly, only in eroticism is there a fundamental possibility of silent understanding. Only lovers can converse with their eyes without leaving anything unsaid, and plump words would only be disturbing. Erotic and expressive play were always sisters [*Minnespiel und Mienenspiel waren von jeher Schwestern*].

The special artistic value of Asta Nielsen's eroticism rests in her etherealness. Her eyes are primary, not her body . . . Her face carries not only her own expression, but almost imperceptibly, yet always noticeable, it reflects as a mirror the expression of the other. Just as in the theatre I can hear what the heroine hears, so can I see in [Asta Nielsen's] face what she sees. She carries the entire dialogue on her face and merges it into a synthesis of understanding and experience (*Erfassens und Erlebens*) (Belázs in Belach et al. 1973:1, 2).

Belázs here makes a central connection between eroticism, visuality and silence that has later been developed by the American literary historian Peter Brooks (1976), who defines melodrama as a "text of muteness": visual knowledge transcends verbal knowledge precisely because it combines sense and sensuality, inner vision and outer visibility. In the silent film, the bridge between these aspects is expression – gestures, posture, movement – lodged in the body. Visible expression is what creates a direct link between character and spectator. This is a main reason why all silent films bear formal marks of melodrama, irrespective of their enunciation. Nielsen's fusion of self and other is an essential visual clue to her filmic star status. While Belázs speaks about the mature Nielsen, who has perfected her repertoire of expressions, he nevertheless explores aspects of her filmic appeal that are equally applicable to *The abyss*, even if the expressive codes are still in the making.

Belázs emphasizes the etherealness of Asta Nielsen's eyes and face. Others stress the expressiveness of her hands, which may be a reason why the Germans dubbed her "die Duse der Kino" (the Duse of the cinema), referring to the Italian tragédienne Eleonora Duse who was said to have "talking hands". In *The abyss*, we see how the bodily elements of expression come together in movement. The dance not only serves to fuse Nielsen's various forms of expression into a powerful whole: her lean and lithe body. Through its movement, the dance actually infuses these expressions with a heightened emotion that transforms the etherealness of posture into an eroticism of pace. Moreover, this visual iconography is motivated by a narrative play on erotic seeming and being: the enactment of jealousy during the dance number is framed by the acting-out of jealousy before and after. In narrative terms, the dance is both performance and experience, a dualism that sustains spectatorial captivation.

However, what ultimately yields the scene its erotic power is its point-of-view structure. In narrative terms, the entire dance takes place on a variety stage during the troupe's performance, with the audience to the right of the picture (some throw flowers on to the stage). But the scene is shot from the film spectator's point-of-view. The gaze is destabilized and questioned, and the invisible screen line demarcating screen and spectator is echoed by a visible barrier between diegetic stage and audience. This Pandora's box yields an extra dimension of spectatorial thrills: the seeming presence of other spectators adds to the obvious voyeuristic pleasure. Yet this pleasure is also potentially unsettling, because it serves to stress boundaries between characters and spectator whose existence film rarely alludes to. From a production perspective, Nielsen's subsequent use of the stage as filmic device can be regarded as a remnant of her and Urban Gad's early theatrical careers. But from a reception perspective, this device certainly is a portent of much later developments in film, when spectacle and direct address became means of meta-commentary and self-reflexion.

Asta Nielsen's persona as indexical sign

The phenomenal success of *The abyss* must be accounted for in terms of Asta Nielsen's charisma, which rests in her unique expressiveness at the intersection between inner emotions and outer forms of signification. On a cinematic level of analysis, this brings me to a more general discussion of Nielsen's star status. As the British film theorist Richard Dyer has demonstrated in his seminal study of the star system (Dyer 1979), it is at once a filmic sign and a cinematic phenomenon. The fundamental point is that the individual star originates at the intersection of these two levels. Following the British film semiotician Barry King, who has recently developed and nuanced Dyer's concepts, one may distinguish between three aspects of the star: the film's construction of a specific character, the "real-life" person and the persona. The persona, according to King, "is the intersection of cinematic and filmic discursive practices in an effort to realise a coherent personality" (King 1991:175). To make these concepts clear, we can see how they operate in *The abyss*: here, the character Magda is physically embodied by the person Asta Nielsen. On a filmic level, the connection between the two is the star image that serves to articulate a space between the real (person) and the imagined (character). Cogently, King asserts that in a star performance the image is coloured by the persona, i.e., an overarching framework of off-screen public conduct that articulates the star as film star. This space of articulation is also the locus of interpretation for the actual cinema audience: it is precisely the distance between the real and the imagined that opens a mental site of interpretation operating between the poles of empathy and distance (Drotner 1991). In the case of *The abyss*, a central question is how does the filmic image of Asta Nielsen fuel the development of a star persona (which subsequently reverberates on to her film image)?

In answering this, the American philosopher C.S. Peirce's theory of semiotics offers a useful approach, since it prioritizes the processual character of signification. Peirce operates with three relations between an external object (the audience) and any given sign (the star): an iconic, an indexical and a symbolic relation. These relations denote rising degrees of convention: an iconic sign works by resemblance, an indexical sign works through connection, while a symbol works through convention.[1] Relating these abstract categories to the elements pertaining to the star, we can immediately see that the "real" person Asta Nielsen has an iconic relation to the physical body actually appearing on the screen. Equally simple, the character Magda is a symbolic sign, inasmuch as her personage bears no necessary likeness to the actress who plays her, but is a matter of convention. This leaves us with the more complex indexical sign. I propose that this can fruitfully be related to the persona (and its filmic "double", the image): the star persona cannot exist without the real person Asta Nielsen's physical shape (she could not be a man, her weight could not be 100 kg without this drastically changing her persona). The persona is motivated by the person to apply a Barthesian term, but even so it covers more than likeness. Conversely, the persona colours the character, as is evident in type-casting, but the audience knows the two are different (this difference, as often noted, is part of filmic allure). The persona, then, is an indexical sign operating at the intersection of similarity and difference.

If we allow that the star persona may be regarded as an index in the process of cultural signification, we can specify how Asta Nielsen's filmic image could develop into a star persona. It centres on her body, since it connects inner emotion and outer expression; indeed, several critics note that the body is the *sine qua non* of stardom (Dyer 1979, Gledhill 1991). Gesture, posture, movement, are indexical signs not only because they form bridges between inner and outer, as already mentioned, but also because they form part of a whole body whose expressions can only be understood by an audience that knows how to interpret them. What would these interpretations be, then? Again, Peirce's semiotics offers a helpful clue because it foregrounds the process through which meaning is made in specific contexts. In contrast to the sign theory of semiology, as developed later and independently by the Swiss linguist Ferdinand de Saussure, semiotics operates with a triadic concept of the sign:

> A sign, or *representamen,* is something which stands to somebody for something in some respect or capacity. It addresses somebody, that is, creates in the mind of that person an equivalent sign, or perhaps a more developed sign. The sign which it creates I call the *interpretant* of the first sign. The sign stands for something, its *object* (Peirce 1931–58:228).

The semiotic sign thus contains three aspects: the *representamen* refers to an *object* by creating a new sign, the *interpretant,* in the mind of the interpreter. The interpretant, then, is not a person, nor is it the substance of interpretation. It should rather be understood as the significant aspects to which the process of interpretation gives rise within a specific social and historical context. These aspects may in turn be activated and combined into new forms of interpretation or action. In *The abyss*, we can follow how Asta Nielsen's screen performance serves to create specific interpretants, specific configurations of meaning that together come to operate as a grid of the audience's interpretation: so this is what a star performance looks like. As already mentioned, a crucial frame of reference in constituting this grid is the distance found in the star persona between the real person and the fictional character. What Asta Nielsen does in *The abyss* is to crystallize what this space could look like by offering her audience certain interpretants of stardom.

Nielsen's gift lies precisely in her drawing on a known visual rhetoric of emblems such as colour, light and gesture while transforming this rhetoric into a personal form of expression. Still, the indexical nature of the persona is sustained not only in the audiences' proper construction of interpretants through their knowledge of narrative codes and conventions, it is equally dependent on wider discursive practices of popular culture to assert its viability. As King stresses, the star is distinguished precisely by the persona overriding the image on the screen (King 1991). The persona feeds on its connection both to the image on screen and to the "real" person as a private individual beyond the screen and beyond public appearances off-screen: fandom is the basis of stardom, and the Asta Nielsen case is no exception.

"Die Asta" and the audience

Part of her initial allure was the censorship surrounding her films. The 1910s was an era of sexual struggle and like any new medium, film became a target of intense moral panic that harboured wider social and cultural contradictions (Drotner 1992). On its opening, *The abyss* was X-rated, but according to Asta Nielsen herself, her "tragic face became the fig leaf under whose cover the [Gaucho] dance escaped censorship [in Denmark] as later abroad" (Nielsen 1945:133). Discussions over the morality of her films undoubtedly coloured their reception, and may have induced what the British cultural critic Stuart Hall has termed "preferred readings" of their contents (Hall 1980). As is evident with *The abyss*, too, both main title, programme and part titles certainly served to underline such preferred readings by anchoring visual iconography ("a fateful vow", "tied to her destiny", "towards her doom").

While we may speculate about the possible interpretants of her star persona, it is open to conjecture how Nielsen's films were actually received. Would audiences remember the explicit morality of the films? Would people rather linger on Nielsen's implied visual eroticism? Or would their

Figure 15.2   The downfall of the female protagonist is a standard element in early film melodrama. Asta Nielsen in the final scene of *Afgrunden* (*The abyss*) (Courtesy Danish Film Archive)

captivation perhaps rest in a manoeuvring between different levels of reception? While a major part of the audiences of very early films were often children and young people, few can have been as unaffected as one Danish boy who was asked in 1913 about how Asta Nielsen's film appealed to him: "It was just nonsense. They kissed all the time and there was nobody wearing a uniform" (Sandfeld 1966:155).

Lacking substantive historical studies of the reception of Asta Nielsen's films, I can only venture to infer some possibilities of the interpretive repertoires (Potter & Wetherell 1987) that the interpretants of stardom may have created. Nielsen undoubtedly represented an alternative to dominant constructions of femininity – the vamp and the victim – as seen, for example, in contemporary American film stars and in popular magazines of the day (Winship 1987, Drotner 1988, 1991, Ballaster et al. 1991). With the clarity of hindsight, her star status can be seen as a prelude to the future, her slender body and introvert sensuality offering an image that is more in keeping with the flapper of the 1920s than with the fairies of the 1910s. Her persona, as we see, is shaped at the intersection of intensity and change. She is sensual without being explosively sexual. For men, this persona may have been particularly pleasing, since it sustained a voyeuristic gaze without endanger-ing their male power.[2] Following this line of analysis, it is no coincidence that male critics such as Belázs and Pabst emphasized particular aspects of Nielsen's persona, namely her etherealness and bodily parts (hands, face and eyes), while neglecting her dynamics and her more open expressions of sensuality.

Conversely, for women I would suggest that it was the very complexity of Nielsen's persona that lay at the core of her mythic status. Its condensed dynamic admirably signified the ambiguities facing women at a time when many of them were situated between the demands of traditional, privatized femininity and the more unbounded, and less inscribed, public trajectories. The indexical nature of Nielsen's persona rested on its suspension of and challenge to demarcations fixed between inner and outer embodiment, pri-vate and public spaces. Fundamentally, these demarcations also operated, as they continue to do, as gendered relations of power. Hence, Nielsen's star status may have been shaped by its early articulation and questioning of the paradigmatic opposition between public and private power at a time when many women in her audiences sought to redraw those very boundar-ies. Her entire oeuvre may be regarded as explorations of the limits within contemporary femininity (Jerslev 1995:30). Her fans' intense preoccupa-tion with "die Asta" is witnessed in a plethora of paraphernalia: in Germany, one could buy Asta Nielsen creams and perfumes, signalling the import-ance of the star persona's body to a female audience. The output of statuettes, pictures and postcards could naturally be enjoyed by both sexes, as could the sandwiches and special dishes named after her (Sandfeld 1966:203)!

In her book on German cinema during the Weimar Republic, the Amer-ican film historian Patrice Petro suggests that Nielsen's fame with her female fans of the 1920s rests on a "particular combination of female bisexuality and melodramatic expression" (Petro 1989:153). Conversely, I contend that Nielsen's star status is shaped by a particular Nordic, perhaps even Danish, experience of gendered modernity: her fame was firmly established already before the First World War and thus cannot be attributed solely to her intriguing recombination of the problems facing women of the 1920s. Rather, the ambiguities of her persona resonate with the wider ambivalences facing women in modernity. And those ambivalences were already evident to large numbers of women in the 1910s, even if few of them had to negotiate their consequences to the degree that was seen in the 1920s.

Nielsen's own life history amply bore out contemporary female dilemmas, and hence served to consolidate her star persona: she had her first, and only, child as an unmarried mother at the age of 20. She subsequently suc-ceeded as a career woman to a degree which, already prior to the First World War, made her German director note:

In Asta Nielsen . . . lies an industry of the world . . . I build her a huge studio in the Tempelhof, I offer her a large production team. This woman possesses everything. It is the first time that a large firm is being founded because of a woman (quoted in Seydel & Hagedorff 1981:50).

In addition, Asta Nielsen married three times – the last time at the age of 88, barely six years after the suicide of her daughter and just three years before her death ("I have never been completely content, completely happy, in my life. Now I am" (quoted in ibid.:252). If melodrama is not only a film genre, but equally "a mode of experience", as Thomas Elsaesser professes (Elsaesser 1991:49), then Asta Nielsen's star trajectory is a good case in point. Her autobiography, which she wrote in her sixties, is shaped by two discourses: film is an art, and the actor's profession is an art of authentic expression. These discourses colour her evaluations just as they seem to have permeated her life. Her films are the best proof that these were more than discursive strategies. Significantly, the German film critic Lotte Eisner – one of the only women publicly to discuss Nielsen's work – makes the following retrospective evaluation: "Perhaps her first film is her best: *Afgrunden* [*The abyss*] where she looks like a daguerreotype figure come to life" (Eisner 1961).

Nielsen's subsequent critical oblivion naturally raises the question of why it is the childlike Mary Pickfords and the vamplike Theda Baras, not the eroticized Asta Nielsens, who have gone down in film history as the early film stars. Is it because gender ambiguity cannot be accommodated within an academy largely defined by a male discourse? Or is it because the critical canon is still predominantly shaped by an Anglo-American view of the world? Whatever our answers, Nielsen's critical fate serves to highlight the fact that film history is shaped as much by the elements we leave out as by the ones we choose to include.

(Unless otherwise indicated, translations are by the author.)

Notes

1. It is important to stress the relational character of icon, index and symbol. They are not three different signs as such, but they denote three different relations between sign and object. Thus, indexes may have iconic aspects (a photograph is an example of this), and symbols may possess both iconic and indexical aspects.
2. For example, Lulu in Frank Wedekind's play *Erdgeist* (1895) is an epitome of a man eater (Dijkstra 1987), and thus a much more ambiguous figure in this respect. Conversely, Nielsen plays Lulu in the film *Erdgeist* (1923) with a heightened sense of tragic insight.

Filmography

Afgrunden (*The abyss*) 1910 Kosmorama. Producer: Hjalmar Davidsen. Script: Urban Gad. Director: Urban Gad. Camera: Alfred Lind. Cast: Asta Nielsen (Magda Vang), H. Neergaard (Peder Svane, parson), Robert Dinesen (Knud Svane, engineer), Poul Reumert (Rudolph Stern), Emilie Sannon (Lilly d'Estrelle), Oscar Stribolt (waiter).

References

Altenloh, E. 1914. *Zur Soziologie des Kino: die Kino-Unternehmung und die sozialen Schichten ihrer Besucher.* Leipzig: Spamerschen Buchdruckerei.

Ballaster, R. et al. 1991. *Women's worlds: ideology, femininity, and the woman's magazine.* London: Macmillan.

Belach, H. et al. (eds) 1973. *Asta Nielsen, 1881–1972.* Berlin: Deutsche Kinemathek/ Danish Film Museum/Academy of Arts.

Brooks, P. 1976. *The melodramatic imagination: Balzac, Henry James, melodrama, and the mode of excess.* New Haven, Conn.: Yale University Press.

Diaz, P. 1920. *Asta Nielsen.* Extract quoted in Seydel & Hagedorff 1981:50.

Dijkstra, B. 1987. *Idols of perversity: fantasies of feminine evil in fin-de-siècle culture.* Oxford: Oxford University Press.

Drotner, K. 1988. *English children and their magazines, 1751–1945.* New Haven, Conn.: Yale University Press.

Drotner, K. 1991. Intensities of feeling: modernity, melodrama and adolescence. *Theory, Culture & Society,* vol. 8, no. 1, 57–87.

Drotner, K. 1992. Modernity and media panics. In *Media cultures: reappraising transnational media,* K.C. Schrøder & M. Skovmand (eds), 42–62. London: Routledge.

Dyer, R. 1979. *Stars.* London: BFI.

Eisner, L. 1961. Til Asta Nielsens ære (In honour of Asta Nielsen). *Kosmorama,* vol. no. 51.

Elsaesser, T. 1991. Tales of sound and fury: observations on the family melodrama. In *Home is where the heart is: studies in melodrama and the woman's film,* C. Gledhill (ed.), 43–69. London: BFI. Originally Published 1972.

Engberg, M. 1967. *Asta Nielsen.* Bad Erms: Verband der deutschen Filmclubs.

Engberg, M. 1977. *Dansk stumfilm,* bd. 1–2 (Danish silent film, vol. 1–2). Copenhagen: Rhodos.

Fønss, O. 1930. *Danske skuespillerinder: erindringer og interviews* (Danish actresses: reminiscences and interviews). Copenhagen: Nutids.

Gledhill, C. 1991. Signs of melodrama. In *Stardom: industry of desire,* C. Gledhill (ed.), 207–29. London: Routledge.

Hall, S. 1980. Encoding/decoding. In *Culture, media, language.* Stuart Hall et al. (eds). London: Hutchinson. Originally published 1973.

Jerslev, A. 1995. Asta Nielsen, kvindeligheden og de store følelser (Asta Nielsen, femininity and passion). *Kosmorama,* vol. 41, no. 213, 26–35.

King, B. 1991. Articulating stardom. In *Stardom: industry of desire,* C. Gledhill (ed.), 167–82. London: Routledge.

Metz, C. 1971. *Langage et cinéma.* Paris: Larousse.

Neergaard, E. 1957. *Historien om dansk film* (The history of Danish film). Copenhagen: Gyldendal.

Neiiendam. R. 1955. Afgrunden (The abyss). *Nationaltidende* (National Gazette), 9th March, 3.

Nielsen, A. 1945–6. *Den tiende muse,* bd. 1–2 (The silent muse, Vol. 1–2). Copenhagen: Gyldendal.

Peirce, C.S. 1931–58. *Collected papers,* Vol. 2. Cambridge, Mass.: Harvard University Press.

Petro, P. 1989. *Joyless streets: women and melodramatic representation in Weimar Germany.* Princeton, NJ: Princeton University Press.

Potter, J. & M. Wetherell 1987. *Discourse and social psychology.* London: Sage.

Reumert, P. 1940. *Masker og mennesker* (Masks and people). Copenhagen: Gyldendal.

Sandfeld, G. 1966. *Den stumme scene: dansk biografteater indtil lydfilmens gennembrud* (The silent stage: Danish cinema until the advent of sound). Copenhagen: Nyt Nordisk, Arnold Busck.

Seydel, R. & A. Hagedorff (eds) 1981. *Asta Nielsen: Ihr Leben in Fotodokumenten, Selbstzeugnissen und zeitgenössischen Betrachtungen.* Berlin: Henschelverlag.

Waldekranz, R. 1985. *Filmens historia,* bd. 1 (The history of film, vol. 1). Stockholm: Norstedts.

Winship, J. 1987. *Inside women's magazines.* London: Unwin Hyman.

CHAPTER SIXTEEN

Oscillations: on subject and gender in late modernism

Lis Wedell Pape

It is the aim of this chapter to illustrate why the question of subject and gender – and, more specifically, the question of "femininity", of "woman" – should not be asked solely within the confines of traditional biological, anthropological, sociological or philosophical schemes. Rather, considering the way in which this question has been (and is still) discussed during the 1980s and 1990s, a different approach to framing the question is needed. Though necessarily dependent on the traditional way of thinking sexual/ gender difference in terms of systems of oppositional structure, the crucial task of this procedure will be to question the basic ideas inscribed in them in order to be able to transcend them.

Historically, the question of gender is closely connected with a mode of thought prevalent in Western thinking: that of the (androcentric) sovereign subject as mastering nature and being constitutive of knowledge and experience. Consequently, a rethinking of gender involves reflections upon this classical modern subject, tending to dismantle its sacrosanct position as the foundation stone of human thought. Thus, the chapter presents itself as an essay in deconstructive practice, and attaches to Martin Heidegger and Jacques Derrida's works on the disclosure of metaphysics and the dissolution of the subject figure as the ultimate basis of thinking as well as being.

The area suitable for a rethinking of the subject figure is, however, not philosophy in its classical sense. In Western culture philosophy since Plato and up to the twentieth century has been tantamount to metaphysics, the basis of which has been/is the idea of "the first and final entity" (whether termed the Idea, God, the Subject, etc.) that endows life with meaning and truth. Historically, this idea saturates argumentative philosophical language as well as ordinary communicative language, both of them being consistent with *logos* as their essential *raison d'être*, and both being inscribed in a law/ *nomos* of terminal – and transcendental – meaning and truth. Hence the area of rethinking must be sought in discourses that tend to break this law, or at least are working on the margin of discourses guaranteed by this law.

In this respect the critique of metaphysics gives priority to poetic discourse over philosophical reasoning. As distinct from philosophy, the poetic discourse is characterized by its equivocal signification potentiality, its non-referential, non-transparent language and its meta-poetic consciousness of being a *mise en scène*. This goes especially for modernist and late modernist literary texts that point themselves out as texts-being-produced, thus drawing attention to the very process of signifiance.* A substantial part of this chapter will, therefore, consist in an analysis of a text from a work of poetry by one of the most outstanding Danish late modern poets, Inger Christensen. In this connection it should be noted that Inger Christensen's poetry does not merely repeat or mime philosophical thought, but produces it and displays it.

The poetic discourse

What's written is always one thing

and what's described something else again
Between them is the undescribed
which as soon as it is described
opens up new undescribed areas

It's undescribable[1]

From a philosophical point of view the poetic discourse is characterized by the indeterminability of its utterance. In this respect it eludes determinate truth, which underlies the proposition of classical thought as its tacit prerequisite. The basic idea of metaphysics, that truth is situated in a *primo et ultimo*, and in a more recent (post-Renaissance) world in the *sub-iectum* as the general, transcendental basis of knowledge, is thus undermined. Though necessarily embedded in metaphysical thought, the poetic discourse invites subversive reading, challenging the *nomos* of the androcentric, self-present subject. So, the poetic discourse has the potential to destabilize metaphysical thought from within. Modernist and late modernist poetry, however, not only has this process as a theme, it also displays it as a strategy on the level of enunciation.

Within late twentieth century modernism the works of the Danish poet Inger Christensen (b. 1935) form a weighty contribution to the poetic discourse described above.

---

* "Signifiance" denotes *the fact that* signification and meaning is *possible*, whereas "significance" denotes the actual display of meaning in an utterance.

Since her debut in 1962 Inger Christensen has published six collections of poetry, two novels, two major narratives and a collection of essays.[2] She is a major representative of the Danish modernism of the 1960s and the so-called "systemic poetry" of the 1970s. Furthermore, her work shows a development towards "deconstructive poetry" from the late 1970s up to the present with regard to form and composition as well as themes. In addition, Inger Christensen's works are extremely coherent in the sense that her poetic writings elaborate crucial problematics of her philosophical essays and vice versa.

Inger Christensen's poetry and the critique of metaphysics have many features in common. First and foremost her texts deal with the dismantling – or, to use her own term, *afrealisering* (de-realization) – of the androcentric subject as constitutive ratio throughout her works, and explicitly in the essay "*Afrealisering*" of 1979.[3] Secondly, although the question of gender is a rarely manifested theme in Inger Christensen's works, it is, however, included in the criticism of the subject figure. Moreover it is worth noticing that neither masculinity nor femininity occur as "pure" terms or positions in Inger Christensen's texts; gender is never posed or fixed within a classical oppositional scheme, but is nevertheless indicated in the various ways of enunciation, i.e., in the way the texts present themselves and deconstruct themselves.

As the following analysis of one of the poems in Inger Christensen's collection, *alfabet*(alphabet; 1981), will try to show, the poetic discourse allows for a different way of thinking subject and gender. The important thing here is that neither gender nor subject should be thought within the hierarchical oppositional scheme, but as a matter of the potentiality of oscillating positions. This poem, which is placed at a turning point within the collection as a whole, is in itself deconstructive and does not only interact with the remaining texts of *alfabet*, but with several other discourses, poetic as well as philosophical.

> *nætterne findes, natskyggen findes*
> *natsiden, navnløshedens kåbe findes*
>
> *bevidsthedens nordgrænse findes, dér*
> *hvor det drømte åbner og lukker sin*
> *nordlige krone i nastiske drejninger*
>
> *uden at dagen og natten bestemt er*
> *placeret, uden at nadir og zenit er*
> *lodret under eller over og uden at*
>
> *naos, det inderste rum som er cellens*
> *vil røbe om frøet i en indvendig himmel*
> *samler bevidsthedens grænser i et punkt*

et blomstrende punkt hvori som lidt solskin
istiderne findes, istiderne findes

hvori som lidt ild insekternes vingeløse
Nike findes, og der hverken er sejr
eller nederlag til, kun ingentings trøst;
navnenes trøst, at ingenting kaldes ved
navn, at navnløshed kaldes ved navn

at navnene findes, navne som narhvalen
nælden, navne som nelliken, natuglen
navne som natravnen, nattergalen, nymånen
navne som natlys, najader, og de anderledes
navne hvor et ord når det nævnes er en duft
som narhvalens navn for de arktiske have,
som nældernes navne for feber, som nellikens

navne for genskær af lys i fabrikshvide
nætter, som natuglens, natravnens navne
for fjer, som nattergalens navne for det at
være jordsanger skjult i de fugtige krat
som nymånens navne for Jorden og Solen
som natlysfamiliens navne for slægtskab
najadernes navne for det at være vandaks
og hviske najadernes navne i vinden[4]

nights exist, nightshade exists
the dark side, the cloak of namelessness exists

the northern limits of consciousness exist,
where what is dreamed opens and closes its
northerly crown in nastic turnings

without day and night being definitely
placed, without nadir, zenith
straight below or above and without

the naos, the innermost place of the cell
revealing whether the seed in an inner sky
gathers the limits of consciousness into a point
a flowering point where like a bit of sunshine
ice ages exist, ice ages exist

where like a bit of fire the insects' wingless
Nike exists, neither victory nor

defeat, only the solace of nothing;
the solace of names, that nothingness has
a name, namelessness has a name

that names exist, names like narwhal,
nettle, names like carnation, tawny owl,
and nightjar, names like nightingale, new moon,
evening primrose, naiad, and the other kind of
name in which a word when named is scent
like the narwhal's name for arctic seas,
the nettles' names for fever, like carnations'

names for light reflected into factory-white
nights, like the tawny owl's, the nightjar's names
for feathers, the nightingale's names for being
an Old World warbler hidden in moist thickets
like the new moon's names for Earth and Sun
the evening primrose family's names for kinship
like the naiads' names for being pondweed
whispering the naiads' names in the wind

Thematically, in consequence of its cosmological dimensions, the poem could be seen as an ontological text, displaying a denomination of beings to their coming into being, especially manifest in the two last stanzas. But the text also deals with a "rendering present"[5] on other levels. This "presenting" is effected by a deconstruction of the implicit subject of enunciation in the text.

The text starts with a designating naming (stanza 1 to middle of stanza 5). This procedure is replaced by a processing appellation and self-naming in the last stanzas. At the same time there is a change in the point of view of the text: from a designating implicit subject to a rudimentary one, only lending its voice to let the phenomena speak for themselves. The rudimentary, non-posited subject in the last two stanzas is an intermediary for the coming into being of the work in progress. Thus, emphasized by the fact that several of the selected n-phenomena are taken directly from a dictionary, there is an anchoring of the text in a (symbolic) lexical norm, but also the current motility of a semiotic[6] level is displayed, semantically and stylistically, the words, seductively, intoning and invoking each other. Through the turning of designation-naming into self-naming, signifiance is brought to work in the text, and through the continuous spiral process of re-naming and self-naming signifiance is never brought to an end, but is carried on within the labyrinthine structure of the text.

The poem falls into two clearly distinguishable parts (stanza 1 to middle of stanza 5; middle of stanza 5 to stanza 7). The first part consists in a movement towards a zero point. In stanza 2 it becomes clear that the discourse is displayed on the borderline between the conscious and unconscious in the subject of enunciation ("what is dreamed"). The oscillation between conscious and unconscious is structurally connected with a biological level ("crown", "nastic turnings"). What is dismantled on these different levels is any form of (transcendent) referentiality: time and space are dissolved (stanza 3), which in turn leaves an inner lack of orientation, the process from macro-cosmos being repeated in micro-cosmos. This deconstructive movement moves on in a series of syncretisms: the sacred (*naos*) + the biological ("cell" – Latin for the Greek *naos*); the mythological (*Nike*) + the biological ("wingless"), and by allusion further on to another mythological figure: the striving Icarus. The text proceeds in a series of negations, where eventually any mark of orientation has been disrupted to (and within) consciousness, and any possibility of acting has been definitively demolished.

But from this zero point a new movement is initiated along with the dissolution of normal syntax, and the text turns into (invoking) appellation. A new presentation of cosmos takes place, but in this case cosmos as (self-)differential topos, disconnected from definite mythological–cultural classification: water ("narwhal"), fire ("nettle"), earth ("carnation") and air ("tawny owl") designate the universe. The second part can be read as a corrective reflection of the first, a sort of inverted Creation. Cosmos regains orientation, but now in the virtue of its naming of itself, and without any light of an act of rigid *logos* to overshadow it. On the contrary: concealed from the perceiving eye, the new (black) moon here names "Earth and Sun", just as eventually biology ("pondweed") inscribes mythology ("naiads") in its own *topos*.

The processuality of becoming

loquor, ergo sum
Maurice Blanchot

The movement of the n-poem is down and then up. Thematically any order, be it spatial or temporal, is dissolved. In the spiral flow of the text any classificatory act of a naming subject is de-qualified when what was previously a designated object is being brought to occur as for the first time in its own significance and in its fundamental differentiality and ambiguity. The poetic discourse makes the phenomena come into being and to appearance without de-signating and con-ceptualizing them, and in this process the idea of an innermost "point" (stanza 4), a fixed depositing of truth, is disavowed. Insofar as the designating subject is present in the last two stanzas it is as an alien element ("factory-white"), which is dismantled and subsequently embedded in the movement of self-naming, the negative propositions of the first part being replaced by a play of indecidability ("whispering", stanza 7: the only verb indicating activity) and mere motility.

315

The coming into being of the universe of the poem is in this respect a coming into word. What characterizes the *mise en scène* of the text is precisely Being's[7] coming into word as beings. This is what is at work and at play as signifiance. Owing to the break, the irruption, signifiance is there as a rhythm, a whispering, mediated by a voice which is instrumental in bringing about the work in progress.

Naming Being

It is crucial to emphasize that this movement of the text is not a "back-to-nature" move that would have its origin in a pre-cultural, amorphous continuum beyond culture. What the text displays in terms of nature naming itself is rather the very potentiality of language not centred in the encyclopaedic rationale of the *res cogitans* (in Cartesian terminology). The text sees the endeavour of enlightenment of this ratio with its desire for absolute knowledge and self-realization ("factory-white nights") as destructive enclosure of the room of experience and life. Hence the peeling off of the conventional content of proper names ("the insects' wingless Nike"), hence the deconceptualizing deconstruction of the order of the canonized worldview, and hence, eventually, the declassification of what is left: the merely lexicographical definitions of phenomena in stanza 6. In this way the text lays its main stress on different functions of language in two aspects of naming: giving/having proper names and naming as classification, de-qualifying them both in the light of the assertion that there is some "thing" which cannot be appointed with determinate names in a speech act of a subject.

This some "thing" is Being. The relation established in any naming is one of identity and intimacy, and its temporality is (generalized) presence. The name is the answer to the question: "What is that?" But this question cannot be asked of the fact that something is without being meaningless (: "What is Being, what is is?"). This is, however, exactly what happens in the logocentric way of asking and naming of which the (generalized) self-present subject is the alpha and omega, and in so doing (as Heidegger argues) the subject mistakes beings for Being and locks itself up in a logocentric circle. What Inger Christensen's poem draws attention to is the possibility of disclosing this circle, letting beings, the phenomena, evolve from their Being, and displaying this activity as a dynamic process of difference. So, Being is not an existent, and can therefore not be named. Being "is" only insofar as it is an effect in beings being there, and can never be grasped or conceptualized in it "self". Being eludes definition and description and only shows under certain circumstances where its indeterminability is differentially related to phenomenological beings: "Being is never an existent. But, because Being and essence of things can never be calculated and derived from what is present, they must be freely created, laid down and given" (Heidegger 1949:305). As shown above, the poetic discourse with its non-referentiality and non-fixedness can display this ontological difference (in the Heideggerian sense), and the work of poetry can thus be seen as the privileged arena for its *mise en scène.*

Naming as the essence of poetry

The n-poem is a crucial text in *alfabet*/alphabet, which belongs to the "systemic poetry". This means that *alfabet* is not merely a collection of poems, but a work that integrates each text into a whole, generated by a specific and unique system. The actual system consists in a combination of the letters of the alphabet with a series of numbers known as the Fibonacci series (in which any number is the sum of the two preceding numbers). Thus the first poem, the a-poem, consists of one stanza of 1 verse, the second, the b-poem, has two stanzas of 1 + 1 verses, etc. From the fact that the Fibonacci series is exponentially increasing it is evident that the system is bound to break down before it gets to the end of the alphabet. In fact, after a few excourses the ultimate break down starts in the n-poem, precisely in the middle of the alphabet. From that point onwards the system is more or less defunctionalized, and an inversion takes place in the last poem, counting the work down to one (and zero).

Thematically *alfabet* is an apocalypse. The texts state the existence of the world of phenomena ("apricottrees exist apricottrees exist", goes the first poem), but from the very start this world is seen to contain its own destruction (the b-poem: "bracken exists; and blackberries, blackberries;/ bromine exists; and hydrogen, hydrogen") so that in this sense the unfolding of the theme repeats the uncontrollable growth of the system. What starts as "big bang", organic beings coming into existence and growing, ends up as "big crunch", melting down into nothingness.

Through its system *alfabet* brings a world into being, a world which – with its different levels: cosmology, mythology, sociology, science and individuality – can be understood as a replacement for the universe we cannot grasp. Hence in its poetic discourse *alfabet* draws attention to the very process of coming into being as an act of naming.

Poetic language names things to their being, and at the same time it places human being in the world, in the middle of things, ex-sistent, standing out from the phenomena in a socio-historical context. Naming in the poetic discourse, however, is basically not a unilateral activity, but has in itself the character of conversation. In the work of poetry the processuality of the difference between Being and being is brought into the open in the double movement of speaking and listening. In Inger Christensen's terms, Being is what is "left out", that which can never be "defined" or "described", but to which the poetic text listens and relates itself. In an essay, "Terningens syvtal" (1977), she puts it this way:

God is not dead, I tell myself. God is the conversation
human beings carry on with the universe, or conversely:
the conversation the universe carries on with human
beings in order to become conscious of itself.

(Christensen 1982:117[8])

The poetic work is a *mise en scène* of this doubleness of addressing and
being addressed, that is of conversation as the fundamental characteristic
of language and of being. This is the essential theme and display of the
n-poem specifically, and of *alfabet* as a whole.

The work of poetry

poetry is the inaugural naming of being and of the essence of all
things – not just any speech, but that particular kind which for the
first time brings into the open all that which we can discuss and
deal with in everyday language. Hence poetry never takes language as a raw material ready to hand, rather it is poetry which first
makes language possible (Heidegger 1949:307).

In Heidegger[9] the work of poetry holds a special position concerning the
play of the ontological difference. This is owing to two circumstances: its
non-graspable heterogeneity and the fact that it is a work of language,
which enables it to establish and show the relation between Being, being
and human being (*German: Sein, Seiende* and *Dasein*):

Language is the house of Being. In its home man dwells. Those
who think and those who create with words are the guardians of
this home. Their guardianship accomplishes the manifestation of
Being insofar as they bring the manifestation to language and maintain it in language through their speech (Heidegger 1977:193).

To Heidegger the *dýnamis* between different ways of "being", put forward and momentarily revealed in the language of the poetic work, is truth.
So, truth is not conceived as something fixable (as absolute knowledge or
anything final), but as some "thing" that happens, only to bear its own
disappearance with it. In this respect the question of truth is analogous with
the question of Being. Though, in the poetic work, language in naming
"nominates beings to their being from out of their Being",[10] "the God
[ultimate truth, the ultimate Name] remains afar".[11] Being is absent, non-
identical, always deferring; but in the *mise en scène* of the ontological difference displayed in the openness of the poetic work as work its working
can be glimpsed momentarily. Thus the poetic work reveals truth as processuality. What it perpetuates in its setting is the difference between Being

and being, not Being as such, for which there cannot meaningfully be asked. At the same time, however, Being cannot be said or say itself except via ontic metaphor.

In Inger Christensen's text a similar comprehension of "being" and truth is expressed, and not only concerning theme. It is also indicated on the level of enunciation, in the specific non-propositional rhythm of the text, and most importantly in the word *findes*. The Danish wording *findes* is the operative word of the text (and functions as a kind of leitmotif throughout the whole of *alfabet*). Where the English translation ("exist") etymologically (Latin *ex-sto*) in this context calls attention to the standing out of beings from Being, the Danish original in its very grammatical–syntactical form involves the particular processuality of the middle voice. The form *findes* has a great many connotations. Being neither decidably active nor passive it has (at least) the following significations: be/be there ("exist", ex-sist); find oneself; be thought of/invented; be found by somebody; be placed; be extant; occur (semantically analogous with the impersonal German *"es gibt"* and French *"il y a"*). All of these significations are at play in *alfabet*, but the last one ("occur") is the most interesting here, because grammatically it seems to imply the same kind of indeterminability regarding subject and object as *findes*. In the middle voice the subject "is well and truly inside the process of which [it] . . . is the agent",[12] that is, "the subject effects something and in so doing is affected himself".[13]

When the middle form is posed as the outset of Inger Christensen's text and pervades it, it means that to whatever extent the text might seem propositional the enunciation is thoroughly a-thetic and non-referential. It displays itself as a "substitute universe" in relation to its nature of a setting. Here the middle voice implies, too, that the very position of enunciation questions its own possibility. Thus, the apparent paradox of this position when articulated in the middle form, that it voices "an operation which is not an operation",[14] cannot be dissolved. When *alfabet* is considered a substitute universe, a coherent work that opens a world and keeps it a-becoming, the indeterminability of this paradox must be maintained as operative for the text as a whole, as a work. As such the crux of the text is to show that the truth of being is becoming.

Subject and gender in the middle voice

I write as the beating
heart writes
the hands the feet
the skin the lips
the sex their whisper[15]

The poetic text as work bears some consequences for the reader involved as analyst, whose analytic strategy, of course, should not be an impediment to the project of the text. This means that any method that insists on establishing an Archimedean point from which the text can be viewed will fail in the sense that it will miss the very nature of the text, turning it into a delimited and fundamentally transparent object of interpretation. Due to its polylogue character the text eludes such endeavour, and the analysis is led to downgrade the thematical elements (the what) of the text and give priority to the ways these elements are organized (the how). Being receptive rather than appropriative, and respecting the heterogeneity of the discourse and seduced by its multitude of signification, the analyst enters into an infinite interchange with the text, the non-transparent language of which invites the reader to stick to the "surface" and not look beyond for a hidden essence or truth. In this process not only the implied subject of the text, but the analyst subject as well are destabilized. This being so, no ultimate reading is possible, and the analyst finds themself "posited" a subject-in-process.

As argued above, the poetic work is the privileged arena of the display of the ontological difference. With its transgression of *nomos*, its discourse exposes a radical otherness, which is not exterior or oppositional to any other discourse, but immanent in its very display, and which inscribes into the text a pervasive indeterminability. The deconstructive text *par excellence* puts the reader in a kind of non-position. Like the text itself, the reader is neither subject nor object, but part of the displaying discourse. If the text is a substitute universe, a work that shows what "being" is like, this state of the "subject" can be generalized, affecting the philosophical way of rethinking the subject.

Différance

The poetic text in question here, the n-poem from *alfabet*, can be thematically characterized by Heidegger's terminology, but concerning its prosody Derrida's notion of *différance*, of play and of writing is far more relevant. In this respect Jacques Derrida's deconstructive strategy seems prolific.[16] A main point here is that deconstruction operates within metaphysics, since any attempt to exteriorize metaphysics and oppose it is in itself a metaphysical manoeuvre. Historically there can be no beyond metaphysics. In short, the deconstructive move consists in an emptying of the conventional sense of basic, dualistically and hierarchically posited elements of a text by reversing them. The reversed terms are deplaced and generalized. So, the strategy of deconstruction is not that of a neutralization, as is the case in the Hegelian dialectical *Aufhebung*.[17] Far from synthesizing the elements the deconstruction lets them appear in their differential play as an open middle, a medium, a milieu, in which the coincidence of the opposites is perpetually deferred.

320

> The medium in question is no static coincidence of opposites . . . And its undecidability is not that of an included middle . . . The lieu of the milieu is not a position or a proposition. It is instead in stead, in lieu, of a position, at most a pro-position, an Etsatz (Llewelyn 1986:88).

Just as the middle voice of Inger Christensen's text, this milieu opens a semantic void which makes possible the opening of opposition and thus the disclosure of metaphysics. Due to its undecidability this semantic void does not signify anything specific. What it signifies is spacing, deferring, articulation, in other words: the possibility of signification. This play of signifiance is what Derrida notes *différance*. Being milieu, *différance* is not beyond or outside the language of metaphysics, but rather in the middle of it, differing and deferring its conceptual architecture, and this being so, *différance* as self-differing is constitutive for any differing and identifying movement on the phenomenological level. As was the case with the Heideggerian Being, *différance* is not. It can neither be represented nor conceptualized; a prerequisite of actual differing practice, it only shows as an effect in this practice, to which it is in this sense "prior". The particular prosody of poetic language with its grammatical voids and stream of signifiers allows for a special attention to the play of *différance*.

Writing as "woman"

The fact that this play of *différance* is a theoretical fiction that cannot be determined, conceptualized or named definitely is emphasized by its multitude of transliterations. In Derrida some of its various notions are: play ("*jeu*"), trace, *archèécriture*: writing (as processual, different from the written text). Common to all these notions is, then, that they denote the *différance* or differing that is the prerequisite of language, a "writing before the word and in the word".

In his reading of Nietzsche (and Heidegger's reading of Nietzsche), *Éperons les styles de Nietzsche* (1978),[18] Derrida elaborates on the coherence between writing and "woman". Departing from Nietzsche's notion of "woman" as seductive, elusive and self-different, at a distance and staging herself, he draws a parallel to the scene of writing, to *différance*. Metaphysically, woman as opposed to man, as man's derivative and other, has been an inaccessible, but necessary object of thought, incarnating the veiled essence of truth pursued by the (male) self-centred subject. The deconstructive strategy, the endeavour of which is the displacement of all binary oppositions, centres and centrisms, reverses (male) centre and (female/woman) margin, and generalizes marginalization without a replacement of centre. By this move not only man, but the metaphysical subject in general is de-centred, deprived of its sovereign position.

Thus, the deconstructive strategy is a femininization of traditional philosophical praxis. Having as its starting point Nietzsche's elaborations on
"woman", and as its strategy the displacement of any oppositional scheme
based on centrism, deconstruction is significant as critique of androcentrism.
And at the same time it is a cogent argument against a gynocentric discourse in opposition to androcentrism. By its strategy deconstruction not
only discloses and invalidates dualism, it also demobilizes the dialectical
way of thinking sexual difference, in which the neutralization of the difference turns out to be but a tacit positing of the neutralized, unmarked sex as
masculine, denoting the generalized subject. To deconstruction "woman" is
neither subject nor object, neither truth nor untruth, not essence that could
be unveiled, and consequently not being or existing, in short conceptual
thinking is suspended in "woman", and "woman" cannot be conceptualized. Undecidably, veiled and unveiled at the same time "woman" oscillates
as milieu, as both centre and circumference, a non-place and a non-position
("*le non-lieu de la femme*"[19]). If the patronymic is the quintessence of the
androcentric discourse which coincides with the history of Western metaphysics, "woman" is a name for that which cannot be named, for displacement – the specific mark of deconstruction.

It should be emphasized that this notion of "woman" is not attached to
anatomical, biological, sociological or anthropological definitions of sex
and gender. Rather, it is congenial with the de-realization of the subject,
elaborated above. In an earlier poetic work, *det*/it (1969) Inger Christensen
phrases *afrealisering*/de-realization as a number of attitudes that might be
called existentials, and all of which concern the decentring of the subject:
erotic attempts "all that unifies us/is what/divides us"; magical attempts "to
trust in language/as part of biology/to trust that on its own language will/
produce the necessary/feelings thoughts"; and "Eccentric attempts/to move
your core/out of yourself/into something else/into others".[20] So, the poetic
discourse keeps the questioning open, exposing and displaying it in a
multitude of references. "Woman" is one of the "names" for the non-position
advanced here. In its non-substantiality it might seem a bit airy, but for a
radical rethinking of subject and gender, and a clearing away to tackle the
question of masculinity and femininity it seems necessary to attempt to
think through the classical oppositional schemes and centrisms. This does
not, of course, preclude discussions of gender difference on an ontic level.
But as is the case with Heidegger's distinction between Being, being and
human being/*Dasein*, the Derridaen way of thinking *différance*, writing and
"woman" might, in its radicality, prove prolific for further reflections on
gender and subject. In an interview with Christie V. McDonald[21] Derrida
comments on Heidegger's analysis of the neutrality of *Dasein*:

> The analysis emphasizes the positive character, as it were, of this
> originary and powerful a-sexual neutrality which is not the neither-nor

(*Weder/noch*) of ontic abstraction. It is originary and ontological. More precisely, the a-sexuality does not signify in this instance the absence of sexuality – one could call it instinct, desire or even the libido – but the absence of any mark belonging to one of the two sexes. Not that the Dasein does not ontically or in fact belong to a sex; not that it is deprived of sexuality; but the Dasein as Dasein does not carry with it the mark of this opposition (or alternative) between the two sexes. Insofar as these marks are opposable and binary, they are not existential structures. Nor do they allude in this respect to any primitive or subsequent bi-sexuality. Such an allusion would fall once again into anatomical, biological or anthropological determinations. And the Dasein, in the structures and the "power" that are originary to it, would come "prior" to these determinations.

The ungraspability of Heidegger's ontological difference and *Dasein's* relation to it, and the undecidability of the Derridaen "woman" and *différance* remain, but in the discourse of the poetic work as their privileged *mise en scène* they can be glimpsed. This kind of setting might also be appropriate to a rethinking, not only of the subject figure in question, but of the question of gender, which is so closely attached to that of the subject, as well. In the middle voice.

Notes

1. Inger Christensen 1969:54.
2. Cf bibliography.
3. In Christensen 1982:129–35, German translation: *"Entrealisierung"*, in *Teil des Labyrinths* 1993:157–65.
4. Christensen, *alfabet*/alphabet, the n-poem: letter-text no. 14 (ibid.:60–1).
5. In Heideggerian terms.
6. Cf the Kristevaen distinction between symbolic and semiotic, Kristeva 1984/1974.
7. I use the Heideggerian distinction between Being and beings, on which the following exposition leans rather heavily (Heidegger 1927).
8. German translation (p. 141).
9. Cf especially Heidegger 1950.
10. Heidegger 1975:73.
11. Brock 1949:191. Brock comments on Heidegger's essay "Hölderlin and the essence of poetry" (1936).
12. Emile Benveniste, *Problèmes de linguistique générale* (Paris: Galimard, 1966), vol.1; here quoted from Llewelyn 1986:91.
13. Llewelyn 1986:91.
14. Cf Derrida 1972:9.
15. Christensen 1981:59.
16. As it is practised from *De la grammatologie* (1967) and henceforth.
17. Cf Llewelyn 1986:1–16. In Derrida's own wording:

> La déconstruction ne peut se limiter ou passer immédiatementà une neutralisation: elle doit, par un double geste, une double science, une double écriture, pratiquer un *renversement* de l'opposition classique *et* un *déplacement* général du système. C'est à cette seule condition que la déconstruction se donnera les moyens *d'intervenir* dans le champ des oppositions qu'elle critique (Derrida 1972:392).

18. Derrida 1979.
19. Ibid.
20. Christensen 1969:229–230; my italics.
21. Jacques Derrida and Christie V. McDonald, "Choreographies" (Derrida 1982).

Bibliography

Brock, W. 1949. *Existence and Being*. London: Vision.
Christensen, Inger 1962. *Lys*. Copenhagen: Gyldendal.
—— 1963. *Græs*. Copenhagen: Gyldendal.
—— 1964. *Evighedsmaskinen*. Copenhagen: Gyldendal.
—— 1967. *Azorno*. Copenhagen: Gyldendal.
—— 1969. *det*. Copenhagen: Gyldendal.
—— 1976. *Det malede værelse*. Copenhagen: Brøndum.
—— 1979. *Brev i april*. Copenhagen: Brøndum.
—— 1981. *alfabet*. Copenhagen: Gyldendal.
—— 1982. *Del af labyrinten*. Copenhagen: Gyldendal.
—— 1991. *Sommerfugledalen*. Copenhagen: Gyldendal.
Derrida, J. 1972. *Marges de la philosophie*. Paris: Minuit.
—— 1979. *Spurs. Nietzsche's styles/Éperons.Les styles de Nietzsche*. Chicago/London: Chicago University Press.
—— 1982. Choreographies. Interview with Christie V. McDonald, in *Diacritics* vol. 12. Baltimore: Johns Hopkins University Press.
Heidegger, M. 1927. *Sein und Zeit*. Tübingen: Tübingen University Press.
—— 1949. Der Ursprung des Kunstwerkes. In *Holzwege*. Frankfurt am Main.: Klostermann.
Hofstadter, A. 1975. Martin Heidegger. *Poetry, language, thought*. New York: Harper & Row.
Kristeva, J. 1984/1974. *Revolution in poetic language*. New York: Columbia University Press.
Llewelyn, J. 1986. *Derrida on the threshold of sense*. Hong Kong: Macmillan.
Pape, L.W. 1993. Tælleværker, *Kvinder køn og forskning* **1**, Copenhagen.
—— 1994. *Mellem-værender. Om subjekt og køn i det senmoderne/ Inter-mediations* (On subject and gender in late modern texts – with special reference to some features in Inger Christensen's works). PhD thesis, Department of Scandinavian Studies, Aarhus University.
—— (ed.) 1995. *Sprogskygger – læsninger i Inger Christensens forfatterskab*. Oxford: Aarhus University Press.
Spivak, G. 1983. Displacement and the discourse of Woman. In *Displacement. Derrida and after*, M. Krupnik (ed.). Bloomington: Indiana University Press.
Waterhouse, P. (ed.) 1997. *Ein chemisches Gedicht zu Ehren der Erde. Einer Auswahl ohne Anfang und ohne Ende*. Vienna: Residenz.

CHAPTER SEVENTEEN

Rationality and identity in Norwegian feminism

Hildur Ve

Introduction

"All that is solid melts into air"
This quotation from Marx may stand as an illustration of the author's experience during the last decade of chaos resulting from the simultaneous signs of disintegration of the welfare state within Western societies, and the postmodernist deconstruction of theories and concepts within feminist thought. The former development constitutes a serious threat to the public sector which – however inconsistently – has served as a basis for job security and influence for women; the latter implies a dissolution of the analytic tools which have enabled women to understand and criticize – at least in the Nordic countries – part of the ideological basis for male dominance and power, and consequently to achieve some measure of political influence.

One of the main objects of writing this chapter is to take a closer look at postmodernist deconstructions of feminist concepts. More specifically, I want to discuss relationships between social responsibility and autonomy, using a sociological discourse on the concepts of identity and identity construction as a point of departure. I shall start with a presentation and analysis of the concept of responsible rationality as it was developed in the late 1970s and early 1980s within certain parts of Norwegian feminist sociologist milieux, in conjunction with a brief description of the social context within which this development occurred. I shall then examine various aspects of the changes within feminist discourse in the late 1980s and early 1990s which may partly be understood as resulting from political developments, partly as originating in the impact of postmodernism. I shall give some intimations of the possible interrelation between these events and then discuss the concept of identity and present some aspects of the formation of identity as it originates in sociological theory. In conclusion I shall examine some of the relationships between the concepts of responsible rationality, identity and autonomy.

The relationships between technical limited and responsible rationality

In the late 1970s and early 1980s, especially within sociology, the concepts of responsible rationality (or carework rationality), and technical limited rationality were considered to be productive in Norwegian feminist theorizing about differences between men's and women's actions, attitudes and thought patterns. The sex role or gender role concept, which had been central to the debate in the late 1960s and early 1970s, had been more or less abandoned along with the critique of the structural functional paradigm.[1] This shift may in part be understood as deriving from the influence of Marxism, in part from Max Weber's "Verstehen" sociology where concepts such as "the actor", "meaning" and rationality were central. Also the impact from exchange theory with concepts such as "interest" and "strategic action" was important in furthering this change of focus within feminist thought.[2] Another important contribution to the change in perspective was the publication of an article in 1976 by social psychologist Berit Ås on women's culture in which she presented an analysis of women's special experience and thought patterns (Ås 1975).[3]

The areas or fields of research within which the concept of responsible rationality was applied as theoretical instrument were both working life and the educational system. The context was the Norwegian welfare state with a strong Labour Party and labour unions, a very low general unemployment rate and increasing numbers of women entering the workforce. Furthermore, because of Norway's oil economy, even though the economic recession in the Western world was felt, still, in the early 1980s the general atmosphere may be defined within the perspective of modernity. This includes a strong belief in the possibility for change and progress in addressing gender inequality by means of influencing welfare state politicians and bureaucracy through the publication of research and theoretically based interpretations of women's situation. In Norway the growth in numbers of women politicians within both parliament and government played an important role in creating a rather optimistic atmosphere within feminist social scientist groups in this period.

The first woman sociologist to introduce the concept of women's responsible rationality and contrast it with men's technical limited rationality was Bjørg Aase Sørensen who had done research on women industrial workers (Sørensen 1982). She argued that for feminists it must be an important objective to describe and interpret women's actions and thought patterns from a standpoint of women's dignity and abandon the tendency to explain women's behaviour as inferior or lacking in comparison with men's (e.g., fear of success, fear of conflict, being irrational, no understanding of labour unions, etc.). Sørensen's theoretical point of departure was Weber's concepts of instrumental and value rationality from which she developed the idea that specific to women's approach in situations of conflicts of interest was the tendency to identify with those in need of care (e.g., their own children, elderly workers). In interpreting her data, Sørensen discussed how this tendency should not be understood as "mere" emotional reactions, but as rationally developed standpoints based on everyday experience. One of the main points in her data on the perspective of women workers was that people must not be considered and used as means to achieve ends, only to be discarded when, because they show signs of stress or exhaustion caused by their tough work conditions, they might pose problems for their employers.

For many feminist sociologists the binary concepts of responsible and technical limited rationality, and the idea of conducting research from the standpoint of women's dignity proved to be very productive. In various fields of research on women working in typical welfare state jobs – i.e., as home helps, nurses, teachers, social workers, etc. – traits particularly associated with women, and mostly ignored by earlier research, such as empathy, emotional engagement, committedness and solidarity, could be interpreted as necessary conditions for doing a good job. Also, girls' and women's choices of education and career paths, which had often been criticized by social scientists for being traditional or conforming to role expectations, within this new frame of reference could in fact be understood as based on rational reflection.[4] The importance of meaning in this approach, when compared to the earlier focus on norms, had effects on the use of methods and resulted for many in a switch to qualitative research designs.

Furthermore, from the perspective of responsible rationality, many feminist sociologists started to analyze critically various types of male social science research which they found to have been influenced by the values within technical limited rationality, especially regarding the positive value given to efficiency within various welfare state institutions (Wærness 1982). In my own research and theoretical work on gender differences in the educational system and in the workplace, in order to interpret various types of data, it became necessary to somewat differentiate the concepts of technical limited and responsible rationality (Ve 1983).[5] It may be divided into three subconcepts: (1) technical rationality, which has efficiency as its basic value, i.e., that persons and machines together make the largest possible product quantity with the least possible use of energy and time; (2) economic rationality, which has as its basic aim the largest possible profit with the least possible input, achieved by the buying and selling of commodities in free markets where manpower is also regarded as a commodity; (3) bureaucratic rationality which has as its basic aim a type of administration that at the same time accomplishes both the aims of technical and economic rationality. Individuals are assigned to positions at different levels in the bureaucratic hierarchy according to rules of competency in technological, economic and juridical matters, and not according to favouritism.

Rationality and the meaning of being human

It may be argued that these three types of rationality strongly influence ideas in Western societies of the meaning of being human. When human labour is regarded as something that may be measured and controlled, along the same lines as machines, workers may become objectified and alienated. The tendency may be strengthened by the fact that manpower is considered a marketable commodity. In the market human beings become competitors for various positions and for the size of wages or salaries. The message of commodity production for the market is that each person must fend for him/herself. This implies a tendency to individualization. At the same time, however, when personal considerations are not permitted to enter into the various decisions, people may not be valued as unique individuals, but become interchangeable means with respect to the aim of creating ever larger profits. Responsible rationality or carework rationality is considered to be related to Weber's concept of value rationality, but the former is developed in order to capture the relational aspect of carework for dependent persons.

In Norway, a number of women sociologists carried out various types of research and engaged in theoretical discussions in order to gain insight into what are the chief aims of unpaid and paid carework for dependent persons (Wærness 1984, Ve 1983). This chapter will focus on aspects typical for paid work in the public education, health and social service sectors, with special attention paid to the challenges connected to teaching in primary schools. Research data indicate that important aims of these types of occupation are to create a high degree of psychological as well as physical wellbeing for the dependent "clients". In many occupations it is also of importance to make such clients better able to manage their own various life situations. In the education sector, one of the main aims is to create an atmosphere of trust and confidence in order to stimulate the children to use their abilities in the learning process, and to develop both independence and a sense of solidarity with their fellow pupils.

While tendencies to individualization and objectification are typical of human relationships within capitalist commodity production, the relationships between those in positions of trust as care workers and those dependent on them are shaped by the willingness of the former to identify with the interests of the latter. This implies a very complex set of action patterns: in order to be able correctly to interpret the emotions and thought patterns of those dependent on them, care workers must empathize with them, and familiarize themselves with their circumstances. However, at the same time care workers must be able to maintain a certain distance in order to convey to those dependent on them the importance of observing certain general norms and rules. In other words, in order to develop those types of situation which further the learning process as well as the development of independence and solidarity, teachers must make each pupil feel that he or she matters to them as a complete and unique human being, while equally the teachers must appear as just in the eyes of all the pupils in the class.

Control and predictability with respect to the use of manpower are important aspects of commodity production. This implies the division of tasks into basic units, routinization and methods of measurement of output per unit of time. If similar methods of organization and assessment of learning are used in schools, the result may be that the pupils lose their sense of the world as a continuing reality and of wholeness. Furthermore, the pupils may not develop their ability to make independent judgements and to use their knowledge to new situations. Responsible rationality differs from technical limited rationality in that the idea of humaneness contains other elements: the most important difference is that within the former perspective human beings must not be used as means in relation to aims which lie outside the wellbeing of those concerned. Furthermore, in care work the whole person matters, and the partners in the interaction may not be considered as interchangeable. In the teacher–pupil relationship a certain degree of individualization is important in order to foster the growth of independence. However, if the message of the market, i.e., that each person must fend for him/herself, is introduced into the interaction patterns in the classroom, the possibility of developing solidarity between the pupils will be severely impaired. More generally, within this perspective learning and education must not be considered as instruments or as a means only.[6] Education may serve to improve the situation of the pupils in the labour market, and also to create a larger GNP. However, first and foremost education should be considered as an end in itself.

Rationality and socialization

An important aspect of these new feminist theoretical attainments was the understanding that human beings learn from experience and practice in work situations, and that subsequently, the differences in rationality between men and women in industrial societies may be explained not by biological differences or "nature", but by the fact that to a much greater extent than men women take care of dependent people both in paid and unpaid work. As a consequence, it was argued by some that men's inclination towards technical limited rationality might change in so far as they started to take on their fair share of work for dependent people.

When in the early 1980s the psychoanalytical theories on differences between men and women of Dorothy Dinnerstein and, first and foremost of Nancy Chodorow, became known in Norwegian social science milieux, they seemed to correspond to the ideas within the responsible rationality perspective (Dinnerstein 1977, Chodorow 1978). The perspective of Chodorow's theory, which seemed to support that of Norwegian feminist sociologists' on differences in rationality between men and women, is her understanding of the consequences of the division of labour between the sexes. This implies that, because the fathers' occupations prevent them from taking part in the upbringing of children, the mothers become the prime object of both infant boys' and infant girls' affection, and the person with whom in their first years of life they most deeply identify. However, since from the age of two boys begin to understand that as grown men they will be different from women, boys must endeavour to distance themselves from their mothers and especially that part of her behaviour which they consider not to be male, i.e., her care for children. Girls, on the other hand, who understand that they are the same sex as their mothers, do not feel the need to distance themselves from this aspect of mothering and, on the contrary, model themselves in the image of their mothers.

In addition to this theory, which implies that girls use their mothers as role models, other perspectives regarding socialization were developed. The concepts of meaning and actor's point of view were focused upon. For some, the sociological perspective developed by G.H. Mead and his concepts of the particular and generalized other were given importance. His analysis of the self as consisting of two parts – the "I" and the "me" – implies the possibility that a person (equally a young girl) may reflect upon the norms and expectations they encounter within various social situations.[7] Thus, concepts of expectations, norms and roles were not entirely abandoned, but the understanding inherent in structural functional theory of a more or less automatic acceptance of and adaptation to the norms of the older generation by the younger was no longer adhered to. Furthermore, Carol Gilligan's theoretical discussions on the ethics of care and of rights in her analysis of differences in moral levels in girls' and boys' thought patterns, as well as her data on how these patterns were expressed, were included in the Norwegian feminist discourse on the development of responsible rationality in girls and women (Gilligan 1982). Regarding my own theoretical development, I was also influenced by ideas on learning through practice (praxis) inherent both in the work of John Dewey and Marx.

A critique of new tendencies

Of great importance for Norwegian feminist sociologists working on the development of the concept of responsible or care work rationality was the notion that this theoretical framework might serve as an instrument in the fight for women's emancipation. In the late 1980s, however, in discussions with feminist social scientists in other Nordic countries, the Norwegian approach was sometimes described as "special species ideology" (*särartsideology*), indicating that women's experiences and thought patterns were being idealized (Widerberg 1986). The differences in opinion voiced in these discussions may be analyzed by referring to a pair of concepts called Alpha and Beta bias (Hare Mustin & Marecek 1988). Alpha bias means focusing on and exaggerating differences between men and women in a way which may serve to deter the fight for equal rights for women in the labour market, politics and organizations. Beta bias, on the other hand, means focusing on the similarities between the sexes with regard to intelligence, staying power, etc. This approach may be problematic in societies where men and men's action patterns serve, more or less openly, as the ideal for women.

Towards the end of the 1980s, within the Norwegian feminist discourse regarding the concepts discussed above, certain new tendencies were appearing. One such tendency was to be found within the work of feminist sociologists who used a social class perspective (Ve 1989).[8] In my own research on social class differences in young girls' choices of education, future family life and paid work, I found a certain degree of variation regarding my informants' plans for how to combine care of any future children with paid work (Ve 1986). On one end of a continuum might be placed those of my informants who wanted to share equally the responsibility for the care of children with the father, especially in the infant stage, and later also to make use of childcare facilities. On the opposite end of the continuum might be placed those who wanted to take care of their children themselves until the children were of school age (7 years old). The rest of the informants might be placed closer to the former or closer to the latter end of the continuum. Regarding social class differences, in the former group were only girls from upper middle-class homes (although only half of the informants belonging to this social class wanted this type of situation). The latter groups consisted of girls from upper middle-, middle- and working-class social backgrounds, with most of the working-class girls wanting to stay at home while their children were under school age. Also of interest is the fact that many of these girls, and none from other classes, informed me that for economic reasons, they did not count on being able to stay at home although they might want to.

For me, when interpreting the above-mentioned differences within a frame of reference of responsible rationality, the most productive solution seemed to be to describe the upper middle-class girls who wanted to share care for infants with the father, and after the first year to send the children to daycare facilities, as modern, and characterize the other groups as more traditional. However, I was not quite satisfied with the use of the concepts modern and traditional as they seemed to imply some kind of hierarchy of values, with a higher ranking given to the values of middle-class girls compared with those of working-class girls.

Another problem appeared within the field of methodology. Again, as mentioned above, when developing their concepts, the women sociologists had made use of the Weberian ideal type approach. The Weberian ideal type is an instrument by which social scientists may construct an "average meaning" attributable to a plurality of actors, or even meaning for hypothetical actors in particular types of activity (Timasheff 1965). Even though the users of the ideal type of responsible- or care-work rationality were aware of the danger of overgeneralization inherent in this methodological approach, often, when writing about and interpreting women's action patterns in various places of work, this type of rationality was presented without taking account of the way sociologists evaluate statistically significant differences. In other words, readers might be led to interpret the results so that they imply that all women share these thought patterns, and that, consequently, they may be understood as part of a women's biological nature, or essence.

The problems regarding social class differences and methodology did not of themselves seem to undermine the fruitfulness of the conceptual framework of responsible and technical limited rationality. However, within various groups of feminist social scientists, new discourses were developing. From several angles the perspective within which the concepts were developed, i.e., paid and unpaid work, was criticized for being too narrow (Widerberg 1986). One of the most important of these groups was the one whose members carried out research on rape, incest and prostitution.

Until the end of the 1980s the expansion of the Norwegian feminist discourse, of which only some of the various development has been described here, resulted in many debates.[9] However, some kind of basic consensus seemed to prevail in respect of assumptions about male power/dominance over women.

Postmodernism

This chapter has mainly discussed developments within Norwegian sociological feminist discourse. All along, however, influences from other disciplines, e.g. social psychology, social anthropology and political science, have been of importance. During the last ten years other disciplines have entered the field: history, philosophy and literature. While the theoretical development within French philosophy and literary analysis, originating in the works of Michel Foucault and Jaques Lacan, has to a very great degree altered the feminist discourse in Norway, these new approaches have at the same time seemed to undermine sociology as a discipline.

The postmodernist deconstructivism carried out by, among others, Beaudrillard and Lyotard had as some of its main targets the so-called "grand narrative" of Marx, Weber and Parsons (Lazarus 1991). Consequently, concepts such as class, surplus value and exploitation were deprived of their meaning. If one were to accept the typical postmodernist postulate, "Truth is local", socio-logical generalizations would be made impossible.

Within feminist thought, important concepts were crumbling. With respect to theories of responsible rationality, of particular importance was the fact that the idea of a universal women's identity came under attack. Joan F. Scott in a very influential article, criticizes essentialist approaches and argues that research on differences between women must be a kind of main goal for women scientists (Scott 1989). Gradually this view came to be accepted by many feminists in the Nordic countries. As a consequence, concepts such as "responsible rationality", and "women's different voice", had to be deconstructed along with all other generalizing perspectives regarding women, and the relationship between women and men. Furthermore, the growing influence from French feminism led to a gradual fading into the background of questions about inequality. "Gender in transition" became the new catchphrase and displaced the more traditional interest in doing research in order to further equality between women and men. Concepts such as sisterhood, or male dominance seemed to become old-fashioned. Increasingly, the study of culture was focused on, while among feminists a decline in an interest to study society took place. The importance of the concept of identity increased steadily, and now replaces that of the rational actor.[10]

Regarding socialization, some of the new and challenging propositions imply that within the present cultural epoch, to a much greater extent than their counterparts in history and in other cultures, girls construct their own identities.[11] The idea typical of some traditional sociological approaches, that socialization is the process by which earlier generations transfer their expectations and norms to new generations, has been defined by many postmodern feminists as deterministic and old-fashioned, and has been discarded. In particular, the idea that girls more or less automatically internalize values of mothering has been vigorously attacked or deconstructed. Psychological theories on universal stages in child development were also criticized, which meant that Gilligan's theory about gender differences in moral development was deconstructed, along with Chodorow's theory about gender differences regarding distance and relatedness respectively.

Critique of postmodernism

However, in the early 1990s some new viewpoints appeared within the sociological discourse on modernity and postmodernity. Sociologists, disagreeing with some of the main tenets of postmodernism, put forward critical analyses, one of which appears in Zygmunt Bauman's book, *Intimations of post modernity* (Bauman 1992). Bauman discusses the extreme relativism of postmodernism, and asks on what basis postmodernism itself may be exempted from the relativistic approach. Just as other theoretical frameworks, postmodernism may be defined as a grand narrative constructed within a certain historical context. Bauman argues that postmodernism could not in earlier historical epochs have developed as a perspective and captured the minds of so many. He discusses the results of the fall of Eastern European socialism and the victory of capital over labour, and maintains that market forces are being celebrated as the only truly liberalizing mechanism of our day. These forces constitute a climate in which consumption plays an ever increasing role. In order to keep the wheels of capitalist production turning, rapid changes of taste are becoming vital to generate demand. In his analyses, Bauman maintains that there is a kind of correspondence between the present economic development and postmodernism. The idea of extreme relativism "suits" the market forces of our historical epoch. Among others Bauman refers to Pierre Bourdieu, who argues that while a main aim of socialization in modernity was self-control and the ability to postpone gratification, the aim of socialization in postmodernity is to turn children into consumers. Internalization of norms is no longer necessary for integration in society. Seduction has taken its place, in what Bauman defines as the "playground of freedom", where "anything goes". Even though Zygmunt Bauman does not discuss postmodernist attacks on theories within feminism, his analysis is relevant for the theme of this chapter.

Identity – a sociological approach

As mentioned above, one important aspect of the postmodern discourse within feminism is the use of the very complex concept of "identity". The way it is used gives little room for an understanding of how a person's identity is – in part – shaped by influences from others (e.g., mothers, teachers, etc.). Nor, it seems to me, does discourse on identity include responsibility for other people. To trace the connections between the concept of identity and that of responsible rationality within a sociological perspective became an important project.

In recent work within sociology, two of the classical perspectives, that of Durkheim (within which the concept of the sex role has been developed) and that of Weber, have been analyzed in order to question whether they yield any insights into the recent interest in the concept of identity (Korsnes 1994). Within the Durkheimian tradition the main aspect of identity is social identity, which is understood as a result of biography – i.e., within a time dimension. The identity of grown-ups is described as a relatively stable phenomenon. Within the Weberian perspective, the space dimension is considered to be more important, which means that identity is constantly being shaped in a system of social interaction where all participants form a conception of each others. When arenas are changed, the conceptions of the actors also change, as do the actor's identities. Accordingly, identity is conceived as a phenomenon of more variability and instability than within the Durkheimian perspective.

Research on young people within educational institutions indicates that both of these approaches give some insight into how identities are shaped. However, at the same time researchers must take into account the young people's own identity work, i.e. their ability to reflect upon their situation, to make choices and to justify for themselves these choices while they interact and negotiate with institutional partners in order to get them to accept and make legitimate the young people's plans (ibid.). In the on-going debate within sociology on the relationship between actor and structure, the concepts of negotiation and transaction inherent in Korsnes' analysis indicate more possibilities for actors' influence than Bourdieu's concept of seduction.

In my opinion, with regard to the problem of the possible existence of a common women's identity, these new theoretical and empirical contributions within sociology show that a totally relativistic and individualistic approach, regarding peoples' ability to construct their own identity, may not be very productive. On the other hand, however, the new perspectives make room for a greater degree of choice on the part of the actor than was allowed by the more traditional sex role perspectives.

In struggling with a sociological conception of identity the Danish philosopher, Hans Fink's presentation of two different approaches to the concept of identity seems instructive (Fink 1991). He argues that one important approach is influenced by Aristotle who defined identity as that which is like – identical. He analyzed identity by dividing it into three aspects: numeric, generic and qualitative. In this short presentation I shall discuss the concept of generic identity only. It refers to the likeness between phenomena which belong to the same category. Categories may be age groups, nations – and also the two sexes, men and women. Within the other important approach to the concept of identity, various social scientists often define it as self-identity or identity consciousness. According to Fink, these definitions originate in ideas developed by Eric H. Ericsson in the middle of the twentieth century when he initiated a new tradition within psychology focusing on the ego and ego strength. Within this individualistic perspective persons may seek identity, lose identity and also to a certain extent construct their own identity. In my opinion, it is within this latter perspective that the critique within the works of many postmodern feminists of a common or shared or universal women's identity originates.

If we take into account Aristotle's concept of generic identity, we may find that in spite of the critique by many feminists of the use of universalizing concepts, in certain circumstances it may be productive to analyze women as a category. In a very illuminating article on essentialism and universalism published in the journal *Signs*, the American feminist philosopher Jane Roland Martin has discussed the use of categories in order to clarify their advantages and limitations (Martin 1994). She maintains that "the category-banning policy assumes that a concept or category or term that has been given an essentialist definition, must always and everywhere be defined in that way. This represents a faulty view of language." She goes on to argue that categories such as motherhood or reproduction have been understood as a priori phenomena. But only Platonists will maintain that a category exists independently of those who use it. Categories are what we make of them. We may choose which categories we want to use, and we may ourselves decide how to use them. The important thing is not to use categories in bad ways, as in making false generalizations. An example of a false generalization would be to define what a human being is on the basis of research carried out only on men (ibid.).

Constructivism, deconstructivism and power

To me as a sociologist, reasoning like that carried out by Jane Roland Martin serves to clarify the differences between the concepts of the general and the universal. Her analysis indicates that for certain purposes it is legitimate to discuss women as a category that in some aspects may be considered to be different from the category of men. One important part of this approach is that it makes room for, or reintroduces, the fact that women are often defined, and consequently treated by men – i.e., constructed by men – as a category with common traits. Furthermore, within sociology, and especially within the symbolic interactionist perspective, the power to define – or construct – the identity of a group of people is understood in many instances as a very serious or even dangerous type of power. The concepts of labelling or stigmatizing are developed in order to demonstrate the grave effects of these processes for those who are the victims of stigmatization. One of the results is that those stigmatized often internalize the derogatory interpretations of their actions and make them a part of their self-identity.

From a somewhat different angle, within research in schools, Rosenthal & Jacobson carried out a famous experiment in which teachers were led to believe that the researchers had developed a test capable of demonstrating that certain pupils in their classes were ready to take a great forward "leap" in learning ability during the next year (Rosenthal & Jacobson 1968). In fact, there was no such test, but by leading the teachers to characterize certain pupils as "leapers", the teachers' attitudes and modes of action towards these pupils changed, and the pupils actually did much better than expected before Rosenthal & Jacobson introduced their non-existing test results. Their research demonstrates that the power to define or characterize may serve positive as well as negative ends.

Within symbolic interaction theory the concept of a self-fulfilling prophecy is developed in order to describe the phenomenon that a group's or individual's patterns of action are influenced by other people's definitions of them. W.I. Thomas developed his famous theorem based on these insights: "When people define situations as real they become real in their consequences" (Thomas & Znaniecki 1937). History demonstrates that such definitions may be deconstructed, e.g., by social science research results. At the same time research also shows the sometimes destructive consequences of social constructions.

Regarding the way men within the power structure may be able to define women, according to a universal idea of the category of women, the treatment in Norwegian courts of women who have been raped may serve as an example. Many of the women lawyers who have specialized in helping such women advise their clients not to take their cases to court on account of the great risk they run of losing such cases, and the very rough verbal treatment the women may receive from the lawyers defending the men as well as, on occasion, the judges. The women are often defined by the defending lawyers as too inviting or too willing. In these situations the postmodernist argument that women construct their own individual identities is of little help. Individual women may protest that the identity ascribed to them by the courts does not correspond to their own self-identity, but such protestations may have little impact. The consequences of this power to define the situation on the part of men is that a very small percentage of rapes are actually reported, and that many rapists avoid any form of punishment. Another serious consequence, both of the act of rape itself and of the treatment of the raped women in the courts, is that their self-identities become negatively influenced.

From another perspective, the American social scientist Charles Murray in an article in the *Guardian* entitled "Get the poor off our over-taxed backs", is constructing a very frightening concept of "the single mother" (Murray 1994). He argues that unmarried mothers are unable to socialize the disruptive energy of their sons. To give them social benefits is to encourage the birth of numbers of potentially criminal men. If his definition is accepted as valid by politicians in the US, it may have very serious material consequences for single mothers in that country. We also see some similar negative tendencies concerning political analyses of this group in Norway. Data on single mothers indicate that their self-identity is being influenced by the negative constructions in the mass media of "the single mother" (Syltevik 1994).

If we look at the approaches of many postmodernist feminists from the perspective of symbolic interaction we may see that the deconstruction of the universal or essentialist concepts of "girl" and "woman" may have been necessary in a certain period – on the one hand in order to criticize all the unfavourable stereotypes of the category of woman developed by men in power – on the other hand to include the critique from women from an ethnic-minority or working-class background who claimed that white middle-class women had constructed an idea of women's identity which to them was totally irrelevant. But nevertheless, men's derogatory constructions of the category woman goes on. In the continuous fight against this practice, feminists must, in certain situations, feel free to analyze women as a category in that they – in certain places and at certain times – share the same destiny, and accordingly, may develop some common dimensions of identity. Within this perspective, responsible rationality may be understood as one such common dimension within many women's otherwise different identities.

Responsible rationality and autonomy

In the last part of this chapter I shall discuss the concept of responsible rationality from a somewhat different angle. As mentioned above, the point of departure in developing the concept of responsible rationality was to extend the Weberian concepts of instrumental and value rationality in order to include a dimension of relatedness, and construct a basis for criticising the extreme individualistic tendencies within technical limited rationality. Looking back, it appears that the understanding of individualism discussed was based on utilitarian or exchange theory perspectives. Within this discourse the Kantian perspective on moral autonomy, which forms an important part of the Gilligan–Kohlberg dispute on ethics of care and ethics of rights, was not taken into account. Recent research on Norwegian girls and boys in schools indicates that it is important to clarify the relationship between responsible rationality and moral autonomy. This research, which deals with women teachers' patterns of action in respect of the two sexes, reveals how the girls, through their own descriptions of the teachers' recommendations, experience that they are given the responsibility for interpreting the boys' action patterns and solving conflicts between themselves and the boys (Gulbrandsen 1994). The consequence of the teachers' admonitions is that an asymmetrical relationship develops in which it is possible for the boys to achieve their aims at the girls' expense. In itself this is not a new observation. Many researchers have found similar patterns. But what, in my opinion, is of particular interest is how the researcher, psychologist Liv Mette Gulbrandsen, interprets her data. She argues that our individually oriented, cultural code system makes it difficult to analyze relationships. For girls it might be especially productive if future research were to illuminate and interpret relational patterns and the cultural code systems that create these patterns. Among other things this might make it possible for girls to make social responsibility an explicit theme for transactions with boys, and with teachers.

Regarding the argument about how people with power define girls, the above-mentioned data demonstrate how girls are treated as a category which differs from the category of boys. In addition, however, the problematics of the relationship between the concepts of individualism and social respons-ibility are demonstrated.

Extrapolating from my own experience in a research project on equality between girls and boys, which lasted from 1987 to 1990, I have drawn conclusions somewhat similar to those of Gulbrandsen. This was an action reseach project in which I worked together with another researcher and 14 teachers in order to strengthen the girls' self-reliance and increase the boys' ability to care for dependent persons (Ve 1991). The theoretical basis of the project was in part influenced by the concept of responsible rationality. The group of teachers and researchers had very probing discussions about the meaning of the concept of equality. However, we agreed that one import-ant condition for equality between the sexes is that men must begin to share with women the responsibility for care work for dependents. Conse-quently, some of the pedagogical measures developed had as their object-ive to give both boys and girls experience of various care-giving tasks (e.g., taking responsibility for the wellbeing of younger pupils). Although we discovered that boys, in favourable settings, are able to develop social re-sponsibility, the part of the project which had to do with furthering the pupils' moral autonomy seemed to be much more in tune with the ped-agogical interests of the teachers and of the Norwegian school system in general.

In an article in which she takes as her point of departure G.H. Mead's concept of the particular and the generalized other, Seyla Benhabib dis-cusses what to me seems a related theme (Benhabib 1992). She contrasts moral ideals of autonomy with Gilligan's theoretical framework. Benhabib ends her article in this way:

> What Carol Gilligan has heard are those mutterings, protestations and objections voiced by women who were confronted with ways of posing moral dilemmas that seemed alien to them and who were faced with visions of selfhood which left them cold. Only if we can understand why this voice has been so marginalized in moral theory, and how the dominant ideals of moral autonomy in our culture, as well as the privileged definition of the moral sphere, continue to silence women's voices, do we have a hope for moving to more integrated vision of ourselves and our fellow humans as general-ized as well as "concrete others".

At the moment, within general sociological discourse in Norway, interest in the concepts of autonomy and freedom have increased while concepts of relatedness, solidarity and workers' collectivity are receiving less attention than earlier (Lysgaard 1961). The concept of responsible rationality was partly inspired by research on solidarity between workers (Sørensen 1982). In one of the most recent Norwegian works on socialization by sociologist Ivar Frønes, the ideal of moral autonomy which Benhabib contrasts with Gilligan's ethics of care, is very clearly articulated (Frønes 1994). Frønes argues that "The individual is the nucleus of European culture. Solidarity and justice is understood with basis in the free, independent individual."

Going back to Bauman's description referred to above of capitalist society in late modernity as the "playground of freedom", one may understand that the concept of autonomy may be interpreted in different ways. One way is related to the idea within economics of competition and freedom in the market as liberating forces. As mentioned above, the concept of technical limited rationality orginates from this perspective. The other way is related to the idea within moral/political philosophy of autonomous persons being able to make up their own minds and defend their ideas against pressure from others (Eric H. Ericsson's concept of ego identity is related to the latter).

Responsible rationality, interpreted as a dimension of women's identity, may be contrasted with both these perspectives of autonomy. It contains an understanding of relatedness that transcends the image of the human being as "an island unto himself" inherent both in economic theory and moral/political philosophy. At the same time, in the ideal typical description of the relationship between care workers and dependent persons presented above, often the aim may be to foster the development of both autonomy and solidarity, which implies very complex types of action patterns. Gulbrandsen's research points to the rather common solution where girls are being socialized to accept the responsible role in relationship with boys, while the latter are permitted greater degrees of individuality (Gulbrandsen 1994).

Conclusion

Returning to the discussions on the ideal type of responsible rationality, it may be argued that while the presentation in the early 1980s lacked nuance and often evaded some of the problematic, power-related aspects of responsible rationality, the concept may still function as a productive tool for the interpretation of (fairly) common dimensions in women's identities. I agree with Gulbrandsen's conclusions about making social responsibility an explicit theme in negotiations between girls and boys – and between men and women – at the same time as I emphasize the importance of not underestimating the enormous power and attraction of the idea of autonomy, both in its moral/political and economic/liberal sense, for people of both sexes in our Western culture.

Notes

1. Within sociology, the concept of role has been defined in various ways. However, it may be argued that the concept of sex role most often has been used in order to explain why in many areas of life members of the two sexes behave in distinctly different ways. This is thought to be effected by the consistent norms directed towards girls and boys, men and women by members of society and by the negative and positive sanctions connected with behaviour which correspond with or break with these norms. Socialization is thought to be the mechanism through which society achieves this type of control of its members.

2. Within Norwegian sociology one of the most influential works within the exchange theory perspective is *Makt og avmakt* (Power and powerlessness; Hernes 1975).

3. The concept of "women's culture" was inspired by the theoretical framework developed by Gunnar Myrdal in "The Asian drama" where he carries out an analysis of the situation of inhabitants in developing countries in the Third World.

4. In a paper on education and equality, the authors argue that some of the differences between girls and boys in respect of educational attainment may be interpreted as resulting from boys' instrumental and girls' ritualistic attitudes (Hernes & Knudsen 1976).

5. In my analysis of the three dimensions of technical limited rationality, I have, among others, found the conceptual framework presented by Berger et al. in *The homeless mind* very helpful (Berger et al. 1974).

6. At the moment, changes in Norwegian educational policy are occurring which to a greater extent than in earlier periods are based on an instrumental conception of education. The first indication of this change is to be found in a public document entitled "Med viten og vilje" (With insight and resolution) presented in 1988.

7. Regarding this perspective, of importance is also the optimistic view on the possibility of children learning from experience implicit in John Dewey's conceptualization of "learning by doing". Mead and Dewey were colleagues and good friends.

8. In this period I found it a challenge how to understand theoretically the social class position of women care workers, especially from a Marxist perspective. In Norway, in several instances, nurses and teachers (and male as well as female representatives of these occupations) have organized various types of political demonstration in order to put the interests of patients and pupils on the political agenda. Within the "Klasse für sich" frame of reference, this kind of expression of responsible rationality seems to be transcending the traditional notions of class interests.

9. In the book "Forståelser av kjønn" (Understandings of gender) (Taksdal & Widerberg 1992) a number of aspects of this discourse are presented and analyzed.

10. In their article "Når kjønnet kommer i skole" Bjerum Nilsen & Rudberg (1992) present an interesting analysis of certain aspects of this development within Norwegian feminist discourse as seen from a pedagogic perspective.

11. In 1992, Alice in Wonderland, the First International Conference on Girls, was organized in Amsterdam. In many of the papers presented there, as well as some of the panel debates, the discourse on girls and girlhood contained very radical criticisms of the conceptions of girls inherent in traditional social science theories.

References

Bauman, Z. 1992. *Intimations of post modernity.* London: Routledge.

Benhabib, S. 1992. The generalized and the concrete other. In *Situating the self,* ch. 5. Cambridge: Polity Press.

Berger, P. et al. 1974. *The homeless mind.* Harmondsworth: Penguin.

Chodorow, N. 1978. *The reproduction of mothering.* Berkeley, Calif.: University of California Press.

Dinnerstein, D. 1977. *The mermaid and the minotaur: sexual arrangements and human malaise.* New York: Harper & Row.

Fink, H. 1991. Identiteters identitet (The identity of identities). In *Identiteter i forandring,* H. Fink & H. Hauge (eds). Århus: Århus Universitetsforlag.

Frønes, I. 1994. *De likeverdige. Om sosialisering og de jevnaldrendes betydning* (Peers. On socialization and the meaning of peers). Oslo: Oslo University Press.

Gilligan, C. 1982. *In a different voice.* Cambridge, Mass.: Harvard University Press.

Gulbrandsen, L.M. 1994. Blant hester og gorillaer i skolegården: Utvikling i en kjønnet kultur (Development in a gendered culture). *Psyke og Logos,* no. 1.

Hare M.R. & J. Marecek 1988. The meaning of difference. Gender theory, post-modernism and psychology. *American Psychologist* **43**, 6.

Hernes, G. 1975. *Makt og avmakt* (Power and powerlessness). Bergen: Bergen University Press.

Hernes, G. & K. Knudsen 1976. *Utdanning og ulikhet* (Education and inequality). NOU 1976:46. Oslo: Universitetsforlaget.

Hernes, G. 1988. *Med Viten og vilje* (With insight and intention). NOU public report, no. 28.

Korsnes, O. 1994. Yrkessosialisering og former for yrkesidentitet (Forms of workplace identity). In *AHS.* Serie B; 1994–3. Bergen: Universitetet i Bergen.

Lazarus, N. 1991. Doubling the new world order: Marxism, realism and the claims of feminist social theory. *Journal of Feminist Cultural Studies,* vol. 3, no. 3.

Lysgård, S. 1961. *Arbeiderkollektivet* (The workers' collective). Oslo: Oslo University Press.

Martin, J.R. 1994. Methodological essentialism, false difference, and other dangerous traps. *Signs,* spring.

Mead, G.H. 1934. *Mind, self, and society.* Chicago: University of Chicago Press.

Murray, C. 1994. Interview, *Guardian,* 17 September.

Nilsen, H.B. & M. Rudberg 1992. Når kjønnet kommer i skole (When gender goes to school). In Taksdal & Widerberg (eds) 1992.

Rosenthal, R. & L. Jacobson 1968. *Pygmalion in the classroom. Teacher expectation and intellectual development.* New York: Holt, Rinehart & Winston.

Scott, J.F. 1989. Gender, a useful category of historical analysis. *American Historical Review,* vol. 91, no. 5.

Sørensen, B.A. 1982. Ansvarsrasjonalitet (Responsible rationality). In *Kvinner i fellesskap* (Women in collectives), H. Holter (ed.). Oslo: Oslo University Press.

Syltevik, L. 1994. Finnes alenemødre? Om konstruksjonen av undersøkelsesenheter (Are there any single mothers?). In *Forskningsprosessen – utfordringer og muligheter.* Bergen: Sosiologisk institutt, UiB Skriftserie.

Taksdal, A. & K. Widerberg (eds) 1992. *Forståelser av kjønn* (Understanding gender). Oslo: Ad Notam Gyldendal.

Thomas, W. & F. Znaniecki 1937. *The Polish peasant in Europe and America.* New York: Dover.

Timasheff, N. 1965. *Sociological theory. Its nature and growth.* New York: Random House.

Ve, H. 1983. Likhetsidealer i velferdsstatens skole (Ideals of equality in school of the welfare state). In *Utdanning og likhetsidealer,* M. Haavelsrud & H.H. Hartvigsen (eds). Oslo: Aschehoug.

Ve, H. 1986. Ansvar oj protest (Responsibility and protest). In *Familien i endring,* J.K. Kristiansen & T.S. Wetlesen (eds). Oslo: Cappelen.

Ve, H. 1989. Byråkrati och Velferdsstat (Bureaucracy and the welfare state). *Sociologisk forskning* no. 4.

Ve, H. 1991. Children and teachers in exceptional learning situation. In *Talent, teaching and achievement,* John Radford (ed.). London: Kingsley.

Wærness, K. 1982. *Kvinneperspektiver på sosialpolitikken* (Women's perspectives on social policy). Oslo: Oslo University Press.

—— 1984. Caring as women's work in the welfare state. In *Patriarchy in a welfare society,* H. Holter (ed.). Oslo: Oslo University Press.

Widerberg, K. 1986. Finnes det en nordisk modell i kvinneforskningen? (Is there a Nordic model in women's research?) Arbeidsnotat nr.5. In NAVF's Sekretariat for kvinneforskning: *Den samfunnsvitenskapelige kvinneforskningen fram mot år 2000 Utfordringer og visjoner.*

Ås, B. 1975. On female culture. An attempt to formulate a theory on women's solidarity and action. *Acta Sociologica* vol. 18, 2–3.

CHAPTER EIGHTEEN

Nordic women's studies and gender research

Bente Rosenbeck

What constitutes the Nordic element?

Does a specific, Nordic profile within gender research and women's studies exist? Posing this question begs another: does anything exist that could be called specifically "Nordic"? When a historical scholar such as Benedict Anderson ends up defining a nation as "an imagined political community", doubt must necessarily be cast upon calling anything inherently Nordic (Anderson 1991). Anderson could not reach a "scientific definition" of the nation concept, and concluded that nationality and nationalism are "cultural artefacts of a particular kind". Worldwide, scholars within women's studies have similarly reached the conclusion that it is impossible to define Woman with a capital W. Nor have we been able to unearth any scientific definitions of gender; rather, we have been compelled to deconstruct the "big narratives" unfolded about woman, about gender and about what constitutes femininity and masculinity.

Common, perhaps, to gender identity and national identity as well as to racial and class identity is that they are phenomena of discourse, all constructed at distinctive junctures in time, and for specific purposes. These identities are not observable in their essence; they are but modes of discourse and myths, owing their effect in part to their intrinsic tinge of universality. And through their pervasive effect, these constructions become reality.

Nations may well be imagined communities, but people still die and fight wars in the name of these constructions, or fictions; in other words, they work. And in the middle of the nineteenth century, when Denmark felt threatened by Germany, many were convinced that political and military support from Sweden and Norway might help form a Nordic bulwark against their daunting southern neighbour (Østergård 1994, Rerup 1994, Linde-Lauersen & Nilsson 1991). But when the chips were down, the Danes had to march alone to war in 1848 and 1864. Yet the concept we call "Nordic" has long been a factor some people believed in, at home as well as abroad. N.F.S. Grundtvig, renowned clergyman and founder of the Danish folk high school system, based his historical writings on the conviction that Christianity reached its true and proper fruition only among the Nordic peoples, according to which view this northern population has a unique position in the history of humankind. The Nordic heritage formed a basis for the "folk high school movement" and numerous, related popular movements (particularly in Denmark, Norway and Sweden). Grundtvig conjured up a fascinating mythology about free-spirited, Nordic heroes as a means to bolster the emergent, emancipatory peasants' movement's struggle to end centuries of repression.

There were many other contexts, abroad as well, in which "the Nordic" was idealized. Thus, the concept of the "unsullied Nordic element" was employed by the Pan-German dreamers of the nineteenth century who applied this term to the "genuine", unspoiled Germanic people; a notion subsequently brought into utter disrepute by Nazism. The invention of "the Nordic" can, in fact, be traced back to the nineteenth century. This was the era when the word "Viking" began to surface in a number of contexts, wielded by philologists of a nationalist-Romantic persuasion who had culled it from the Icelandic sagas (Roesdal 1994). Alongside the spread of a nationalist discourse within the individual Nordic countries, the nineteenth century saw the proliferation of a transnational ideology extolling a Scandinavian or Nordic spirit of communality. Interest in the uniquely Nordic past was part of a national, as well as a Nordic call to arms.

This spiritual call to arms was accompanied by a political one. In the 1830s, the political idea of a common, Nordic "Scandinavia" emerged in quixotic poets' and students' coteries. The Scandinavian movement ran parallel to contemporary nationalist movements in Italy and Germany, the only difference being that Scandinavianism never succeeded in forming an alliance with the military prowess of a strong state, as was the case in Italy and Germany.

Following the defeat in the war of 1864, the dream of a political and military coalition between Denmark and Sweden–Norway collapsed. But the grand-scale political vision was replaced by cultural coalitions working in civilian society, safeguarded by the once so quixotic students who had in the meantime become civil servants and politicians. Political utopianism was replaced by pragmatic co-operation. Legislation became the means for this co-operation, seeking Nordic unity and harmonization. In 1910, women were allowed to participate in the preliminary work leading to unified Nordic legislation on domestic relations, i.e., before female suffrage had been achieved.

Collaboration also took place within the folk high schools, the workers' movement and the women's movement. In the nineteenth century, a few Nordic meetings were held by women's organizations (in 1888 and 1902) but no foundation was laid for continuous co-operation, since the women's movements were swayed more by international movements in those years. In 1914, however, co-operation was initiated between the Nordic women's organizations as they strove to create a uniform, Scandinavian legislation on domestic relations. This proved a successful endeavour and the result was in fact a unified, Scandinavian matrimonial legislation. In the period from 1918 until 1927, a number of domestic relations bills were introduced in Sweden, Norway and Iceland, as well as in Denmark, placing spouses on an equal footing and introducing a mutual obligation of support (Melby 1995, Statens beroende av familjen 1996). This legislation, granting women the same fundamental rights as men, was regarded as epoch-making, since it meant that male supremacy – at least formally – was abolished in Scandinavia ahead of other European countries.

Within pedagogics, a lively collaboration existed between female members of the teaching profession in the Nordic countries. The co-operation that took place between 1898 and 1905 has even been characterized as a unique brand of Scandinavian female pedagogics leading to a number of practical, pedagogical initiatives. In the early nineteenth century, when education for schoolmistresses was established, pioneers saw this as a national achievement, but they also carried a strong Scandinavian commitment as part of their ideological baggage, along with an irrefutably strong dedication to the women's movement.

The collaboration, which from 1870 onwards evolved at regular, inter-Nordic teachers' conferences, dealt not only with educational politics but also with female suffrage and social policy. This collaboration was intensified in 1889 as the Danish periodical *Bog og Naal* (*Book and Needle*) was given the subtitle *Nordic Journal of Female Upbringing and Education.* Hereafter, a formal co-operation existed between girls' secondary schools and women's teacher-training colleges in the Nordic countries. Collaboration between Nordic (Norwegian, Swedish and Danish) female teachers provided a professional forum for addressing pedagogical issues regarding girls' education and the training of female teachers in particular. Behind this co-operation lay a wish to draw the countries' educational systems closer together and a determination to promote the Nordic dimension in teaching, especially within subjects regarding the mother tongues and history; and also to provide mutual support in the common endeavour to secure an equal footing for women versus men – in schools as well as in society at large. At this stage, where women's suffrage had not yet been won in the Nordic countries, such collaboration was an important prerequisite for building strategies towards the advancement of equality between the sexes. However, because of the difficulties arising between Sweden and Norway, this practical, pedagogical developmental work stalled after 1905. Annual inter-Nordic conferences were still held, and *Book and Needle* was still published, but co-operation of a more binding nature came to a standstill (Hilden

1994). Still, collaboration between women within the fields of politics and business is no novel occurrence.

Indeed, Nordic co-operation builds on a very long tradition; especially as regards cultural collaboration in civic segments of society. Not only teachers, but members of the legal profession, natural scientists, painters and writers maintained close ties through Nordic conferences and in inter-Nordic, specialist journals.

Nordic collaboration within the field of literature was intense from the end of the nineteenth century. A case in point was the great 1880s' controversy about sexual morality fought in the Nordic countries under the name of "*sædelighedsfejden*". In the years from 1882 to 1888, a complex array of problems relating to sexual morality were debated publicly in the Nordic countries in a manner the likes of which could not be found in other European countries, according to Elias Bredsdorff (Bredsdorff 1969). Nearly every Nordic writer of note, including many women authors, entered into this fray which filled magazine articles, newspaper leaders, commentaries, letters to the editor, lectures and public debates. In 1888 in France, *Le Figaro* mentioned this polemic under the heading "*La polygamie en Scandinavie*", tracing the controversy back to Henrik Ibsen's play *A doll's house* which had generated a series of virulent confrontations in 1879. The main bone of contention was that Nora, in the play's final scene, abandoned her children; so contentious was this that many alternative endings were proposed. Thus one German actress simply demanded that a happy ending be added before she would agree to play the part (Ericsson 1994).

The great controversy concerning sexual morality is but one example of a public discussion with a Nordic scope. Formal as well as informal networks flourished in the Nordic countries. These networks were much more efficient and productive than the great, quixotic visions found within politics – precisely because they had realistic goals. Cultural journalism boasted a sense of communality; the major publishing houses initiated a collaboration still in existence today; Nordic exhibitions were organized, a Nordic museum was established, and so on. Consistently, the practically oriented extensions of Nordic co-operation worked the best, while the more quixotic ideas about, say, a pan-Nordic empire with Gothenburg as its capital (a notion fostered around the years of the First World War) as well as more serious ideas such as a common Nordic defensive alliance (which arose after the Second World War) failed. But even though cultural co-operation has generally proven to be the most successful, often at the grass-roots level, there has also been a long tradition of political co-operation. Regular interparliamentary meetings between the Nordic countries have been held since 1907 (Larsen 1984).

Modern, Nordic collaboration exists as a result of the nation states, not as an alternative to them. The Nordic Associations ("*Foreningerne Norden*") were created in 1919, i.e., after Norway had gained its independence in

1905, Finland likewise, in 1917, and, finally, Iceland as well, in 1918. The foundation for Nordic co-operation was the unassailable status of national sovereignty. However, this co-operation worked most effectively within the civic areas of society, steering clear of the more comprehensive domains of politics, economics, security issues and foreign policy. In many ways, the Nordic countries are not as different from the other European countries as ideology would sometimes have us believe. And, yet, a certain distinction does prevail. Even though it is difficult to speak of a bona fide "Nordic model" as such, throughout the twentieth century most Nordic countries have undergone a more seamless process of modernization than have most other countries in Europe, and the welfare state has stood its ground. This is not only because of the labour movement but also due to the various popular movements; and it is possible to see a clear line from the religious revival movements to the subsequent political, cultural and economic movements arising at the end of the nineteenth century. In an early phase of industrialization, labour unions succeeded in being accepted as negotiating partners by management as well as government. This gave rise to the tradition of collective bargaining and may be the reason for the high level of union membership in the Nordic countries.

Another salient feature of the Nordic countries is that they are homogeneously Lutheran. Protestantism has moved more vigorously in favour of women's equality than has Catholicism, even though the Protestant ideology was far from woman-friendly, actually advocating a quite restricted role for women. The nineteenth-century movement for women's rights never quite caught on in the Catholic countries while Protestantism provided a basis for refuting traditions, including those striving to keep women in their place. The basic tenet demanding individual freedom of the spirit encouraged independence, so, in the nineteenth and early twentieth centuries, Protestantism created a more benevolent climate for the education of girls and for women's rights movements. This is also the reason why European women living in Protestant countries – more specifically, in northern European countries – won the right to vote a generation ahead of women in southern, Catholic Europe.[1]

In the twentieth century, Nordic co-operation has primarily been cultivated by the Nordic Associations, created in 1919. Among the significant achievements are reciprocal social legislations and unified passport laws. Many of the policies of collaboration endorsed by the Nordic Associations in the 1920s were in fact implemented in the 1950s.

In 1952, the Nordic Council (Nordisk Råd), an interparliamentary Nordic body, was created. The Nordic Council of Ministers (Nordisk Ministerråd) was formed in 1971. After the Second World War, cultural collaboration was intensified, gradually encompassing research as well. In 1947, Nordforsk, a Nordic council for research in the natural sciences, was created, primarily by the national research councils for the technical and natural sciences. The Nordic council recommended that similar, collaborative strategies be adopted for other areas of research, as did indeed happen during the 1960s. This collaboration was strengthened in 1968 through the founding of several Nordic committees, types of Nordic research councils that awarded funding for research projects.

Nordic researchers within women's studies have benefited from these collaborative frameworks. In broad summary we may distinguish two principal lines of Nordic collaboration. One focuses on founding Nordic institutions; the other aims to make Nordic co-operation a standard activity within Nordic national organizations – public as well as private. Research within women's studies has benefited from both lines of approach.

What constitutes Nordic women's studies?

"Nordic", then, is in many ways an epithet used to designate an imagined community; so the strong, Nordic woman who would seem to form part of this picture – what about her? Does she exist? And is it at all possible to speak of a distinctive profile characterizing Nordic gender and women's studies?

The impossibility of arriving at a universal female subject has not caused researchers within women's studies to cease their endeavours. On the contrary, theoretical reflections are currently flourishing more than ever, since the former project of gaining visibility has now been supplemented with a project of deconstruction from which women's studies can garner many advantages. The intention behind deconstruction, of course, is to insist on ambiguity and investigate the ways in which femininity as well as gender, class, nationality and "the Nordic element" have been constructed.

In the interest of our common (as well as separate) history it is important neither to relinquish the visibility aspect, nor the Nordic element. The question facing us is whether traditional historical research, because of its nationalistic slant, has repressed the significance of the Scandinavian ideology in constructing the Nordic welfare state. Works on Nordic history have been, and still are, being written. Remarkably, many of these deal with the history of everyday life. Once again, the unifying factor is an interest in society viewed from a down-to-earth angle, rather than from the perspective of high politics. Do we still feel the need to nurture our imaginations about Nordic society? We ourselves participate in perpetuating the articles of faith on which the imagination of things Nordic is built. But we do not merely confirm this imagined entity, we keep changing it, even as we oscillate between our similarities and our differences.

The Nordic countries are also characterized by proximity, in a geographical as well as a cultural, social and linguistic sense.[2] This is the background for the existence of a networked, Nordic community on the civic level encompassing a significant number of institutions, including research institutions, which have been helpful for gender and women's studies. One of the most recent examples of this has been the setting up, in 1995, of the Nordic Institute for Women's Studies and Gender Research, located in Oslo. So Nordic gender and women's studies do in fact exist, having quite a long tradition as well.

As early as the 1950s, research was undertaken into Nordic gender roles and social structure, influenced by structural functionalism in the United States.[3] Nordic researchers did, however, adopt a position more radically critical of society and gender roles than that of the leading functionalists. The dominant Nordic perspective on gender roles that prevailed in the 1960s was fundamentally radical and inaugurated many changes in terms of equal rights. One such change came in the form of more education for girls, the underlying assumption being that it was the female gender role which needed to be changed. But pretty soon ideas surfaced that emphasized that the male gender role also needed to be transformed. Thus, Nordic gender research in the 1960s presaged many of the themes that were to surface as the new women's movement and women's studies emerged in the beginning of the 1970s.

Very early – to wit, in 1973 – Berit Ås introduced the concept "women's culture" into the Nordic scientific discourse. She identified a series of cultural dimensions which defined the fundamental difference between women and men and outlined an array of repressive techniques which had considerable impact, even abroad (Ås 1975). As opposed to "gender roles", which was very much a 1960s concept, the concept of women's culture emanated from the new women's movement which was to characterize the ensuing phase, beginning in the 1970s.

In the constructive phase leading to what we might call new women's studies, Nordic collaboration again played a prominent part through the institution called NSU (Nordic Summer University), a pioneering institution not only for Nordic collaboration among academics but also for introducing new scientific approaches and especially for advancing interdisciplinary perspectives. Intellectual currents from abroad have always been quickly reflected in Nordic collaborative efforts, and the NSU has actively contributed to the developments within these currents. Starting in 1973, the NSU initiated a collaborative research effort in women's studies under the heading "The characteristic situation of women under capitalism". This work was initiated the previous year during a winter symposium in Denmark with the participation of the British researcher and activist Juliet Mitchel – which goes to show that external influence was present from the beginning. The workshop research under this heading continued for some years, and was followed by other headings or themes. Most recently, in 1994, a research group focused on male gender research was launched, entitled "Between men and masculinities".

350

From the NSU, women's studies slowly spread to the universities; here, starting in the mid-1970s, courses were offered and networks founded, while the 1980s saw the inauguration of centres all over the Nordic countries. At present, more than 20 centres exist in the Nordic countries, and at least one, sometimes several journals, both national and local, are devoted to research in gender and women's studies in each country.[4]

1981 saw the founding of the Nordic Forum for Research on Women in the Nordic Countries (Nordisk forum for kvindeforskning i Norden), which, at that time, experienced some difficulties in getting many of its ideas across. However, the inter-Nordic collaboration between researchers within women's studies did result in an interdisciplinary conference in 1983 and in the founding of a university summer school at the Nordic forum of 1988 in Oslo.[5] This conference, consisting of an official as well as a grass-roots conference – almost as a parallel to the United Nations' Women's Conference – drew more than 10,000 participants. One result was the appointment of a Nordic co-ordinator for women's studies, affiliated with the Åbo Academy in the period from 1991 to 1995. The project leading to this appointment was launched by the women researchers and achieved through lobbying by, among others, the network Nordic Forum for Research on Women in the Nordic Countries. This co-ordinator became involved in the Nordic action programme for equal rights (1989–93), based on the realization that the equal rights effort presupposed a basis of knowledge on which to work.

The Nordic co-ordinator project was successful; among its achievements has been the ensuring of continuity in the Nordic areas of co-operation and the inauguration of fresh initiatives, including the founding of *Nora, Nordic Journal of Women's Studies*. This English-language journal commenced publication in 1993, with its main editorial staff located in Oslo, and it has contributed towards the internationalization of Nordic women's studies. While the main editorial staff moved to Åbo in 1995, the co-ordinator position was now in Oslo.

That same year saw the inauguration of the Nordic Institute for Women's Studies and Gender Research (Nordisk institut for kvinde – og kønsforskning (NIKK)) with Fride Egg-Henriksen acting as institute director in the period from 1995 to 1998. The desire for a Nordic institute, in view of the many such institutes that exist throughout the Nordic countries, had been felt for many years, but not until the Nordic Forum at Åbo in 1994 did the necessary political, and thus financial, endorsement materialize. At that same 1994 Åbo conference, where the current state of research in women's studies was presented to 15,000 women from the Nordic countries, the Nordic Association for Women's Studies and Gender Research was established, the purpose of which is to support *Nora* and further develop inter-Nordic co-operation.

The Nordic platform has also given rise to a series of researchers' courses; not just of an interdisciplinary nature but also more general courses on

351

method and theory; these took place in Finland in 1989, and in Iceland in 1992.

Another reason for the significance of inter-Nordic co-operation has been the comparatively small size of the separate research communities at the individual universities. The co-operation has unfolded within individual subjects, disciplinary fields and interdisciplinary studies alike; one course of action has been to organize larger interdisciplinary conferences, as well as conferences devoted to more wide-ranging political issues of women's studies. Oddly enough, the first disciplinary conference was launched as a Dutch–Scandinavian venture in 1975 (Silfwerbrandten et al. 1975). Subsequently, an initiative arose from the research organizations in the Nordic countries. As a case in point, the Joint Committee of the Nordic Research Councils for the Humanities held a conference on women's studies within the humanities in 1979. Seventy individuals gathered at this conference, the goal of which was twofold: to discuss methodological and theoretical questions within women's studies; and to establish contacts between researchers in the Nordic countries so they might discuss potential fields of Nordic co-operation. This work was followed up 10 years later by a conference entitled "Future strategies for women's studies in the humanities". It was on this occasion that the proposal for a Nordic institute was put forward.[6] Nordic conferences on strategies with a political dimension regarding research (organized as joint colloquia involving politicians, administrators and researchers) have been held in 1983 and 1993. On the first occasion, the initiative came from the Nordic Council of Ministers; on the second, from the Nordic co-ordinator.

This considerable array of networks established over the years – some largely *ad hoc*, some more enduring – has been of significant importance to Nordic gender and women's studies. One of the first, very sizeable networks was Women in Politics, which, in 1983, published a comparative study on the position and role of women within political systems in the Nordic countries. The report, entitled "The incomplete democracy" (*"Det uferdige demokrati"*) was also published in English (Haavio-Mannila 1983).[7] A follow-up report is now being prepared. The project, funded by the Nordic Council of Ministers, is called "The other half of power. Nordic women's path towards democracy and equal rights" (*"Den halve magt. Nordiske kvinders vej til demokrati og ligestilling"*) and will also result in a book, to be published in 1998.

One of the networks currently very active is the project entitled "History of literature by Nordic women". This project, which ran from 1993 to 1996, is set to publish a comprehensive history of literature written by women in the Nordic countries, consisting of five volumes: four volumes of text and one reference volume, amounting to a total of 6 000 pages. In the four text volumes, approximately 100 contributors from all the Nordic countries present an exhaustive account, from a Nordic perspective, of literature written by women from the Norse era up to Samic and Greenlandic women's literature.[8]

Scholars concerned with Women's history have also been active on a Nordic scale, having held regular Nordic conferences covering the Middle Ages as well as contemporary history, in addition to which several Nordic research projects have been initiated through the years. Nordic co-operation renders otherwise unrealistic projects possible; an example worth mentioning is the three-volume women's world history, result of a predominantly Danish-Norwegian collaboration, published from 1992 to 1993.[9]

It remains beyond doubt that Nordic co-operation has had an immense effect on the initiation of research, even in the case of individual and national projects. Only by thinking beyond the boundaries of each individual country has it been possible to bring together sufficient numbers of researchers in comparable fields. Even within larger fields such as that of women's history, this has proven to be the case; and the imperative has been even greater in the narrower more specialist fields such as musicology, philosophy and art history. Some networks are centred on specific disciplines, while others are of a more cross-disciplinary or thematic nature. Different libraries, likewise, have for many years maintained contacts (Larsen & Wedborn 1993).

Nordic collaboration has oftentimes operated as a structural umbrella for co-operation and inspiration rather than as a motor for striving towards an integration of subjects. Even when the subject matter is the Nordic countries, each individual country is dealt with separately. The principal model for collaboration has been the collation of more or less co-ordinated national reports which are then published in the same volume, preceded by a short introduction. Given the rising level of internationalization, if it is wished to underline the significance of Nordic co-operation it is important that the Nordic perspective takes precedence over the nationalist elements. An example of an inter-Nordic, integrated project where the nationalist principle takes a backseat is that entitled the "History of literature by Nordic women". Here, a comprehensive view of literature by Nordic women is presented, making it possible to see Nordic trends in a clearer light than would be possible through a national approach to the subject.

So far, a definitive profile of Nordic women's studies is difficult to pinpoint, due to the cornucopia of activities within the area. But it would not be entirely off the mark to stress the fact that women's workaday chores have been a central theme, so central in fact that it has prompted Karin Widerberg, a Swedish-Norwegian professor of sociology, to voice the opinion that women in the Nordic countries have been made to look "strangely sexless. They just work and work – as if we women lived by and for work alone" (Widerberg 1986). There can be no doubt that, so far, the productive sides of women's lives have been the ones highlighted; along with a certain stress on gender and class, this maintains an emphasis on materiality.

The Danish-Norwegian professor Harriet Bjerrum Nielsen has pointed out that precisely because Nordic research in women's studies has been so strongly centred on issues of equality, areas such as education, work, politics, social reproduction and the organization of daily life have been the pivotal focus of research while, for instance, research into the body, identity formation, socialization and mentality has been less prominently featured, only to be embarked upon in more recent years (Bjerrum Nielsen 1994). But it will always be possible to name projects and researchers that go against this grain, for in the Nordic countries, just as elsewhere, there is a traceable critique of the worker's paradigm dating back to around 1980.

The greater emphasis on workaday life which is an undeniable fact might well also be related to the Nordic welfare model, a model that has given rise to research into the welfare state as such. Similarly, we see a close interrelationship between the fight for equal rights and women's studies. Over a number of years, the Nordic Council of Ministers has prioritized equal rights, sponsoring a committee for equal rights issues made up of council officials as well as setting up the post of official equal rights consultant, a position later renamed equal rights advisory officer. A variegated series of projects has been initiated. One of the most extensive was the Bryt Project, aimed at developing and testing methods to combat the sexist allocation of work within the labour market.[10] The latest action programme from 1995 to 2000 sees mainstreaming as an important tool in the Nordic co-operation towards equal rights. Equal rights must be integrated into every policy area of society.[11]

The Nordic forum of 1994 gave rise to several publications which were then translated into English to coincide with The UN World Women's Conference (Fougner & Larsen-Asp 1994). The project of having a coordinator was also part of this action programme, just as the Nordic Institute came into being after the subsequent action programme which covers the period 1995–2000. There has been a general recognition of the fact that research and researchers within women's studies can contribute substantially to the equal rights effort. Research in women's studies provides the knowledge and facts needed for an effective equal rights effort.

The emphasis on equal rights between the sexes has also meant political support in favour of research in women's studies in several countries. Often, women politicians have actively demanded that women's studies be allocated more funds; while support from within, from the academy itself, has been more subdued. The proportion of women politicians is comparatively high in the Nordic countries (in excess of 30 per cent) compared to other countries; while, on the contrary, the same is not true when it comes to women engaged in research. In Denmark and Norway, particularly, the figure is less than 20 per cent. Therefore, the on-going initiatives for the next few years concentrate not only on supporting research in gender and women's studies but also on getting more women into research. Along with the hightened priority now given to men in equal rights politics, research in men's studies has also become an increasingly important area, boasting Nordic as well as international networks.

It is by no means easy to expostulate iron-clad characteristics that are specific exclusively to Nordic research in women's studies as opposed to women's studies in other parts of the world; and yet certain features hinting at a Nordic profile in gender and women's studies do seem to emerge. Hitherto, Nordic women's studies have had a closer affiliation to Anglo-American women's studies than to research in these areas from other European countries. But currently, as European integration grows stronger, this too is changing. Being situated as we are, in the Nordic countries, at the interstices of Anglo-Saxon and continental intellectual movements, we should be more determined to make this geographical and academic fact work to our advantage.

Nordic women's studies will come to possess a new value of its own and faces a challenging future; particularly if more emphasis is placed on the Nordic than on the national aspects; more emphasis on comparative studies and the collaborative efforts that thus become more than a mere umbrella. The Nordic countries make up a region eminently suited for more stringent, comparative investigations. Nordic co-operation, therefore, has many inherent, innovative possibilities for development.

Notes

I should like to thank Solveig Bergman, Marianne Laxen and NIKK for their help.

In relation to this chapter, a larger bibliography containing literature in the Scandinavian languages as well as an overview of Nordic networks has been prepared and may be obtained through NIKK, Nordisk Institut for kvinne-og kjønsforskning, Universitetet i Oslo, Postboks 1040 Blindern, 0315 Oslo, Norway.

1. Jean Baubérot points out an inherent contradiction: women gained access to education, while a similar access to certain positions was blocked. "In many cases, this contradiction was resolved by making it the mission of the Protestant woman to assist her husband and serve as his partner. The married couple and family therefore proved both emotionally appealing and culturally and socially ascendant" (Baubérot 1993:198).
2. The Nordic countries are: Denmark, Finland, Iceland, Norway and Sweden, plus three self-governing regions: the Faroe Islands, Greenland and Åland. "The Nordic countries" designates the entire area, while "Scandinavia" includes Denmark, Norway and Sweden only. In medieval times, the Nordic peoples were linguistically very close, but the national languages have since developed in somewhat separate directions. Today, the linguistic community comprises only Norway, Denmark and Sweden. Finnish is a member of a separate family of languages, but Finland does have a Swedish-speaking minority, and Swedish is taught as an obligatory subject in schools.
3. Berit Ås, Harriet Holter and Erik Grønseth from Norway; Rita Liljeström and Edmund Dahlström from Sweden; and Elina Haavio-Mannila from Finland.

BENTE ROSENBECK

Acta sociologica Special issue on sex roles, vol. 14, no. 1–2, 1971. (The editors were Elina Haavio-Mannila, Harriet Holter and Rita Liljeström.)

4. Solveig Bergman (ed.) 1994. *Women's studies and research on women in the Nordic countries.* See also *European women's guide*, Utrecht, 1993.

5. *Women's studies and research on women in the Nordic countries.* Uppsala: Uppsala University, Centre for Women Scholars and Research on Women, 1989.

6. NOS-H. *Kvinneforskning i de humanistiske fag. Konferenserapport: Nordisk konferanse avholdt på Hurdalsjøen hotell, Norge, 7–10 may 1979.* Oslo, 1979. NOS-H. *Framtids-strategier för humanistisk kvinnoforskning. Konferensrapport: Nordisk konferens Hanaholmens kulturcentrum i Esbo, Finland 28–30 may 1989.* Helsingfors, 1991.

7. About Nordic women in general, see Lauri Karvonen and Per Selle (eds) 1995. *Closing the gap. Women in Nordic politics.* Dartmouth.

8. E. Møller Jensen, *Nordisk kvindelitteraturhistorie*, vol. 1: *I Guds navn*, and vol. 2: *Faderhuset* were published in 1993 and 1994, respectively; in both Danish and Swedish, by Rosinante/Munksgaard, Denmark, and Bra Böcker, Sweden. Vol. 3: *Vide verden 1900–1960* was published in 1996 and vol. 4: *På jorden 1960–1990* was published in 1997, both in Copenhagen. Volume 5 is forthcoming.

9. *Cappelens Kvinnehistorie.* Cappelen, Oslo, 1992–93, vols 1–3. *Kvinder fra urtid til nutid.* Copenhagen: Politiken, vols 1–2, 1992.

10. Nordic Council of Ministers 1990. *The Nordic Bryt-projekt. Final report.* The Nordic Council of Ministers has also published: D. Dahlerup (ed.) 1989. *Køn sorterer: Kønsopdeling på arbejdspladsen.* Copenhagen: Nordic Council of Ministers.

11. "Program för det nordiska jämställdhetssamarbejdet 1995–2000." *TemaNord 1995:* 529. "Women and men in the Nordic countries. Facts and figures 1994.", *Nord 1994:* 3.

References

Anderson, B. 1991. *Imagined communities. Reflections on the origin and spread of nationalism.* London: Verso.

Andersson, J.A. 1994. *Nordisk samarbete: Aktörer, idéer och organisering 1919–1953* (Nordic co-operation: actors, ideas and organization 1919–1953). Lund Political Studies 85, Lund.

Ås, B. 1975. On female culture: an attempt to formulate a theory of women's solidarity and action. *Acta Sociologica*, no. 2–3, 25–41.

Baubérot, J. 1993. The Protestant woman. In *A history of women in the West*, G. Duby & M. Perrot (eds), vol. 4, 198–212. London: Harvard University Press.

Bergman. S. (ed.) 1994. *Women's studies and research on women in the Nordic countries.* Åbo:Institute for Women's Studies.

Bjerrum Nielsen, H. 1994. *Notat til den nordiske planlægningsgruppen for forskningsprogrammet Norden og Europa* (Note to the Nordic planning committee for the Nordic research programme, The Nordic Countries and Europe) Norden och Europa – et nordisk Forskningsprogram. *TemaNord* 1994: 584, 75–81. Copenhagen: Nordic Council.

Bredsdorff, E. 1969. Moralists versus immoralists: the great battle in Scandinavian literature in the 1880s. *Scandinavica: International Journal of Scandinavian Studies*, vol. 6, no. 1, 91–111.

Ericsson, E. 1994. Att vara eller inte vara – 1800 – talets aktriser och kvinnligheten (To be or not to be – femininity actors in the eighteenth century). In *Det evigt kvinnliga. En historia om förändring* (Eternal femininity. A story about change), U. Wikander (ed.), 162–87. Stockholm: Tiden.

Fougner, B. & M. Larsen-Asp 1994. *The Nordic countries – a paradise for women?* Copenhagen: Nordic Council.

Haavio-Mannila, E. 1983. *Unfinished democracy: women in Nordic politics.* Copenhagen: Nordic Council.

Hastrup, K. (ed.) 1992. *Den nordiske verden,* (The Nordic world), Bks 1 and 2. Copenhagen: Gyldendal.

Hilden, A. 1994. Nordisk lærerindesamarbejde omkring 1900 (Nordic co-operation between female teachers around 1900). *Den jyske Historiker* **69–70**, 79–87.

Larsen, J. & H. Wedborn 1993. Nordic women's documentation centres. *Nora,* vol. 1, no. 1, 125–30.

Larsen, K. 1984. Scandinavian grass roots: from peace movement to Nordic Council. *Scandinavian Journal of History,* vol. 9, 183–200.

Linde-Lauersen, A. & J.O. Nilsson 1991. Nationella identiteter i Norden – ett fullbordat projekt? (National identities in the Nordic countries) Nordiska rådet: *Nord* 1991:26. Stockholm.

Melby, K. 1995. Kjønsforholdets politikk. Ekteskapsloven av 1918 og Ektefælleloven av 1927 (Gender and politics. The marriage laws in 1918 and 1927). Centre for Women's Research. Trondheim University, series 6/95.

Nordic Council (ed.) 1990. *The Nordic Bryt-project. Final report.* Copenhagen: Nordic Council.

Østergaard, U. 1994. Norden – europæisk eller nordisk? (The Nordic countries – European or Nordic?). *Den jyske Historiker* **69–70**, 7–37.

Rerup, L. 1994. Nationalisme og skandinavisme indtil Første Verdenskrigs udbrud (Nationalism and Scandinavianism until the First World War). *Den jyske Historiker* **69–70**, 79–87.

Roesdahl, E. 1994. Vikingerne i dansk kultur (The Vikings in Danish culture). *Fortid og nutid,* vol. 2, 158–72.

Silfwerbrandten C., S. Govaarts Halkes, T. Govaarts Halkes, M. de Swart 1975. *Feminology. Proceedings of the Dutch-Scandinavien symposium on woman's position in society, June 8–11, 1975,* University of Nijmegen, The Netherlands.

Statens beroende av familjen 1996 (The state and the family) Helsingfors: Publikationer av projektet Kvinnan i rätten – kvinnans rätt.

Troels-Lund, T. 1879–1901. *Dagligliv i Norden.* (Daily life in the Nordic countries). Copenhagen: Gyldendal.

Widerberg, K. 1986. Finnes det en nordisk modell i kvinneforskningen? Om velfærdsstatens krise som kvindeforskningens legitimering (Is there a Nordic Women's studies?). *Den samfunnsvitenskapelige kvinneforskningen fram mot år 2000: Utfordringer og visjoner.* Seminar report. Work no. 5/86. NAVF, 62–71.

Wikander, U. En utopisk jämlikhet. Internationella kvinnokongresser 1878–1914 (Utopian equality. International women's congresses 1878–1914). In *Det evigt kvinnliga. En historia om förändring* (Eternal femininity. A story about change), U. Wikander (ed.), 7–27. Stockholm: Tiden.

Index

phenomenological theory of 284–6
and stardom 303, 306
Bombelles, Ida 140
Book and needle 346
Borg, K. 180
Bourdieu, P. 130, 334
Branting, H. 26
Brantsæter, M.C. 176
Brentano, F. 277
Bringle, R.G. 212
Brooks, P. 301
brotherhoods 217, 218–19, 223–5
sexuality in 229–30
Brun, F. 125, 126, 141, 142, 143
Bryt Project 354

Campbell, B. 185, 187, 188
care work 189, 190, 328–9, 330
categories 335–6
Centrala Kvinnorådet 38
change *see* organizational change;
social change
changing the world, as goal of
Icelandic Women's Alliance 81–2
child care 11, 33, 35, 220, 250
class and 34, 331–2
in nineteenth century 25
childbearing 31, 285–6
Chodorow, N. 330
Christensen, Inger 15, 16, 311–12, 322
alfabet 312–15, 316, 317–18, 319, 321
class 23, 26, 27
child care choice and 34, 331–2
clinical gaze 225–6
collective action 49, 54–6
Collett, C. 128, 143
conflict of interests 35, 36–8, 49–50, 52
contraception 251
control 192, 221
emotional 228, 230, 234
conversations, in salons 123, 136–7
Cronstedt, M. 127
cross-gender interaction at work
199–201, 210–11
cultural co-operation 347
cultural heritage 93, 95, 96
cultural identity 129
culture 108, 233–4, 333
gender and 249–50
nature and 106, 111

Dagny 32
Dahl, B. 60
Dahlerup, D. 47, 179
Dahlström, K. 37
Danish Golden Age 139
Dasein 322–3
deconstruction 104, 312, 320–2, 337–8,
349
Denmark 160, 344–5
cross-gender work relations 202, 205
films in 296, 298
Labour Exchange 161–72
professions in 220–1
rural society 295–6
salons in 126–7, 131–42
Derrida, J. 106, 320, 321–2
Descartes, R. 273, 287, 288n
différance 320–1
differences 30, 31, 32, 82, 99
alpha and beta bias 331
in rationality 326–7, 330
among women 80, 244, 249
see also equality/difference
dichotomy
donation of egg/sperm 182–3
Donzelot, J. 218
dramatists, women 148–55
Durkheim, E. 334
Dyer, R. 302

economic independence 31, 34
Edgren Leffler, A.C. 152–4
Eduards, M.L. 49
education 329
for girls 346, 350
Egg-Henriksen, F. 351
Eisner, L. 307
Elmbrant, B. 45
Elsaesser, T. 307
emotions
cognitivist theory of 275–84
control of 228, 230, 234
rationality of 273–6, 281–3
women and 272, 273, 274–5
at work 203–9, 211–12
see also feelings
Engels, F. 24, 25
envy, in work relationships 204, 207,
209, 212
equal rights research 354–5

nature 92, 93, 105, 107
and culture 106, 111
Paglia and 107–8, 109, 112, 115–16
women and 33, 98, 131
negotiation of gender 257–62
Neumann, E. 96, 98
New Women's Movement (Iceland) 71
Nielsen, Asta 14–15, 294–5, 306–7
The abyss 295, 296–302, 304
star status of 301, 302–6
Nietzsche, F. 321, 322
night shifts, women banned from 30, 37
'non-issues' 47, 60, 61
Nora, Nordic Journal for Women's Studies 351
Nordforsk 348–9
Nordic Association for Women's and Gender Research 351
Nordic Associations 347–8
Nordic Council of Ministers 348, 354
Nordic Film Company 296
Nordic Forum for Research on Women in the Nordic Countries 351, 354
Nordic heritage 345–9
Nordic Institute for Women's and Gender Studies 351
Nordic Summer University 350
Nordic women's studies 349–55
Northern Europe, in nineteenth century 124
Norway
salons in 127, 128, 129
working women in 192–3
nuclear proletariat 188, 194
nursing 222–3
Nussbaum, M. 274, 275–6, 280–2, 286–7, 288n, 289n

Oehlenschläger, A. 137, 139
Ólafsson, E. 94, 95
one-act plays 148–59
Organization for Married Women's Right to Private Property 28
organization of women 28–9
organization theory 160–1, 164, 183
organizational change, gender and 162–73
organizations 7
gender in 161, 177, 183
Orozco, M. 127

Paglia, Camilla 6, 7, 104–5, 210
Sexual personae 106–16
pain 285–6
Palme, Olaf 44, 45, 57–8, 59–60, 61
Palmer, M. 192
Pankhurst, Christabel 70
parental leave allowance 65n, 220
feminist revolt over 54–62
Parkin, W. 176, 186, 211
parliaments, women in 71
Parsons, T. 226, 228, 229
participation in politics 46, 48, 51, 70, 85
party politics, women in 46, 48–9, 50
see also Icelandic Women's Alliance; Social Democratic Women's Federation
paternity leave 54, 55, 62
patriarchy
Paglia and 112, 115
see also brotherhoods
Peirce, C.S. 302–3
persona, of Asta Nielsen 302–4, 305–6
personal choice 251–2
personal development 248–9
gender-specific modelling of 254–5
social change and 248, 253
personal/professional roles 189
Petro, P. 306
phenomenology 14, 278–9, 285, 287
Phillips, A. 75
physiology, and emotional states 283–4
poetry 15–16, 134, 311–20
politics 22–4
and taste 136–7
women in 5–6, 11, 44–62, 69–70, 250, 326, 354
women's issues in 28–33, 36–8, 39
postmodernism 7, 17, 104, 109–10, 325, 332–3
critique of 333–4
Paglia and 107, 109, 115
in medical profession 231–3, 236
power 13, 49, 64n, 84, 265, 266, 337–8
brotherhoods and 218–19
and conflicting interests of women 36–8
masculinity and 187–8
Weber and 219
of women 113
women's lack of 153, 154, 155